PEMBERTON:

The History of a Settlement

Frances Decker, Margaret Fougberg
and Mary Ronayne

Consultant and editor: Gordon R. Elliott

PEMBERTON PIONEER WOMEN
Pemberton, British Columbia

PEMBERTON: The History of a Settlement

MAJOR FUNDING PROVIDED BY NEW HORIZONS PROGRAM

Published by
Pemberton Pioneer Women
Pemberton, British Columbia V0N 2L0

First Printing — October 1977
Second (revised) Printing — June 1978

Typeset, printed and bound in Canada by Hemlock Printers Ltd.,
Burnaby, B.C., Canada.
Design and Technical co-ordination: R. Neville Wrigley
Cover Design: Ian E. Staunton

TABLE OF CONTENTS

Olav Slaymaker

INTRODUCTION

Dividing the Coast Mountains from the Cascades the Lillooet River Valley is a trough gouged out by glaciers, and originating in a vast glacier itself the Lillooet River meanders along the flat valley floor for miles, swinging freely from one side to the other until restrictive man-made dykes regulate its flow and curb its wandering. Then, about sixty miles from its source, the river enters Lillooet Lake, passes through, and speeds south to the Harrison system. Over the thousands and thousands of years the flooding river has repeatedly laid down rich layers of sediments over the debris left by the glaciers.

The Lillooet River of this book is the Upper Lillooet, the river flowing into the lake, but because in the past the name "Pemberton" denoted a region larger than the Lillooet River Valley itself this history of Pemberton deals with events taking place in lands drained by the Lillooet River and its tributaries, and by the Birkenhead River. Lying along the Pemberton Portage road which was built during the Gold Rush of the 1860's to link Lillooet and Anderson Lakes, the Birkenhead River section of the area is part of the "Portage", a name old-timers have always given to the narrow valleys through which that road winds. It was during the Gold Rush period that throngs of miners rushing through this country gave the name "Pemberton" or "Lillooet Meadows" to these farmlands close to the lake, but nowadays most people speaking of Pemberton Meadows refer to farmlands farther north, to those around the site of the former Pemberton Meadows Post Office and the Pemberton Meadows School in the Upper Valley. The rather vague boundary between Upper and Lower Valley probably lies not far from the bridge over the Ryan River, a stream once officially known more modestly as Ryan Creek.

Rivers and streams, most of them glacier-fed, have strongly influenced the lives of all who have lived in the area. From unrecorded time waters moving through the valleys have provided fish for food, and from unrecorded time the rivers have carried sediments which have created the richness of this fertile farmland. And through recorded time rivers have certainly continued to flood these farmlands, though since the flood control program of 1945-51 the Lillooet has carried away a greatly increased load of sediments. In the summer of 1972 geographers from many parts of the world climbed the hill overlooking the north end of Lillooet Lake to look down on the massive deposits from all the streams which form the Lillooet River.

With their lakes the rivers were not only the ready-made highways of times past, but the rivers have also carved out the space for land routes linking Pemberton with coast and interior. The most important one from the south follows the Cheakamus and the Green; the one from the north, the Birkenhead. Roads that were once mere trails make Pemberton the hub for highways from Lillooet, from Port Douglas, and from Squamish. And the road that once followed the meandering river from one side of the Valley to the other now cuts almost straight down the middle.

Besides temperature and precipitation, among the factors affecting the climate of the Pemberton area are the shadows cast by the mountains, and the directions in which those mountains run. Shadows from lofty peaks, many 8,000 feet and higher, greatly reduce sunlight in the narrow valleys. Pacific air blows up the canyons through which the Cheakamus and the Green twist, but beyond Pemberton Village, its altitude 692 feet, the continuing north-west swing of the mountains bordering the Lillooet River reduces coastal influence.

In 1909 Jack Ronayne estimated that winter temperatures averaging 23 degrees Fahrenheit at his farm in Pemberton Meadows were 10 degrees colder than those at the junction of Owl Creek and the Birkenhead. In 1916 his weather station recorded the lowest temperature since he had settled in the Valley, 30 degrees below. A month later he discovered "nearly all fruit trees winter-killed, but the hardy apples from Ottawa." In 1949 weeks of intense cold stopped all outside work except the most essential: caring for livestock and carrying wood and water into homes. At Pemberton Meadows the thermometer dropped to 44 below.

Prepared in 1974 *Pemberton Valley Agriculture* states that "The temperatures at all stations in the valley have been similar during the growing months. . . ." At the Pemberton Meadows weather station, its altitude 730 feet, July temperatures have averaged 66 degrees. Because nights are almost invariably cooled by snowfields and glaciers high above homes and farms, soaring daytime temperatures account for that average. The record is 100 degrees. For many varieties of vegetable the fast summer growth compensates for the rather brief frost-free period of 120 to 150 days.

Much of it snow, most of the annual 40-inch precipitation falls from September to April. Again the average does not indicate the wide variations. In January 1916, 5 feet 9 inches of snow lay on Ronaynes' fields, but in 1931 the greatest depth of snow was about 6 inches which melted so early that Lower Valley farmers were plowing in February. Residents can expect little precipitation during the growing season: the long-term average, just 7 inches, explains contemporary farmers' investments in irrigation systems. Before river control the abnormally high water table supplied crops with all the moisture necessary.

Pemberton Valley Agriculture also comments that "weather conditions in the Pemberton Valley can be extremely variable — for example: snowfall has ranged as high as 360 inches in 1971-72, and the frost-free period can range down as low as 70 days." Looking over their gardens and fields one morning in 1909 Upper Valley settlers saw saddening proof of a short growing season: frost had damaged beans, potatoes, and corn. Thc date was the fifth of August.

Until recently the area had only two main settlements: Pemberton Village and Mount Currie. Pemberton Village is a mile from the Lillooet River and nearly one hundred miles from Vancouver by Highway 99 which has been completely paved since 1969 and is always cleared of snow in winter. About four miles east of Pemberton, Mount Currie lies between the Lillooet and Birkenhead Rivers.

Pemberton: The History of a Settlement touches on early exploration, but deals mainly with settlement, tracing developments through more than a hundred years. Ending with events of 1966 this history of the Pemberton area describes the major results of the drainage of the Lillooet River Valley, the reclamation project which saved the Valley from depopulation. This history also touches on the Lillooet Indians of Mount Currie because many names and events indicate that since Europeans first entered this region they have mixed with the native people, but Mount Currie people should really be writing their own history, as indeed they have started to do. Though our early section referring to the Indian people is based on works of early authorities, it also includes recent writings by and about Mount Currie people themselves.

When we started work on this history one of our major difficulties was in finding any book with more than a chance reference to Pemberton. For information we therefore went first to our friends, those residents past and present of not only Pemberton and Mount Currie, but also of communities to the north and to the south. Many of those people gave us oral and written accounts which we have used freely. We happily acknowledge information sent by Roman Catholic priests and Protestant ministers formerly working in the area. We thank, too, both past and present Pemberton Secondary School students for details they obtained during their own research and we particularly thank the young Mount Currie people who permitted us to print accounts they wrote while in school. Always patiently and generously a few individuals have been contributing reminiscences at intervals for more than twenty years. If our presentation unintentionally distorts anyone's story, we pray that the contributor will forgive us.

For a framework on which to develop our account we needed records. For those we are indebted to many local organizations and to several churches; to the local headquarters of the British Columbia Forest Service; to the village clerk at Pemberton who, being also secretary of the Pemberton Dyking District, helped us find facts about both village incorporation and the reclamation of the Lillooet River Valley; to the secretary-treasurer of the Howe Sound School District; to the administrator of the Squamish-Lillooet Regional

District; to the editors of both the *Bridge River-Lillooet News* and *The Squamish Times;* to *The Vancouver Sun* and *The Vancouver Province;* to the B.C. Indian Arts Society; to British Columbia Hydro; to the British Columbia Telephone Company; to the Royal Canadian Mounted Police; to both the British Columbia Railway Company and the Canadian Pacific Railway Company; to government offices in Lillooet, Kamloops, Victoria, and Ottawa, particularly in Victoria where numerous officials have helped; and to librarians at the Vancouver Public Library. For great and continued help we thank the staff of the Provincial Archives, but especially the former Provincial Librarian and Archivist, Dr. Willard E. Ireland.

For our illustrations we have cast a wide net. The Provincial Archives, of course. But neighbours have been most generous in lending valued old photographs, and appearing in this book are those which we think best illustrate our history. Many others have been saved for the museum which is to be built in the future and to which our profits will be assigned.

Shortly after organizing, the Pemberton Women's Institute began to collect material for a local history. Frances Decker, Margaret Fougberg, and the late Kathleen Lundgren formed the first history committee and were joined in 1973 by Mary Ronayne. The wish to make our work available to more than only members of the Institute developed into a plan to publish a book. Teas and sales of work raised considerable funds for this purpose, but were insufficient in the mid-'seventies, even with a generous gift from the late Margaret Green. Fortunately an organization known as the Pemberton Pioneer Women, an organization of older members and friends of the Institute, applied successfully for a Federal government New Horizons grant, for which we are extremely grateful. We are grateful also for assistance from Neville Wrigley of Hemlock Printers Ltd.

In 1974 we were fortunate in securing the aid of Gordon R. Elliott, son of pioneer residents of this area — Ray Elliott, a homesteader and packer, and Margaret Mellish, the second school teacher. As our consultant his experience and his concerned attention to every phase in the preparation of this history have helped immeasurably.

Added to all such help has been the help from our families: without their co-operation we never could have completed this project.

The Squamish Times

Going Fishing

Provincial Archives, Victoria, B.C.

Sorting the Crop

THOSE WHO WERE ALWAYS HERE

THOSE HERE FIRST

The native Indian peoples were the first inhabitants of the Pemberton Valley, but no one knows where they came from or how long ago. One theory is that these first settlers were Asians who came to this continent by way of the Bering Strait and the Aleutian Islands some twenty to thirty thousand years ago, and indeed a ten-inch long caribou-bone scraper found in the Yukon has been radiocarbon dated as being 27,000 years old. These migrant peoples lived off the land, following the migrating herds of animals on which life depended, fashioning their clothing and their tools and their shelters from the materials at hand, and these earliest arrivals had drifted southward into Mexico, into Central America, and on into South America long before the Spanish conquests in the sixteenth century.

The Indians at Mount Currie — or "Slalok", as they called the village — belong to a branch of the Interior Salish which lives between the Fraser River and the Coast. The branch is generally thought to have been called "lil'uet", or "Onion People", because the wild onion was so plentiful in this area, but legend tells of an old Chief whose name was "A-ihl-ooet" and tells that wherever he camped became known as "A-ihl-ooet's". Whatever the source, though, the name Lillooet has been used by non-Indians for some time too: the "Lillewhit" River appears in a Hudson's Bay Company census dated 1839, and both Lillooet Lake and Lillooet River appear on a map prepared by Alexander Caulfield Anderson, the surveyor, between 1832 and 1851.

This Indian Band at Pemberton was the most westerly of the Interior Salish and inhabited an area which was approximately one hundred miles square and which included much of the Bridge River; the confluence of the Bridge and the Fraser; and Seton, Anderson, Blackwater or Birkenhead, Duffy, Green and Alta Lakes — an area reaching as far southward as Harrison Lake. During the hunting season the people would go into the headwaters of the Lillooet River and beyond the mountains which they could see from the Upper Pemberton Valley.

These Pembertons were bounded on the east by the Thompson Indians, on the north-east by the Shuswap, on the north-west by the Chilcotin, on the west by the Tlahus and Sechelt, and on the south-west by the Squamish. The Interior Salish with their fine features and aquiline noses were a taller and finer built people than were their coast neightbours, but marriage with non-Salish had perhaps enhanced their physical appearance, and their strenuous hunting travel had created a strong symmetrical development — the Coast Salish who lived by the sea travelled mainly by water and were consequently of a heavier build.

The main settlements were on the Lower Lillooet River, on Lillooet Lake, at Port Douglas, and on the upper section of Harrison Lake. A small settlement approximately nineteen miles from Port Douglas was called Skookumchuck and this the Band used during the salmon run but it wintered at Port Douglas. The valley was probably never really thickly populated and there is little remaining evidence of people at all — a few ceremonial stones, an odd stone wedge or hammer to split cedar trees for canoe-making, and a few pumice stones hollowed out for medicine bowls. In fact, the kekuli holes, the dwelling sites at points where the salmon run in the fall, the rock paintings along Lillooet Lake and at a few points in the valley, and the absence of trails except a few in the mountains — all would indicate that travel was mainly by canoe and that people were never numerous.

Those first white traders travelling southward from Kamloops in the early nineteenth century saw a husky and well built people with broad chests and strong arms, and dressed entirely in skins. They were milder in disposition than the other tribes and were noted by the early explorers as being less warlike and more peaceful. They were intelligent, receptive, and quiet; they were good-natured and kind; and they were honest, industrious, and hospitable. And perhaps moody: suicide because of shame or jealousy or severe depression was common in the early days.

The thick black hair cut straight across the forehead fell either loose or in long braids at the back and the sides. The very old and the very young had their hair cut straight across the brow and wore it loose on their shoulders while warriors tied knots on the tops of their heads and at the back. Short hair signified a slave; hair trimmed across the shoulders, a mourner; hair covering the ears, a young unmarried woman; and a woman's half-shaven head declared her to be an adulteress. Salmon oil was the usual "pomade", and combs were of maple and dogwood.

Some of the people were tattooed, and often both men and women wore ear and nose ornaments of bone and horn with incised designs filled with paint and decorated further with shells, teeth, or tassels. Face painting was universal, with stripes of red, yellow, white and black. Necklaces of grizzly bear claws could only be worn by a Shaman who had that animal as his "Manitou", and feather necklaces by those who could claim the eagle or hawk as "Manitou", though headbands decorated with feathers warned that warriors were on the move. Glass beads and coloured threads became popular later.

The life of these people in the early days was a continuous struggle against hunger, against marauding tribes such as the Chilcotins and Thompsons, and against the ever-changing elements. With utmost ingenuity they had to create their tools, build their houses, make their clothes, gather their food, store it, and protect themselves.

For tools the Indian people depended upon stone which they cut, worked and flaked, and to some extent upon jade. They created knives and spear heads from sharpened stone, and used glassy basalt for chipping and flaking arrow heads, spear heads, knives and adzes. The pieces which flaked off became skin scrapers, but beaver teeth and deer antlers were sharp enough to split hides. Making hammers, cleaving wedges, cutting knives and adzes required painstaking effort, though sandstone was a help in shaping tools and in hollowing stone dishes. Birchwood provided the good cooking spoons and the harder maple supplied the pestles.

Of the trees, though, the Lillooets revered the versatile cedar, and when cutting the roots of the cedar for basket-making the Indian women would pray: "Oh, Friend, I come to ask you for your dress. I pray you do not be angry on this account, Long Life Giver." In the Pemberton Cemetery there is a grave of a young Scot who had come into the Lillooet Lake area seeking gold in the 'thirties and had dug under the roots of a large cedar which fell and killed him. Some Indians say that he had been disrespectful of the Cedar.

With only stone or bone tools the men would split cedar wood which they could mould by steam. Cedar provided canoes, paddles, domestic utensils, balers, and fish hooks, and cedar provided planks for houses, and shredded cedar became rope to tie those planks to the framework. Cedar also provided cradles and the primitive looms upon which the women wove cloth from the finely spun fibres of cedar bark or from the wool of dogs kept especially for their hair and for food. Twisted young cedar roots and twigs became ropes and lines for fishing nets and harpoons, and where the strain was severe animal sinews strengthened the cedar ropes. Shredded into soft padding cedar bark became bedding and mats for cradles. The jelly-like cambrian layer found in the spring on the inner surface of cedar bark became food. The long supple roots of the cedar tree form the base material of the baskets for which the Mount Currie people are justly famous.

From time immemorial the Indian women have made baskets, baskets for cooking and storing food, deep baskets for carrying berries, long baskets for carrying babies, baskets for storage chests. Gathering materials for basket-making takes time and effort. The basketmaker first digs out the roots of the cedar tree, taking care to obtain roots with few branches or knots, discarding unsuitable material, and leaving the thickest portion near the tree trunk. Cedar saplings supply the splints for the firm base, and cherry bark and grasses the decorations.

After a few days of drying, the roots are ready for splitting. First the worker peels off the outside bark, and then gripping the larger end of the root

Carrying on the old tradition

The Basket Makers

The Basket Makers

Dorse McTaggart

in her teeth uses both hands to pull off long thin strips, working carefully to keep them smooth and of even width. She then ties the split roots into bundles and stores them until she is ready to go to work. With a wide sharp knife she splits the saplings into inch-wide splits. Some of the cherry bark she leaves in its natural state to provide the red colour, and the rest she buries for a year in order to blacken it.

An early settler of Pemberton Meadows described the preparation of the grasses: "All the younger women would go to the upper end of the valley and spend the day gathering roots and bark. The old women would tend a fire in the pasture. When they had a good fire started they would gather green branches and leaves to keep on the fire and produce a great volume of smoke. The swamp grass was then moved to and fro through the smoke until well cured and bleached."

With all her materials at hand and a bowl of water nearby to soften her material, the basketmaker sets to work. First she cuts the sapling splints into the desired shape for the basket base, binding them together roughly with roots. She makes the first row by binding the long splits round the stiffer splints, attaching the next row by punching holes with a small sharp awl and pulling the strand through the hole. After finishing the base she builds up the sides of the basket in the same way, using the heavier splints to supply firmness as needed. For the sides she uses her best root splits, trimming them carefully to make them smooth and taking care that the best side faces outward. She makes her decoration by weaving in the cherry bark, both black and red, and the bleached grasses, and uses all her skill to make the patterns work out evenly. The basketmaker then winds splits smoothly over the upper edge, or finishes the basket with coiled roots to produce a firm, durable edge.

Another method, possibly older, is coiling the basket. The basketmaker binds together a bundle of root splits and winds the whole to form a coil, gradually building up the sides to form a very tight, almost waterproof, basket. The women improved the waterproof qualities of these baskets used for cooking by working a mass of fresh berries into the crevices, or by smearing the gum of balsam buds into the baskets. They also mended holes with yellow pine pitch or rewove parts so that the life of a coiled basket often extended over fifty years. To cook in one the women heated stones in the fire and dropped them into the basket which contained the food.

When contact was made with the white population the basketmakers added extra decorative touches to their wares to suit them for trade or sale. From the earliest days these fine baskets were exchanged for food or clothing, some of the loveliest changing hands for a bucket of rendered lard. The basketmakers adapted their craft to the needs of the settlers and made trays, and tables, and even match containers with the word "matches" worked into the pattern. Mrs. Johnny Sandy was a noted basketmaker of the early days and the most famous of the present-day basketmakers is Matilda Jim who continued to work when in her nineties and almost blind.

When the roads were fit for travel in the spring the Indian women would go up into the farming community with their winter's weaving carefully wrapped in white cloth. The trading procedure was entertaining and prolonged. After the farmer's wife had chosen her basket she would ask how much. The reply was, generally, "Some clothes." The farm wife raided her cupboards and put down an armful of clothing beside the basket. Garment by garment, the basketmaker picked them up and carefully investigated them for wear and tear. Having inspected them all and having made her choice, the basketmaker would finally ask for some fat. After a tin full of fat was added to the clothing, her next request was for some money. Unless the farmer's wife was prepared to spend some money, or had a friend visiting who wanted a basket and would pay cash, the deal was ended and, gathering up their baskets, the Indian women would go on to the next farm house.

Housing for the native peoples was no real problem except in winter. Summer houses were fairly easy to build: they were oblong or conical lodges covered with brush or bark and skins. An even more temporary shelter was made of merely rush mats and cedar boughs. Winter housing had to be less temporary, and was of two types, the semi-subterranean kekuli and the truly subterranean dwelling.

After choosing a site for a kekuli, usually close to a salmon stream, the men crossed two ropes at right angles on the ground to enable the builders to mark out a circle. They then scooped out the earth within the circle and saved it for later banking. The men set strong posts within the perimeter and upon these erected an ingenious pattern of rafters and braces to form a domelike structure which they then covered with skins, bark, grass and dirt. The fire was placed in the centre of the floor with a smoke hole directly above it. In bad weather when the ground level entrance was blocked, people used this hole as an entrance, the ladder being a notched log.

Exterior of kekuli house B.C. Provincial Museum

The truly subterranean communal homes were of logs and planks, and rectangular in shape with cedar posts at each corner supporting the framework and roof. These houses were deep into the ground, some completely buried, and well protected on the outside with slabs of bark and an earth-covered roof. In many cases the entrance was by ladder only. Inside, small compartments on either side separated the half-dozen families and a centre aisle served for the cooking fires. Chief Bill Pascal used to point to a spot across the street from his home in Mount Currie and indicate the remains of one in which his grandmother had lived.

Clothing was as important as housing, and clothing too came almost directly off the mountainside and from the swamps. Snares caught small animals like marten, muskrat and mink; trained hunting dogs ran down deer, panther, lynx and coyote. And the bow and arrow was most important. Like those of the Thompson Indians, the flat bows wound with cherry bark or backed with a sinew were basically made of yellow cedar, yew, cypress, maple, dogwood or vine maple, while arrows were of service berry bush, from dogwood, hazel nut, and sometimes cedar. Winter hunting required snowshoes with frames of vine maple, yew and occasionally cedar, and the fine mesh webbing of twisted rawhide woven in an elaborate pattern. Two general types of snowshoe were common, the round "bear paw" for short trips and the long narrow kind with its wooden cross bars and even more elaborate webbing for longer trips. Construction of the two was essentially the same, with the harness fitted to allow the foot to be easily removed in case of breaking ice.

Clothing suited the weather. In fact summer clothing was negligible. For men, a breech-clout and a head band; for women, a breech-clout and a short vest because the breasts had to be covered. Children ran naked. But other seasons demanded other clothes which came from animal skins and shredded bark fibres, and the wool of the mountain goats, mountain sheep, and dogs. The skins of small animals became decoration as well as pieces to hold clothes together. Dried grasses lined the decorated moccasins in summer, and woven socks of animal hair lined them in winter. Summer head bands were of buckskin or dyed cedar bark and winter caps were of coyote skin. The fringed leggings were of buckskin. Men's shoes were made of deer hide, and the fine slippers of the women were of fish skin, the soles treated with fir or pine resin mixed with earth or sand for durability. Dried moss supplied diapers, and the underbark of cedar, or goat and dog hair, provided material for woven underwear.

Preparing buckskin for clothing was arduous and time consuming. After being stretched and dried the hides were rubbed with the decomposed brains of animals, with marrow or salmon oil, salmon roe, and occasionally with rotted wood. The women repeated the process three times before finally drying the skin in the sun and wind, and then again stretching it on a framework of poles and beating it until it was soft. Special beaters' pins were made of thorn, needles from bone, and thread from fine willow fibres. Buckskin was sometimes coloured by smoking before being shaped into a garment.

The detail and decorative work must also have been time consuming. The women excelled in elaborate quill and beadwork, using quills of porcupine, swan and goose feathers, seeds and shells, and later using glass beads and shells obtained by trade with the coastal peoples. Claws and tails of small animals like weasel and mink also became ornament. The fringes on garments usually concealed the seams. Although the women of some groups wore soft clothes beneath their breech-clouts and dresses the local women did not do so, but older women in the Mount Currie Band do remember weaving cedar bark into underwear.

Besides supplying clothing, the mountains and valleys also supplied the food. Some animals provided several necessities: porcupine, for example, was used for both food and decoration; grizzly bear and panther were valuable for claws, meat, and skins; swans and geese were both food and a supply of quills and feathers.

But game in general was plentiful throughout the area: mule deer, black-tailed deer, mountain goat, black bear, marmot and porcupine. Smaller animals such as lynx and coyote were acceptable when other meat was scarce. Carrying service berries with them for food the hunters went out with the trained hunting dogs used to run down the game, and at times various types of camouflaged pitfalls captured large game to be finished off by the hunters' arrows. Berries were abundant in summer when they were dried for winter use and for men to carry on the hunting trips. Service berries, or saskatoons, were most common.

It was the responsibility of the women and children to gather the abundant edible leaves, ferns, huckleberries, service berries and soopolallie; snow lily and tiger lily roots, wild onion, wild carrots, bracken roots, and wild clover; roots of Indian potatoes and of camass and dog-tooth violet; hazel nuts, and kernels of white and yellow pine cones. Young wild raspberry and salmon berry shoots were cooked as a vegetable: tied into bundles they were boiled and served with fish oil. Wild raspberry shoots taken in early spring and eaten raw were a sure cure for a stubborn cough. Edible mushrooms, such as the meadow mushroom of the fall, the large, firm mushrooms of the forests, and the morels that flourished in the spring under the cottonwood trees, provided extra flavour and, when plentiful, were dried for winter use. Young shoots from berry bushes gathered in the spring, eaten raw or boiled in fish oil, provided the needed leaven of fresh vitamins.

The lakes abounded with trout and dollies, but the Pacific salmon travelling up the lakes and rivers to their spawning grounds were the Lillooets' most important food. A rich source of protein and fat, the salmon is rich too in vitamins and minerals, and the iodine content prevented the Indian people from suffering from the goitre that plagued the early white settlers and their animals. First up the rivers are the Spring or Tyee and in the late summer and fall come the Sockeye and the Cohoe. Anderson Lake provided the land-locked Kokanee. Of all the varieties, the dark red sockeye is the richest and most valued.

Indian women drying soopolallie B.C. Government photo

The Indians set nets in the lakes, and bag nets and traps in the streams, and in the shallows speared the fish with sticks. The favourite fishing locations were Skookumchuck rapids, the upper end of Lillooet Lake, and the Pole or Birkenhead River, and the lower Lillooet River. Above the present-day Pemberton Village, at Salmon Slough, the Lillooets gathered to catch and dry salmon for winter.

Some of the women still use sheds and frames for drying salmon in the old way. They drive four or more posts into the ground and lay crosspieces from post to post, and on this framework rest other poles from which to hang the split fish. The women keep a slow cool smoke from daylight to dark and cut the flesh of the salmon in a criss-cross pattern to facilitate the drying. The end product is very hard and very dry, and younger housekeepers prefer to freeze or can their food for winter use.

But generation after generation carefully stored the salmon oil for winter medicine and for use in flavouring food. Extraction was done, when possible, along the river banks where water action had hollowed out depressions in the rocks, and these depressions served as rendering kettles. The young men would build a good fire in which they heated stones to throw into the kettles which contained water and the heads and fatty parts of the salmon. The water would boil and the oil would rise to the top where it was carefully skimmed off, often with the horn of a mountain goat. The same technique was used to render oil in baskets.

Salmon on drying racks Provincial Archives, Victoria, B.C.

Oil was stored in fish skins, the tears and natural openings of which were sealed with gum. When the skin was filled the top was tied fast and sealed with gum made from salmon which the women had patiently chewed until it reached the proper consistency. The oil was also stored in hollowed stone dishes. Lack of fish oil caused serious illness among the Indian population, and marauding bands could often keep the local people away from their annual catch.

These native peoples had several ways of cooking food. They roasted it in hot embers, broiled it on sticks supported over the fire or boiled it in water heated in baskets. Fish cooked in water was first wrapped in leaves or bark to prevent its breaking into pieces.

Stone ovens, however, served for cooking most food. These were oblong pits lined with stones and heated by fires in the pit. When the stones were hot the debris from the fire was removed and the food, wrapped in bundles, was placed on the stones, and the oven carefully covered over with grass and earth, leaving a small vent for steam to escape. When the people returned from a day of hunting or gathering food they had a hot meal waiting for them, a meal which could have included a kind of wild potato.

The remains of such stone ovens have been found in three places in the Pemberton Valley. Walter and Margaret Green found one when clearing land, and the stones, when pushed, disintegrated into powder. Another is located on the John Decker property at Mount Currie, and Howard Ayers found some large ovens near the old road which led over the Harvey Nelson Hill to Mount Currie.

Because baskets could not hold a great amount, other storage techniques had to be devised. A framework of poles covered with fir boughs, bark or hides, was all right, but offered little protection from raiding animals. More resistant were the very strong caches of logs raised on sturdy poles, or the deep pits lined with bark and covered with heavy stones, or the caches made in trees, a platform across the branches being strapped on with leather thongs. Dug out cellars carefully made and lined with bark were called "Powa'wan" and into these went food wrapped in bundles of bark. All surplus food not needed for winter stayed in the Powa'wan until spring and the food so stored was known as "Ka'za". Made with less care and entered during the winter according to need, another type of cellar, the "Sqo'zeks", stood near the house.

Not only did the Pemberton people have to shelter, clothe and feed themselves, they had also to protect themselves. Early settlements were small, but the native people soon realized that they had to establish larger villages in order to fight off raiding parties from other bands. Though mild in disposition, they called themselves the "Knife People" because of an old legend about a mythical monster which had "thrown a knife" to them.

Their greatest fear came from the northerly Chilcotins whose prisoners never returned, but the Shuswaps, too, in a long war with the Lillooets came in small raiding parties to steal fish and kill any Lillooet in sight. At one time these Shuswaps took possession of a large section of the Lillooets' territory along the Pole River and to Anderson and Seton Lakes, and to Lillooet Lake. They even dammed the Lillooet River about eight miles above Lillooet Lake and built a fortified camp there to keep the Pemberton Band from its main supply of salmon. Parties from this camp harassed the bands located on Lillooet Lake and those living between present-day Mount Currie and Anderson Lake. The intruders also cut off the Pemberton Indians from the usual hunting, and the upper Lillooet people were so short of food at home that they went to winter with people of the lower Lillooet River who finally had to retreat to an area between Warm Springs and Douglas. The people of Green Lake, and Anderson and Seton Lakes also feared the Shuswaps who thus held the central area by dividing the local bands. When spring came the Shuswaps left, taking with them many young women and boys as slaves, and large quantities of dried fish. Such invasions they repeated in the following two years and for about fifteen years uncertainty continued.

Older people tell that one old woman of the Lillooets was so very much annoyed by this raiding that she persuaded her sons Nxemo'tenetc and Isa's to train in order to rid the area of the Shuswap menace. They trained for several years and became very skillful and strong, but when a party of raiding Shuswaps finally did come its strength was such that the brothers could do nothing, although one visited a Shuswap fish trap where an alert Shuswap stabbed him. The brothers then made an underground shelter on the north side of the Lillooet River just opposite the present Mount Currie Reserve, a shelter with several subterranean passages, one leading to the river bank. The next Shuswap raiding party was smaller, but it found the house and set fire to it. The brothers, though, escaped. A Shuswap saw them emerging from a tunnel, chased them, and fired arrows at them. Nxemo'tenetc and Isa's pretended to be wounded in order to induce the Shuswaps to follow. They did follow and the brothers led them into the swamp at the foot of Pemberton Meadows, where the brothers ran across the quaking bog and all but two of the four hundred Shuswaps sank. The brothers told the two survivors that their lives would be spared if they returned to their own country with the story of the massacre of their comrades, and the threat of the Lillooet Indians to kill all the Shuswaps should they dare to raid again. The brothers being kindly people also told the Shuswaps they would like to be friends and that if the Shuswaps needed salmon they could come in peace to fish. The Shuswaps never came again in any combative force, but small groups did come to fish and to visit. Francis Wallace of Mount Currie told of a graveyard on an island off Boulder Creek for burying local Indians killed by enemies from the Fraser and Thompson Rivers.

Father Chirouse Provincial Archives, Victoria, B.C.

Further trouble came from the Thompson Indians during a potlatch at Hope when a quarrel arose between a Lillooet and a Thompson and the Lillooet was killed. Later the son of the Lillooet avenged his father's death by slitting the throats of a group of Thompsons while they slept. Seeking revenge, the Thompson band killed a young Lillooet woman who had gone alone to prepare a place for drying berries. Relatives found the body and in the ensuing fight a Thompson fired a gun, the first gun-fire the Indians of the Lillooet Band had ever heard. Following this incident the Lillooet poeple, having driven out the Thompsons, built several fortified houses on the west side of Lillooet Lake and River and those people living on the other side moved across, only venturing back to the east side in daylight. In spite of their precautions, two small parties of Lillooets who ventured across to the east side of Lillooet Lake the following summer met a party of Thompsons who killed them.

MEETING THOSE COMING LATER

Before the coming of the white man, and long before that first rifle shot, the Indian traders in their dug-out canoes had travelled the lakes and rivers to Cayoosh in the north — later known as the Village of Lillooet — and to Scowlitz, or Harrison Mills, in the south. Undoubtedly the first contact with the white men was made by these Lillooet traders during their visits to the neighbouring tribes.

The first known traders to visit the Lillooet Indians were the Hudson's Bay men who came south from Kamloops looking for a new route to Fort Langley, and it could have been from these men or through earlier Indian traders that the people along the meandering Lillooet River and living on its rich silt-laden flood-plain obtained their first cultivated potatoes. Joe Joseph says that the land he inherited from his grandmother grew the first potatoes in the valley and that before the Gold Rush, when she was only six, his grandmother had travelled to the coast with relatives and there visited a Mount Currie woman who had moved away from the valley and was then living somewhere in what we now call the Lower Mainland, perhaps around Fort Langley. When Joe's grandmother and her relatives were leaving to return to their Lillooet River homes the woman they had visited gave them a pail of "skinny", long, "lady finger" potatoes, and said to plant them all that year, but to save the whole crop of the first year and plant that crop with the coming of the second spring. Then, she said, the Mount Currie people could eat some of the potatoes they would dig up the next fall. The returning visitors followed directions because the cultivation of domestic potatoes fitted well into the gardening practices of Indian women who dug them with forked sticks, and early miners making their way north to the Fraser River gold fields stared in astonishment at the potato fields of Joe's ancestors.

The coming of the white man certainly changed the way of life of the Indian people, but every new influx of settlers or passers-through created work for them. The Hudson's Bay traders, such as Alexander Caulfield Anderson who came through in the spring of 1846, would hire Indian canoeists to take them down the sixteen miles of Lillooet Lake. In the Gold Rush days some twelve years later, "willing and active" Indian crews helped to unload freight from any incoming steamer, among them Paul Dick's father and Dr. Joseph of D'Arcy. Stores set up to supply the packers and miners traded also with the indigenous population, offering knives, iron pots and guns in exchange for smoked fish, meat and labour. The end of the Gold Rush in the 1860's saw the return of the local population to their traditional ways and with the removal of the machinery from the old steamer *Prince of Wales* travellers were again hiring Indian canoeists. In addition, early farmers moving into the area to supply the miners passing through often married Indian women. John Currie, for whom the area was later to be named, married a Lillooet woman, and they raised two sons and a daughter.

The opening of the Squamish trail provided Indian men with opportunities for employment as packers, both this route and the route by lakes and portages to Lillooet being in use at this time. Mack Seymour packed for McKenzie, Francis Wallace travelled with his father who was bringing blasting powder to road foreman James Punch, and Harry Dan rode on Billy Williams' pack horses that brought supplies to Sam Spetch, the first of the traders to remain in the area.

Andrew Joseph was the first mail carrier, serving the Post Office at the Currie ranch. Later mail carriers from the Indian village, men such as Charlie Wallace, Felix Sam and Bill Pascal, often combined their mail trips with packing goods to and from the stores, and early settlers came to rely on these men for advice and assistance. Paul Dick paddled new settlers such as Maria Poole and Ernest and Gladys Blakeway on lakes and down rivers, and even after the first world war carried Frances McCulloch, a Scottish warbride, in his dugout to her husband's cabin on the shores of Lillooet Lake.

In 1881 some 5,000 acres of land, the main portion of which stretched from present-day Mount Currie down to Lillooet Lake, was reserved for the Indian community. When Commissioner Peter O'Reilly of the Department of Indian Affairs visited the village, Chief Stager pointed out that the 160 acres on which the principal village stood had been given to the Indians by Governor Douglas some twenty years earlier, but no record of the gift could be traced at the land office. By the early 1900's the Indian people were raising fine crops and cultivating fruits such as plums, cherries, apples and currants. A further 1200 acres were added to the reserve over the next thirty years, including some 800 acres purchased for the Catholic Church by Bishop Durieu in 1886 and turned over to the Indians in 1905. A great part of these later additions consisted of mountainsides rich in timber, but unsuitable for cultivation.

Early settlers in Pemberton Meadows employed Indian helpers who either camped out in their home-made shelters or slept in barns or sheds. Sometimes they ate at the settlers' family table, but in fine weather they usually cooked their own supplies over campfires. Women like Mrs. Johnny Sandy worked at housecleaning and washing, weeding crops, thinning turnips, planting and picking up potatoes. Two Indian women could keep up with six men digging

Mrs. Johnny Sandy

Paul Dick, former chief, in 1959 Provincial Archives

potatoes with spades. Much of the payment was in kind and few references are made to the actual amounts paid in wages, which could not have been much because in 1914 Indian workers were digging potatoes for 12½c a sack. Indians like Sam Jim helped in the construction of barns and other buildings, and cleared the site for the fish hatchery at Owl Creek. In 1912 Gabriel Abraham cut one thousand fence rails for 2c each. In addition, the Indian people traded apples, greengages, huckleberries, baskets, salmon and venison, for butter, bacon, beef and vegetables. Teams of horses loaned to white settlers were often paid for with hay and foods such as butter or pork. Upper Valley farmers bought seed corn from the Indians and sold them both wheat and oats.

Indian children rushed out barefoot to greet the first train to stop at Chilsampton, to be known locally as Creekside or the Rancherie from the 'twenties to the 'fifties when the name Mount Currie was finally chosen to replace both the railroad name of Chilsampton and the Post Office name of Creekside. The special fares offered on the railroad enabled Indian workers to travel to the Fraser Valley and Washington for hop-picking and fruit harvesting.

The influx of settlers to Pemberton Valley in the 1920's and 1930's brought even more opportunities for seasonal work for the Indians on the local farms. By that time most farms had a small shack, often with an old stove or heater, to accommodate their Indian help. In the fall the Mount Currie women would travel up the valley with baskets of huckleberries which they sold for $10 a hundred pounds.

With the introduction of the chain digger on the farms in the late 'forties much larger Indian crews were required for picking potatoes. Instead of staying on the farms in cabins, the workers were picked up daily outside Spetch's store and transported to the farms, usually crowded onto the back of a pick-up truck. They carried their own lunches though the farmers' wives supplied hot coffee and cookies mid-morning and mid-afternoon. The standard rate of pay for potato pickers in 1950 was $5 a day, a rate gradually increased over the next ten years. The crew boss was sometimes paid an extra dollar, as were the men who loaded the potatoes onto the wagons. These cheerful, hard-working crews would each pick an average of two tons a day in all kinds of weather; only pouring rain, impossible mud, or hard frost would deter them. Heading back to Mount Currie the farm pick-up would be loaded down with sacks of potatoes — a welcome supplement to the wages.

The expanding potato production of the late 'fifties meant most of Mount Currie's able-bodied men and women were pressed into service for the season, and children in their early teens often spent their Saturday holidays in the potato fields, but by the mid-'sixties the potato combine began to replace the old chain diggers. Big crews were then no longer needed and only a few Indians worked at sorting, planting, or at the Co-op grading table.

Hand-logging was also lucrative. During the hand-logging era the Indian and non-Indian men worked side by side on the crews, and the expansion of the logging industry in the 'fifties offered many more opportunities for work in the bush. The Indian men proved to be good bush workers from the start, and in later years they were to harvest their own reserve timber, and to run their own outfits.

Besides occasional employment and trade goods, the white men also brought problems for the indigenous population. Traditional ways continued in the early days, but were gradually restricted. Early diaries mention parties travelling up the Valley in the fall on hunting trips, sometimes on horseback and sometimes with wagons and teams, but though the Indians fished and hunted as they had always done, the traditional method of dogging deer had brought severe criticism from the game department, and the native peoples gave the first fisheries officials a cool reception.

The white man also brought diseases for which the local population had acquired no resistance. An early epidemic of small-pox wiped out one settlement at the south end of Lillooet Lake, and tuberculosis continued to be a horror until the introduction of the immunization program. The 1918 flu claimed many lives in the little Indian villages and such diseases as measles had a virulence unknown in the white population. By 1933 the census showed only 350 Indians on the Creekside reservation, and the graveyard proves that many of them did not survive babyhood and early childhood.

As in other places, the break from traditional ways was not always beneficial, but governments did make some efforts over the years. The introduction of the Indian Health Service was the first step back to better health, with Sally Purden as part-time resident nurse from 1936 until 1971. Better housing was much slower to come and by the time it did more generous relief and dental health services had had some results. The most significant improvements came with the housing programs of the late 'sixties and with the expansion of the logging industry.

The Indian community also changed over the years as trading facilities improved and expanded. Trading stations and little stores had come and gone during the gold rush period and after, but Sam Spetch who established the Pemberton Portage Post Office and store at Owl Creek became the "father" of storekeeping in this district. Bill Kiltz of the Lillooet Lake Trading Company built Creekside's first store in 1923, and after it burned he built close to the station where the school stands today. By 1937 Sam Spetch's son Bill had moved his store and post office over to Creekside to serve the Indian village, where George and Adelina Williams were already operating a small family store in their home on the reserve and which they operated until the early 'fifties.

During the early 'forties, the businesses in Creekside changed little from the depression years, but in the late 'forties and early 'fifties went through a period of change and expansion. On joining the army in 1940 Bill Spetch sold out to his brother Walter who rented the business to Jack and Alice McKay. The McKays purchased the store in 1943 and four years later sold it back to Bill who was then home from the army with his Scottish-born wife Jean. An energetic and enterprising businessman, Bill was partners with George Walker for several years in a logging operation while George McDonald ran the store. To serve the now rapidly increasing Indian population Bill embarked in the mid-'fifties on a series of store expansions. In 1955 he opened a dry goods store, first run by Bill Pascal near the railroad, and then in a fine new building opposite the old grocery store. This store, known first as Penny's and later as Mount Currie Dry Goods, was the first in the area to specialize in clothing.

The *Bridge River-Lillooet News* in 1965 had a comment: "One can find lots of different accents in Canada made up as it is with adventurers from all over the world. In the ready-to-wear store in Mount Currie you will hear a Scotch brogue for sure. Mrs. Spetch operates this busy shop far from her native Scotland and hasn't any desire to go anywhere else away from Mount Currie. . . . Jean says she hasn't the headaches some businesses have in other places where there is a high welfare rate and a shifting population. 'Everyone knows everyone around here and there is no dishonesty,' says Mrs. Spetch. 'There is no trouble with unpaid bills as a result'."

Bill Spetch next built the hardware store to which he moved the post office. This store he rented first, briefly, to the Pomeroys and then, in February 1957, to Fred and Eleanor Collister who later purchased the business and were to remain there for nearly twenty years. Fred was soon involved in a thriving electrical business and Eleanor ran the store, keeping house in the apartment behind. In 1965 the *Bridge River-Lillooet News* reported on them: "we found Mrs. Collister, peppy and busy, selling chains, bolts and all manner of things pertaining to a man's world with the aplomb of long experience. . . . Mrs. Collister answered phone calls, handed out mail, made out money orders and sold electrical appliances, all the while welcoming callers like ourselves."

In 1957 Jack and Ada Graham took over the grocery store from Bill Spetch, remaining there until Jack's retirement. During his years as Justice of the Peace, Jack took a sympathetic interest in the problems of juvenile offenders, working with the leaders of both the Indian and white communities. Closely allied to this work was Jack's chairmanship of the Family Court committee of 1964, whose other members were Band Chief Francis Wallace, Indian Agent Vaughan-Jones, Father Wilfred Scott, Adelina Williams, Leo Nelson, Joe Joseph, Edward Paul, Slim Fougberg, Jim Buss, Assistant Forest Ranger Burnie Salter, and Justice of the Peace Jack Decker.

Just down the road from Mount Currie Hardware, Gerry Boulanger ran a small cafe in a cabin built by Bill Spetch in the 'forties as a construction camp cookhouse. Gerry also ran a taxi service between Mount Currie and Pemberton, and for the first time residents of Mount Currie without cars were able to travel with ease to Pemberton for shopping. In the 'sixties, a cafe operated out of a converted railroad coach just south of the station; among the proprietors were Dave and Marion Janzen and Adelina Williams. Nearby, Harry and Frances Erickson had a small gift shop which sold souvenirs, mainly driftwood fashioned into ornaments and lamps by Frances.

Selling groceries, hardware, basic clothing and some medical supplies, the little general store at the station, owned by Bill Kiltz of the Lillooet Lake Trading Company, was run by Bill Simpson and Fred Sweet from the mid-'thirties until 1946 when Gerry and Florence Cowell took over and managed the business for some four years. Their sons, Jack Matthews and Roy Cowell, started a trucking business in 1946, hauling ties and lumber for George Walker, gravel for the P.F.R.A., and potatoes for the valley farmers. After the Cowells, Hector and Adele Harwood used the store building as a restaurant, while Adele's mother, Henrietta Boeur lived in the small house built by Roy Cowell at the time of his marriage to Ruth Shore of Pemberton. Because this building was on reserve land, it was pulled down when the school was expanded in the 'fifties.

At the Second Dicennial Conference on Native Indian Affairs William Pascal of Mount Currie spoke of his experiences managing a store:

"I should not be speaking on this subject, for there are a number of Indians in this Province who are running much bigger enterprises than mine. In fact, I am only a merchant by accident, but perhaps for that reason, and because of the very casual way that I got into storekeeping, what I have to say may be of some value to others.

"I am quite sure than any Indian who is reasonably honest, and who is willing to do a little planning, can make a success of a small business. I knew nothing whatever about running a store when one day the white man who ran the little business where I live handed me the keys of the building and the combination of the safe, and asked me to keep the place open for him while he was away for a few days. Actually, he stayed away for a month, and when he came back he looked at the accounts and said 'You are doing just fine. Keep on running the store for another month.' So I kept on for another month, then for another six months, and then I ended up by running the business altogether.

"I had managed to collect all the bad debts, to put the business on a sound footing and to make it pay. There have been a few ups and downs since then, but it has been a reasonably successful undertaking. There must be a number of places in the Province where the opportunity for a small business is at least as good as at Pemberton, and there is no reason at all why an Indian should not grasp the opportunity."

After the coming of white traders, and using the same routes, came the Roman Catholic Missionaries to minister to the Indian villages along the shores of Lillooet Lake. The earliest baptismal certificates in existence in Mount Currie are those of Pierre Jim and his wife, Margaret, dated 1859. Margaret Jim died in March of 1957.

In 1861 Oblate Fathers Fouquet and Grandidier, at the invitation of the Skookumchuck chiefs, made a three-month trip through Harrison Lake, Douglas and Lillooet River districts as far as Alexandria. They started from New Westminster, travelling to Scowlitz, Chehalis, and then by canoe to Port Douglas. The native people did not at that time live on reserves, but lived in small family settlements at points advantageous for fishing, trapping and hunting, and moved frequently from place to place according to the foods provided by the seasons of the year. The missionaries established two centres where they built churches, Skookumchuck and Shalalth.

For many years missionaries visited these points once or twice a year, staying a week or two at each place. They taught the Indians prayers and hymns, appointed church chiefs and watchmen who, besides fulfilling duties when the missionaries were present, also formed a nucleus of local authority among the Indian bands, and acted as leaders and councillors. During this period the Indians were encouraged to move from their poorer holdings along the lakes to the river meadows of the present reserve. For the church services they journeyed either to Skookumchuck or Shalalth where the Oblate Fathers held their missions. Many of the Indians intermarried and a significant proportion of the present-day Mount Currie families are descended from the natives of these two centres.

By the time Commissioner Peter O'Reilly visited the area in 1881 a church had been built in the principal village on the meadows between the Lillooet and Birkenhead Rivers. This building was destroyed by fire and replaced during the ministry of Father Chirouse in 1896. The church at Tenas, built around the same time, burned in the 1930's after sitting unused for a number of years. The church still standing at Skookumchuck was started in 1905 and required ten years to complete, and another ten years for the congregation to pay for the stained glass windows. Built mainly of hand-hewn timbers, the church boasts an altar and pews made by the Indians themselves. The Indian men pulled wagonloads of lumber to the site because the horses were neither large enough nor strong enough to do the job. Chief Harry Peters, Captain Alex and Captain Jim were among those who worked at building this church.

Father Chirouse also travelled up to Pemberton Meadows to minister to the white settlers there. Among the babies he christened were James and Sis Punch, and Norman Dermody. On one of his visits Father Chirouse, a saintly absent-minded man, spent the night at Dermody's, and when the time came to pack up he could not find his nightshirt. He turned out his suitcase and searched his room, but no nightshirt was to be found. "Is it possible, Father", said Mrs. Dermody from the stove where she was busy preparing the after-Mass breakfast, "that you are still wearing your nightshirt?" And indeed that proved to be the case.

Father Rohr, who followed Father Chirouse, stayed for more than thirty years in the Lillooet area. In 1908 he was marooned at the Punch home during a flood and the Indians came up from the reserve in canoes to fetch him. In a letter written when he was an old man he said, "Often my thoughts are wandering in the lands where I spent the most glorious days of my life. Pemberton has been and is still the spot in British Columbia where I loved to go and visit the Indians and the whites. Everywhere I went I was a welcome visitor. . . ." As an old man he made a pre-Christmas trip to Port Douglas by way of Harrison Lake and held midnight Mass at the church at Skookumchuck. From far and near came 200 Indians to attend that Christmas service and to visit with their old friend.

Congregation of St. Christopher's Church, early 1900's Provincial Archives, Victoria, B.C.

The first resident priest was Father Patterson who came to Mount Currie in the late 'forties. During his ministry the old church burnt down and was replaced by the present church and priest's residence in 1953. Because this church served all the Catholics in the area, it was not built on reserve land but in the small pocket of privately owned property near the stores. Father Patterson was followed by Father Wilfred Scott in 1954 and then by Father Coffin in 1956. In 1963 Father Scott returned to Mount Currie where he continues his ministry today.

Through the boarding school at Mission the Catholic Church extended its influence to the education of Mount Currie children. In 1958 the one-room elementary school built in the mid-'thirties in Mount Currie village was replaced by a larger building with several rooms and a staff residence. Under the principalship of Sister Mary Immaculata, the school was soon entirely staffed by the Catholic Sisters of Christ the King. The *Bridge River-Lilloet News* in January 1965 reported on the school:

"A great part of the interest in the Mount Currie village centres around the day school. The Principal is Sister Mary Immaculata whose dainty and gentle appearance belies the precision with which she carries out her difficult job. The old original building houses the grade ones and kindergarten tots. The other end of the large sprawling building contains the classrooms and the living quarters of the devoted sisters of Christ the King, who teach all grades to seven.

"During the rainy winter weather there is no shelter for the children outside. So, when things get too bad the gym classes are taken to the old rancherie to use the Community Hall there for games such as basketball, volleyball and other indoor sports.

"The school rooms are bright and modern looking and kept in good repair and, from reports, the parents are all proud of the advantages of education that their children are getting both on the reserve and at the high school in Pemberton where the older children from grade eight are taken by bus.

"The teachers are from Quebec and New Brunswick . . . are all delighted with the climate . . . and find the children most respectful, easy to teach and very lovable.

"One of the most successful of their school enterprises is the participation in sports. Last year, before the grade eights were bussed to Pemberton, the boys' soccer team travelled to Sechelt, Pemberton and Mission and were very successful. The Indian children show marked ability in this game and have always been champions in contests around the area. Now that the highest grade is seven the teams have fewer good mature players to call on but they are in training for the next year when they can be of use to the High School now being completed in Pemberton. The children are very fond of basketball, and play outside until weather forbids.

"The school has a very fine Girl Guide and Brownie pack. The Guides, some 24 to 30 girls with Guide captain, Sister Mary Immaculata, are divided into four patrols with Christine and Mabel Leo, Annie Jones and Matilda Pascal as patrol leaders. These patrol leaders went to a leadership camp at Wilson Creek near Sechelt.

"This was a wonderful and instructive weekend for the girls for they went by themselves and joined with 60 other patrol leaders from other areas. They were very proud to be the only Indian band from the area. . . .

"The Brownies, about 24-30, are coming along very well under the leadership of Sister Mary Clements who is the Brown Owl of the pack. Everyone has a spanking new uniform and is bent on making their club the best in B.C. This year another all Indian pack has been started in Anahim so that the Mount Currie groups will have competition. . . .

"Another useful part of the school picture is the Kateri Club. This is a relative of the PTA club in the Province and was so named in honor of an eastern Indian girl, who through good works was Canonized. . . .

"This Kateri Club on the reserve has been indeed helpful to the school. The president, George Leo, is a very able speaker and an excellent leader, realizing with a minimum of quibbling what is needed. He is looked up to and depended on for his wisdom and help. Agnes Pascal is the vice-president and one of the sisters is the secretary.

"One of the projects this year was buying Guides and Brownies their uniforms. Some of the other things done by the Kateri Club were the buying of a record player and records. . . .

"One of the very fine parts of the school is a tiny chapel for the sisters' use. . . . It is only a tiny corner but has an air of quiet peace and joy."

May Queen and her attendants

BY AND ABOUT

REMINISCENCES OF BETSY JACK

Born, Port Douglas 1888
Died, Vancouver 1974

When the white men came, everybody got married. My mother-in-law for six years had lived with my father-in-law before they were married. Old Goodwin Purcell married a woman named Mary. They were married in the old church.

The first church at Douglas was made of rough lumber. Old Basil Charlie's father made the altar; it was lovely. The benches were lovely, too. We pulled the old church down when we built the new one. Both were St. Joseph's.

Skookumchuck Church is the Sacred Heart. The Indians had to pay to get the three towers. That church cost a lot of money. There was just a little trail for the Indians to drag the lumber. Bishop William Duke blessed the church.

The men, they were clearing at St. Mary's School. Boats and canoes took them right down to Mission. Some Indians walked down in moccasins every year, so it was a long time ago.

Ignace Jacob started the Mount Currie band. He had learned music at St. Mary's in Mission, and he had learned English so fast. Then he took a correspondence course in music.

When I was about five my father died. We couldn't afford shoes and stockings. My uncle's mother used to trap little squirrels that got apples in our cellar, and made me stockings and moccasins. It was a tough life, with my stepfather just about killing me.

These whites that came first gave me twenty-five cents and fifty cents. I gave the money to my grandmother. She put it away and saved it for my shoes. I had fur inside my shoes for stockings.

In 1908 when I was going to be married, they took me to New Westminster with my mother. It was the twenty-fourth of May. We got to New

Exchanging News

Westminster and there was a message from the priest. I was going to get married to the guy that took me down. "No, Lord", I said to the Bishop. "I'm not going to do that." The third time he blessed me. I kneeled down a long time with the Bishop, Bishop Dontenwell. I had my last confession. I was going to be married tomorrow. I didn't want to.

I had eleven kids. Girls of mine married into the White Act. Boys married into the Indian Act. My husband died in 1951.

SALISH MARRIAGE HYMN

Now for you there is no rain,
    For one is shelter to the other.
Now for you there is no sun,
    For one is shelter to the other.
Now for you nothing is hard or bad,
    For the hardness and the badness is taken
By one for the other.
    Now for you there is no night,
For one is light to the other.
    Now for you the snow has ended always,
For one is protection for the other,
    It is that way, from now on, from now on.
Now it is good and there is always food,
    And now there is always drink,
And now there is comfort. Now there is no loneliness
    Now forever — forever, there is no loneliness.

MY GHOST

By Richard Sam, 1968

Ever since I could understand the old people, my grandparents have told me ghost stories. They told me a ghost was out every evening looking for young boys and girls to take them and eat them piece by piece. This got me scared and I asked my grandpa how I could tell when the ghost was around. He told me it makes a cuckooing sound, just like a cuckoo clock, but a lot faster, and that it made the sound toward the end of the evening. I used to stay outside and listen for that sound. By God, I did hear it. That was enough to send me running home. I was too puny to be eaten.

Not until about five years ago did I find out what that cuckooing sound was. When I was riding my horse out by the pond, I began to hear the sound. Right away I started for home at a gallop. Because I was a little older though not much braver by this time, every time I heard the sound I would look to see where it came from. From what I could see it was coming from a bird. The bird would fly up and glide down, and gliding down it produced a cuckooing sound. If I hadn't stayed out there I probably still would believe I heard a ghost. My grandparents had used a good way of getting me home at night.

THE LEGEND OF GUNSIGHT MOUNTAIN

From Paul Dick

Look up Tenas Lake on a clear day, and you can't miss seeing Gunsight Mountain. That mountain has two high peaks, all rock. One log lies between them. Where did it come from? Maybe from the flood.

THE CHEHALIS LEGEND

By Darryl Stager, 1970

This story took place in Chehalis quite a while ago. The people there always used pitch for kindling.

Henry Sam, an old man, was the guy who collected pitch from up the hills. On one of his collecting trips he hadn't realized how high he had gone. Suddenly he turned a corner, and there on a great flat rock he saw a hairy creature lying sleeping. Henry thought "Sasquatch", and started running. He ran until he reached home.

He told all the people in the village about the sasquatch. They prayed and they locked their doors and windows.

That night Henry went to the outhouse. As he came back to his house he heard slurping and munching. He went to look at the garbage pit, and once again he saw the sasquatch. Henry didn't run this time; he watched for at least

Honoured at centennial celebration in 1958

The Squamish Times

three minutes. Then he walked very quietly to his home and told his wife. She came out and saw the hairy sasquatch. When she turned and started off to tell some neighbours, she stepped on a twig. The sasquatch heard the cracking sound and leaped out of the pit. Henry and Sue ran into their home just in time. The sasquatch tipped the house about three inches off the ground, then left.

The people of Chehalis have never seen the sasquatch again, but from that time they have talked about his visit to their village. Today they still find prints of his feet.

STORY FROM MY GRANDFATHER

By Paul Dick

Most of the people and all the animals were on the other side of the mountain. On this side everybody was starving. A chief said to the porcupine, "I think you're the people who can make it to the other side".

"I'm only small, but I'll try."

So the porcupine put on snowshoes. He dived through the snow to the top of the mountain. He rolled down the other side. Then he said, "Call the people to come".

SAM CHARLIE WINS

By Marie Joseph, 1969

It happened in the 1930's when everyone was having a bad time. Sam Charlie, an Indian, had a hard time. There was no work, so Sam fished and hunted to feed his family, but he needed money to buy other kinds of food as well as clothes.

So Sam figured out a way he might get some money. A white man named Mike Smith owned a trapline not far from the Reserve. That trapline was real good for trapping martens. Sam thought he might steal some of those martens and sell the furs.

Mike suspected something was going on at his trapline and he wanted to know what it was.

Sam did what he always did, went to see his traps, and there was a marten caught in one of them. Sam was just starting to skin it, when he heard crackling of bushes behind him. It was Mike. Sam never had a chance to run or do anything. Mike grabbed Sam, socked him, and knocked him down.

"Well, so it's Sam Charlie, eh? You jest get the hell outa here before I do something worse than sock you in the eye," Mike said angrily. "And I'm reporting you to the R.C.M.P.," he shouted. Sam didn't say anything, but got up and hurried away.

The next morning, a police car stopped in front of Sam's house. Sam stood in the doorway.

"All right, Sam, get in the car, I'm taking you to the courthouse," said the cop.

Sam didn't say anything, but got into the car.

Mike and the judge were waiting in the courtroom when Sam and the cop got there. The judge asked, "Sam, did you set your traps on Mike's trapline?" Sam didn't say anything, but nodded.

"Do you say you are guilty or not guilty?" asked the judge.

"Guilty, I guess," said Sam.

"Can you pay fine, fifty dollars?" asked the judge.

"No, can't pay fine, I go to jail. Somebody look after my family. I go to jail," said Sam.

"You can borrow, can't you?" asked the judge.

"No, can't pay back, no money, I go to jail," said Sam.

"You can pay back a little at a time," said the judge.

"Can't pay a little at a time. No money. Can't pay fine. I go to jail. Somebody look after kids. I go to jail," said Sam.

"Sam, policeman will take you home and I'll talk to Mike. O.K.?" asked the judge.

"O.K. I see family before go to jail," said Sam.

The police car stopped in front of Sam's house and Sam got out.

"I'll come tomorrow morning at eleven o'clock," said the cop.

The next day Sam was waiting for the police car. It never showed up until five after twelve. The tall R.C.M.P. officer got out and came to Sam.

"Ah, Sam, I want to tell you that. . . ."

"No, no more talk, somebody feed my kids, I go to jail," said Sam in an angry voice.

"Look, Sam, you won in court, so you stay home, no jail, no fine, O.K.?" said the policeman.

"O.K.," said Sam. "I get black eye. I win, I stay home with wife and kids."

DR. JOSEPH JOE

Report of the passing of Dr. Joseph Joe, Indian medicine man, at the age of 105, at D'Arcy, was received in Lillooet on Wednesday, but no further details have been available.

Dr. Joseph was widely known throughout this section of B.C. and at 105 was surprisingly active. In fact, he expressed a desire, about a month ago, to come to Lillooet to visit the dentist, being, at the time of his death, still in possession of his own teeth.

— from the *Bridge River-Lillooet News,* December 22, 1955.

Dr. Joseph worked on the sternwheeler on Lillooet Lake doing odd jobs. He remembered the first white people going through, some from Squamish, some coming up the Lillooet.

— William Pascal

Dr. Joseph saw the camels going to Cariboo, and remembers the steamboat on Anderson Lake and cutting wood for a steamboat captain who paid him in money; he threw it into the lake, not knowing what it was.

— James Landsborough

THE OWL

By Marguerita James, 1970

Long, long ago, a little girl was playing in the woods when an owl looked down from the tall tree he was sitting on. He thought to himself that he wanted this beautiful little girl. So when night came, he flew to the house where she lived. Then he started to talk.

"Ha, who, who, who,
Where's the little girl?"

Then the wind howled and a gust threw the little girl's bedroom window open. The owl flew down and sat on the window sill.

"Ha, who, who, who,
Where's the little girl?"

He went to her bed and picked her up and put her into a basket of writhing snakes, croaking toads, scaly lizards, long-legged spiders, and many other loathsome creatures. She was frightened of these things that the owl ate.

Then the owl flew back to the tree tops with the little girl in the basket. She shivered from the coldness of the night and from the strange surroundings. Then she started to think how she could escape and thought of the sticky pitch on the trees. She told the owl that this was good medicine. The owl believed her and she started to apply some to his ears, his mouth, and his eyes.

Her claim about the good medicine wasn't true. With the pitch she made the owl deaf, dumb, and blind. Then to escape she climbed down the tall tree, using the branches like the rungs of a ladder. When she got down she ran home.

The owl was trying to take the pitch off his face. Finally, after trying very hard, he managed to get it off. Finding that the girl wasn't with him, he went to her house and started to talk.

"Ha, who, who, who,
Where's the little girl?"

The little girl's parents showed the owl her sister. The owl said,

"Ha, who, who, who,
She's not the one I had.
Where's the little girl?"

They argued. Finally, the owl flew away without either of the sisters, because he couldn't get the little girl he had before.

HOW WE BEAT THE BLANKETS

By Arnold Ritchie, 1969

Years ago, in the time of my ancestors, a drastic thing happened to my people. About the year 1850, during the best season for hunting and trapping up in the Chilcotin, the Hudson's Bay Company traders came with some blankets to trade for all the furs they could get. Immediately after they got rid of all the blankets, which they touched only with gloved hands, they went back to their boats and rowed to their ship and left. The Chilcotins immediately began to use the blankets. Then smallpox struck. It killed almost all the Chilcotins, who had been the biggest tribe in British Columbia.

Hearing of the pestilence farther north, the Indian doctor in D'Arcy foresaw that the disease would come to his village. He told his people that if they went to a certain mountain the smallpox would go right past. Some of the people would not leave home, but the doctor's followers left and lived up on the mountain for about one month.

When they came down they found all the people who had not gone up the mountain lying dead on the roofs and the trails. At the direction of the doctor, his followers buried the victims of the smallpox.

At the time the D'Arcy doctor saw the disease coming, the doctors in my village, too, prepared for it. They told their people that the disease would kill if they did not rub their bodies with skunk tallow and wrap skunk skin around their necks. If you already were sick and put on tallow you would get better, but live with the marks of the disease. My father saw some of the men who lived through it, and he says that their skin was pocked until they died.

Down on the coast, the doctors' way of battling the disease was with wolf grease, used the same way my people used the skunk as a cure, for at home there were a lot of skunks, but down on the coast there were a lot of wolves. That is the way we Indians beat the blankets.

MOUNT CURRIE HOMEMAKERS

With the over-all aim of improving their community, women of the Mount Currie Homemakers have worked together for years. In 1965, a *Bridge River-Lillooet News* item stated that

"Mrs. George Williams and Mrs. Adolph Leo reported for the Homemakers on their recent activities, which included the purchase of an adequate sink for the Community Hall kitchen, $220.50; donation toward Church repairs, $10; donation toward the Sisters' Christmas party for school children, $50; donation toward repairing a house for a young married couple, $70; and smaller projects. Funds are raised by rummage sales and bake sales, a bank balance of $330 showing good management. . . ."

A year earlier, the same newspaper had reported on a special committee of the Homemakers:

"One of the new signs of progress in the Mount Currie Indian Village is the interest young married women are taking in improving facilities of their reserve for the benefit of their young families and the betterment of life around. A good example of this new spirit is the Indian Health and Welfare Committee set up and working for over two years."

In its first years committee members included Mary Williams, Felicity Nelson, Rose Andrew, Rosie Joseph, Margaret Lester, Adelina Williams, Agnes Pascal, Marie Leo, Deanna Jim, Celina Dan, and Ann Peters. All of these women were busy with membership in other clubs, working in their gardens, freezing and canning food, and caring for their families, "but you'd never know it from the things that have been done and are in the planning stage". In general, these volunteers tried to help their neighbours "help themselves in times of stress", but at the same time, they worked to improve "home and sanitation conditions on the reserve". Money for improvements was always lacking. One woman who had never done any carpentry work studied a picture of a room divider, then built a very attractive one between her living room and her kitchen. On the living room side she stored books and magazines; on the kitchen side, her children's books and shoes.

Adelina Williams' 1965 report gives more details of Health and Welfare Committee work:

"Since last annual report we have made good use of the three sewing machines in our little sewing centre, which we have painted, furnished with cupboards and provided with new curtains. Several quilts were made by group effort; each woman who helped was entitled to use material to make a quilt for herself. . . . We purchased materials for sewing meetings, purchased a community sprayer, and medicines not immediately available through Health Service. We also purchased plywood and bolts to construct a septic tank form that can be taken apart and used over again. This will be put to good use this summer."

The correspondent for the Lillooet paper reported that one of the committee's best ideas was the "Beautify Mount Currie Project". In the fall of 1964, visitors to the Reserve saw lovely gardens and improved homes — positive evidence that the community had worked to realize the women's dream.

VISITING PORT DOUGLAS

Not many years after the British Columbia Electric Company had built an access road down Lillooet Lake, Mr. and Mrs. George Williams took a trip down to Port Douglas to renew the memories of the same trip taken twenty-nine years before. The mode of travel was different and the time much less, but to Adelina Williams the drive brought back happy memories.

This time she accompanied the resident priest and travelled by jeep. The time before she had gone with her husband and her five-year-old daughter by canoe down Lillooet Lake and through a connecting stream which was very narrow and rough, into Tenas Lake, near which they camped for the night.

The next day they walked into Skookumchuck, a distance of nine miles. George Williams had the camping supplies strapped onto his back, and his wife had their daughter strapped onto hers. They stayed at Skookumchuck over night, then walked into Port Douglas the next day, another twenty miles.

Today the trip takes three hours by jeep; it had taken the Williams three days.

ABOUT LONG AGO

By Karen (Pascal) Gabriel, 1968

One night I spent the night with my grandmother and she began to tell us what her great, great grandmother had told her.

"When there were no such things as roads, the people of the village used to travel by the river on some sort of raft. The people were dressed in skins which had been scraped by a certain rock, and the children had nothing to wear until they reached a certain age. In those times, the Indians had long hair, and great strength. The women had to work just as hard as the men. They scraped the skins of animals, hunted for firewood, and fished for the meals which they had to cook for their families. When the Indian men used to go on a hunting trip, they wore some special skins that had been scraped until they were very light and thin. Then, one day when the women were cooking for their children, all of a sudden they heard terrified cries coming from their men. They dropped the clay bowls which they were holding and ran to see what was happening. The sky darkened and they could see a huge, huge snake cross from hill to hill. They ran into the caves they were living in and never came out until the snake had disappeared onto the next hill. The people began to pray to their gods, because they thought the gods were angry and had sent the snake after them. They began to worship any snake they saw afterwards."

NIMICH MOUNTAIN

Seen from the door of the Valley Market, the mountain whose name to the white man sounds like Nimich stands directly across the valley. Bands of horizontal strata are conspicuous. They were made during the recession of flood waters. At each successive water level, the ark grated heavily against the mountain, cutting into the rock.

SKOOKUMCHUCK

By Kenny Peters, March 11, 1960

Skookumchuck is a little Indian village nine miles from Port Douglas. The village consists of about fifteen to twenty, or less, occupied houses. Not many people stay there though. Some go down to Port Douglas to live during the winter. During spring and fall the place is active on account of the fishing done there, also because of the cherry picking and the Graveyard cleaning. During summer most of the people go to the States to pick strawberries. The people are very good fishermen with nets, gaff hooks, and line and pole. During fishing season the people put away plenty of salmon which is salted and saved for the winter. There is no electricity in Skookumchuck yet. There isn't any store either. The people go down to Port Douglas to shop for groceries. Skookumchuck some day will be a big Reserve like Mt. Currie.

Skookumchuck B.C. Government Photo

ANNUAL GRAVEYARD CLEAN-UP

During three days in July 1965, Mount Currie people worked at the annual clean-up of the Graveyard. They cleared away weeds, cut the grass, planted flowers, and painted the crosses. In the Community Hall, Mrs. Victor Frank and a committee from the Homemakers' Club took charge of preparing and serving meals for all the workers. Among those helping Mrs. Frank were

Mrs. Francis Wallace, Dorothy Pascal, Maryanne Dan, Rosie Wallace, Dorothy Wallace, and George Williams, as well as several of the teen-age girls. Mr. Williams did all the heavy lifting.

LEGEND

By Sylvia (Lester) Shanoss, 1968

Every year the people of Mount Currie climbed up to Owl Mountain to pick huckleberries in the month of August. This was to be my first trip.

We began preparing a couple of days before, gathering together Indian picking baskets, buckets, and boxes. We only took as much equipment as we needed. To pick too much would mean too much to carry down. Our next concern was our clothes. Everyone who has ever been up Owl Mountain knows you need protection against mosquitoes and the bushes. I was advised to wear long sleeves and sturdy jeans and runners.

"Your uncle will be here to pick us up at 6 o'clock in the morning; you had better go to bed now," advised my mother.

I said goodnight to everyone and went to bed. Tomorrow was going to be a busy day.

At 5 a.m. I heard someone yelling at me. It was Mom.

"You better get out of bed right now. We're not waiting for anybody, and you need time for a good breakfast."

"I'm coming," I answered, and I jumped out of bed and washed and dressed. I was in the kitchen in five minutes.

At a quarter to six we were dashing around looking for insect repellent and string to tie up our boxes.

At six, when my uncle came, we invited him in for a cup of coffee while I looked for the string. At last, ten minutes later, we were off.

When we arrived at the foot of the mountain, we all gathered our stuff together and stood rubbing insect repellent on our hands, faces, and necks.

We then started the climb up the mountain. Everyone was silent. I then asked Mom how long people had been climbing this mountain.

"Well," she said, "some people my age can remember when they used to come with their grandparents."

"And still these trails are narrow," I said.

"I guess the people always walked one behind the other," she answered.

The ground was rather damp, but I noticed one spot was dry. I asked Mom about it.

"Many years ago," she told me, "a frog lived here; he owned this pool. He was the only frog that lived here and he always sat on that rock. People used to stop and drink on their way up and down. One man did not like the frog sitting there, so he killed it. The pool dried up. It has been dry every since the frog was killed."

By then we reached some berry bushes that no one had picked yet.

"There is so much!" I exclaimed.

No one answered; they were all picking. I picked too.

At three-thirty we ate our lunch and took time to look at the scenery. We could see the stores and part of the old reserve.

We then went back to picking and no one spoke again. We would only hear an occasional slap and a scream if someone was stung. After we had filled our baskets, boxes, and buckets, Mom brought the basket which we were to fill for our uncle.

When it was filled we started down the mountain for it would soon be time to meet our uncle.

"To think for years and years people have been picking berries on this mountain; it's a lot of work," I said. "Now think of canning them."

"CUP OF TEA AGGIE"

To pick berries or to gather materials for basket making, Aggie used to walk up from the Reserve to the Salmon Slough in the Upper Pemberton Valley, where she had a small shack. On the way up she visited each farm home and asked for a cup of tea, which was always given to her together with some biscuits or cookies. She became known as "Cup of Tea Aggie".

TWENTY-FOURTH OF MAY CELEBRATIONS

For farm families the one big outing of the year was a trip to see the parade and races at Mount Currie on May 24. Never were children so helpful with farm chores as from mid-May onward! When the big day arrived, lunches packed, children excited, we set out in whatever mode of transportation we possessed. Some rode bicycles, some went in farm wagons behind teams, some in vehicles of uncertain vintage called buggies, and some in two or more old Ford trucks. At that time the road led over the Red Bridge and the Harvey Nelson Hill, then down into the Indian Reserve, where all was gay with bunting and flags. The one street, with houses on both sides, is what is now called "the old Reserve". Gay in bright shirts and dresses, the young boys and girls perched on the roof tops, like flocks of birds.

The parade was already forming at one end of the road. Soon we heard the boom of drums, and the band stepped forward in marching order. These men all wore band uniforms and hats; this day, clothes freshly brushed and instruments gleaming, the musicians made a proud showing. Each instrument had a sheet of music attached; extra sheets were tucked into tiny baskets woven by the women and suspended from the men's necks by leather thongs.

The wrestling match

The time for the parade to start depended on an assessment of the assembled crowd. When a substantial audience had gathered the parade began. Following the band, a wagon decorated with greenery and streamers carried a group of lovely young maidens, all dressed in white with floral headbands; at centre sat the crowned May Queen in all her finery. Clowns and riders followed, excited horses prancing and sidling, giving their riders an opportunity to show off their horsemanship — as if we did not know what daredevils they were!

Getting ready for a race Provinial Archives, Victoria, B.C.

Following the parade sometimes a captive sasquatch lumbered, bearded and with tousled head, making fierce, growling noises and fighting the ropes and the men who bound him. Children clung to their mothers' skirts; many had to be picked up, their eyes shielded from the awesome sight. The performance was so dramatic that the children would not believe that the sasquatch was only a man dressed up!

Now the crowd scattered to find a quiet place for the mid-day lunch, after which the horse races commenced. These were run down the main street of the village. It was a case of "standing room only" on the roof tops and verandahs of the Indian homes lining the street on both sides. On the verandah of a house at the finish line, Bill Pascal had set up his betting stand. During and after the parade the men-folk had been studying the horses and talking to their riders — soon there was a crowd of bettors around Bill's stand. Here we learned of Bill's amazing memory. He took all bets, but had no pen, pencil, or paper to record either the names of bettors and the amounts bet, or the names of horses and riders. All this information was carried in his head and, races run, he handed out the winners' gains in the exact amount required by the odds.

Now the May rodeo is a much more sophisticated affair, but nothing will erase from the memories of the older people and their children the excitement and joys of the old Mount Currie twenty-fourth of May celebrations.

PAULINE FRASER

Aggie visited Al Fraser's farm, which lay across the Lillooet River opposite the Mitchell place. Al's wife was an Indian woman, Pauline. Pauline also visited around in the farming community on the more settled side of the river, even walking up to the Ronayne land and beyond. Pauline never came empty handed. A few trout, some berries, or fresh vegetables from her garden were her calling card. Pauline was always an interesting caller — she had news of the Lower Valley from Al, who frequently went down to One Mile, as Pemberton Station was called. Pauline will never be forgotten in Pemberton. Mount Pauline in the Upper Valley was named for her, because she was the only woman ever to ride a horse to the top of that small, rounded mountain.

CLASS HISTORY

By Florence (Peters) Andrew, June 1967

In September of 1956, thirty-five eager students rushed into the Pemberton schoolhouse to start the first year of their education. We were happy, care-free, and ready and anxious to learn. (It's too bad the enthusiasm died off as the years went by.)

As each year passed some of us made it to the next grade and if we didn't, we tried and tried again. We were the typical average school kids; which means we weren't very average or typical. We needled our teachers as much as any other class did, but we weren't so bad; we weren't so good either, but I won't go into that.

We all had our share of awards, threats, praise and detentions which helped to pull us through. After we finished Grade 6, we were all enthusiastic again, because we had half our education already, and had only six more years to go.

Then they told us about this new system they thought up, where they changed the math, science and the whole education system. We not only had to know what two and two made, we had to know WHY. That year, five years ago, was the turning point in our school life. We were separated into categories, the academic and the non-academic; if you knew what 2 and 2 made, and why it made 4, you were academic; if you only knew it made 4, you were non-academic.

In our eighth grade, the school board decided that they would have the Mount Currie students over at Pemberton. So they brought us over and most of us had our first taste of public school. We decided it wasn't so bad, so we stayed the next four years.

In Grade 9, our class was made up of about twenty-eight pupils (this is thirty-five, according to the new math) altogether considering the ones who left and the ones who came, and those who stayed.

In Grade 10, there were about twenty hopefuls still pushing pencils, needling teachers, and frustrating parents. We lost the other eight to other schools or to the cruel working world. I think this was the best year our class had together. We learned, needled and worked quite hard so at the end of the year we were rewarded with a class picnic!

We ended our fun-filled day by throwing our teacher into the icy waters of Anderson Lake. It wasn't even swimming season, but it was all in fun though, as was the rotten egg fight we had coming home. We never did have another class picnic.

In Grade 11, we realized we had to get down to business, so we did. We were exceptionally good, exceptionally studious; you name it, we were the exceptions.

Grade 12 was another matter. We started the year with only thirteen students. (I don't really know what happened to the other twenty-two we started out with in Grade One.) We crammed and crammed and crammed some more as our last school year came to an end. Through some unknown force of circumstance I'm proud to say we all made it; and as we stand here tonight you can be sure we are as ready to fight the world as we were when we started twelve years ago.

GRAND OPENING
OF
MOUNT CURRIE COMMUNITY HALL
April 26, 1968

Program

1. Mt. Currie Brass Band
2. Mt. Currie Indian Dancers
   — Eagle Dance
   — Princess Dance
3. Opening Speech — Chief B. Ritchie
4. Cutting of Ribbon by Sam Jim — 101 years old
5. Bar Interlude
6. Banquet — Grace by Rev. Father Kelly, O.M.I.
7. Guest Speakers
8. Speeches
9. Entertainment
   — Mt. Currie Children's Choir
   — "Supremes"
   — Tap Dancers, Lois Nelson and Janet Peters
   — Indian Dancers
10. Closing Speech — Chief B. Ritchie
11. Brass Band

The Squamish Times

Brass Band, 1959
"The Pemberton Meadows [Mount Currie] Indian band gave a concert on Columbia St. last night." ***The Columbian,*** *August 18, 1902.*

Joseph Despard Pemberton Provincial Archives, Victoria, B.C.

Alexander Caulfield Anderson Provincial Archives, Victoria, B.C.

Ship of the Gold Rush, after one hundred years

PEMBERTON BEFORE WORLD WAR II

THE FIRST PEMBERTON

Although it is probable that Lillooet Indians of the Pemberton area had heard of Europeans before 1827, that seems to be the year in which Hudson's Bay men first penetrated the valleys of the Birkenhead and Lillooet Rivers. Francis Ermatinger arrived then by way of Seton and Anderson Lakes, and James Murray Yale came three years later, having made the trip north from Fort Langley. In all likelihood both men were searching for a safe route for fur brigades between Kamloops and Fort Langley, for a route to bypass the lower Fraser River canyons.

Not until 1828, however, did the company's Governor George Simpson become convinced of the dangers of a canoe descent through those dangerous waters: "I should consider the passage down to be certain death, in nine attempts out of ten." Some years later, in 1846, Alexander Caulfield Anderson travelled through this country with the same purpose: to decide if company horses could make their way from the Fraser to present-day Mount Currie and on, by way of Lillooet and Harrison Lakes, to Langley. By now the lower Columbia River, the main link with the interior, was American, and for that reason Governor Simpson considered a new route "mostly highly important".

Not far from the confluence of the Bridge and Fraser Rivers, Anderson and his party sent their horses back to Kamloops, the men themselves travelling on foot and by canoe to the south end of the lake later named for the leader. They continued by what Anderson described as "a very good trail", camped over night, and set out again early on May 21. Following the Birkenhead River they reached the Mount Currie area by late afternoon.

There on a good-sized grassy island three miles above Lillooet Lake they found what Anderson called Lillooet Village where fifty men lived with their women and children. As usual in May fishing had been poor and the people could sell no fish to Anderson, but they did supply him with two canoes and canoemen to take the party down Lillooet Lake and beyond.

What Anderson called Lillooet Village was not what we today call Lillooet. The present town of Lillooet is situated on the banks of Cayoosh

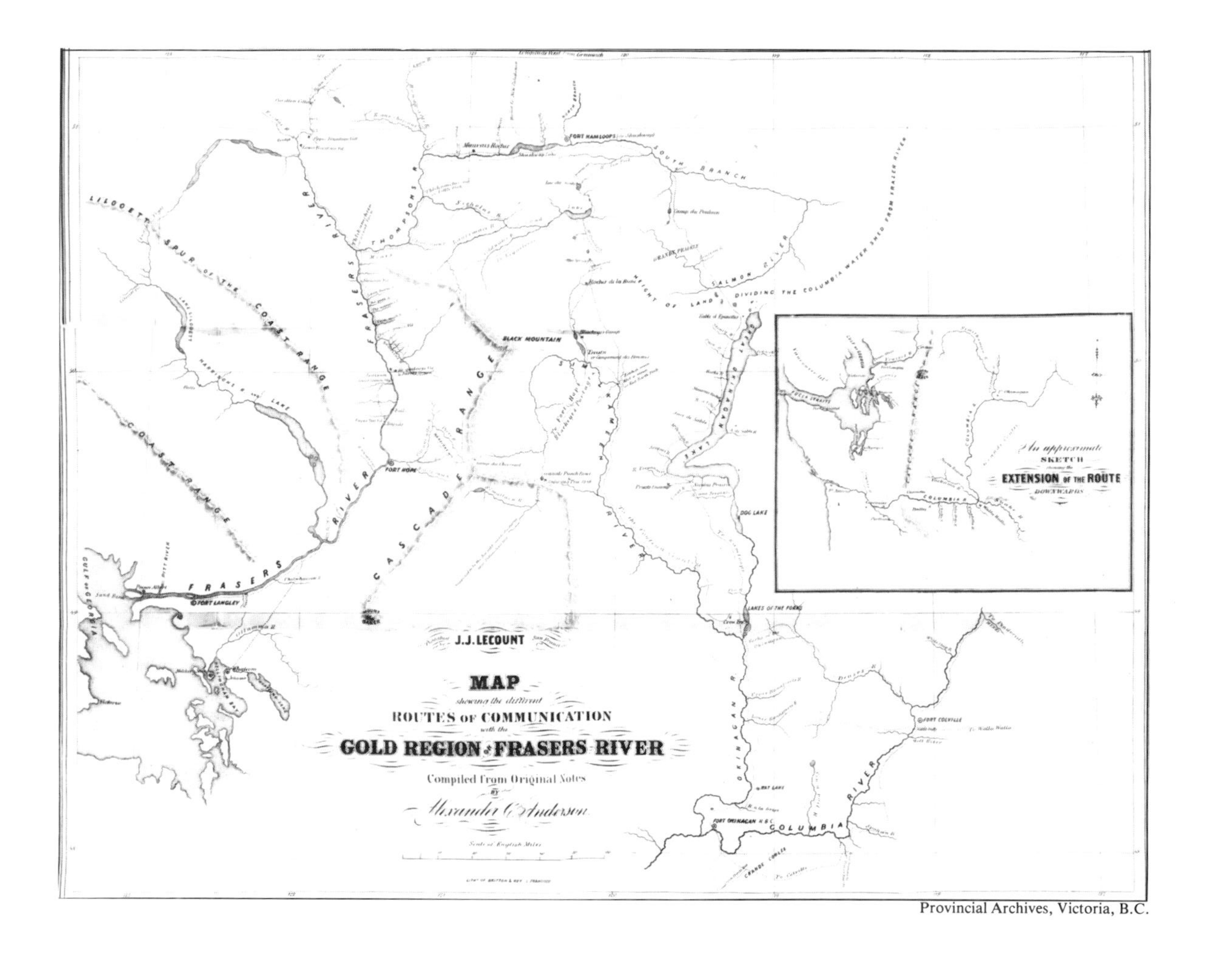

Provincial Archives, Victoria, B.C.

Creek and the Fraser River, about fifty-five miles from where the Lillooet River runs into Lillooet Lake. Early people called present-day Lillooet "Cayoosh", and did so until 1859 when the name changed because "the trail by Lillooet Lake and River here joined the Fraser".

The Hudson's Bay men were the first of many Europeans who would examine routes through Pemberton in order to link the interior and the coast. Some used the waterway connecting Cayoosh and Langley; others climbed up and down the rocky hills between Pemberton and Howe Sound. The explorers of the 1850's and 1860's, unlike the earlier men, were concerned with the transport of gold, not of furs.

For a few years after Anderson's visit people living along the Birkenhead and Lillooet systems, as far as is known, had little contact with white men. Then came the Fraser River gold discoveries that would lure thousands of transients and some settlers into these peaceful valleys. Probably few, if any, could understand the feelings of the Lillooets as they saw strange men from Canada, the United States, Europe, and Asia pouring through the country. As they saw some of the strangers settling.

In 1858 the miners who had somehow reached the Fraser gold-fields and intended to stay through the winter created an urgent problem for Governor Douglas of Vancouver Island. They needed food, and that food had to be transported to regions above the lower canyons of the Fraser, into the Mainland area to which there were no roads.

Even though not Governor of the Mainland until November, Governor Douglas felt he had to act. Because he knew that twelve years earlier A. C. Anderson had travelled from Cayoosh by a chain of lakes to Langley, in July Douglas asked the fur-trader to survey a route linking all lakes between the north end of Harrison Lake and the Fraser. The total length of trail would be just over sixty-eight miles, the total length of all lakes nearly fifty-six miles.

Five hundred miners eager to reach the gold-bearing Fraser River bars volunteered to build the trails. They established Port Douglas and constructed a trail called Douglas Portage to the south end of Lillooet Lake and there raised a building at what would be known as Port Lillooet. Then in early September a party of men climbed out of row boats that had taken them to the north end and prepared logs for a house which would stand a few hundred yards from an Indian village. *The Victoria Gazette* correspondent described the event in these words: "We went to work with a will at building another log house at the spot designated, which I believe has been named Port Pemberton." The name honoured Joseph Despard Pemberton, Surveyor-General of Vancouver Island.

That log building was probably Port Pemberton's first. The little port developed to serve the Gold Rush, and a nearby farming settlement grew as mining traffic increased on its way to Eldorado. Then very quickly, when traffic shifted to a route better than the one between Harrison Lake and Cayoosh, most of the settlers moved on. One of the assets of the area would become

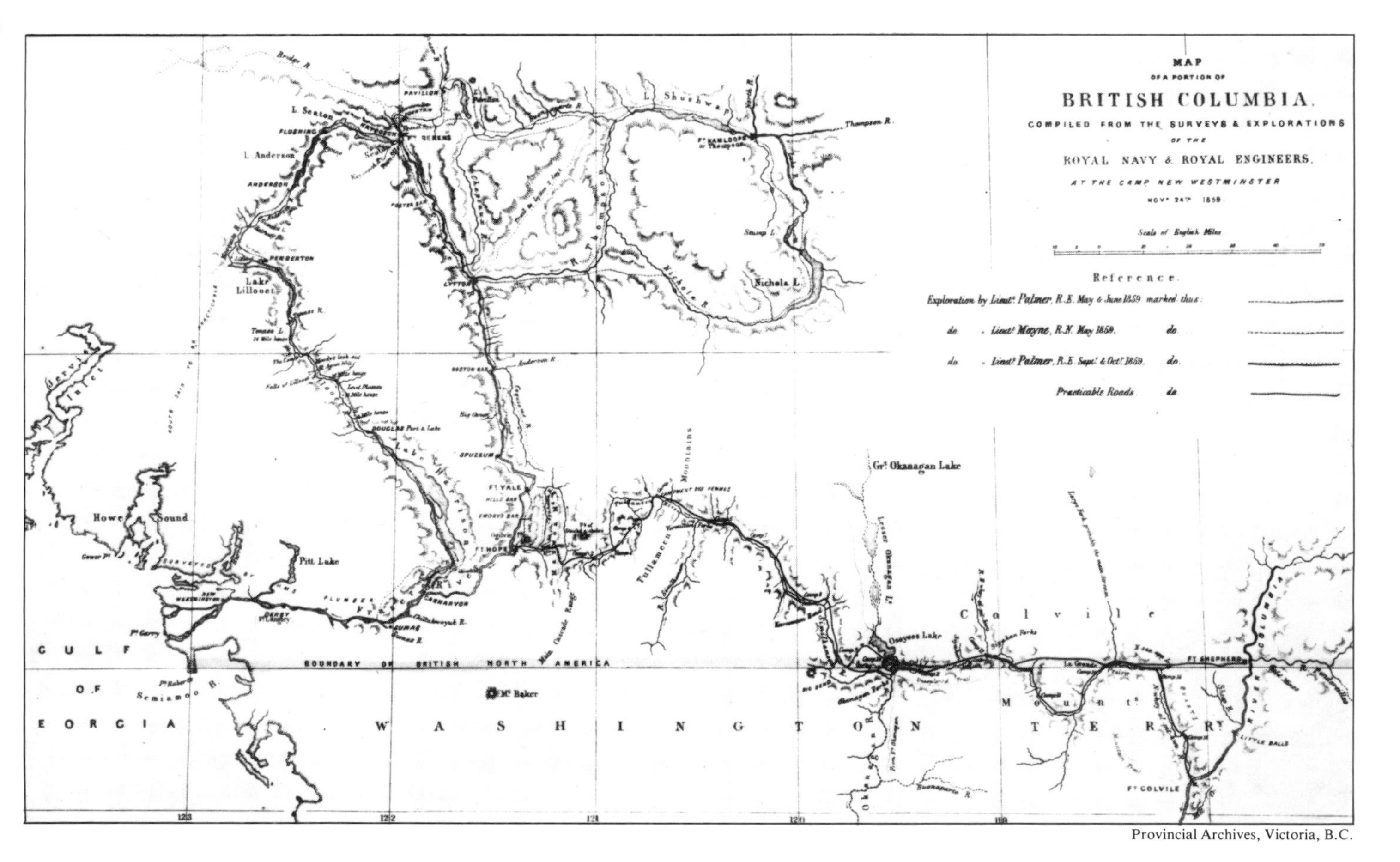

Provincial Archives, Victoria, B.C.

widely known — the richness of the land — and small waves of settlement would continue until a new Pemberton would replace the first Port Pemberton.

Named after a man who probably never saw the place, Port Pemberton was poorly situated, being crowded between steep bluffs and a lake with wide variations of high and low water. A year after it was located on its rocky site Lieutenant H. Spencer Palmer of the Royal Engineers was surveying the wagon roads which would soon replace the trails of the Harrison-Lillooet route and he advised dredging one of the mouths of the Lillooet and relocating the Port to a point where steamers could reach it at all seasons. He thought farmers would then be encouraged to work "the exceedingly rich prairie land", but the town remained where it was.

Through September and October 1858 trail construction went on. Though slowed by lack of enough mules to pack provisions, by mid-October the rough twenty-nine-mile Pemberton Portage trail to Anderson Lake was nearly ready for men and pack animals, and the miners who had decided to winter above the lower canyons of the Fraser would not starve. By agreement, two weeks after the trail-builders had completed their job others would scramble and sweat along the rugged track. Port Pemberton received the increasing hordes of people who for various reasons but mostly in hope of wealth rushed to the gold-fields. Some of them were women. All of these people headed to several areas: around Lytton, to the Bridge River, and by 1860, the Cariboo.

Some did not live to see Pemberton, much less the mining areas. Early in September an old man from Wisconsin who died while packing up a steep hill was buried beside the road. Several men attempting to go upriver in boats were drowned, one of them being buried beside the river in his "dark frock coat, two woollen shirts, brown ribbed pants, and cotton socks, one blue, the other white."

Soon mule trains wound along both Douglas and Pemberton Portages. Freeman Company's Atlantic and European Express even in August 1858 offered to send goods "by every steamer to all the Principal Bars" on the Lillooet River. But the snows of the 1858-59 winter forced mules off the trails, and then the Indians did the freighting, some carrying 100-pound sacks through the deep snow, others bringing up goods in their canoes. Their charge of 5c a pound was 10c less than that of the packers.

For a time flat-bottomed boats moved regularly between Port Lillooet and Port Pemberton. While the trail-builders had slashed and grubbed out the trail, another group of men had taken out timbers for two boats large enough to transport animals as well as freight over the lake. Officials of the road-building party tried to stop freighting across the lake by any except their own men, but in October a Chinese company was still ferrying provisions across Lillooet Lake. Then in June 1860 the locally built sixty-five foot *Marzelle* began carrying the assorted cargo for mines and miners. At least one creature who embarked on the little ship did not survive the trip: Henry Guillod's horse, Old Moke, kicked an ox overboard into the lake.

By August 1860 Port Douglas merchants had imported a number of wagons. By 1863 from that port, along the narrow, rocky valley of the Lower Lillooet, a four-horse stage sped north daily, numerous heavy wagons lumbered after oxen and mules, and trains of pack mules creaked their way toward the mines. Lieutenant R. C. Mayne, R.N., reported that the Engineers' road connecting Douglas with Tenas Lake was very good in spite of its very steep hills. During the year camels plodded the Harrison-Lillooet route, some shipments suffered, and lawsuits followed some accidents. "At the first whiff of a camel," according to one writer, "mules and oxen did everything but climb trees."

Anderson and Seton Lakes also had steamer service. In September 1860 Governor Douglas reached Anderson Lake "just in time for the trial trip of the *Lady of the Lake"*. Traffic began to increase even more rapidly.

Lillooet Indians like Dr. Joseph of D'Arcy and Paul Dick's father were hired to transfer the stacks of freight from shore to ship and back to shore, or to sand during low water at Pemberton. Provincial records show that river steamers preferred Indian crews because they were "most willing and active".

Captain Goulding, the owner of the *Marzelle,* must have foreseen the need of a larger steamer to carry the mountains of freight and numerous passengers disgorged from freight and stage lines. Somewhere along Lillooet Lake he built the 115-foot *Prince of Wales,* "as big as four others" according to Paul Dick. On June 7, 1863 Goulding wrote Governor Douglas, and heading the letter "Prince of Wales" said that the new steamer was making regular trips directly from the 29-Mile House on Tenas Lake, six miles south of

The 29-Mile House Provincial Archives, Victoria, B.C.

Lillooet Lake, to Port Pemberton. While the ship was under construction he had been building the dam recommended four years earlier by Lieutenant Palmer in order to bring Tenas and Lillooet Lakes to the same level. The dam was incomplete, but until dam completion in September Goulding expected to be able to operate from the lower lake during high water. He probably had his fine ship winched through the dangerous passage between the lakes: Joe Peters used to tell of Indians winching steamers through such waters.

The great volume of traffic required some accommodation at Pemberton. By 1859 the port had five or six log cabins — shelters and eating places for the men who rowed the large boats, for the mule drivers, and for the travelling public. The two restaurants offered the usual Gold Rush menu at the usual prices: bacon and beans, bread and butter, tea or coffee for one dollar. The 1860 Royal Engineers' map shows fourteen buildings of various sizes, with three named: shed, mule shed, and Lake House. None was far from the lake, but some stood in rocky gulleys which long ago recovered their original moss which is dotted in May with the pinkish blooms of the rare calypso bulbosa.

The year before launching the *Prince of Wales,* Captain Goulding, along with some sergeants of the Royal Engineers and contractors W. T. "Billy" Ballou and Kwong Lee, became involved in his proposed road extension to a new place to tie up at in Pemberton. This extension would lead from the port to an all-seasons landing with room to turn a team farther down the lake shore. Officials must have believed heavy traffic would continue through Pemberton: at the time the Royal Engineers were planning port improvements the Governor had already approved an alternate route to the Cariboo. The contractors wished to secure and complete the Pemberton job, then move their men to the new Fraser Canyon road.

They sent letters and sketches to Colonel Moody of the Royal Engineers and these sketches of the proposed road extension show a large building belonging to P. Smith and Company, Nelson's barn, a Spaniard's cabin, and Pemberton House, as well as the Indian village. Squatters' cabins made up part of the town, and in March 1863 some squatters received notices that their buildings would be moved to allow for road construction, which began a month later.

Records give names of two businessmen operating in early Pemberton. Mr. Drinkall's Pemberton House catered to travellers, offering them meals and spaces to sleep. Otis Parsons' store offered a variety of goods to miners and to residents. Robbins and Waldron in 1859 bought thirteen pounds of bacon for $9.75, a horse for $75, and brandy for which they paid $50. Payment was partly or altogether in gold dust.

Whether the buildings bordering the road that wound through the port could accommodate the six hundred pack-mules said to have wintered in Pemberton in 1861 is doubtful. Those animals could have spent much of the winter grazing near the lake, for many animals have survived in that way. Several large buildings sheltered the freight animals which regularly left the

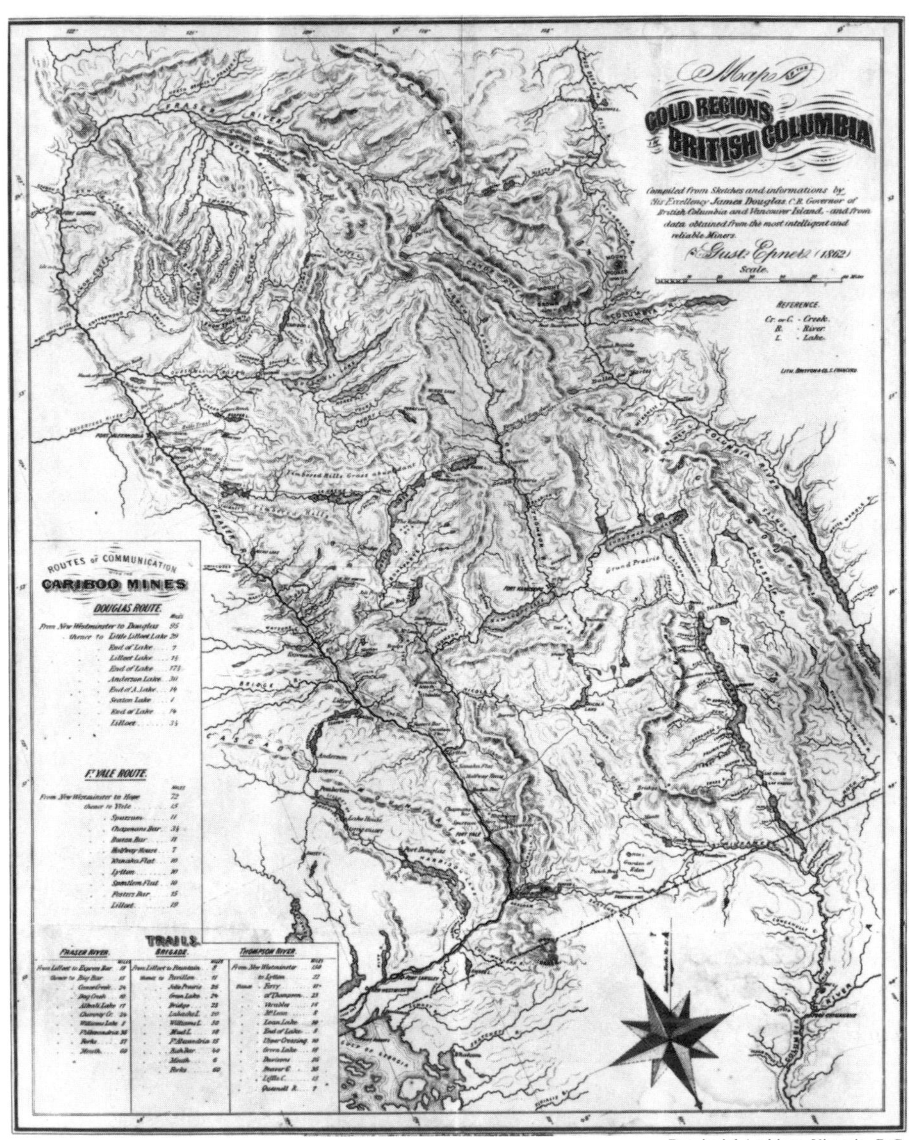

Provincial Archives, Victoria, B.C.

settlement and returned to it, and one of these stables was the only structure damaged in the rockslide that roared down towards Pemberton in 1864. Of all the buildings in Port Pemberton, those stables must have been the busiest, noisiest, and smelliest. Otis Parsons, packing for Nelson, used one of them; Billy Ballou, another. Billy Ballou was a packer from Douglas until his rival, Frank Barnard, took over his business.

Imagine early mornings beside the lake: lanterns bobbing as men in charge of animals hurried out to water and feed; men forking out hay hauled from lands near the town; later, men packing mules and camels; a general clanking and shouting; barking dogs. Wagons, loaded the day before with tools, clothes, food and whiskey for the mines. Oxen led out and hooked up to their loads with shoes and wheels grating on rocks; the crack of whips, and more shouts. No quiet for late sleepers. But with everybody pushing either themselves or freight northward, few could be interested in sleeping past dawn, anyway.

The route to the gold-fields opened a route for farmers to reach the meadow lands above Lillooet Lake, Pemberton or Lillooet Meadows. According to Governor Douglas, these new people settled about five miles from the port. Even during the first years of Port Pemberton's existence they were staking land below the wall of Mount Currie, land that was among the first privately held land on the mainland. Gold Rush traffic, both two- and four-footed, provided them with a market larger than later farmers would reach until construction of the Pacific Great Eastern Railway and the resulting link with Vancouver.

Fresh vegetables had been extremely scarce and dear. For these reasons, in 1859 Chief Justice Begbie gave several seasonal permits for use of land: "40 acres, being 5 acres each to 8 men, at the Halfway House" between Anderson Lake and Lillooet Lake. A Mr. Bryant applied for 250 acres near Pemberton.

With tomatoes selling for as much as seventy-five cents each and cucumbers at a dollar, farmers never did better. In 1859 one settler had cleared "upwards of 240 pounds sterling" an acre growing potatoes. Prices dropped in half once the wagon road was finished as far as Tenas Lake, but the "oldest and principal settler", having the next year a much larger crop, expected to make even higher profits. Ketterel, a Virginian on Pemberton Portage, cleared $2,000 in one year after the completion of the wagon road to Anderson Lake and then had enough money to buy the Halfway House property pre-empted in 1860 by Peter Dickenson.

Pre-empting land meant driving corner posts, or staking, around the acreage allowed, then recording the pre-emption with a magistrate. The settler had to live on and improve his land, have it surveyed, and finally pay for it at the rate of $1 an acre. He then received a Crown Grant.

The first Pemberton pre-emption was recorded at Douglas by P. Smith and Company who were heavily involved in Gold Rush business. They were packers, they were owners of a stopping place at Pemberton and, according to more than one account, they were the builders of the wooden tramway between Anderson and Seton Lakes. Joe Taillefer said the tramway was still in use in 1912: "a cart coasted one way and was pulled back by a horse". The company filed their pre-emption in January 1860, just a few days after the Government's Pre-Emption Proclamation. Rich land and heavy grass had figured in the reports of such men as J. W. McKay, who was commissioned to find a route to the interior by way of Howe Sound, and of Chief Justice Begbie when on his way south from Cayoosh. That grass had fed Smith's pack animals before 1860.

In February John Shaw recorded the second pre-emption. His 160 acres, with Smith's 320, formed part of District Lot 98. William Jones, pre-empting 260 acres the same year, occupied Lot 99. Both lots are now part of Mount Currie Indian Reserve in the general area once known as both Lillooet Meadows and Pemberton Meadows. In 1861 David Douglas and James "Scotty" Halliday staked land near Port Pemberton and two years later David Douglas staked the Rowntree Ranch.

Because all these early pre-emptors recorded their land at Port Douglas they would travel down Douglas Portage to do their business, probably with J. Boles Gaggin, who for several years was magistrate at the Port. The Royal Engineers by this time had reduced the highest hill and converted the Douglas Portage trail into the twelve-foot-wide Cariboo Highway, the first highway on the mainland.

St. Agnes' Well, 1958 Provincial Archives, Victoria, B.C.

As the farmers travelled they had a choice of stopping houses, spaced to accommodate speed of movement. Begbie's 1859 map shows wayside houses at the south end of both Lillooet and Tenas Lakes, and at the Hotsprings, or St. Agnes' Well, which had been named after Governor Douglas' daughter. One miner described his mineral water bath in a wooden tub as the only cheap comfort in British Columbia, but those gnarled apple trees which still bear fruit at the Hotsprings provided another pleasure for travellers. More houses sprang up, including one at Rogers Creek.

On his two-day trip home from Douglas in 1863, Lillooet's Anglican priest counted twelve farmers in the Pemberton area. These may have included some men of whom there are the scantiest of records: George Dunn, John Rogers, Frederick Sylvester, and R. Taylor. R. C. Mayne met some of the early settlers in 1860 during his survey of the route between Jervis Inlet and the Fraser River, and passed men harvesting crops, sawing lumber, and building houses. It was a bright morning, "as July mornings always are here", Mayne wrote in his report, and he enjoyed the delicious perfume of the tall grasses.

Some of the early farmers took Indian wives. In 1862, at the height of Port Pemberton's importance, a Scottish resident and his wife became parents of a daughter. One of the first born to a settler, this child was sent to school in Scotland where, while living with her aunts, she learned to sing Scottish songs and dance the Highland Fling. But she longed for home, returned to British Columbia, and later married Alonzo Roberts. The son of a later settler and a native woman, William Currie, loved the Pemberton area as had Mrs. Roberts. After a long absence he described this country as he saw it in his youth as "the most beautiful place in the world" and spoke of masses of fireweed in bloom, the dazzling hues of hummingbirds, and the beauty of the short rose bushes in flower.

Passing through were men whose descendants would later live in post-railway Pemberton. George Turner of the Royal Engineers came first to Pemberton in 1859 and helped survey the improved road to the mines. His great-grandson, Lorne Monford, was Pemberton agent for Imperial Oil one hundred years later. With "Gassy Jack" Deighton of Gastown, Sam Fiddick passed close to the area where his grandson, John Decker, would farm and serve as magistrate.

Early travellers writing of William Currie's beautiful valley tended to write of tangibles. The Governor wrote of excellent crops of oats, corn, potatoes, and hay. After exploring the route leading up Cayoosh Creek and down to Lillooet Lake, Sapper Duffy mentioned the steep hill leading down to the lake. Dr. Cheadle, one of Canada's first tourists, reported on the great number of drinks the magistrate at Douglas had consumed on his way north to Pemberton.

Soon after Viscount Milton and Dr. Cheadle went to the Cariboo most of the traffic through Pemberton switched to the Fraser Canyon. The inconveniences of the Harrison-Lillooet route had hastened the building of that new road. The frequent shifting of freight from steamer to wagon or pack train and back again, eight handlings between Victoria and the Cariboo, combined with road closures during heavy snowfalls, had created annoying and expensive delays. At the conclusion of a trial launched by an irate citizen who thought his goods had been unduly delayed, Chief Justice Begbie ruled that forty days was a reasonable time for transport of goods between Douglas and present-day Lillooet. Because of the delays and because freight rates varied at every stage of the trip and were all based on weight at the start, Williams Creek miners in 1862 were paying "famine prices" — flour at $2 a pound and butter at $5.

The new Cariboo Road up the Fraser, begun in 1862, was completed from Yale to Clinton the next year and the exodus from Pemberton commenced. In 1864 Dodge and Company had 160 animals in transport, but complained that both Douglas and Pemberton Portages were almost impassable in places. Without a transportation system the people had no choice but to uproot themselves and move elsewhere. Ten years later, in 1874, only a few settlers remained and the Lillooet Indians affected by the frenzied pace of five or more years were returning to their traditional ways.

Having no reason for continued existence, Port Pemberton soon died. Only rock foundations show where buildings sheltered men and animals of the Gold Rush. But the area was never totally forgotten, and for many years before the building of the railway, Vancouver papers carried glowing reports about the land and its potential.

Oven used during the Gold Rush

GRASSY TRAILS

After the opening of the Fraser Canyon road public transport systems soon stopped operating between Douglas and the Cariboo gold-fields, but some sort of road maintenance continued until 1867. W. R. Gibson of Douglas contracted to keep the road from Pemberton to Anderson Lake in condition for heavy traffic, all "stones larger than can be put in a man's mouth to be removed", and in 1866 the road was in good condition for large wagons, but for light ones rough and stony. Six years later grass and brush covered much of the once heavily used highway. After Gustavus Blin Wright had removed the machinery from the *Prince of Wales* in 1869 to install it in a steamer on the Upper Fraser, the few visitors to the Pemberton area had to hire Indian dugouts to cross the lakes.

A few settlers remained, about six living on Lillooet Meadows, now known as Pemberton Meadows, not many miles from Port Pemberton. The transient population having moved on, general conditions were little different from what Ermatinger had found close to fifty years earlier. In 1879, after one of the settlers met a violent death, most of those who remained packed up and moved to the Cariboo.

But before the last of the farmers moved away national and provincial demands for new routes brought more strangers to the Lillooet River Valley and Pemberton Portage, although not in the hordes of Gold Rush years. Searches for routes again publicized this country. In 1873 Marcus Smith, the leader of the first railway survey party in this area, was attempting to locate a line for the first Canadian transcontinental railway and wanted to cross more or less directly from the Pacific Ocean to Yellowhead Pass. He supervised a survey that brought him up from the head of Howe Sound and on by way of the Birkenhead River, Anderson and Seton Lakes, to Lillooet, following the route the Pacific Great Eastern Railway would take forty years later.

As he travelled north from Howe Sound, Smith included in his notes a reference to the earlier bursting of a mountain lake, which by washing down boulders and other debris had created Daisy Lake. In 1858 J. W. McKay had reported seeing the same evidence. Smith described crossing either the Soo River or Rutherford Creek on "an Indian bridge of the most slender construction, a few poles lashed together and suspended from the top boughs of a leaning tree which reached about two-thirds across the river, and fastened at the other end to a stump." His party strengthened the bridge, but "the passage was anything but pleasant with a swollen mountain torrent rushing beneath."

A little farther on they looked down on the Lillooet River Valley, "this great basin in the heart of the Cascade Mountains". The survey party had spent four hot August days travelling thirty very rough miles "from the Surveyor's camp". After resting at One Mile Lake the men followed the Pemberton Portage road and camped near the Halfway House built in 1859 by Peter Dickenson, but by this time owned by Thomas Poole, who was a farmer described as efficient as Dickenson. Of the stopping house and its surroundings James Douglas had said in 1860 that "It is prettily situated on the mountainside overlooking a rich expanse of arable land covered with a profusion of potatoes, beets, carrots, tomatoes, cucumbers, and other vegetables, certain proof of the great capabilities of the soil and climate."

At the Halfway House Marcus Smith learned that a large canoe was ready for him at the head of Anderson Lake. Learning too that a small pack train of mules was waiting at Lillooet — known earlier as Cayoosh — he hired a wagon from Poole and sent all his packers back over the way they had come, but the leader himself continued into the interior.

In the year of the Canadian Pacific Railway survey, workers had started to build a cattle trail from Lillooet on the Fraser to pass through Pemberton, on to the head of Howe Sound, and through the mountains to Burrard Inlet. People spoke of it as the Burrard Inlet Trail, the Howe Sound Trail, the Lillooet Trail and, referring to the section between Pemberton and Squamish, the Pemberton or Squamish Trail. Lillooet and Pemberton people with ranches and Burrard Inlet sawmill operators who wanted meat for their employees had urged the construction of this new route south for up-country cattle. Lillooet ranchers argued that there was more feed by way of Pemberton than through the Fraser Canyon and moreover, that travelling by the proposed trail their cattle would not have to meet the freight teams hauling on the new Cariboo Road. Pemberton settlers needed a way to the coast, cut off as they were from markets.

The 32-mile trail along Seton and Anderson Lakes, to cost $5,180, followed the Canadian Pacific survey. All along the lakes high rocky bluffs made the workers' job extremely difficult; in one section, impossible. There the men built a floating platform and secured it to the shore, but unfortunately the platform floated away.

When they reached the far end of Anderson Lake the workers made use of the Pemberton Portage which was badly in need of repair, with all its bridges rotting and breaking down. The trail crew, according to 1876 legislative records, proceeded "thence south-west across Jamieson Creek and to the

After the Gold Rush B.C. Government photo

Lillooet River and Pemberton Meadows, about six miles further, crossing the Meadows a short distance above where the C.P.R. survey ran." From Pemberton the trail again followed the railway survey as far as Howe Sound. Apparently mismanaged throughout, construction was completed in 1877.

In 1878 a legislative committee held hearings to investigate complaints by Robert Carson, a Pavilion rancher who had driven his herd to Burrard Inlet the year before over sections he described as entirely unfit for the passage of cattle. Through Pemberton his animals were "mired to their bellies" because Halliday's cattle had broken up the brush so hopefully laid down and covered with earth. Here the survey made by the engineer hired in 1876 had not been followed. Leaving the meadows of Pemberton and climbing up the mountain trail, Carson's animals had bruised their legs on the rocks as they moved along a trail which for long stretches had no meadows for pasture. Fred Magee, Carson's brother-in-law, as a young boy listened to accounts of the famous drive, and years later spoke of the misery of the cattle and of the men herding them as rain fell almost continuously.

Others besides Carson gave evidence at the hearings. Their statements, along with the official reports, reveal a little about the men living along the trail. As with later construction projects, those in charge employed some local men and bought some local supplies. A number of Indians were hired, but their names are unavailable. Of the Pemberton settlers, Scotty Halliday, W. McBeth, and Dan Carey all worked on the trail, Carey as a foreman. P. Smith's brother, A. W., a Lillooet merchant, supplied groceries; Thomas Poole, on the Portage, provided meat and other staples. Wattis "Wattie" Burgess, who lived somewhere below the site of the present secondary school, with Halliday packed for the trail builders and supplied beef, driving cattle after the party; one steer would provide meat for two weeks. Halliday, however, at one stage refused to drive cattle over what he called "that mountain".

In 1877 H. A. McLellan had been in charge of trail building, but Carey thought he had not taken his duties seriously. Much of the time, Carey testified, the supervisor was not on the job because he had brought along Mrs. McLellan. She probably caused some of the unnecessary delays and expense Carey complained about because her being in the party meant that every time camp was moved several horses were put at her disposal — one for her to ride, others to carry her trunks and carpets — and on reaching the new campsite several men had to clear paths for her.

The hearings ended, but no rancher after Carson drove cattle beyond Howe Sound. With the Canadian Pacific Railway line settled, pressure from Cariboo ranchers for the Pemberton route disappeared and it was left to local ranchers who used it until the Pacific Great Eastern Railway was built.

The year following the hearings into complaints about the cattle trail, Thomas Poole and his children were murdered on the Portage. Several trials, the last involving very distinguished legal men, failed to solve the mystery surrounding the grisly murders. Several versions of the story circulated.

One version has been pieced together mainly from accounts given by Arthur Phair, son of the Lillooet coroner who in 1879 travelled down to the Portage to examine two bodies. Poole, the owner of the Halfway House, had sold cattle in Lillooet and had accumulated $2,000, all in $20 gold pieces. When his body was discovered in the potato patch, stabbed, and the bodies of his children in the burned ruins of the house, an Indian was arrested but later released. Then suspicion shifted to a white man. This man's Indian wife testified in court that when she was riding with him near Poole's house, he had told her to go to the ford on the Birkenhead River and make dinner, and when he eventually galloped up to the crossing on his lathered horse he tossed her his bloodied shirt and told her to wash it in cold water. The trial ended in acquittal.

A variation of this story tells of three suspects, all working on the Portage road. They too were acquitted. But one later hanged himself; the second, "a sly-looking fellow, went crazy in his cabin up the Fraser, where he always had a gun standing by the window"; and the third, Scotty Halliday, had "quite a bit of money" and "died a few years later".

Still another version of the story was written by a former Assistant Superintendent of the British Columbia Provincial Police. In this account, Jim Queen, brother of Poole's dead wife, found the Halfway House burned right down to the piles of smoking potatoes in what had been the basement. Lying there side by side were the bodies of Poole and his 11-year-old daughter, Mary. Nearby bones might have been the remains of 8-year-old Perry, whose cap was found hanging on the branch of a tree.

When coroner Caspar Phair arrived on the scene from Lillooet, he discovered that both Poole and Mary had been shot. Some time later, on a tip from Scotty Halliday, Hunter Jack was arrested on suspicion of murder and taken by way of the cattle trail to Lillooet and on to Clinton for trial. When he was found not guilty, suspicion fastened on Scotty himself.

Earlier Halliday had appropriated Hunter Jack's wife, Jennie, whose conversation with her friend Sophia was part of the evidence at Hunter Jack's trial. Jennie told that Scotty arrived home with his helper, Tenah, and some pack horses two nights before Queen discovered the deaths of the Pooles. Scotty sat down to supper without removing his coat, and not until bedtime did Jennie see that the arm of his shirt was bloodstained from cuff to shoulder.

The policeman assigned to the case, Livingstone, ferreted out more details. After dusk on April 21 Halliday and Tenah pulled into the Halfway House with five horses loaded with peas, barley, and flour, and planned to eat with the Pooles and spend the night with them. After the meal, the quick-tempered Scotty quarreled with Poole, and the next morning, as the quarrel continued, Poole reproached Scotty for stealing Hunter Jack's wife. Tenah went out alone to get the pack horses ready to move on and was half way to the Indian village where Halliday lived with Jennie before his employer caught up with him, riding at a gallop.

Scotty's neighbours, Dan Carey and Wattis Burgess, came to supper that night, and during the next day, Jennie revealed, Halliday and Burgess had a long conversation in private. The following day Jim Queen reported that Poole's house had burned down with its occupants in it. Before galloping off with William McBeth to see what remained after the fire, Scotty pushed a roll of bills into Wattie's hands. Later Wattie and Tenah saddled up and headed off along the road to Lillooet Lake, on their way to Victoria.

Having collected a sheaf of signed statements, Livingstone arrested Halliday, rode off with him to Clinton, and there wired the Victoria police and told them to arrest Burgess and search him. When the jury disagreed at the Clinton trial, Scotty was taken to New Westminster and waited twelve months, until November 1880, for another trial. The judge's summing up of fourteen days of evidence lasted from 2:30 one afternoon until 11 at night, and the jury came back at 1 a.m. the next day with a verdict of not guilty.

For a few years after Halliday's acquittal evidence of white settlement in Pemberton is slight. Halliday and McBeth were on the 1880 tax rolls, but by 1881 Burgess, Carey, and Halliday, the last a twenty-year resident, had taken the trail to Clinton. The 1882 Lillooet voters' list had only one name with a Pemberton address, that of McBeth.

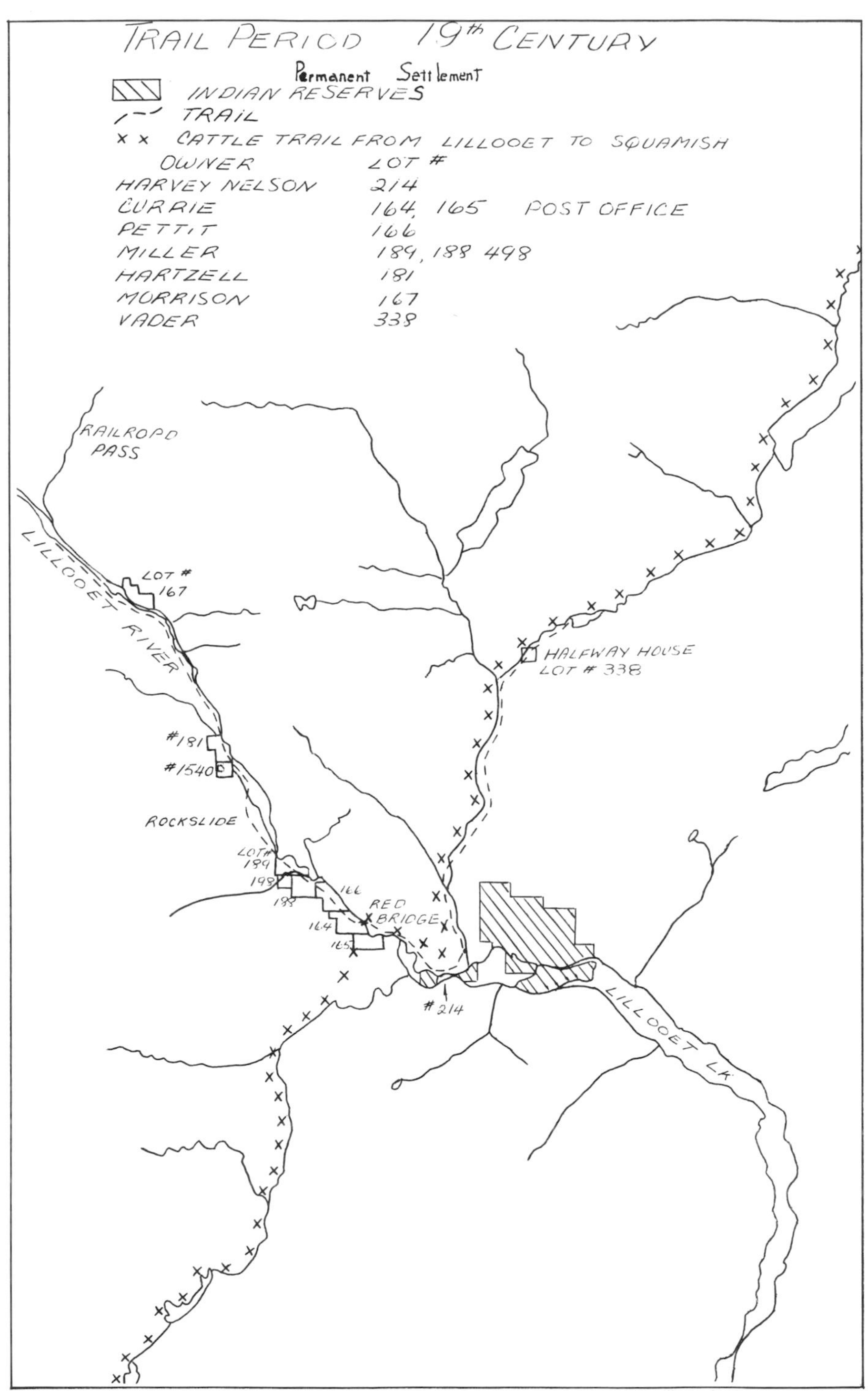

Permanent Settlement

PERMANENT SETTLEMENT

Not many years after the departure of all or most of the few lingering post-Gold Rush settlers, new settlers arrived in Pemberton. By 1900 several had established themselves and would remain, despite isolation, floods, and mosquitoes. They knew that the land was good, and must have looked forward to a time when additional settlement would induce those with financial or political power to convert the trails into roads. While these men worked and planned some of them provided for themselves and chance visitors a few essential services, like stopping houses and stores.

The new settlers included John Currie whose name had appeared earlier on the Lillooet tax roll, but not until 1885 with a Pemberton address. With his partners, Dugald McDonald and Owen Williams, he held 960 acres on which he pastured a number of hogs, cattle, and horses. In 1888 Currie and McDonald applied for survey of District Lots 164 and 165, an area including the present secondary school site and extending south beyond the line where trains would be running twenty-six years later. In 1890 a surveyor, William Allan, described the pre-emptors' holdings as "well improved, with splendid buildings". In the year that Currie and his partner made their application, Sylvanus Pettit applied for survey of DL 166, land extending north from the present Shore property and including the present Summerskill farm. The following year G. W. Terry applied for survey of land near Miller Creek. William Vader had probably settled in the early 'eighties, taking over the Poole place and building the first section of the second Halfway House on the Portage. In 1891 a barn he had built without nails sheltered twenty-five cows and two horses.

Just previous to the survey applications Charles E. Wood had surveyed some of the first pre-emptions in the Pemberton area, DL 98 and DL 99, now part of Mount Currie Indian Reserve. Ten years after Wood's survey the provincial government issued crown grants "in two portions" to lot 98: 320 acres to the original pre-emptors, P. Smith and Company and John Shaw, and the remaining 200 acres to the Reverend Paul Durieu, the Roman Catholic Bishop

The Early Years Provincial Archives, Victoria, B.C.

W. M. Miller Provincial Archives, Victoria, B.C.

of New Westminster. Prior to the survey a search had started for Shaw who was thought to be in the Cariboo Mountains and whose children were at a Roman Catholic School at Williams Lake.

Like others before them, Dugald McDonald and his wife decided to leave the Valley and move to the Cariboo, and in 1890 when they moved away they had three children, Flora being the small baby. The McDonalds left just when interest in Pemberton land had increased markedly. In 1890 and 1891 twenty-three individuals, some in partnerships, applied for thirty-three parcels of land extending from the borders of Indian Reserve Number One all the way up to DL 167, a distance of about nineteen miles.

There are several reasons for the suddden desire to acquire land in a remote valley, but the interest could have been developing since 1886 when the first passenger train reached Port Moody and when every train brought new settlers. Dealing in land and timber, many Vancouver residents quickly became wealthy. Rail transportation opened up new resources and interest grew in opening up still more wealth with railway lines. To encourage the building of new systems, the provincial government offered land, timber, and mineral rights to prospective builders, and before 1913, not surprisingly, the legislature had approved 211 railway schemes.

In 1890 McClaren Ross Company decided to build a railway from Vancouver to their property at Daisy Lake, anticipating that Pemberton Meadows would be "filled up soon" and make passenger traffic profitable. In 1891 John Hendry was prominent in a group who proposed to construct a line — the Vancouver, Northern, Peace River and Alaska Railway — which would head from Vancouver through Pemberton to a terminus well north of Fort George as Prince George was then called. Rumours of planned railways, rumours which circulated years before incorporations, stimulated both land and timber speculation.

In 1890, throughout the Valley William Allan and G. T. Burpee surveyed close to 5,000 acres for which a flood of applications had been received. Land speculators quickly bought over 4,500 acres and as quickly resold them. That many of the new land owners spent much time in the Valley is doubtful. The 1891 tax rolls listed eleven resident owners, of whom only Currie, Pettit, and Vader owned animals, and though the 1892 tax rolls included forty-three farmers, the 1893 Pemberton voters' list had only eighteen names. Though the McDonalds left, the Curries remained. If they were not the only farm family, they were one of few.

In 1851, at the age of seventeen, John Currie had emigrated from Scotland. His family settled in Quebec, but he ran away from home and struck off for the California gold-fields. Like many other miners he later travelled north to the Cariboo where he could have met McDonald, his partner in Pemberton. Returning south Currie passed through Clinton when smallpox was raging, and continued on to Lillooet. For a number of years after 1868 he farmed between Lillooet and Ashcroft where he pre-empted land.

In 1895, ten years or more after Currie settled in Pemberton with his Lillooet Indian wife, the federal government established a post office on his farm to serve settlers scattered throughout the Valley and over Pemberton Portage. John Currie was the postmaster handling the mail in the little log building in which there was also a store. Willie Currie, John's second son, said that Andrew Joseph was the first of several mail carriers who in all weathers brought the mail from Lillooet. A. P. Barnfield of Squamish described Currie as five-feet ten-inches tall, well built, and probably "skookum" when young, but during his mining years he had developed rheumatic fever from which he never completely recovered. The Curries had three children, two sons and a daughter.

The trail from Squamish led travellers straight to Currie's door where he would welcome them and invite them to stay over night. Brought up from the abandoned steamer at the lake, the Curries' hardwood doors would be more elegant than the common homemade variety, but the inside walls of the addition to the original home were decorated with 1886 newspapers which had been pasted there for insulation. Newspapers on the walls of the Halfway House, on the Portage, served a double purpose: one family used them to play "I Spy".

As in most pioneer homes, the kitchen was the principal room, its wood stove topped with a steaming kettle. This stove provided heat, baked bread, heated water for washing and baths, and cooked the endless meals for the family and for all who happened in. Currie would have built a wood-box close by, and a bench for pails of water hauled up from the well near the door. Not far away stood the long table which was work table and dining table combined. There the wife cut meat, kneaded bread, worked butter, and prepared and served meals. At night, lighted by a candle or a coal-oil lamp, the table was the place where the family and visitors gathered to talk or read.

Currie's grazing land stretched down to Green River and over to the mountains on the west side of the Valley. By 1891 he had one hundred cattle and six horses. Six years later, when his herd had grown considerably, he decided to drive most of the animals over the trail to Howe Sound, and no doubt ship them on to Vancouver, and because he would not be feeding much stock the next winter, he cut and stored much less hay than usual.

He hired dozens of men from the Indian Reserve to help with the drive, but the cattle were quite unaccustomed to being herded and refused to stay on the trail. Currie then fenced sections of the path and tried again, but the animals still went their own ways, up the mountain, or down to a slough running into Green River where many were mired and lost. Rain turned to snow; in just a few days the temperature dropped to eighteen degrees below.

The drive was a complete failure and Currie's supply of hay was far short of the needs of the few animals that did reach home. A. P. Barnfield and his partner, both of whom had helped with the drive, stayed with Currie and cut cottonwoods and willows to help feed the cattle. The animals "would eat sticks as big as your finger", but the twigs and branches were no substitute for hay or grass, and in the winter of 1898 the snow lingered until April. Years later white skeletons still littered the edges of the fields.

Charlie Morris later took charge of Currie's herd. To market them, he would drive only five or six cattle at a time over the trails, at least once by way of Douglas, but like the animals on all other drives, these too were plagued with sore feet.

Currie's relatives finally found him here, more than forty years after he had left home. In 1893 his step-mother reached Pemberton. With her son and her daughter, Ronald Currie and Annie McIntosh, Janet Currie had come from New Westminster, through Douglas, and on to the Lillooet River Valley, travelling by canoe over the lakes and on foot over the rest of the rocky distance. According to Willie Currie, Janet Currie thought Pemberton was "the end of the world", and with her son and her daughter therefore moved on to Lillooet. About 1895, however, another sister came to live with "old John", and Janet McCurdie brought three daughters, Annie, Mary, and Kate. Mary married Charlie Morris; their son John was born in Pemberton in 1901.

Janet McCurdie lived with old John as long as he remained in the Valley. In 1901 he resigned as Pemberton Meadows postmaster and not much later Leonard Neill took over the farm. Currie moved away. In 1910 he died and was buried in Vancouver.

Another early settler, Harvey Nelson, reached this region when a young boy and in 1890 was on the list of Pemberton voters. He acquired land close to the Rancherie, as the Indian Reserve was called, but when his house burned he located farther up the Lillooet, sharing his home with Lame Johnny from

Skookumchuck. The Nelson farmland is now owned by Howard Ayers and is distinct from other land because of that lone old crabapple tree still standing in the middle of a field. On the old road to Mount Currie, the steep hill which overlooks the farm was named for Harvey Nelson. One of his descendants is Matilda Jim, a woman of more than one hundred who still weaves baskets of fine quality.

By the time Currie's relatives had reached his farm, more settlers were establishing themselves. John Long and Mr. R. Taylor came at this time. Paul Dick remembered that when young James Taylor was very small his parents would take him to the fields where they were going to work, and would stuff him into a potato sack for protection against mosquitoes. About the time the first post office was established three more men made their way into the Valley: Carl Abraham Hartzell, William Morgan "Jock" Miller, and Duncan Morrison. Hartzell, a Swede, and Miller had both been at sea and had met in Vancouver where they worked as longshoremen.

Anita (Ronayne) McWilliams describes Hartzell's voice as "rising in excitement until he was almost singing". Wearing a beard, and looking like King Oscar of Sweden, Hartzell sported a straw hat summer and winter, and required outsize collars to stretch over the goitre he had developed. About 1891 he settled in the Soo Valley, his Greta Valley, where others, too, invested; one was Sam Fiddick's widow, who thought she was investing in the Pemberton country her husband had described after his return from the gold-fields. From his high valley, Hartzell at first came down to work at Currie's farm during haying season and returned home with food, but after a few late springs, with their accompanying floods which set his cabin boards awash, he settled in Pemberton.

In the year of Currie's disastrous cattle drive Hartzell was returning from the coast when a snow storm caught him at Green Lake. In leather shoes, his feet were nearly frozen when he stumbled into Currie's house. Janet McCurdie took charge, pulling off his shoes and socks and bathing his feet. To protect his feet in later years he would wrap them in strips of gunny sacking and then pull on his own homemade moccasins — winter footwear the very best for warmth.

Hartzell had located beyond the Rockslide and had built a log house with a roof extension to shelter his wood supply, and a loft above reached by a ladder. He plowed with oxen, one named Spot, but at the time Hartzell broke his land nobody else beyond the Rockslide owned a horse either. He planted a variety of crops, but the farming activity for which he is best remembered is the raising of pigs. One of his friends claimed that Hartzell taught his pigs to eat clover roots under the snow, where they made tunnels with air holes, and that he once thought he had lost a pair of pigs, but they had spent the winter eating cull potatoes along last season's potato rows and had turned up grunting when the snow melted.

Inside the cabin, like several other early Pemberton farmers, Hartzell carried on both scholarly and household activities. Besides working at endless mathematical problems, besides trying to "square the circle", he kept weather records. Until 1904 when he succeeded Currie as postmaster, Hartzell would sometimes leave his farm for a time during the summer. Once he hiked twenty-five miles through Railroad Pass to the Lorne Mine on Cadwallader Creek. In 1900 he made this diary entry: "Water over land in June. Came home in July. Crops and everything all right". To simplify soup-making, over the stove he hung a chunk of meat ready to be immersed in a pot of water, boiled for an hour or more, then returned to its hook. Kathleen (Ronayne) Lundgren remembered his "third brew" which she, as a child, was allowed to sip, a wine brewed from currants, a first, a second, and a third time, the last brew proving less than potent. Some people remember his unique method of hanging out shirts and overalls to dry — spread eagled, and nailed to the wall.

Ian Nicholson has vivid memories of Hartzell's efforts to interest officials — even the King of England — in exterminating the beaver whose dams were flooding his fields. After 1918 another ongoing problem was the contempt in which new settlers held the fences Hartzell had built across the public road at the north and south boundaries of his farm as protection against straying cattle. Despite Hartzell's racing the mile between his gates to guard them, settlers manoeuvered their cart wheels to damage the gate posts. Finally Hartzell's recourse was to a shotgun; the settler's to a justice of the peace. At the trial held on a summer week-end at a table in front of Jack Ronayne's house, everyone was there: "Old Hartzell had a secret up his sleeve. The settler had been courting the teacher and in the evenings they used to go to an old house on Hartzell's property. He comes on with this story, everybody laughs, and Jack Ronayne dismisses the whole case".

Hartzell was a man with a strict code. Once he sold his land, but when the buyer was unable to complete payments, Carl Hartzell returned to Pemberton, took back the acreage and, as he was able, paid back the money he had received for the land. He was a most careful budgeter. His yearly supply of groceries would total $35, about the amount of his annual salary from the post office. One year his expenditures exceeded this limit and only after long calculations did he remember that during the year he had broken his lamp glass and had had to replace it. Once when he counted the matches in a new box he found that he was short the usual number. When the local merchant disclaimed responsibility, Hartzell wrote to the E.B. Eddy Company in Hull and the firm sent him two small boxes. If he seemed to be penny-pinching, he was also generous: every Christmas he gave $1.00 to each child in the Valley, at that time a handsome gift, and he continued to do so until the Green family arrived and brought the number of children up to twenty-four.

Will Miller settled near the creek to be named for him and his brother — in 1895 he pre-empted a district lot. He had reached Pemberton long after he had left the home farm in Scotland at the age of sixteen to enlist in the Argyle and Sutherland Highlanders. He served in Africa and Ceylon. Later as a seaman he sailed several times to the British Columbia coast, and there as a resident of early Vancouver earned a reputation as a boxer and a wrestler and as captain of a tug-of-war team. Then he headed towards this Valley and on reaching the Lillooet River, swam across to the inhabited area.

A few years later Miller took part in one of the cattle drives organized to supply beef for Yukon gold miners. After the men in charge had overcome extreme difficulties and had herded the cattle as far as Teslin Lake, they found that thick ice had formed around barges built to ferry the herd across the lake. The herders could do nothing but slaughter the cattle. Mining out of Atlin, the Ronayne brothers found and used some of the frozen beef, but of course had no idea that one of the men who had driven the cattle north would be their neighbour in Pemberton. Miller himself, after mining at Dawson City, walked on ice along the Yukon River and across Norton Sound to Nome, Alaska. Through the winter he had travelled about 1500 miles.

When he hiked back into Pemberton he had his brother Bob with him. Within a few years the brothers received crown grants to two district lots ad joining the lot already owned by Will Miller, all near Miller Creek. There they cleared land and raised cattle herded by a dog Leonard Neill had given them. About 1950, far out in what had been a swamp, a much later owner of the land plowed up ancient cedar fence posts and rails that could have formed a corral, and the skeleton of Millers' barn still stood beside the creek, the remaining timbers still pegged together. Having packed an axle from the coast and having made wheels from solid cottonwood, Bob Miller built the first wagon in Pemberton and thereby eliminated the use of rawhide, and replaced the go-devil, a rough all-wooden sleigh.

When Jack Ronayne wrote in April 1909 "Neill and Jock Miller firing [burning dead grass and brush]", Bob Miller was already at the fish hatchery at Owl Creek. Not many months later the brothers returned to Scotland for a visit, having by then started transfer of their property to the Howe Sound & Northern Development Company. They signed the quit-claim deed in 1912.

From their vantage point on the trail to the Upper Valley, the Millers had seen other settlers pass on their way to the post office on the Currie farm. Occasionally surveyors, timber cruisers, prospectors, and land seekers travelled into the Valley. If not seeing them, the Millers knew of their passing. The print of a horseshoe indicated a visitor from the coast. Men were known by their footprints. One example of such keen observation Clara Jones mentioned.

One early fall day Clara Jones' mother, Minnie Ryan, decided to walk about six miles down the trail to visit her sister, Mrs. Leonard Neill. "She made herself a couple of sandwiches, and wearing running shoes she started off. She just got past the Rockslide and into the Miller timber when she rounded a curve in the road and came face to face with a big black bear sitting up eating berries from the bushes. Mother stopped dead in her tracks — the bear looked, then lumbered off into the bush. Mother said she just couldn't move, then thought of her lunch — put her hand in her pocket and brought out a sandwich and ate it, then went on. She was at Auntie's an hour when one of the Ronayne brothers came in and said, 'I see you met a bear, Mrs. Ryan.' Mother looked amazed and asked how he knew. He laughed: 'I saw the tracks, and you stood and never moved until you ate a lunch'."

One land seeker reached Pemberton very thirsty in the summer heat of 1897 and, to the amusement of people who regularly used river water, asked if Lillooet water was fit to drink. The newcomer was Duncan Morrison, a tall, blue-eyed, gentle-mannered man. After acquiring his lonely ranch where he believed trains would some day chug past, he would walk fifteen miles to the post office down the road which twisted its way back and forth across the valley floor, meandering like the river.

Born in Cape Breton, he had left home planning to prospect for gold in the Yukon. Some say he made his way into this Valley working on Pemberton Trail maintenance. His niece, Mrs. C. E. Carter, knows that at first he found life here very lonely and she was not surprised to learn that he once decided to leave this country and started to hike out through Railroad Pass where a blizzard turned him back. She said, though, that in later years "the lovely valley" was "Paradise" to him.

Most of the pioneers appear to have developed no adverse effects from their isolation. A few may have suffered. One unfortunate bachelor resented his neighbours. The first had filled a sock with thistle seeds, then strode up the trail twirling the sock around his head to distribute the seeds on the unfortunate bachelor's land; another had trained a crow to steal the bachelor's eggs; and a third came in the dark of the night to ride the bachelor's yet-unbroken eight-year-old "colt".

Those few nineteenth-century settlers lived as we do, facing Mount Currie which is named for the pioneer who farmed below it. In all its shifting colours, from snowy white and blue to summer green and blue, that mountain is the prominent landmark, unchanged over centuries except for some logged patches on its lower flanks. And when the first snows fall at 8,000 feet "old man Currie puts on his nightcap" and "John Currie Mountain begins smoking all day in winter as if to vie with the chimneys in the Valley".

C. A. Hartzell

Duncan Morrison Provincial Archives, Victoria, B.C.

THE SQUAMISH-PEMBERTON TRAIL AND EARLY LOCAL ROADS

Until the 1960's, when a rock-crushing operation obliterated it, everyone who passed could see at Mile 68 on the British Columbia Railway a section of the Squamish-Pemberton Trail, the old link with the coast. In 1881, four years after completing the very rough route, the provincial government spent $400 on its maintenance, but with years of neglect after that expenditure, the windfalls, slides, and rotting bridges discouraged most travellers from using the trail. Then in 1891 the government allocated $1,000 to build a road within the Pemberton Valley. The settlers decided, however, that for a few years longer they could tolerate a local trail because their great need was an improved trail to Squamish. They met at Currie's and decided to ask Victoria officials to reallocate the $1,000.

The result of the request was that a crew of sixteen men started in April to clear the sixty-mile distance to Squamish, to replace bridges and, in a few spots, to improve the grade. A. P. Barnfield, then a pre-emptor on the Lillooet River, was one of nine men who completed the job in July. Even with a twice-weekly steamer from Vancouver to Squamish and an improved trail, though, not all preferred this route into Pemberton. After the turn of the century some pioneer families entered the area by way of Port Douglas or Lillooet Town. Eventually, experience proved that, while still very expensive, food was cheapest packed from Squamish.

Near the end of his long life, Barnfield still vividly remembered the trail: "It was a heartbreaker, built so that it climbed up and down most of the ridges between Pemberton and Squamish." In the main it had followed the Canadian Pacific Railway's temporary pack trail built with one purpose: to move camp as required by the advance of the survey crews.

The government maintained the trail, making yearly grants that provided jobs for residents at both ends. Having allowed themselves only three days to cut out windfalls, one spring two Magee brothers ran out of their staple supplies which were pork and beans and apples. Finding a canoe at One Mile Lake

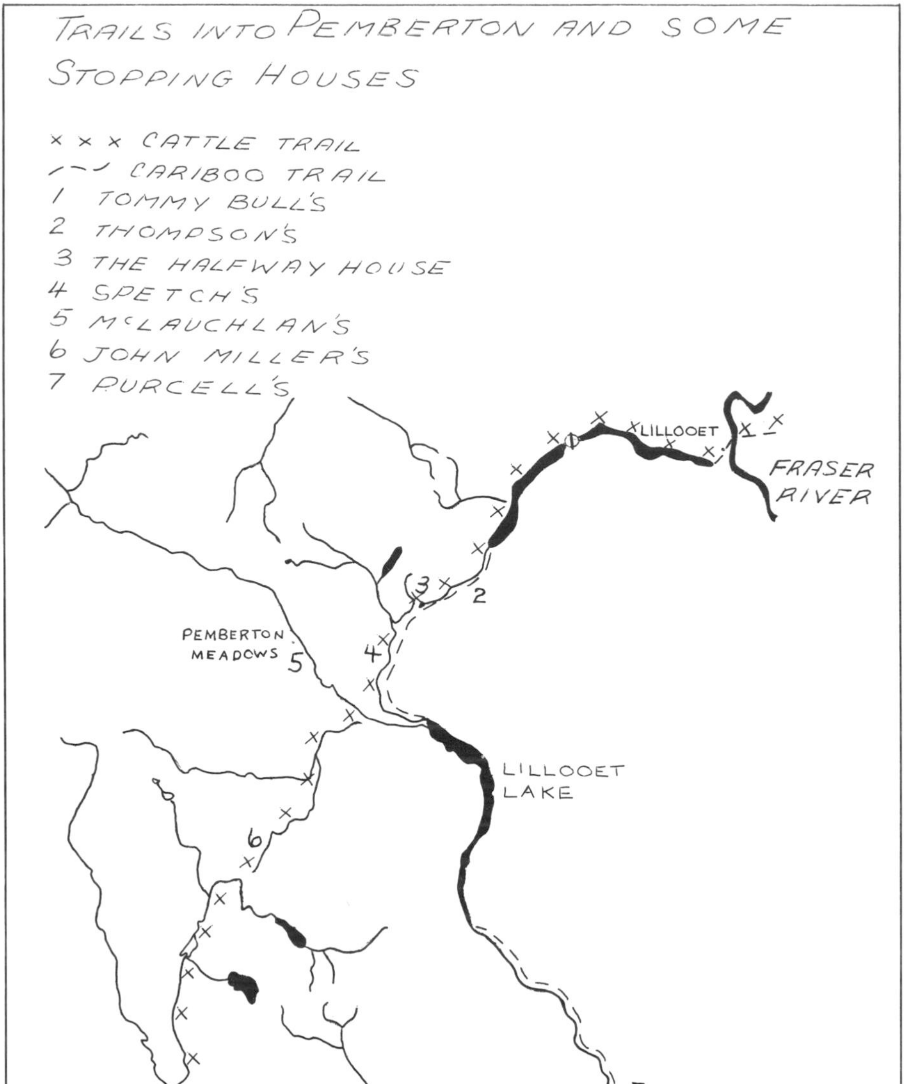

TRAILS INTO PEMBERTON AND SOME STOPPING HOUSES

× × × CATTLE TRAIL
/−/ CARIBOO TRAIL
1 TOMMY BULL'S
2 THOMPSON'S
3 THE HALFWAY HOUSE
4 SPETCH'S
5 McLAUCHLAN'S
6 JOHN MILLER'S
7 PURCELL'S

LILLOOET
FRASER RIVER
PEMBERTON MEADOWS
LILLOOET LAKE
HARRISON LAKE
SQUAMISH
HOWE SOUND
VANCOUVER

The Squamish-Pemberton Trail — Elsie Miller and Janet Miller de Suarez one brother paddled off to an Indian family who sold him dried fish and apples.

Tom Greer packed powder and supplies to men working on the trail in 1902. He describes the section through the Cheakamus Canyon: "The old trail left Cheakamus Flats at Swift Creek, and went up Swift Creek for over a mile. Then, if you missed the trail, you made for the biggest rockslide you could see and continued until you were over Lookout Mountain and crossed Stoney [Rubble] Creek."

Travel by this trail was not for weaklings. Those men who walked from Brackendale to Pemberton in one day, Edward Adie, Felix Sam, and Bert Perkins among them, were strong men. Perkins once set out on foot to race a horse and rider from Pemberton to Squamish. Given a two-hour start, Perkins reached Squamish on the day he left home and then, the story goes, played a mouth organ all night at a dance. The horseman, William Hamill, arrived at his destination on the afternoon of the second day. Another man forced his horse to cover the same distance in one day. That horse died.

Children too walked or rode over the trail, sometimes attacked by angry wasps accidentally disturbed, sometimes making difficult creek crossings. Charlie Barbour's step-daughter, Bebee (Fowles) Ruddock, remembers riding across Rubble Creek with stones rolling and grinding in a May freshet. Vivien (Ross) Lokken remembered a very tiring trip, mostly on foot, with her uncle Edmond Ronayne, when she was only twelve.

That year uncle and niece stayed overnight at John Miller's Halfway House which was located near the present Malloch and Moseley camp at Mile 71 on the British Columbia Railway. Miller had then one of the very few habitations between Brackendale and Pemberton, and once he had opened his establishment Pemberton ranchers preferred it to the camping spot at Daisy Lake. A stopover with "Mahogany John", as the proprietor was known,

Afternoon clean-up at John Miller's Provincial Archives, Victoria, B.C.

meant good substantial food, a soft bed — usually in the haymow — and entertainment. Miller threw slices of bacon from table to frying pan, never missing. When everything was ready "he would remove the stub of a cigarette from his lips and utter the words well known to every Pemberton pioneer, 'Now, gentlemen, please put your feet under the mahogany'." Myrtle Philip enjoyed the fresh vegetables from his garden and considers his pastry the best she has ever eaten. A one-time packer, Cliff Thorne says it did not do to be too inquisitive about the food, because that excellent soup might have been made from goose bones "trimmed by some other fellows". A young girl who rode the trail even earlier than Bebee Fowles and Vivien Ross considered John Miller a queer-looking character: Clara Ryan was troubled by his flattened nose, his booming voice — and the rumour that his gun had more than one notch on its handle.

Early packer Provincial Archives, Victoria, B.C.

A stopping house that did not prosper was Cotton's on Green Lake. On his arrival from India, Cotton bought Cheque-Book McDonald's land and hired loggers and carpenters to build him a substantial log house, and James Landsborough wrote that the crew at Cotton's must have been a happy one to judge by the epigrams on the walls, such as "When pleasure interferes with business, cut out business." Eventually Cotton closed his stopping house and moved on. Landsborough remembered a night when he, Cliff Thorne, and two Vancouver businessmen on a holiday dodged smoke around their campfire outside the deserted establishment. Next morning they got up from their beds on the ground to enjoy the aroma and taste of sizzling bacon, Shelley's 4-X bread with Malkin's jam, and cups of Nabob coffee.

In 1909, on her way to school in Vancouver Clara Ryan travelled with her uncle and her aunt, and Ray Elliott, a packer. At the end of one day, continuous rain had made the child so cold that she could hardly get off her horse. She describes how Neill and Elliott made sure that she and her aunt would spend a warm night: "When we stopped the night at Daisy Lake, Uncle and Ray took a huge stone and put it in the fire and got it hot, then rolled it in sacks and put it in Auntie's and my bed — cedar boughs in a tent — and we hugged it to get warm."

Wildlife along the route was more plentiful than it is today. Willie Currie and Bill Spetch used to find Alta Lake alive with fish, and sometimes when passing Daisy Lake heard loons calling or wolves howling. Once Bert Perkins saw seventeen wolves within a stone's throw of his camp at Nairn Falls, but on the far bank of the river.

Some never forgot the beauty of the trail. Seventy years later Bebee Ruddock remembers the lovely May woods she rode through as a child. Landsborough, writing of "the home run along the west side of Green Lake and down the Green River Valley", mentioned the remarkable flowers of the syringa and the dogwood, and said that: "The trail is bordered by kinnikinnick, lupines, twisted stalk, and thimbleberries. Here and there huckleberries tempt the packer, so that he has to 'hurry up to catch up'." His colour-blindness did not blunt that rancher's joy in his environment.

Packing a stove Provincial Archives, Victoria, B.C.

Several men made their living by packing, spending three days each way on the trail to Squamish. Tom Greer returned to the work in 1907 to pack at intervals for some settlers, particularly when they wanted stoves which, he says, were articles not popular for packing. He packed too for the new storekeeper, John McKenzie. In 1911 when she and her husband were returning from Pemberton and Alta Lake, Myrtle Philip remembers meeting Bert Perkins and his pack train, fifteen horses loaded with stuff for Pemberton. Until the railway put him and other men out of business, Ray Elliott continued packing up and down the trail.

Francis Wallace was only a small boy when he travelled the trail with his father's pack train and hung onto the tails of the horses as they climbed steep hills. The older Wallace often loaded his horses with blasting powder for James Punch, the road foreman at Pemberton. Another child, Harry Dan, was only ten when he worked with packer Billy Williams who, when packing for one of the early stores, loaded seven horses with sugar and flour, and seven with coal oil. The child helped with the loading: he would stand under a can and support it with his head while the load was being fastened and then when all were ready to travel he would stuff the bell of the lead horse with hay, spread his blanket over some sacks of flour, climb up to his resting place and go to sleep. Sometimes when the pack train would reach the Soo River and find it a raging torrent, Williams would tie little Harry onto the back of the horse.

Packers and ranchers themselves took charge of cattle drives, slow trips to Squamish lasting eight days or more. One very convenient camping place for men driving animals over the trail was the meadow ten miles out of Pemberton where grass grew in abundance. Furthermore, memories of the bears at Hell's Gate, through which the men had just driven the herd, killed the cattle's desire to return home. Landsborough said that some riders made sure no animal would escape: each horseman took charge of two steers tied together, head and tail. The usual method, though, was the slow drive which allowed the animals to feed along the way and not lose over-much weight. On one occasion Ed Ronayne and Will Miller drove out a herd which they slaughtered at Squamish and sold at 6c a pound, an unprofitable conclusion to their enterprise.

Speaking in Squamish in 1906, a provincial politician promised that if his party were elected it would build a road to Pemberton. Men in his audience would have remembered that in 1899 the government of that day had already started a road to Pemberton, but stopped at the Cheakamus. All machinery bound for the Valley had been packed in either on settlers' backs or by pack trains, and for having equipment packed in over this route in 1902 Leonard Neill is said to have paid $1,500. Whether buying or selling, settlers could not escape the costs resulting from their isolation, and for many long years, speculation about road or railway building must have cropped up every time these people came together.

No road to the coast would be completed until the 1960's, but in 1893 the provincial government did start to convert into a road the trail linking Lower and Upper Valley. In that year workers slashed over six miles to a width of 15 feet, excavated 920 yards of rock and built five bridges averaging 12 by 60 feet. Where the road began is uncertain: a 1903 Public Works report explains that "the road to Pemberton Meadows turns off at the Birkenhead Bridge, about five miles from Pemberton [Lillooet] Lake." But before the federal Department of Fisheries built a hatchery at Owl Creek, a trail, not a road, turned off at the Birkenhead Bridge. That trail crossed land where Samuel Spetch later established himself, and which George Walker bought still later. Bill Spetch,

P.G.E. tote road, 1913

John Currie home in 1952 Provincial Archives, Victoria, B.C.

Packing up Bear Mountain Provincial Archives, Victoria, B.C.

Samuel's son, says that instead of heading south to present-day Mount Currie the cattle trail continued in a westerly direction to Harvey Nelson Hill, from which travellers made their way down to the Lillooet. Once there they walked over the river on log jams, forded, or crossed by canoe. The trail striking west from Owl Creek never did become a road. In 1893 the Public Works crews must have worked in the Valley and their excavations must have been along the Rockslide, about four miles from Pemberton Village. On an abandoned section of the first road up the Valley, it slopes up from a curve in the Ryan River. Before its diversion in the 'forties, the Lillooet River flowed alongside the

Rockslide, but with the diversion the river has been forced to the other side of the Valley.

Men started to build the first Valley road when funds for provincial construction projects were drying up, and as a consequence what was built was poorly maintained. In 1903 an official reported $325 spent on it, and added that "there is nothing there at present worthy of the name of road. . . .A good wagon road the length of the valley would be the means of bringing new settlers and developing the country."

Again and again early twentieth-century settlers referred to "the trail". Landsborough described it as "in summer like a trench bordered by high grass, thimbleberries, raspberries, rose bushes, and bracken." In such dense growth "it was very difficult to find a horse without a bell."

At times, some men preferred to travel by river where they had estimated visibility of about half a mile. Hartzell and Morrison often used canoes. Jack Ronayne's notes show that others did the same:

"April 1909 Joe brought grub from store with canoe."

"July 1910 Road engineer went down river with canoe."

"April 1912 Went down to Coleman's in canoe with children."

Probably the trail or road was the usual route. In winter, snow plugged it: "Very frequent snowfalls followed by very frequent breaking caused the teamster to become fed up and abandon the double track. The pack horse carried his load from the store. On rare occasions he hauled a rawhide well laden with provisions." Several diary entries tell of winter road conditions and travel:

"After snowfall broke with Tom and rawhide to Hartzell's. Landsborough broke with loose horses to here."

"January 1911 Fanny went to Hartzell's with dog team and children."

"February 1911 I took down Mrs. Ryan with dogs; had to pull myself as well for dogs got tired on account of loose snow."

The twisting track was so narrow that until 1906 when the Ronayne brothers blasted their way through, no settler beyond the Rockslide owned a wagon or a mower. Jim Dermody remembers that as a team pulled a wagon past the same Rockslide, his father threw his weight against the vehicle to keep it from sliding into the river.

Before 1906 the Public Works Department had introduced both road machinery and more modern methods into the Lillooet District to which part of the Pemberton area belonged. By that year district residents "contemplated with more favour" the use of "a grader, two spreading wagons, one horse roller, one engine and a sawmill." In the next few years annual reports listed a pile driver, four forges, and a gasoline hoist.

In 1909, sixteen years after Public Works employees had started to build a road to the Upper Valley, settlers circulated a petition. Through their member in the legislature, F. Carter-Cotton, seventeen men asked that "the road up the valley be put in condition for wagon traffic." Probably in response to that petition the Department of Public Works appointed the first local road foreman, Robert Hutchison, who in November of that year was hiring men.

Jim Dermody says that the first big change in the Valley road was its diversion from the banks of Ryan Creek to its present route through the Miller property. That project was a big one which made work for local men and their teams. Because most men were hours distant from their homes the foreman set up tent camps in which Ernest Ward was an early camp cook, as were Dunc Morrison and Mrs. Tom Bubb.

In March 1910 James Punch was road foreman and, in addition to his regular maintenance work, started to build a road on the east bank of the Lillooet. That road, which headed towards the Dermody farm, was never completed, but even in recent years loggers have used the section built then.

The year before Punch took charge the Public Works Department had built a bridge over the Lillooet at a site to be reached now by following the Pemberton Farm Road. According to Mabel Boeur, an early teacher, Douglas Adie worked on that bridge along with Johnny Punch. The approach and the two spans measured 289 feet, all constructed for $1,876. At some time somebody must have painted the structure, because many years later the weather-beaten crossing was still known as the Red Bridge.

In 1914, following the north bank of the Lillooet Public Works crews started to build a road from the Red Bridge towards the Indian Reserves, or present-day Mount Currie, grading two miles and scattering gravel over three-quarters of a mile of that distance. The next year they finished the last four miles. Before that section of road was built people could travel along the south bank of the Lillooet from the Reserves to present-day Pemberton, but only during low water.

From year to year throughout the Pemberton area the sums for government road maintenance fluctuated. Until 1913 annual appropriations for the Portage Road were only a few hundreds of dollars. The amount zoomed from $962 spent in the previous year to $2,833 when heavier traffic associated with railway construction required improvements. Amounts spent on the Pemberton Meadows Road varied too, but generally in an upward direction; by 1912 the allocation was $7,250. In 1914 for the first time crews spread gravel on Valley roads.

Until 1916 men continued to repair both the Anderson and Seton Lake Trails. In that year railway construction destroyed the trail along Seton Lake, but in the same year a gang "cleared, grubbed, and made general repairs" to a new road, the road to the Pemberton depot. Two years before, the Pacific Great Eastern Railway had replaced the Pemberton Trail, in fact had obliterated parts of it and of the Portage Road. "Pat Welch," as Barnfield said, "laid his ties and steel on the nice level stretches."

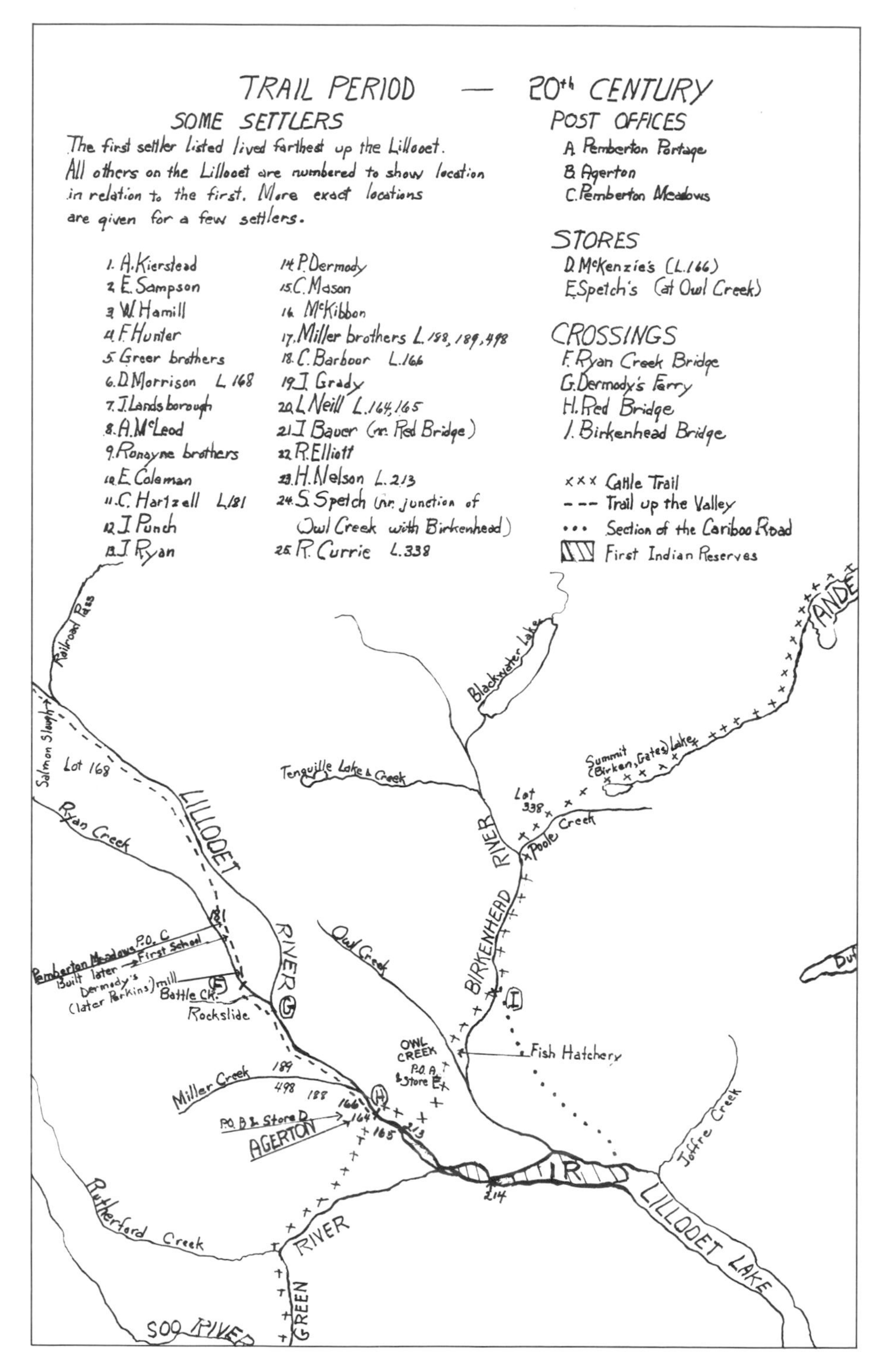
TRAIL PERIOD — 20th CENTURY
SOME SETTLERS
The first settler listed lived farthest up the Lillooet. All others on the Lillooet are numbered to show location in relation to the first. More exact locations are given for a few settlers.
1. A. Kierstead
2. E. Sampson
3. W. Hamill
4. F. Hunter
5. Greer brothers
6. D. Morrison L 168
7. J. Landsborough
8. A. McLeod
9. Ronayne brothers
10. E. Coleman
11. C. Hartzell L/81
12. J. Punch
13. J. Ryan
14. P. Dermody
15. C. Mason
16. McKibbon
17. Miller brothers L. 188, 189, 498
18. C. Barboor L. 166
19. J. Grady
20. L. Neill L. 164, 165
21. J. Bauer (nr. Red Bridge)
22. R. Elliott
23. H. Nelson L. 213
24. S. Spetch (nr. junction of Owl Creek with Birkenhead)
25. R. Currie L. 338
POST OFFICES
A. Pemberton Portage
B. Agerton
C. Pemberton Meadows
STORES
D. McKenzie's (L. 166)
E. Spetch's (at Owl Creek)
CROSSINGS
F. Ryan Creek Bridge
G. Dermody's Ferry
H. Red Bridge
I. Birkenhead Bridge
xxx Cattle Trail
--- Trail up the Valley
••• Section of the Cariboo Road
First Indian Reserves
Railroad Pass
Salmon Slough
Lot 168
Ryan Creek
LILLOOET
Tenquille Lake & Creek
Blackwater Lake
Summit (Birken, Gates) Lake
Lot 338
Poole Creek
BIRKENHEAD RIVER
RIVER
Owl Creek
Pemberton Meadows P.O. C
Built later → First School
Dermody's (later Perkins) mill
Battle Ck.
Rockslide
OWL CREEK P.O. A. & Store E
Fish Hatchery
Miller Creek
189
498
188
166
P.O. B & Store D
164
165
213
AGERTON
214
IR
Joffre Creek
LILLOOET LAKE
Rutherford Creek
RIVER
GREEN
SOO RIVER
ANDE

SETTLEMENT 1900 to 1914

During the first years of the twentieth century lives of Pemberton settlers changed little. One new development did occur, though: the establishment of the Dominion Government Fish Hatchery at Owl Creek. Built in 1905 the hatchery gave part-time jobs to some men and provided a limited market for farm products. In spite of ever-present difficulties, little by little the population increased.

Under the government of Richard McBride, premier from 1903 to 1915, British Columbia prospered and attracted more and more settlers. McBride encouraged railway building and promoters planned ten railways to head north to Fort George. The belief that Pemberton would be opened up in a few years encouraged settlement in the Valley and on the Portage, settlement by some families as well as by bachelors. Parents bringing children into areas without schools or without any medical services must have had misgivings, but available land, combined with the expected railway link, was a powerful magnet.

In 1901 Carl A. Hartzell wrote to the *Daily Province* stating that 20,000 acres of Pemberton land were out of reach of flood and that an acre in the driest sections could produce 1,500 pounds of grain or 12 tons of potatoes. Appearing in the same paper as Hartzell's letter was one from Charles Barbour who lamented that the government's lack of foresight in failing to build a road from the coast to Pemberton prevented annual production of $1,000,000 worth of agricultural products. Some selling at $18 an acre, Pemberton land was cheaper than Fraser Valley land which, in 1900, sold at an average of $45 an acre. This comparative cheapness attracted some settlers, but inevitably local prices increased as a railway became a probability and in 1910 one settler stated that he would not sell his holdings for $50 an acre. The next year 100 acres sold for $10,000.

The settlers made their way, singly or in groups, over the lonely trails which like the spokes of a wheel converged on Pemberton. Some rode; many walked. James Ryan and Arthur Keirstead took to the trail after buying cayuses in Squamish. Ryan pre-empted on a creek later named for him, and built his first house, a shack twelve feet square. Two years later, with her daughter, the widowed Minnie Hall came to visit her sister, Mrs. Neill and after a few months in Pemberton, Mrs. Hall married James Ryan. The Neills, with their daughter, had come by way of Lillooet to operate the former Currie ranch. Keirstead pre-empted 160 acres close to the confluence of the Lillooet with Twin Creeks, now North and South Creeks, in that area where a rockslide and a creek have been named for him. He too built a house and lived in it until the river swept house and land away. Then floodwaters deposited sand up to the eaves of a house he built farther upriver. In between trips packing for the government and for the owners of Britannia Mines, Bert Perkins also came and looked the country over and for a time seems to have alternated between logging in Squamish and trapping here.

The 1905-06 tax rolls show sixty-eight landowners. Besides those already mentioned others lived here for short or long periods, or not at all. Tom Greer's brothers, Jack and Will, lived up the Valley; Frederick Hunter gave his name to an Upper Valley bridge; Claud Mason's swamp was where an expanse of fields now extends above Ryan Creek Bridge; and Edward Milton died in his far up-valley shack as he was trying to start a fire in his stove. Alex McLeod was known for his mining activities: the McLeod Trail switchbacking up to Crown Mountain, McLeod Creek, and "the old McLeod place" commemorate this man. Sixteen-year-old Tom Steinbrunner of Gibson's Landing freighted lumber across the Lillooet by canoe in order to build J. Lovering's house.

The Landsborough brothers had travelled far from their Scottish home before settling here on land well beyond the Rockslide. Walter had lived in New Zealand; James had herded sheep in Argentina. Jim Landsborough spent little on himself: he usually wore blue denim pants and a matching jacket, and when going into the mountains he would sling his new boots around his neck, ready for use when the old ones gave out. But he often generously shared his house and all that he owned. When young Francis Wallace was about to go off to school at Mission, Landsborough made his way over the trail to Lillooet and bought the boy a watch, new pants, and a .22 rifle. Jimmy, as he was affectionately known, loved books and encouraged a love of books in others — at intervals a Vancouver bookseller received Landsborough's gift orders for Pemberton children. His obituary showed another side of his character: "He loved dogs, and when going to the defence of his Airedale, Smitty, an enraged cow attacked him."

About the time the Landsboroughs acquired the Currie pre-emption in the Upper Valley, Jack Ronayne bought land from Charles Barbour for himself and his brothers Edmond and Joseph. Descendants of the three Ronayne brothers, and of Will Miller and his wife, Teresa (Ronayne) Miller, now form a considerable portion of the Valley's farmer population. Jack Ronayne was a keeper of a diary, the original of which has been given to the Provincial Archives in Victoria. In another record he described the arduous trip with his brothers into the Lillooet River Valley: "Ronayne Brothers and C. Barbour brought their supplies, including mowing machine, rakes, ploughs, wagons, and heavy horses by train to Agassiz, by road using their own horses to Harrison Lake, by scow and tug to Port Douglas, by wagon to Tenas Lake, and by Indian canoe at 3½c a pound to Pemberton, the horses being taken by trail around Lillooet Lake.

"We were advised at Agassiz to take a box of blasting powder to remove a slide near Skookumchuck; the powder was not needed there, but came in handy later in widening the trail at the Rockslide in Pemberton, to allow the wagons to pass.

"Our wagon was the first to reach the upper valley; this was made possible by the above blasting and by detours and slashing where spaces between large cedar trees on the trail along the banks of Ryan Creek were too narrow, and by manoeuvering around stump holes in the open country farther up."

Charles Barbour settled on the land which he had bought some years earlier from Pettit. In May 1906, after three and a half days on the trail from Squamish, Barbour and his wife Dora and their two children reached Pemberton. While he was building their log house, the family lived for a few days in the old part of the store and that summer Pemberton experienced such a serious flood that "the whole place was like a river." Barbour's step-daughter, Bebee (Fowles) Ruddock, recalls that "one of the worst spells" of mosquitoes followed that flood, and that her stepfather would fling open the door, then quickly close it; between the opening and the closing, he would throw in an armful of wood.

Still early in the century, James Punch and his son John acquired the land that is now Petter Kuurne's. After mining in the boundary country at Phoenix, where Punch's son-in-law had been his foreman, Joseph Bauer too settled here with his wife. They lived in the new log house which the Barbours had occupied only during the 1906 summer, and would not re-occupy for several years because they had moved to Squamish. Later the Bauers lived across the Lillooet near the site of the yet-to-be-built Red Bridge. Mrs. Bauer was well known for her onion pies and friends wanting to enjoy them crossed the river by dugout.

The year after Punch arrived, his daughter Katherine also arrived from Phoenix with her husband, Patrick J. Dermody, and their family, the youngest only a few weeks old. With all their goods, including flowering plants, they had travelled by canoe to the head of Harrison Lake and there hired horses to pull a wagon which jolted and pitched so wildly over the old gold trail that Dermody carried the baby nearly thirty miles to Tenas Lake. After two days of rough travel the family spent about three days at the lake with the widow of Goodwin Purcell. Then they travelled up Tenas and Lillooet Lakes by canoe, poled up the Lillooet River, and landed, Jim Dermody says, somewhere near present-day Pemberton Village, at what until fairly recent years was called One Mile, a name originating in Pemberton Trail days. There at Pemberton the trail came down to the Valley floor, one mile from Currie's farm.

Carrying on from the river, the Dermodys walked several miles to the Bauers' house, then travelled on in Joe Bauer's wagon to the Punch home where they lived with the Punches until their own house could be built from lumber produced from their own mill which pack trains had freighted in shortly after the arrival of the family. Dermody set up his mill at the falls cascading into Ryan Creek close to the Lex Ross home-site of today. In 1909 a carpenter from "outside" completed the house, finishing the inner walls with lath and plaster. When it was finished, the family moved down the river in a canoe to their new home — the first Valley house across the Lillooet River. There the Dermodys lived until in August 1914 the house was destroyed by fire.

Somewhere along the lake or river when she was making her first trip into Pemberton, Katherine Dermody — "a very pretty woman" — had chosen a shamrock from among her treasured plants, which included the first white phlox brought to the Valley, and gave the shamrock to the late Saraphine Lester; and from that original stock, many years later Saraphine gave a shamrock plant to the Bill Spetch family. Derived from Katherine's gift, shamrock plants have therefore lived on in both the Indian and the white community. Jim Dermody remembers that on cold winter nights his mother wrapped her house plants in newspapers, and Bebee Ruddock recalls that Katherine Dermody, who "delighted in gardening", would arrive at their door "with the first green things of spring, lettuce or onions".

In 1907, the year the Dermodys reached the Valley, the Samuel Spetch family arrived at Birken, having come to Canada not long before from England. Travelling by way of Lytton and Lillooet they had brought with them to their new land, the Summit Ranch, horse harness, a knitting machine, and bolts of printed cloth. In June 1908, already operating a store, Samuel Spetch became the first Pemberton Portage postmaster. In August, however, when he moved his family to Owl Creek he moved the post office too, reasoning that the post office should be located at the main centre of population. But postal authorities did not hear of the new location until six months had passed, and one postal inspector jokingly advised Elizabeth Spetch to watch her husband's suitcase to make sure that he did not have the post office in it.

About the time the Dermodys and Spetches settled, a number of single men were arriving. In 1905 Robert Hutchison pre-empted 160 acres in the upper reaches of the Valley where successive floods silted his cabin to the window sills and buried his abandoned sewing machine. William Hamill met Bert Perkins on the trail, each riding one horse and leading another with a pack. "They came on together and kept together, more or less, friends for the rest of their lives," according to Mildred (Graham) Hamill. Hamill located on what is now the Perkins' Echo Ranch, and built his home from lumber sawn at Perkins' mill. Bert Perkins' son Phillip says that Hamill was a popular man, and most of the local men helped with the building. Tom Greer walked in from Clinton, staked land now belonging to Max Welti, then walked on to Squamish. Arriving from Edmonton, Ray Elliott met Jim Ryan and Len Neill who were on business in Vancouver, returned with them and their pack train to

Pemberton, and pre-empted land on the south side of what is now called Suicide Hill. Not many years ago, his cabin was still standing. Stella Shantz' uncle, James Duff, came at this time. John McKenzie opened a store on the Barbour place, and a small lake a few miles to the north is named after him.

In May 1908 a girl walked into the Valley accompanying Ann Strutzel, a crippled woman, and her two young children. The girl was Maria Poole, recently from Wales. She arrived sunburned and mosquito bitten, but to the Ryan's young daughter she was "as pretty a girl as you'd see in a day's travel, her hair so curly gold." Before long she would marry Johnny Punch and later, after being widowed for many years, Nelson Fraser. Her son and her grandchildren still live in the Valley.

Surveyors' camp on the Lillooet Provincial Archives, Victoria, B.C.

The two women had reached Lillooet by horse-drawn stage. From there Charlie Wallace, the mail carrier, arranged transportation for them, but before they left Lillooet they supplied themselves with lunches, as Mrs. Egan, the postmaster's wife, had advised. Then, after they had walked to Seton Lake and embarked with the collie dog sent as a present to Katherine Dermody, who was Ann Strutzel's sister, an Indian canoeman paddled them down towards the portage between lakes. The trip was an ordeal for the women. Never having known an Indian, perhaps they were less concerned with the fierce heat of the sun beating down on them and the children than with their fear of the man paddling, but Maria stayed outwardly calm as she sat on a crate of St. Charles milk and held the baby. Then they were left stranded on the Short Portage until Wallace arrived along the lake-side trail with his pack horses and insisted that the canoeman walk with the women to Anderson Lake. That lake they travelled in greater comfort, sitting on quilts in a flat-bottomed boat. At present-day D'Arcy, Wallace sent them off by horse and wagon to Charlie

Place who probably lived in the community now called Gates and who next day drove them to the Halfway House then owned by Ronald Currie, and Currie drove them on over the Portage to the Rancherie. From there Paul Dick and others paddled them to Harvey Nelson's farm.

Then they were on their own, a young girl, a crippled woman, and two infants, all following the mosquito-infested trail through the cottonwoods, Ann Strutzel limping and the baby crying. Passing the Neill farm at milking time, they trudged on to Bauers' stopping house where they spent the night, and then waited until Charlie Wallace could take news of their coming to the Dermodys.

After the Bauers had left the Barbour house, Barbour's nephew, Bob McLauchlan, took it over and continued to run it as a stopping house in which guests slept in bunks built around the four walls of the upstairs area. When the Barbours returned to the Valley, McLauchlan moved to a log house, probably the present Shantz home, where Margaret McLauchlan, Bob's mother, and his sisters, Della and Rita, lived with him.

While trails were still the only ways into the area more settlers came to spend a few years or many. From the farm adjoining the Ronaynes' in Ireland, Mrs. Jack Ronayne's brother, Frank Buckley, arrived, worked a few years at the fish hatchery, and then, chased out of this country by mosquitoes, he settled in Squamish, becoming the third locomotive engineer to work for the Pacific Great Eastern Railway. Douglas Adie too worked at the hatchery, and lived with his wife and his son in a house built on land now owned by Tom Ranson.

One-eyed Pete Petersen rode a one-eyed horse and ranged the country, living at several locations. George Williams saw him once carrying tobacco leaves up into the loft of a shed in a field near his house below Miller Creek. In one of Pete's homes he had a collection of surplus items from which he selected a gift for Mrs. Johnny Punch: three pots which she treasured. One Valley resident visited Petersen in his last home, close to the Ayers' home of today. Pete was about to cook eggs for his next meal, but lacking both the sense of taste and the sense of smell, and having collected his eggs at irregular intervals, he had to test each one. He sat cracking eggs, throwing those with chick embryos into the slop pail beside him, and easing fresh ones into a frying pan.

Eric Coleman lived across the river from the present Mitchell farm on land later acquired by Al Fraser. With the help of a neighbour, Coleman built a boat and bought an engine to install in it, but he left his land and his home to fight in the First World War. After Coleman died overseas, Vivien Lokken remembered the "dainty little wife", Mrs. Coleman, coming to see where Eric had lived.

Not long before the coming of the railway, more settlers arrived. From Eustace Bubb of the Howe Sound & Northern Development Company, George Groat bought several lots close to Miller Creek. Bubb assured him there was no possibility of water failure in summer, but no one told him that the danger was not in drought, but in flood. Jack Grady settled and became a good source of loans for some neighbours. Bill Fowler remembers him walking with his hat clasped to his back, even when heading out into the rain. Stella Shantz used to speak of Grady sitting reading under a tree, then walking off, leaving his book. On Easter Sunday in 1913 E. N. Sampson and his wife arrived from Squamish, having walked on the crusted snow. Since 1911 Sampson had held a pre-emption located on the "east side of the mouth of the locally named Sampson Creek, which flows south from Mount Samson [sic]." Nathaniel Baker bought the Neill farm and had his cousin, Popham, work for him.

Two years before the railway reached the Valley, Gladys and Ernest Blakeway learned in England from Baker's cousin that Baker needed a couple to help on his ranch. Gladys Blakeway, a Goldsmith College student, later told of answering a question about "what steps" she intended to take regarding her college program: "I'll take two steps: the first across the Atlantic, and the second across Canada". Towards the end of her second step, she and her brother rode the stage from Ashcroft to Lillooet.

When travelling down Seton Lake in a small steamer, she was wearing her London finery, a navy blue suit and a rose-bedecked hat. After the short walk between the lakes, the travellers found that they had missed the mail boat on Anderson Lake and, with some others, had to hire Indian canoemen. The wind blew strongly northward and finding the water too rough the paddlers landed midway down the lake, stormbound overnight in the pelting rain. To protect the fashionable young woman James Creighton gallantly erected a small canvas shelter.

After walking four or five miles the next morning the Blakeways met Baker coming with his team and wagon to take them to his ranch, but first he drove on to Anderson Lake, over the miles they had just walked, to rest and water his horses and turn them around. Following a night at the Halfway House, they continued over the rough road. After one violent lurch of their vehicle, Baker and the newcomers crashed down so hard on the wagon seat that it broke under them. By evening they had reached the historic farm where Gladys immediately set about making baking powder biscuits and cooking a meal for twelve men, one of them Ed Ronayne, her future husband.

Still more bachelors came about 1912. Jake Lokken and Olus Lee arrived together, Lokken to clear land now farmed by George Purden. Joussilana, a Finn, built a house and farmed in a small way, probably farther up the Lillooet than any other man. He and Sampson came down to help build the Joe Ronayne house.

The Barbour family returned from Vancouver, where they had lived since 1907. After Cyril Keyes came to live with them, Dora Barbour organized Pemberton's first milk route. She made a sack to be fastened over a horse's back, and made the sack with compartments on each side to hold glass milk bottles so that Cy could deliver milk to One Mile, or Pemberton Station.

Sunday jaunt Provincial Archives, Victoria, B.C.

Then, when the railway was under construction, and knowing that Pemberton was "mosquito land", Joseph and Annie Ronayne and their baby Margaret made their way into the Valley by a variety of conveyances. A Canadian Pacific train took them from Vancouver to Lytton where they caught the motorized stage competing with the horse-drawn stage on the run to Lillooet. According to Joe Taillefer, for the privilege of making the more than forty-mile trip lasting from 9 a.m. to 4 p.m., each passenger in 1912 paid $30 and pushed on the hills. In Lillooet the Ronaynes met Carl Hartzell, who was waiting for the old-style stage. He mistrusted motor cars: they could not be safe, he reasoned, when they depended on just a few screws.

Annie Ronayne's description is more detailed than Taillefer's: "Little rocks were rolling down the mountain side. Sleet was coming down, so the driver stopped to put on chains. There was much hauling of supplies for railroad workers, with large hooded wagons drawn by four and six horses. These animals appeared to be very frightened of our auto and would start into the bush or rear on their hind legs. One driver sitting up high could not control his horses and jumped down, his pant leg catching on the brake lever. With the roaring river on one side and very little room on the other, there he hung for a moment before the pant leg tore. Then he was on the ground and cursing loudly."

By 1913 powered boats plied both Seton and Anderson Lakes. Aboard the Seton Lake boat which had its deck piled high with freight, Annie Ronayne sat below with her baby, next to a hot engine. After a night at Lame Johnny's, the mother and baby were able to ride in a surveyor's wagon, while with a mattress on his back Ronayne walked behind. They managed to escape flying rocks at construction sites all along the Portage and their third night out from Lytton they spent with the Spetch family. From Owl Creek they travelled in the mail carrier's democrat to the site of their new home.

Throughout the summer, and longer, while their log house was being built, the Ronaynes slept in a tent and cooked in a shed. By various stratagems the young couple minimized the biting of the persistent mosquitoes surrounding themselves and their baby day and night. Joe had lived with these insects before and Annie had anticipated them. The Ronaynes used cotton mosquito netting to make screens which they fastened securely around the baby's cot and above their own split cedar bed. Avid readers, in the evenings the couple lay under their screens and read by the light of a coal-oil lamp, and to escape the mosquitoes during the day, the mother often took her baby up into the haymow. When his wife was cooking supper, Joe Ronayne would lead a horse close to the shack. The animal attracted swarms of mosquitoes which Ronayne swiftly squashed as soon as they had settled.

The year before, the very small pre-railway white population had been reported as not exceeding thirty. Now it was at least thirty-three.

Left to right: Rene, John, and Daisy Ronayne Provincial Archives, Victoria, B.C.

The Spetch family at Owl Creek, 1909 Provincial Archives, Victoria, B.C.

The Joe Ronayne family, 1913 Provincial Archives, Victoria, B.C.

ABOUT PIONEER LIVING

Because all things brought from outside the area had to be transported sixty miles or more from one of three points, pioneers brought in few items not needed in everyday living. The largely self-sufficient life required regular work, year round, with intervals now and then for recreation and get-togethers with neighbours. Emergencies did arise and these the iron-willed settlers dealt with as best they could.

Furnishings of all kinds were few, simple, and improvised. Many of the people sat on homemade benches or chairs. James Ryan made a rocking chair which, according to his daughter, had "four kinds of wood in it — cottonwood, birch and alder in the chair, and maple in the rockers. Mother wanted him to bring it out to Vancouver, but he wouldn't. She was so proud of it and had made the old-fashioned padded cushion and back, and oh, it was a treasure!" Ryan made a couch which his wife topped with a pretty quilt and which made a soft resting place for some calves that wandered into the house after the family had fled to the attic during the 1906 flood.

Maria Fraser used lids from baking powder cans as muffin tins, and used ground pumice as well as grass for scouring pots. Years would pass before she could discard the heavy ironware dishes which were in the Punch home when she first married, and replace them with the fine china she used more recently.

Months before the annual shopping trip to Vancouver, which for the Punch family meant buying at Woodward's Store, they prepared long lists of essentials: coal oil, flour, kegs of molasses, cases of soap, dried fruit, salt, tea, and coffee — not forgetting sugar. During the first winter of their marriage Maria Punch and her young husband used their sugar too extravagantly, making candy, and lots of it, until they realized that the sugar supply would not last. Then they sweetened old James Punch's desserts and ate sugarless puddings themselves. One husband blamed his unlucky wife for omitting coal oil from the yearly list and for their having to borrow to keep the lamps burning.

In the interests of survival, most pioneers would agree with "Waste not, want not", but some economies may have been unduly rigid. Having butch-

Mountain trip Provincial Archives, Victoria, B.C.

ered a beef, James Punch would decree that no cuts might be eaten until liver, heart, and tripe were gone. At one time just before an election the family had finished all the preliminaries except the tripe, and the polling to be held in her house, Maria decided to serve tripe to all voters who called. When the poll closed, old James found his daughter-in-law happily frying steaks.

Fuel for the stove

Many of the foods eaten daily were from the farm or the hills or the streams. Women made butter from cream often skimmed by hand from pans of milk that had been sitting long enough for the fat to rise, and sometimes had enough surplus butter to sell to the store or to road camps. They used "water glass" to preserve eggs for the cold season when hens were unlikely to lay. They pickled supplies of beef and pork, or preserved them in glass jars. Most families ate venison: to be good providers most husbands were generally good hunters.

In pre-freezer days, women bottled and processed in a hot-water bath most of their fruits, vegetables, and meats. Imagine on a hot summer day a woman stoking her wood fire for up to three or four hours to make sure that the water in the canner never stopped boiling, and canning during the day because canning in the cooler evening raised the house temperature too high for comfortable sleep. Taking advantage of the hot stove, the woman might do some baking, or ironing, having heated the flat-irons on the stove top. A canning day was not entirely pleasant, but the result was a supply of food costing very little and providing almost instant meals for unexpected guests.

Andy Anderson had his own method of preserving wild raspberries. Having filled his jars in the bush, he took them home, covered the fruit with boiling syrup, capped the jars, and rolled them in his sleeping bag until they were cool and the tops had set. Unfortunately, this relatively cool process could not be used generally.

Throughout much of the season for gathering and preserving fruits and vegetables, mosquitoes filled the air, inside the house and out. Their incessant humming sounded like a threshing machine and everyone went around for weeks wearing a veil, even at times drinking water through the veil. A smudge was some help: smouldering shavings in a pan, with grass and leaves thrown on top. A repellent later in common use, pyrethrum powder, was unavailable in the early years.

After the main rush of summer work and after the snow had melted sufficiently at higher elevations, people could escape mosquitoes by spending holidays in the surrounding mountain country. Jack Ronayne described how these annual mountain trips began: "It was not until 1912 that I found behind the valley horizon, at an altitude between 4500 and 7000 feet, a charming land of little upland valleys gaily decorated with alpine flowers of every hue, parklike open spaces ornamented with clumps of balsam and pine, tumbling streams and pretty lakes crystal clear to the deepest blue in colour and, for contrast, grim solitudes of snow and rock; altogether an ideal pleasure resort, especially for the leisure hours of the workers in the deep adjacent valley. In 1913 Jim Landsborough accompanied me to the same scenes for a week's holiday and after that, every year between haying and harvest an enthusiastic party of all ages took to the hills for their vacation."

Even before those unforgettable days in the mountains, families found interesting ways to fill their leisure time. In summer, mosquitoes permitting, people enjoyed picnics. For a picnic women "dressed up" in their wide-brimmed hats, and in their freshly washed, starched and ironed blouses billowing over the waist bands of long skirts. Men and children too wore freshly laundered clothes. Then, after the team had been hitched to the wagon, all climbed in as best they could and proceeded to some grassy spot to share the goodies the women had prepared.

A picnic party Provincial Archives, Victoria, B.C.

Clara Ryan spent hours in Neill's meadow "watching the beavers build their dam to keep their little lake as they wanted." One winter James Ryan built his daughter a sleigh "like they used in the Yukon", and made a harness for her dog. She was then able to drive her mother miles down the Valley, over the frozen snow, to visit Mrs. Neill. Rene Ronayne paddled a canoe over the fields in water left by melting snow. And there were books to read.

At intervals, children with their parents visited neighbours' homes, riding in the wagon or on the sleigh. Upper Valley families like the Dermodys, Punches, Ronaynes, and Ryans could return the same day after visiting, but a trip to the races down the Valley on July 1 included an overnight stay with friends. Visiting the Spetch home required a day both going there and coming home. Travelling to the Halfway House on the Portage, operated after 1900 by Ronald Currie and his sister Annie McIntosh, meant two days both going and returning, the first night visiting the Bauers or the Neills, and the second at the stopping house. It was a small house, but to accommodate visitors Mrs. McIntosh would arrange mattresses on the floors and provide blankets for all.

Sometimes the routine of work and occasional visiting was interrupted by emergencies. At least one story tells of a man racked with pain, appendix close to bursting, riding over the trail to Squamish, and travelling from there to Vancouver before he could get help. One known instance of nearly succumbing because of Pemberton's isolation is the experience of James Duff who froze both feet. Few details survive of how he reached Lillooet, except that the

Ronayne brothers put him on a horse and took him to Anderson Lake where they broke the ice to allow a boat to get away and head up towards the Short Portage between Anderson and Seton Lakes. A *Bridge River-Lillooet News* account printed thirty years after the event tells that Duff "dragged himself from Pemberton." Dr. Greene "decided to cut off the frozen feet in order to save the man's life", and called in Joe Russell, a Lillooet prospector, to help give Duff an anaesthetic. "Then while Joe helped, the doctor amputated the man's feet. For weeks Duff lingered between life and death, then decided to get well. He recovered, bought himself two artificial feet and went back to Pemberton." After that Duff continued to work at the fish hatchery, a "man of iron will". One time The Freight Shed Gang — youngsters who did a lot of good deeds in the community — could not understand Duff's rage when they bought him a can of sewing machine oil to lubricate his squeaking ankles.

The James Ryan family and the Neills' daughter

Ronald Currie and Annie McIntosh Provincial Archives, Victoria, B.C.

Provincial Archives, Victoria, B.C.

Jack Ronayne in 1932

SERVING THE PUBLIC

Some pioneers set up and operated such minimum services as stores, post offices, and stopping houses. Otis Parsons, at Port Pemberton, may have been the first storekeeper in the area, though through the years, other stores were established farther north. Paul Dick, a former Mount Currie chief, remembered the first store on the John Currie ranch: "a little log house; you could touch the roof." Probably located in this same building was Butler's store. Like most pioneer general stores, it also served as a post office. When Duncan Morrison arrived, Lang, or Long, had a small store and more than once on early records his name appears as a trader.

Early in this century "after Butler had given up or died", John McKenzie set up business in a cabin on the Barbour place. Bebee Ruddock can still smell that old store: coffee, coal oil, and snoose combined in the rich blend that met the customer's nose. And rock samples scattered over the counter caught everybody's eye. According to Clara Jones, "Maybe you'd go to the store and find 'Gone Prospecting' posted on the door." On the walls of what much later would be the Lundgren bull-pen, McKenzie kept records of his sales. One entry listed snoose and fifty pounds of beans.

Although early storekeepers did stock locally produced butter and vegetables, most supplies had to be packed over trails or hauled, where the width of the track allowed. Mack Seymour brought in McKenzie's groceries and other supplies. Reaching Lillooet Lake with his team, Seymour put the wagon on a raft, and often against the prevailing wind men rowed the raft down the lake while somebody drove the team along the lakeside trail. When team and wagon were once more hitched together, Seymour drove over thirty miles to Port Douglas for provisions freighted up through Harrison Lake. Returning up Lillooet Lake was faster than the trip south because Seymour could hoist a sail to use the wind blowing up the lake. During McKenzie's time and later, Samuel Spetch operated at Owl Creek what Geoffrey M. Downton considered a "well-equipped store". To maintain his stock throughout the year, during good weather Spetch freighted several large orders in from Lillooet. Some customers rode long distances to trade at his store, as Jack

Ronayne's May 1910 diary entry proves: "Joe home with provisions from Spetch and McKenzie."

After McKenzie sold his business, J. F. Brokaw ran it for the Pemberton Trading Company. At the same time he operated the newly established post office serving the Lower Valley. Located probably in a corner of his store, it was not far from Currie's ranch, the site of the first Pemberton Meadows Post Office which closed in 1901. About 1915, after Frank and Fay Brokaw moved away, William Kiltz took charge of both businesses. Before then the businesses had been moved down the road close to the site of the railway station planned by the Howe Sound, Pemberton Valley & Northern Railway Company.

During trail days, mail carriers as well as pack trains connected Pemberton with the world outside. Over two years elapsed between the time of Currie's retirement as Pemberton Meadows postmaster and Hartzell's appointment to the same position when, by the new appointment, the post office was moved about eight miles up the trail, beyond the Rockslide. In the period without a post office, the carriers seem to have continued their service, leaving with each settler his individual mail sack. Weather sometimes delayed the mail carriers. In January 1911 one diary entry reads: "No mail delivery owing to bad weather. Terrible wind storm from Anderson Lake to Rancherie. Snow piled up in drifts."

Willie Currie said that Andrew Joseph was the first mail carrier, bringing the mail from Lillooet. After Joseph, several Indians served for extended periods, a few white men for shorter times. Hugo Westerberg carried the mail from Squamish, but found that route unsatisfactory. Ernest Blakeway spent his first winter in Canada as mail courier between Pemberton and Lillooet, making a round trip every two weeks. Willie Currie saw him pass the Halfway House on his route, Gladys Blakeway and Nellie Spetch travelling with him. Names of carriers related to Mount Currie families, Charlie Wallace, Felix Sam, and Bill Pascal, often crop up in pioneers' stories.

Clara Jones tells of "dear old Felix Sam" who carried the mail by horse, canoe, and snowshoes. "Dear old Felix would come into our home and Mother would make him a hearty lunch. He'd tell of his daughter, attending a Catholic school, and he'd have us read her letters to him."

One mail carrier's routine was interrupted as he was returning from Lillooet. Bill Spetch gives details: "In 1912 there was an attempted hold-up just half a mile south of where Ernie Ward lives now. Bill Pascal was the mail carrier, and he showed me the very spot. He had picked up a man passing through and was giving him a ride. Driving towards Pemberton they met a man who had a rifle, and who said 'This is a hold-up!' The rifle was pointed at Bill. While Bill was hurriedly picking up the letter bags, his passenger pulled up his own rifle, saying 'Now *you* hold *your* hands up.' The would-be bandit dropped his rifle. Bill's passenger kept his rifle aimed at the would-be bandit as they drove on their way. I asked Bill if the police ever got the bandit and Bill said, 'No, we never reported it; we would have lost our rifle'."

Pascal lost a mail sack just once, and Tommy Hurley of Lillooet found it. Another carrier left the sacks all night in Anderson Lake and the mail was like mush when it reached the postmasters. That is a rare example of mishandling of the mail. Twenty years ago, one long-time resident said that "in those days" the pre-railway mail carriers "took better care of the mail . . . than others do now."

Riding on a Pacific Great Eastern train to Lillooet some years ago, through a translator Charlie Wallace told of his seven years' experience carrying mail between Lillooet and Hartzell's farm. He made the round trip twice a month and received $40 each time. He had a canoe on each of Anderson and Seton Lakes. Sometimes, in most favourable conditions, he made the close to 60-mile trip from Lillooet to Mount Currie in one day. In winter, with a dog team and a toboggan and fighting snow as deep as five feet, he might take four days to travel about 15 miles from Mount Currie to Hartzell's. In good weather he travelled alone, but if he expected difficulties he hired helpers and paid them himself.

On one such trip he had three men with him: his nephew, Henry Wallace; Joe Ross; and John McKenzie, the storekeeper, who had pelts to sell in Lillooet. None had blankets or food. Reaching Seton Lake and finding a violent storm whipping up the waters, they decided to spend the night on a bluff. In the morning the waves had calmed, but ice had formed around the canoes. After making a fire to thaw the ice from their paddles and after breaking away from the shore, the men paddled nearly the length of the lake before they stopped at an old Indian cabin and rummaged around for food. They could find only a few dried saskatoon berries, but were so hungry that they lit a fire, heated the berries and ate them before continuing on to Lillooet. On the return trip, finding Seton Lake frozen over Wallace had to make a sled to which he attached a long rope; at Shalalth the ice was breaking and he hired horses to carry the mail to Anderson Lake, and the men then paddled with no trouble to what is now D'Arcy.

Along the routes postmasters would be expecting the carriers. Neighbours would gather and wait for them at the establishments of Samuel Spetch, J. F. Brokaw, C. A. Hartzell, and James Punch, who in 1913 succeeded Hartzell as postmaster. By such men and such methods, carrying, sending, and receiving of mail would continue until October 1914 when the Pacific Great Eastern Railway inaugurated a weekly mail service.

An area which early attracted landseekers, prospectors, timber cruisers, and various officials needed accommodation for the men — and the few women — who after two or three days of hard travelling reached the Valley or the Portage. When Pemberton House on Lillooet Lake had been abandoned for about twenty years, and a few years after the first Halfway House on the Portage had burned down, John Currie established himself and made travellers welcome at his home. Currie's was one of several that through the years supplied strangers and friends with meals and a bed. Throughout his

The third Pemberton Meadows postmaster, his daughter-in-law and her children, and an early Pemberton Meadows teacher

Journal, Jack Ronayne mentioned mealtime and overnight guests. Maria Fraser tells of Chief Stager and Ignace Dick, "probably on their way to ask the justice of the peace, Jack Ronayne, for his signature on some official paper", spending the night at the Punch home and singing Indian songs during the evening.

Taking over the Currie farm about 1903, the Leonard Neills continued the tradition of hospitality. Clara Jones speaks of her uncle as very friendly, and of her aunt as a good cook. She describes one meal which provided "plenty to feed all, with huge dishes of rolled oats, fried potatoes and meat, sauce, homemade bread, eggs, doughnuts and *cookies always.* This was breakfast."

George Miller and Joe Taillefer told of their experiences at Bob McLauchlan's first Pemberton Hotel — Barbour's house. Because neither Miller's heavy boots nor Taillefer's brown cloth-topped patent leather shoes had prevented their feet from blistering on their two-day hike from Squamish, they sat bare footed. Then the mosquitoes attacked. The thought of reaching down to scratch their feet was somehow embarrassing and they sat rubbing one foot against another until Tom Greer and Jack Grady could no longer repress their snickers. After that the cheechakos tucked their pants into their socks.

Another time McLauchlan's guests, including the packer Red Mahan, had finished their meal of bully beef and potatoes in their jackets. Red was used to potatoes like that in the American Mid-West because on cold mornings he had trotted off to school with a hot potato in each hand, the potatoes to serve two purposes: as hand warmers in the morning and as lunch at noon. After that meal at McLauchlan's Lame Johnny entertained the company: wearing a white Hudson's Bay blanket, and brandishing a double-bitted axe, he did a war dance around the heater to the music of a mouth organ played by Stafford, a packer with Red.

An interesting feature of the first Pemberton Hotel was its shake roof. Guests lying upstairs in their bunks could gaze through the chinks in the roof that gave free access to air and mosquitoes, but never to rain. A later occupant remembers shaking out bed sheets and hearing the clatter of dead and dried mosquitoes as they hit the floor boards.

Expecting the railway station to be built near the site of the present secondary school, Bob McLauchlan set up a tent stopping place on the corner now occupied by the C & S garage. About 1914, when the first Pacific Great Eastern station had been located near the existing station site he built the shell of the original section of the present Pemberton Hotel.

Nobody knows much about two buildings started far up the Lillooet among the pines, both intended to serve as stopping houses; one was to operate as both gambling and stopping house. As one story goes, the first was partly constructed not long after the Gold Rush period. In preparation, some Chinese hewed immense logs which Andy Anderson used much later to build his own trapping cabin. By various means, the Orientals had placed several rounds of logs. The second upriver wayside house was built by two partners, McDonald and Schell, close to where North and South Creeks enter the Lillooet. In 1916, with Oscar Johnson, Andy Anderson found the abandoned structure. He learned later that the builders expected a road to cross the river near their property.

Their expectations exceeded those of Dunc Morrison who had settled earlier near Railroad Pass and expected a railway to penetrate the Valley as far north as his farm. Proposed Canadian Pacific routes appear not to have included that pass, though Howe Sound & Northern Railway plans for 1910 did include "completing the survey of a branch from Pemberton Meadows to Bridge River Mining District." Part of a July 1910 record by Jack Ronayne refers to that survey: "Railroad surveyors passed up and hired a canoe". In an age of dream railroads Railroad Pass could have received its name very early, and ideas associated with that name could have encouraged upriver settlement.

About 1900, before the Neills settled, Ronald Currie and his sister Annie McIntosh bought the Halfway House property. Then, for a few years, branches of the Currie family lived both in the Valley and on the Portage. Those on the Portage served the public travelling to and from Anderson Lake, besides timber cruisers and prospectors. Annie McIntosh went twice a year to Lillooet to buy staple provisions, but much of the food she served originated on the farm: fruit, vegetables, and meat. Forty years after the Curries had left the old stopping house, Muriel (Spetch) Grubb told of their kindness, and of her sadness when she passed the house where once they had entertained.

The second Halfway House was only one of the stopping houses on the Portage. Surveying for the British Columbia Government in 1913 G. M. Downton remarked on Mr. Spetch's "excellent accommodation". During one noon hour in railway construction days, with the help of two daughters, Elizabeth Spetch served forty-two meals. Another stopping house, now enlarged and modernized and the home of the Gunnar Gimse family, the Thompson house put up travellers and also put up Marjorie Gimse's father, who was G. M. Downton. Earlier, Mrs. Thompson had operated a guest house at D'Arcy where Gladys Blakeway worked one summer during railway construction.

Lame Johnny's establishment exists now as the log section of a house close to the Portage road, and not far from the row of Twin Peaks resort cabins. One day more than sixty years ago, Lame Johnny had been peddling meat in Pemberton. As he was leaving to drive home he offered a lift to George Miller and Joe Taillefer who were on their way home to Vancouver by way of Lillooet. Lame Johnny's blind wife served the same food for supper that she would cook and place on the table in the morning: bannock, bacon, and baked potatoes. She managed her house as though she were sighted, even operating a sewing machine. When her guests went out to their tent bedroom that night, they found the most comfortable beds they had slept in since leaving Vancouver, beds made up with spotless white sheets. Taillefer said that he and Miller nearly bought that wayside house: "It was boom time. The railway was coming, and towns would spring up every few miles."

Provincial Archives, Victoria, B.C.

Judd's stage met the steamer at Squamish and drove passengers as far as Brackendale

SURVIVAL

Farming by itself could not support the needs of most settlers of Pemberton Trail days because the settlers could market little except "what could walk to Squamish", mainly beef animals. Once the pioneers had made a clearing they were self-sufficient in some foods. Hunting might provide meat and sometimes they bartered and exchanged farm products for fish or venison, or for Indian labour. But because they needed dollars to buy many necessities, life was an unending struggle to develop the farm and, at the same time, to convert goods or services into cash.

A very few managed to stay with their land and year by year put all their efforts into developing productive farms. Most had to seize every rare job opportunity: some worked on bridges and trails, later on roads, and some eked out a living by prospecting. No settler was trapping when Landsborough reached the Valley, but as a child Clara Jones saw Tom Greer come down from his trap line after a winter in which his curly black hair had grown long. After 1905 some men found casual employment at the Dominion Government Fish Hatchery, a few worked at the Dermody, later Perkins, sawmill, a number went to the coast to find work. But in order to "prove up" on crown land the pre-emptors among the settlers had to clear and improve their acreage. One pioneer described the mutual helpfulness of these men. Knowing that he would be away during harvest, one would ask another to cut his oats and pit his spuds if he was not back in time. The answer was always "Of course I will."

In 1895 prospectors were at work on Poole Creek. One seam there, between slate and granite formations, was reported to be very rich in gold, silver, and copper. Two years later, after a summer of exploring for minerals down Lillooet Lake A. P. Barnfield went north to the Blackwater, or Birkenhead, Basin, where miners were excited by copper deposits. Near the Birkenhead River, in the area worked over in the 1970's by Malibu Mines, Will Miller had sunk a shaft. Later, Will Haylmore staked claims at the north end of Birkenhead Lake and carved his name in the logs of a cabin which has recently collapsed beside Phelix Creek.

Prospectors were roaming the mountains on both sides of the Lillooet River. A 1909 *Daily Province* article reported gold, silver, and lead mining activity at Tenquille Lake. In August 1910 Jack Ronayne noted that "Keddy and McLeod made out mining papers." On holiday from keeping store, John McKenzie contentedly searched ridges and valleys for likely samples, and hopeful men, including the once well-known marathon runner Cameron Smith, investigated Owl Creek and staked claims. Just before the First World War, a mining group did considerable work there.

More reliable employment was offered by the fish hatchery at the junction of Owl Creek with the Birkenhead River, one of a number of fish hatcheries built about the same time in this province. A Department of Fisheries official in Ottawa gives reasons for their establishment: "With the rapid development of the salmon fisheries in British Columbia, urgent representations were pressed for the construction of hatcheries by such bodies as the British Columbia Fisheries Commission, Boards of Trade in various Pacific cities, Fish Canners' Associations and Fishermen's Societies. Competent authorities considered that the Pemberton Hatchery would be an excellent one, since the Birkenhead River was one of the most important spawning streams in the Province."

At Squamish in November 1904 Fred Magee loaded his pack horses with hatchery equipment which had been unloaded from the *S.S. Burt.* The trip over the trail to Owl Creek took three days. All the way snow was falling, threatening to cut off return to tidewater until spring.

In the first annual report of hatchery operations, Alexander Robertson, officer in charge, explains the procedures by which lumber for his establishment had been provided: "The contract for the lumber was let to Duguid & Hurlay [sic], of Lillooet, who deserve credit for the manner in which they surmounted the difficulties incidental to bringing a 23,000 lb. sawmill outfit, the 36 miles by raft on Seton and Anderson's Lakes, and 24 miles of mountain road to Owl Creek. They were three weeks on the road coming in and the same going out; the boiler alone weighed 6,000 lb., and they were engaged four months in sawing the 170,000 feet and planing 130,000 feet of lumber of which the buildings were constructed. Mr. Forrester, the building superintendent, started actual construction in May 1905, though previous to that he had a gang of Indians clearing the site, making roads and hewing sills." Skookum Pascal built the first road to connect the Reserves with the hatchery.

In August 1905 carpenters completed the hatchery, a building 150 feet by 40 feet, with a capacity of 25,000,000 eggs. Construction "by day labour" had cost $19,510. Nearby the workmen erected a boarding house, "a two-storey frame building, 16 feet by 24, with an addition containing kitchen, pantry and bathroom. The main building contains dining room, 12 by 16, office 10 by 12 and hall; upstairs there are four bedrooms."

While carpenters constructed buildings, other men worked in the cold waters of the Birkenhead River "building . . . traps for the taking of the parent

The Fish Hatchery

fish." These traps "were located 200 yards above the hatchery . . . at a point where there was a large rock on both sides to protect the banks. The main fence was built on the tripod system. Ten tripods made of 7-inch fir poles were placed at intervals across the stream and filled with rock. The height of the water — four feet — made the job an arduous one. The large boulders in the bed of the stream, which could not be seen, though their effect on the water was plainly visible, contributed to the difficulty. After two weeks' exertion, during which time dry clothes were an almost unknown quality, the tripods were placed in position and the stringers fastened down. The fencing proper consisted of sections 6 feet by 12 feet, made of 1-inch by 4-inch on edge, and bolted together, and had been under construction while the tripods were being placed. They were laid on stringers with a 2 to 1 slant lying down stream, and had a yard of heavy canvas nailed along the heel of them to prevent salmon burrowing; rock was then placed in front, the pens anchored and leads built from the fence to them. There were fifteen pens in use altogether of different sizes, 12 feet by 12 feet, 10 feet by 12, and 6 feet by 12. Two more fences were built after this before the run came, one 100 yards below the first one to keep the salmon from drifting down. . . .Another fence was constructed, one and a half miles above the hatchery, as a safeguard against mishap to the lower ones."

In 1905 eggs taken from trapped sockeye numbered 26,500,000; from "sockeye caught at the mouth of the river by means of a seine", 1,500,000. From these eggs 17,500,000 "healthy fry" developed. In 1910 T. W. Graham, who had succeeded Robertson as officer in charge, refers to liberating fry "during April and May in the usual way, viz., being allowed to depart when they felt inclined."

Transporting salmon eggs was a delicate operation. Bill Spetch tells of hatchery workers first placing the eggs in metal baskets, then putting the baskets into wooden boxes. The men next dipped heavy burlap in water, and placed the dripping fabric over the boxes. Pack horses then carried the boxes to the hatchery. In later years, to transport the valuable cargo Jonathan Lindsay drove a rubber-tired democrat, never a jolting wagon.

The hatchery fence and pens

Wages were considerably lower than present-day wages. "Officers in Charge" received "$1050 to $1500 per year. . . . When the hatchery was in operation", four or five assistants received "$50 to $90 per month". Assistants in the early years included John Martin, David Bothwell, Harry Gibbs, George Stack, C. D. Wray, James Tyner, Logan W. Davis, W. C. Adams; Martin Espeland was cook. "The Officer in Charge and his regular staff were also paid a board allowance of $22 to $32 per month." During the collection of salmon eggs the management hired "about 18 extra men as short term helpers at $3 per day." Among the Valley and Portage residents who worked at the hatchery were Walter Landsborough, Bob Miller, Frank Buckley, Joe Lester, Harvey Nelson, and James Duff who, after surviving amputation of his feet, sat down to his work. According to Ben Cherry, his own ability to play cribbage secured him his job. With a team of horses, Baldy and Blue, Bill Hamill hauled essential supplies, including firewood which was used in great quantities. When Hamill gave up that job Walter Spetch took it over.

Besides giving employment, the hatchery had other effects. A new community which grew up included both single men and families. Employees like Lindsay, Lewis, and Clarence Sayres could build homes at their own expense, making use of the hatchery's water-powered sawmill. Bill Spetch tells of thousands of feet of lumber being hand planed after going through that mill. Douglas Adie built his third home in the area on land that had been homesteaded by Martin Espeland, but out of lumber from the Hindu mill on the road to Anderson Lake. George Stack brought his lumber from the P.G.E. mill at Mons. The new community also created a market for farm products. When farmers took pack horses or drove teams pulling wagons to deliver their meat and vegetables, they spent a night at Owl Creek. Tom Graham made the employees' dining room available to visiting preachers for their services.

Then there were family connections, both between Valley and Portage settlers and hatchery personnel, and within the hatchery community itself. William Hamill married Tom Graham's sister; John Martin married Nellie Spetch; the first officer in charge, Alex Robertson, married a sister of John Martin; and Graham, who succeeded Robertson, married another Martin girl. For dances and other activities the Owl Creek community later built its own hall beside the creek. After the closing of the hatchery and consequent loss of population, the usefulness of the hall declined rapidly, but in the early 'fifties it was still standing and was suggested as a temporary Creekside school.

Finally, in 1936, after thirty-one years, along with other Dominion Government Sockeye hatcheries in British Columbia the Owl Creek establishment closed: "Results from artificial hatching and rearing of this species were not commensurate with the cost involved." At Owl Creek annual maintenance amounted to about $9,000. Ben Cherry still regrets the decision to close, saying that the operation was "very, very successful; at the time the hatchery was destroyed, more salmon were returning to the Birkenhead than had returned at any previous time."

Little remains of the once well-established community, a few vestiges of cement foundations, orchard trees gone wild in the grassy field, and some cork trees, but forty years later visitors still wander down to the scenic hatchery site. Long ago, local people dismantled the buildings and used the lumber to build new homes. Cleveland bought the Pelton wheel that once operated the sawmill and moved it to Bridge Lake. John Decker used the baskets that once held fish eggs in a short-lived new industry. During the Second World War, when European imports were unavailable, the baskets held flower and vegetable seeds produced by that innovative man and his wife.

While men were increasing their incomes in whatever ways possible, farm acreage gradually expanded. In 1902 Tom Greer had found few farmers in the area, but five years later more settlers had arrived. Most were farming only to the extent of keeping a few cattle on their pre-emptions, but a few were able to farm seriously.

Early in this century, the Leonard Neills and their daughter settled on the former Currie farm. They raised beef and as a side line pastured ailing horses sent up by Vancouver business men. Several workers helped during haying, building the hay into huge stacks on the lower part of the farm. In their garden, as others have done the Neills sometimes raised watermelons. John Currie had been proud of the tobacco he grew on that land.

Being long established and long worked, Neills' was then probably the best of the few farms. Most newcomers had to clear their land while they coped with various difficulties and hardships: "The clearing of the land by saw and mattock was slow and laborious for lack of dynamite. Fire was the main agent, but it took many years.

The Neill ranch — Provincial Archives, Victoria, B.C.

"Among the handicaps of early days were mosquitoes in indescribable numbers and ferocity, very deep snow in winter, making trails impassable except for snowshoes, and frequent summer frosts, making it impossible to grow corn. Above all, there was the fact that the young of farm animals did not long survive birth."

Jack Ronayne's diary outlines the varied program of early settlers. He and his brothers Joseph and Edmond were tired of mining and wanted to farm, having come from an Irish agricultural community. As a partnership they farmed the land which they later divided, and which is worked now by their respective sons. Already married and with a family, the diarist stayed on the land, while his brothers sometimes took jobs in other areas.

In mid-April of 1909, with the sweet green smell of the cottonwood already in the air, two feet of snow lingered at Ronaynes', although none remained on Millers' fields seven or eight miles down the Valley. Because the grass was still buried, the Ronayne cattle and cayuses were driven across the river to feed on rushes, and Ed and Joe hauled hay from McLeod's. An ice bridge over Ryan Creek still allowed hauling of boards. Just over two weeks later, Jack Ronayne was planting experimental peas and wheat, while his brothers were plowing, each with a team. Then came seeding and re-seeding, because nibbling mice and heaving frost had destroyed clover previously planted. Oats and peas were broadcast, one fistful to each twelve feet as the sower strode through the fields. Wheat could be sown with a machine that threw the seed thirty feet.

Various other matters took time and attention. One or more of the brothers planted the vegetable garden, set broody hens to hatch chicks, searched for lost animals, or attended to mares brought to be served by the stallion. At least eighteen owners living in the Valley and on the Portage brought their mares to Ronaynes'.

In the long daylight hours of summer, chance travellers saw these farmers hard at work hoeing and thinning their row crops, scything ferns in the oats, and haying. But in every spare moment, and as required, they were clearing land, building a barn, draining wet spots in the hayfields, or building dykes, often in the great heat, and often with humming, biting mosquitoes attacking in clouds. The diary for August 1913 has ten references to mosquitoes and tells of "suffering terribly". What a pleasant respite for Jack when he spent two days climbing in the mountains with his good friends the Landsboroughs!

Keenly observant of everything in nature, Jack Ronayne kept weather records for the government, while at the same time, again and again, he wrote detailed descriptions of weather indicators, the sky and the clouds. He wrote too of "great numbers and varieties of bird songs" that "combined with the beauty of evening and morning landscapes" and made him thankful for "so many free gifts of nature to be enjoyed."

Through September, land clearing, plowing, harrowing, and more seeding continued. In early October, after a chase of several days the wild-as-deer cattle were temporarily corralled, before some were driven to Millers' farm. From time to time they butchered a cow and sold the meat, Ed Ronayne driving off with it, maybe to Bauers' stopping house or to the hatchery.

The Ronaynes carried on with their harvesting into November when they used hoes to extract the last turnips. Gradually, by December, weather had slowed the fast pace of earlier months; by the fifteenth, trails had to be broken through the accumulated snow. Then came time to add finishing touches to the barn. The last days of the year brought soft, fine weather, so fine that the cattle jumped around in high spirits.

Although the fact was not understood for many years, animals brought into the Valley had reserves of iodine that for some time kept them in good condition. Jack Ronayne noticed that animals close to salmon streams ate spawned salmon and remained healthy and able to produce healthy young, but before long, up the Valley, deaths of goitrous calves and foals and of hairless piglets made the future of farming in Pemberton highly uncertain. Losses were very great — about 50% of calves, 80% of foals, and 95% of young pigs —

and for several years the Ronaynes were undecided whether or not to remain in the Valley. In 1917 as a result of careful records kept by Jack Ronayne the way was discovered to ensure the birth of healthy animals. Ronayne had discovered that "Goitre is bad wherever pumice stone abounds" and that "Internal doses of iodine is an adequate preventative."

In January 1967, fifteen years after Jack Ronayne died, Tom Leach emphasized in *Country Life* the importance of the work of the Pemberton farmer: "Few will conceive it possible that a farmer situated in the isolated valley of Pemberton had anything to do with the discovery that goitre was caused by the lack of iodine in the system. But it was through the persistency of that Irish settler, John [Jack] Ronayne, that you have iodized salt on your table.

"It was his day-by-day recording of events in the Pemberton Valley that led to correspondence with medical authorities and which helped them to reach the conclusion that it was a lack of iodine, and not some diabolical disease, that caused the hairlessness in pigs or caused the swelling that choked humans and young foals alike.

"The answers he received to some of his evidence were sufficiently discouraging that the average person would have dropped the matter for fear of being found a fool. But this man was above self concern. He wished to prove what he found as a fact in his neighbourhood.

"It took a long time and several years of noting various events in his diary. But staunchly and steadily he persisted until research took up his task and proved his theory right."

Although pioneers had to face many difficulties, "there were", as one pioneer said, "some assets": "There were few noxious weeds, no onion or turnip maggots, no house mice, and scarcely any epidemics of colds". As a surveyor for the provincial government, G. M. Downton knew the Pemberton area and in 1913 his conclusion regarding its future was that with a railway to the coast and flood protection the agricultural possibilities of the Lillooet River Valley "could hardly be overestimated". He stressed the assets of rapid spring growth from unfrozen ground, and an average land-clearing cost that was comparatively low at $50 an acre. With railway construction proceeding and flood protection under discussion Downton's prediction of profits from garden produce and small fruits seemed realizable. Jack Ronayne too forecast success with fruits, and even then felt that potatoes would be "writ large in the future history of the valley."

During Trail days, newspaper reports of the area seem to have dealt mainly with its assets. In 1910 a reporter interviewed an enthusiastic Robert Hutchison who was a pre-emptor in the Upper Valley, and quoted Hutch as saying that Pemberton was the garden spot of British Columbia: "Every variety of vegetable, apples and all kinds of small fruits attain perfection." Hutchison said that in the five years he had lived in the Valley "thousands of acres had been pre-empted by new settlers" and that Patrick Dermody owned "one of the best ranches and had it stocked with cattle and horses." The report concluded that the only use for crop surpluses was to feed cattle, horses, and sheep.

Prior to railway completion, crops were grown for mainly local use. McKenzie and later Brokaw bought produce to sell in the store; Punch relied on farmers' vegetables, butter, and meat for his road camps; Tom Greer bought hay for horses, and other items for the men of survey parties. Jim Dermody describes how his grandfather, James Punch, once an MLA, made his first money in Pemberton. After harvesting wheat, he would wait for a breeze and then open up the doors on both sides of his barn and flail away at his sheaves. He sold the grain to Indians owning chickens.

During the last months of travel by the Squamish-Pemberton Trail, a reporter from the *British Columbian* made his way through the Valley and commented on what he found. The large area, the Valley above Lillooet Lake, "includes about 1,000 acres owned by Indians who raise fine crops of every description . . . . Owing to lack of transportation facilities, the white settlers, men, women and children, do not exceed thirty. Their land under cultivation totals about 3,000 acres. The lower end of the Valley is subject to occasional inundation by the overflow of the Lillooet River. This, however, will be remedied shortly . . . . The average price of land is $100 an acre, although sales at the rate of $320 an acre were closed during the past summer . . . . The experience of Mr. J. Ronayne, a pioneer, has been paralleled by a number of other settlers . . . . Mr. Ronayne owns about 500 acres, one half of which is under cultivation. He has grown Red Fife wheat giving the phenomenal yield of 100 bushels to the acre. He owns a splendid herd of 500 cattle as well as numerous horses . . . . Wild pea vine, vetch and red top grass on some of this land yields from five and six tons per acre; wheat, No. 1 hard, yields from 40 to 50 bushels per acre . . . . Potatoes give a return of from 20 to 30 tons to the acre . . . . Plums do well even without care. Tons of them were seen bending the trees at the Indian rancherie. The same applies to currants . . . . In Pemberton Meadows the conditions of soil and climate, from a horticultural standpoint, are perhaps more perfect than in any other part of the province."

Until about 1913 cattle and horse raising were more general than the growing of crops, but in that year the British Columbia Hydrographic report noted that both hay and potatoes were being grown "in considerable quantities for railway camps". Jack Ronayne's diary between October 1913 and March 1914 has entry after entry like the following: "McDonald & Mitchell, railway contractors, bought potatoes and hay", and "McDonald's team took away 2298 lb. potatoes, 230 cabbages and 382 turnips". McDonald & Mitchell bought a lot of Ronaynes' Green Mountain potatoes: November 8 — 4,333 pounds; November 10 — 2,859 pounds; November 16 — 2,298 pounds.

Sometimes selling at $35 a ton, baled hay was also in great demand. Probably the expanded market was the Ronaynes' reason for buying a hay baler which Ed Ronayne pulled home with a six-horse team in December 1913. The following spring he and a hired man spent between May 21 and 26 going to Anderson Lake and returning with another baler. Many teams plodded up to the farms and back with hay for the horses at the camps. At long last Valley farmers had not only a temporary market, but also the prospect of a continuing market when the railway gangs had finished their job.

Raking hay

Prospector's camp

THE COMING OF THE RAILWAY

As early as 1891 men incorporated a company to build a railway from the coast to Pemberton and beyond, but not until 1914 did a train run into the Valley. This delay prolonged the hardships of isolation. By pack train from Squamish, charges on freight ran as high as three cents a pound. Isolation increased in winter when depth of snow closed the trails except to travel on snowshoes. In such circumstances the able-bodied could still reach the coast; the ailing were completely cut off from help they might need.

Finally the plans of two promoters resulted in the laying of the first tracks north from Squamish. As early as 1905 James Cavers Gill, then Reeve of North Vancouver, and Arthur McEvoy, a lawyer, had dreamed of a railway to tap the country north of Howe Sound, primarily "the fertile Pemberton Meadows country". Later, with Pemberton land-owner J. W. McFarland, W. E. Burns, and J. C. Keith, a well-known financier, they served on the board of the Howe Sound, Pemberton Valley & Northern Railway. In 1907, when the company was incorporated, its railway was only one of several planned to head north towards Pemberton. Most promoters envisaged their trains reaching Fort George, or points beyond that settlement.

For two years the company kept secret the fact that the engineering firm of Cleveland and Cameron had surveyed a reasonable grade through the Cheakamus Canyon. By 1909, when the feasibility of H.S., P.V. & N. construction made headlines in the *Daily Province,* the railway company had bought most of the tidewater land in Squamish. In Pemberton the company had bought the Neill ranch, as well as the Miller land on both sides of Miller Creek. In 1911 the promoters bought land Tom Greer had pre-empted, and possibly more. One source gives the company's Pemberton holdings as 2,930 acres.

In the beginning the railway men planned to build their road to haul out the timber up the Squamish Valley, but their charter provided for construction from the Squamish River right through to Lillooet on the Fraser, about 120 miles distant. By the end of 1907 ten miles of the line had been surveyed; by the end of 1909, the nearly sixty miles to Pemberton. In 1909 crews laid rails heading towards the Cheekye River. Another promising development: two Baldwin locomotives were on their way to Squamish for service on the new railway. Although initially the few miles of track, including branch lines, served just as a logging road, the directors expected to haul varied freight: timber all along the line, copper-gold ores from the Green Lake Mines, and fruit, vegetables, and livestock from Lillooet and Pemberton.

Patrick Dermody had another plan. According to a January 1909 report in the *Daily Province,* he "suggested that his district and New Westminster be linked by steamers to Tipella City at the head of Harrison Lake, by electric tram to Lillooet Lake, and steamers for the remaining distance." The government does seem to have started to renew the gold miners' route, but not according to Dermody's plan.

Howe Sound & Northern Railway Surveyor's Pack Train Provincial Archives, Victoria, B.C.

Father Patterson, O.M.I., wrote about the road he knew so well, the road north from Harrison Lake. By 1911, he said, all bridges built by the Royal Engineers had been swept away, but in that same year "The provincial government rebuilt the bridges with the purpose of providing an alternate route to the Interior." By that time the railway was becoming a reality and making unnecessary the renewal of the old road.

Meanwhile, the railway company's subsidiary, the Howe Sound & Northern Development Company, managed the land. This company planned two townsites. That in Squamish would be called Newport. The Pemberton townsite, Agerton, was part of DL 164 and lay close to the Lillooet River, much of it on land Neill had recently farmed, and the site extended to below the one-time Red Bridge area. The company subdivided the remainder of the old farm: 74 lots, each containing from five to ten acres, were offered at prices ranging from $100 to $150 an acre. Similarly, the company divided the former Miller property, but into farm-sized acreages. Eustace Bubb, an English immigrant, was land agent in Pemberton. The representative for Europe was based in Glasgow.

Residents have given two explanations of the name "Agerton" for the new townsite. James Landsborough said that the name was suggested by the Latin "ager", meaning "field"; John Ronayne remembers Bubb laughing heartily and talking about "A-gr-ton, a great town."

The tiny settlement that developed close to the planned station site centred at the corner where the Pemberton Farm Road joins the main road linking Upper and Lower Valley. There William Kiltz built the present Patenaude home to serve as both store and post office; nearby he erected a large house and a barn. Eustace Bubb, for his own use, had the Miller house floated down the Lillooet and dragged up to where it stands today, the home of Milton Shantz.

The Howe Sound & Northern Railway Company, as it came to be known, never did extend its twelve miles of line, or complete any other developments. It lacked provincial government backing, and in March 1912 Pemberton people heard that the government had entered into an agreement with Foley, Welch and Stewart to build a railway from Squamish to Fort George. A new company, the Pacific Great Eastern Railway Company, received the government aid the Howe Sound Company had petitioned for and had hoped for.

The June 1913 issue of the *British Columbian* had several articles on the coming of the railway to Pemberton. In one, Jack Ronayne referred confidently to expected new settlers, and to the future of the Valley, saying that Pemberton was then producing "the finest potatoes in the world . . . always with a broad smile on their Irish mugs as they come out of the pot." He considered the pleasure of the city dweller who "might take the train in Vancouver, land in Pemberton four hours afterwards to enjoy, for instance, a sleigh ride." Until 1956 the trip by steamer and train took nine or ten hours, and by the time trains from North Vancouver travelled the approximately 100 miles to Pemberton in about three hours, sleigh rides were pleasures of the past.

In 1913 a rail link with the coast would solve not only difficulties of travel, but also other serious penalties of isolation: the lack of a school and the inability to control streams prone to flooding. Only more settlement could warrant establishment of a school; only a modern transportation system could move in the heavy equipment needed to safeguard the Valley against floods.

For years before the coming of the first train the settlers wrestled with both problems. At a very lively meeting in January 1910, those attending elected the first school trustees and chose a school site. Reports of the period tell of protecting river banks by laying willows along them, of making dykes, and of breaking up log jams. Local manpower and horsepower were pitted against streams often unpredictable in their fluctuations and, at peak runoffs, awesome in their destructive powers. Then they spilled over banks and laid waste the farmers' livelihood. The restricted and meandering channel between Lillooet and Tenas Lakes increased the possibilities of flooding in the Valley to the north.

Settlers began to ask for government help with the flooding problem. In February 1911 Ray Elliott and Jack Nelson, a surveyor, circulated a petition asking for Victoria's help with drainage. In May 1912 the *Daily Province* carried this item: "Property owners in Pemberton Meadows are petitioning the Provincial Government to appoint a commission for the carrying out of a project for draining 15,000 acres." A few months later, Ernest McBride, a superintendent of roads, said that $10,000 spent on blasting out obstructions in the river above Lillooet Lake would save Pemberton from flooding. Cleveland and Cameron, of the Howe Sound & Northern's survey, prepared a report which was to be consulted much later during the reclamation of the Valley. Some early settlers lived to see that reclamation, but in the years of waiting they saw family after family sadly give up the struggle with the water environment and move elsewhere.

Hopes of far-reaching benefits depended on rails. For Pemberton people, the first real evidence of the Pacific Great Eastern's determination to extend the Howe Sound & Northern line came with the building of a rough road from Squamish, a road needed for teams working on construction and for hauling supplies of all kinds. Raised on a farm in Quebec, Allan Fraser travelled the new road butchering cattle for the construction camps, but before starting down the steepest hills, he tied himself to his democrat. Frank Buckley and Ray Elliott herded the cattle to the camps. As these men worked along the tote road, they met the general public moving between Squamish and Pemberton and between Pemberton and Anderson Lake.

Once construction started travellers had a wider choice of stopping places: they could spend the night at railway camps. When Fay Brokaw and Gladys Blakeway rode south from Pemberton, Fay armed with a revolver, they stayed overnight at one of them. Many travellers saw Myrtle Philip working with her father and her brothers, the Tapleys: while Alex Philip earned money in Vancouver to support them all, they were building Rainbow Lodge to be ready to receive guests from the first Fishermen's Special train. Some passers-by saw a mysterious girl in a blue gingham dress who had appeared from nowhere to borrow eggs from Mrs. Philip who had thought herself the only woman living in the vicinity. But camp followers came with construction.

North of Pemberton, as towards the south, survey lines followed close to the only existing route. There it was the Pemberton Portage road extending into the cattle trail following the shores of Anderson and Seton Lakes. Bill Spetch now recalls in particular two men who passed his Owl Creek home, Pat Welch and Ray Elliott. When Pat Welch, one of the railway's promoters, visited the Spetch family he insisted that every man in his party fork out dimes and put them in Bill's piggy bank, but though Bill may have enjoyed the unexpected wealth, he enjoyed even more the occasional ride on Ray Elliott's horse, the finest saddle horse in the country.

Some people bound for Anderson Lake rode in Ronald Currie's stage, behind his fat team, its harness shining from a weekly washing and oiling. To make such trips pay Currie combined his stage runs with delivery of meat from his farm, but finally in 1913 the white-bearded farmer made his last run: the Foley, Welch and Stewart democrat, provided for visiting officials, had reduced the little business he had. Nearing Currie's stopping house, some travellers saw an eccentric who sometimes emerged from his home place riding a mule and talking to the trees. As people passed the Halfway House, they had a view of the cultivated section of Currie's 400-acre ranch, its "broad green meadows and fields of ripening grain . . . fruit trees bending under the weight of apples, pears and plums."

In 1912, reaching Anderson Lake, walkers, horseback riders, or stagecoach passengers could board "a swift gasoline passenger boat" for the trip north to the Short Portage. There, during their half-hour walk to Seton Lake, they saw the iron-reinforced wooden rails of what is considered to be the first railway in British Columbia, a railway built during the great Cariboo Gold Rush. According to an issue of the *British Columbian,* at Seton Lake passengers boarded a small steamboat under the command of Captain Cox who, according to Bill Elliot of D'Arcy, was the owner, captain, and crew of the Anderson Lake boat which had been built by Willie Durban, also of the Lakes area.

Pemberton residents were not the only ones who appreciated the swifter passage over the lakes as a result of railway construction. Some lured by offers of the H.S. & N. Development Company, many strangers flocked into the Pemberton area. The company's advertisements suggested that one crop might pay for the "ideal little farms" created by the subdivision of the former John Currie property. The reader was assured that "the day the railway is completed to Pemberton" land would sell for $500 to $1000 an acre.

A profitable result of construction was the sale of farm products to railway camps. Bill Harding delivered hay and vegetables to those camps with his mule team. Some teams employed in railway building near Pemberton were fed at those "ideal little farms", many of which were then the property of Nathaniel Baker. Until the 1960's, despite the subdivision, much of the old farm continued to be worked as a unit.

In this transition period for Pemberton people, railway and bridge building proceeded steadily. Some settlers worked for the P.G.E.: Willie Currie helped slash the right-of-way; Bert Perkins supplied timbers for the long trestle approaching and crossing the Lillooet River. At first the railway headquarters was near Squamish, down at the end of the Howe Sound & Northern line. Cleveland Hughes, a worker on the 1913 British Columbia Hydrographic survey, said that teams engaged in hauling on some days travelled no more than five or six miles. He spoke of one unscrupulous contractor who took advantage of some workmen's ignorance of the English language by postdating cheques which were then discounted when the men cashed them.

Finally, the first train from Squamish reached Pemberton, reached the station platform that was a structure of "rough planks in a sea of roots". On

Pemberton Station, early 1920's

October 29, 1914, that general roughness was of little concern to settlers boarding the first passenger train south. For the Joseph Ronayne family, travel had been transformed since the year before when they had made the rugged trip "in" by way of Lytton and Lillooet. On his first trip "out" by train James Landsborough gave one of the trainmen a $2 tip. Reaching Alta Lake the train made an overnight stop, and there, for $1, Landsborough shared a double bunk in the boarding house which was a converted sawmill.

Six days after the departure of the first passenger train weather conditions allowed the music of a steam locomotive's whistle to penetrate to the Upper Valley, a signal that Pemberton had entered the age of the railway and was facing a whole new way of life. Packers like Elliott, Greer, Mahan, Perkins, Thorne, Wallace, and Williams were forced to find new careers, but farm families had high hopes of increased services of all kinds, as well as of increased incomes, with all the comforts and conveniences those could supply.

Car barged in for inspection of Portage road after railway construction Provincial Archives, Victoria, B.C.

SETTLEMENT 1914 to 1940

Very soon after railway completion to Pemberton several families arrived to settle, and more came after the war. With vastly improved transport, they could bring with them most of their personal possessions. Dealing in Pemberton real estate after moving away from the area, James Ryan interested the George Thompsons in land north of Hartzell's farm where they settled with their baby. Edna Thompson's parents, the Harrises, and her sisters, were living on the James Ryan place, and the family being musical, with, as one man said, girls who were "the life of the valley", their home was a pleasant place to visit.

The Frank Smiths came to live, first at several locations in the Upper Valley, once farming in partnership with Dunc Morrison. One pioneer woman remembered their team and democrat dashing past her home. In early years George Smith rode a horse many miles down the trail to attend the Pemberton Meadows School. Later the Smiths built a house near the station, the house much later renovated and remodelled by the K. C. Harris family. James Ryan's cousin, Martin Ryan, and his wife Mattie, settled also in the Upper Valley and their children, too, attended the school.

Will Miller eventually returned having met and married in Ireland the widowed Teresa (Ronayne) Ross. After about five years in Lynn Valley he had driven to Fort George and sold all the horses he had used in a freighting business. In March 1915, driving a four-horse team, Ed Ronayne went to the station to meet Will. Miller had three stepchildren, Vivien, Alexander or "Sandy", and Gerald Ross, and, since his marriage to Teresa, had two sons of his own, Morgan and Ronayne or "Ronie" Miller. Teresa Miller had remained behind for the birth of Robbie Miller. The family lived for most of a year with the Ronaynes while Will built a house and cleared the land now farmed by his youngest son Donald.

Several single men also arrived. In the first year of train service young Ian Nicholson travelled into the Valley where he already knew some of the Ronaynes. Of his life in Pemberton he says, "Although I put in only about nine years here, this valley had so much to do with my life. I met and married an English girl who had come to work at Taillefers' stopping place. She got sick and died, and I just couldn't stick it any more." He therefore abandoned the farm at the Agerton corner that he had been buying from Jack Grady, and left the Valley. When Grady died Nicholson had a surprise: the old man had willed him the amount paid towards the purchase of the farm.

Temporary Shelters Provincial Archives, Victoria, B.C.

Arvid "Andy" Anderson came with Oscar Johnson who had been working on the railroad and both went to work at Perkins' mill. Andy, and probably Oscar who was a carpenter, helped build the Miller house. Later Oscar's brother Axel joined him and built a blacksmith shop on the site of Hillstrom's PX garage. Some years later Anderson, with John Arn, constructed one of several cabins along the winding trails beyond Pemberton Station. Eventually Anderson farmed on part of the original Pettit pre-emption; Arn, north of Miller Creek.

Before significant numbers increased the handful of pre-railway settlers, an exodus also took place: men enlisted to fight with the Canadian Armed Forces. The Landsborough brothers left the home farm in charge of James Duff and, like Ernest Blakeway, Jake Lokken, Olus Lee, and Eric Coleman, boarded the train at Pemberton. Men like Ernest Ward, who had homesteaded near Birkenhead Lake, and Law, a resident of the Portage, left from Owl Creek or Birken. Walter Landsborough, Coleman, and Law did not return from overseas. Law was a recent English immigrant who had worked in a London store, but had wanted to farm. He and his wife came to the Halfway House property then owned by Dr. T. V. Devey. About the time war broke out, Mrs. Law gave birth to a baby girl, the first child, she was told later, to be born at the old stopping house. Like many others before and after him Law did not fully realize his dream of farming in the Pemberton area, though flooding and mosquitoes, not death, accounted for the shattering of most such dreams.

Little settlement occurred during the four years of war, but Premier John Oliver, a farmer himself, fully expected that at the end of the war all returning soldiers would prefer farming to other occupations, and in some areas, though not in Pemberton, the provincial government sponsored settlement schemes for soldiers. Nevertheless, whatever the influences, compared with the previous trickles of immigration, the influx into the Pemberton area after the armistice seemed to be a flood.

Many of the new settlers were returned men; and many of the old settlers came back. James Landsborough and Ernest Ward both returned from France. Until the early 'fifties Landsborough continued to live in the Upper Valley; Ward bought the farm at Gates which is still his home.

Followed by his English bride, Blakeway returned and farmed south of Ronayne land. The couple lived temporarily in a tent while Olus Lee built their log house that became a showplace. In partnership, Jake Lokken and Olus Lee built a house and started to clear the land now worked by Lokken's grandson, Donald Summerskill. Lokken married Vivien Ross; and about the same time Lee married Helen Dermody. The Lees lived for a while in a small building that was later incorporated into the Lokken house.

Like Blakeway, Harry McCulloch had met his wife overseas. From Edinburgh Frances McCulloch reached Owl Creek in 1919 by one of the bi-weekly trains. After a night at the Spetch home, of which they would have many happy memories, she and her husband drove off in a steel-wheeled wagon to Lillooet Lake, she wearing kid gloves, suede shoes, and a fashionable blue suit. Paul Dick was waiting for them with his dug-out, and paddled them down the lake to their home. On reaching the McCulloch land, now Potvin's, Frances did not recognize the cabin as a home, and asked where the house was. On learning the truth, she sat down on a log and cried. Paul Dick tried to cheer her by pointing to the hills and saying, "Harry has a gold mine up there." The couple spent only six months in their isolated cabin, then bought the Stack farm at Owl Creek, with its house which Frances described as "the finest in the country". There they spent seventeen years, years she remembered as the happiest in her life. Later, when they bought the Dermody farm and lived on the far bank of the Lillooet, their son rode a horse to the Pemberton Meadows School.

In 1918, with the hope that May Taillefer's health would improve in the country, Joe Taillefer left the Kurtz Cigar Factory in Vancouver to farm his land near Pemberton Station and to raise chickens. Hawks ate the chickens. The first year a flood swept away their house lumber; the second year, with Lloyd Shore, they shipped a carload of potatoes and cleared just $15 on the twenty tons. During 1919 old friends of the Taillefers, George and Isabel Miller, made their move to the Valley. To give them a home, the Taillefers vacated the house they had contrived, despite floods, to build and, Taillefer said, "moved back" to the partly built hotel. There they used packing boxes to make walls and give themselves privacy. After becoming discouraged the Millers packed up and, with their two children and their horse, moved away to raise chickens on Bowen Island. George Miller, who had also worked at the Kurtz Cigar Factory, later moved to Vancouver and eventually became mayor of the city.

Lloyd Shore bought land which for many years had belonged to his family. His uncles, D. E. and Alex McMillan, had been members of an early survey party working in Pemberton, and expecting the present Shore land to be near a future railway station, D. E. and his sister, Adeline Hendry, had secured 160 acres. Years later, in addition to the quarter section, Shore bought two nearby parcels: 26 acres, the home place, and 40 acres to which Norah Bell-Irving had received a crown grant. In the early years on the farm, Harvey Derrick, who had been a stage hand in Edmonton and a milk delivery man in North Vancouver, worked for Shore.

Shore married Lilian Broadfoot, who had been a teacher at Pemberton Meadows School. Lilian had had an outstanding record as a strong swimmer and in the 1920's worked in an early motion picture, *Empty Hands.* A sequence in the film was shot in British Columbia, below the suspension bridge on the Capilano River, and for ten days the high school girl worked there, receiving the "outrageous" wages she had nerved herself to ask, $30 a day. In the icy waters, Lilian's part was to swim ashore from an overturned canoe. She was stand-in for Norma Shearer.

In the summer of 1928, with their two very young children, the Shores lived in a large new house. Then, when Lloyd was at the Tenquille Lake mine he and his cousin were developing, fire broke out at home. Shore's widow, now Lilian Spetch, recalls her ordeal: "Frank was eighteen months, and Ruth, four. Our three guests were asleep. I had to wake them twice, once before I took my children out, and again when I found they had gone back to sleep!

"The elder Barbour girl [Bebee Ruddock] and her daughter came over to try to help. I stayed at Taillefers' that night, and went to Vancouver next day, after Lloyd got back. Everyone clothed us, as we were all in our night clothes.

"A truck driver hauling ties said that the house must have burned down in fifteen minutes; he used to take fifteen minutes to drive from our place to the station, unload, and return as far as our place. Of course, I lost all my trophies, besides two trunkfuls of wedding presents I had never used."

With their son Robert, Basil and Ada Taylor settled on 300 acres in the Upper Valley. They sold 200 acres, leaving themselves with the farm which they retained until after the Second World War. Through many of those years, it was home to Bob and Mary Taylor and their young family. Bob would return there at night from his businesses at Pemberton Station: the Pemberton Express, or PX, office; the gas station; and the garage.

In 1919 the Taylors' pressing need for a part for their car brought their friend Bernard Cherry to the Valley. He arrived with the part, looked around, left briefly, and returned to work at various jobs. The crib-playing Cherry went to work at the fish hatchery and then Olus Lee, the government road foreman, hired him to work with the road crew and keep their solid rubber-tired truck operating.

Harry Gardiner bought 100 acres now owned by the Spetifore family. Allison Johnston said that when the river washed away much of Gardiner's land, discouraged, he sold what remained and, with his brother William, moved away.

The Start, March 24, 1920 Provincial Archives, Victoria, B.C.

Before reaching Pemberton in 1920 Barry and Christopher Girling and their friend, Pierre Souaillard, had met in Montreal, and had then spent a winter studying at the Vermillion Agricultural College. In the Pemberton Valley they bought adjoining acreages. After ten or more years, Souaillard, a veterinary surgeon, sold out to the Girlings, and with his mother moved away.

The Girling brothers' first land purchase included a small house which had been built for the previous owner, Bob Stacey, and in 1977 was still standing. Very early the men arranged to have Olus Lee build a large log house, finished inside with wood panelling, to be ready when their parents, Walter and Beatrice Girling, arrived from England.

At the age of eighteen Walter Girling had worked on an Ontario farm. When he injured his back, he returned home to England, but later, with his wife and sons, moved to the Falkland Islands. There, besides attending to his business, he served as a justice of the peace, as Swedish consul, and as a member of the legislature. After the outbreak of the First World War and the enlistment of their sons, the senior Girlings returned to England and rented a farm. For Beatrice Girling, the transition to life in Pemberton must have been very difficult. On cold winter mornings, when washing and dressing upstairs, she would crowd as close as possible to the warm pipe from the stove in the hall below. On wash days, for a time, she and a house boy took the family laundry out to the river bank and worked on it there.

After twenty years, successive floods drove the sons and their wives and young children off the land. But Walter, by then a widower, stayed on in the small original home, "The Willows". He never lost interest in the community, and in his old age was a weekly Pemberton contributor to the *Bridge River-Lillooet News,* as well as volunteer caretaker of the cemetery.

On April 3, 1920, leaving two daughters at school in North Vancouver and bringing with them their youngest daughter and their son, Walter and Margaret "Mame" Green arrived to spend three years in the Valley. Margaret's brother, John Mee, came to help them settle because both Green and Dick, the son, needed time to recover from severe attacks of influenza. During their years in the country they planned to clear their land and thus reduce their tax bill. Green had travelled by P.G.E. earlier — as a newsman he had covered the railway's inaugural run to Horseshoe Bay. Even earlier, after walking over the trail in May 1909 with his uncle, J. C. Williams, he had inspected the land which J. C. Gill of the H.S., P.V & N. Railway had persuaded Williams to buy.

On that spring day in 1920 the Greens' first concern was to move their belongings up the muddy road and establish themselves. Old Pat, their horse, pulled the wagon piled with their belongings as far as Millers' where they found a mud hole so long and so deep that the horse could not drag the freight through it. They had to unload half their possessions and leave them by the side of the road, and then drive on to their own land and set up their tent. After a night's sleep, they got up early and returned over the now-frozen road to collect the rest of the load.

All were muddy when they returned to the tent and Annie Ronayne just then came along to invite them to a dance that night in the nearby school. John Mee looked at his sister: "I'm not going to any dance with you until you wash your neck." She washed, and they went, and had an unforgettable experience.

During mosquito season life in the tent became unbearable, and the family therefore moved into the school where fumes of burning pyrethrum powder could not drift away, but, instead, killed the insect tormentors. Day by day, though, the house was taking shape, as both parents worked on it. When they completed it, this house had exceptional features for Pemberton: hardwood floors in dining and living rooms, a fireplace in the living room, and a furnace in the basement. In the 1920 summer the family wanted only two things of their house — walls and a roof that would let the pyrethrum powder do its work. As soon as that stage was reached, the Greens moved in.

In 1921, Alexander "Sandy" and Adela Fowler came with their three children to live several miles up the road from the school and across the river, to a house which Tom Steinbrunner, Adela's brother, had built. During the first winter, Bill Fowler remembers Jack Ronayne crossing the river to bring them "a bucket of eggs and a bucket of gramophone records". The next spring, fire destroyed the home. Bill remembers that "after we got out, Edith, the baby, was thrown into a corner, and the three-month-old pig sucked on her bottle". As the Jack Ronaynes and the Dermodys had done before them, and as the Shores, Girlings, Taillefers, and others would do after them, the Fowlers overcame their loss. Besides themselves and their children, about all the parents had saved were a bird's-eye maple dresser, the gramophone, and a trunk. While they lived first in a tent, then in Herbert Steinbrunner's cabin, Herb and Sandy built the log house now belonging to singer Terry Jacks.

Through a relative who knew Beatrice Girling's sister in London, Allison Johnston heard of Pemberton and decided to emigrate.Late 1921 floods and washouts on the P.G.E. kept him waiting for about three weeks in Vancouver, but on reaching Pemberton eventually, he travelled to Girlings' farm in Bill Gardiner's sleigh, stopping at noon for clam chowder with Olus Lee and Jake Lokken. In 1924 he bought the Martin Ryan place.

Joseph Charles "Jay" Mighton and his wife acquired land and a cabin set away back in the bush on the upper side of Miller Creek. In 1921, with Katherine Dermody helping, their first child was born. Like other new settlers Mighton worked at various jobs to help support his family and the farm, and by collecting spawned salmon from the creek bars, he enriched his garden soil and produced vegetables the family took pride in. When Maria Fraser and Kay Handy, a teacher at Pemberton Meadows, visited Ruby Mighton, they found her cutting up home-grown watermelons to make pickles. Working there in her secluded cabin, without neighbours, she often wished she could see the road.

In 1921 Arthur R. Mawbey lived briefly in Pemberton. His varied careers included long service in the Royal Navy, service during the First World War in the Royal Signal Corps, and farming in the Upper Squamish. By 1921 he had joined the British Columbia Forest Service.

In 1923, with two sons, the Hugh Shaws lived in a shack not far from the Gardiner farm, until with the help of John Jack they built a log house with a cement basement. According to Gerald Ross, a neighbour, "they did things right": that house has since been the home of the Barry Girlings, the Hector Harwoods, the Leonard McNoltys, and the Martin Beks, the present owners, who now use it as a farm building.

With this influx of post-war settlers, the John Peter van der Hoop family also arrived, father, mother, and young daughter. The father had spent the 1919-1920 academic year studying agriculture at the University of British Columbia, and when they settled on land adjoining the Blakeway farm, all of the animals were of recognized breeds, not of the mixed breeds common in pioneer areas. According to Ben Cherry, their machinery included a lot of electrical equipment which Ben helped to keep in repair. Another machine rare in Pemberton was a manure spreader. After a few years van der Hoop sold his place to Count van Rechteren, from Holland. Known as "Mac" to his neighbours, the Count farmed the land until he moved to Chilliwack.

Al Fraser and his wife Pauline lived across the river from the present Mitchell farm. He worked at various jobs, but while packing up Mount Garibaldi he cut his leg, and the cut became infected. In the days before anti-biotics, infection often had dire consequences, but though Al lost his leg he continued packing and prospecting. From Montreal and as fluently bi-lingual as his brother, Nelson Fraser joined Al in Pemberton in 1922. For a time Nels lived and worked with his brother, then married the widowed Maria Punch.

Settlers arriving after railway construction and immediately after the war must have bought most of the available and cultivable land. In 1919 Surveyor Downton reported all land suitable for settlement "long since taken up". He had been impressed, not only by the large area of flat land which could be easily cleared, but also by its "rather deserted and neglected appearance". Doubtless much of the uncultivated land belonged to the absentee owners he referred to in 1921 when he stated that a scheme for drainage had fallen through because of lack of interest on the part of those owners. In 1912, a reporter for the *British Columbian* had written that "Large tracts of land in the valley are owned by non-residents, who have made few improvements pending the advent of the railway. These holders include Mayor Findlay, Mr. D. Steinbrunner, the Howe Sound Development Company and Pemberton and Son." Of these owners, Pemberton and Son, if not the others, still held Pemberton land at the time of the 1921 Downton Report.

Certain areas now cultivated were then sedge meadows, areas for trapping and duck hunting, but not for settling. These included several sections, one between Pemberton Village and the Lillooet River bridge, another, the present Guthrie and Gilmore farms and, above Ryan Creek bridge, much of the Dill, Lex Ross, and other properties. Farther north, too, were wet areas, though on a less extensive scale. Back towards Ryan Creek, at the rear of some of the farms, was a favourite cranberry bog.

After the earlier considerable increase in settlement, years went by when few families arrived. Probably the difficulty of securing land and Pemberton's reputation discouraged settlers. In 1924 an English immigrant wrote home to England from Squamish: "Pemberton is not much of a place from what I hear. It is infested with mosquitoes and floods and the market is awkward. The Ry charges are very high."

Some single men were straggling in to work at whatever they could find, a number ambitious to farm when they could afford to do so. These and others, among them young men who grew up in the Valley, bought and cultivated some of the neglected land. Selling marten skins to Bill Kiltz, by 1923 Sandy and Gerald Ross had earned enough money to buy their first 80 acres from Pemberton and Son on which they established themselves in a tent Sandy had brought down from a job at Codman's Mine. During the winter they lived in the tent they built the shack which was home to them until each of them married. On the recommendation of the Count, Frits Tellander, from Holland, worked for the Joe Ronaynes, and later for Landsborough; Frits bought land north of the Miller farm. Both coming initially to the Girlings, the Wilson brothers immigrated from England, first Edward, then Patrick, and bought half the McLeod farm on which they built a house and farmed together. About 1940, Pat, the artist, enlisted to fight in the Second World War, from which he never returned. In 1925 Joseph Gilbert "Scotty" Bennett, born in Canada, but raised in Scotland, came to live with his friend Jim Landsborough and worked for a number of years in different parts of the Valley before moving to Lillooet.

Lucien van Beem arrived from Java in the winter, wearing a white tropical suit. He found friends in the Joe Ronayne family, and after working for them and others, in 1930 he bought land from Landsborough and planted potatoes and turnips in his one-half acre of cleared land. He bought a house already on rollers and within a few days his team had dragged it a mile up the road to his own land where it was home until some years after his marriage, when he built a larger house. Lukie's wife, Doris, described the neighbourhood: "Upper Pemberton Valley was mostly bachelor land and the road a cow trail improved by wagon wheels running over it."

Upper Valley road, 1920's

In 1927, for the first time in several years, Pemberton welcomed married couples with families. The Ernest Coopers and the John Deckers had lived eight miles apart in the Cariboo. There they met twice a year, at Christmas, and on May 24 when they picnicked at a lake midway between their farms. When the Deckers looked ahead to the time when they would have to send their delicate daughter to school on horseback with her older brother, through five miles of uninhabited bush, they rejected the idea. Their alternative was to give up the farm on which they were becoming well established and move closer to a school. They decided, therefore, to explore farming possibilities in Pemberton. At the next May 24 picnic they told their neighbours of their plan, and urged Ernie Cooper, whose daughter, too, was approaching school age, to visit Pemberton with Jack Decker. The trip would be economical: Frances Decker planned to send blankets, beans, and bread with her husband; her father would drive him to Lillooet to catch the southbound train. Cooper agreed, and the two men bought adjoining acreages north of the Ronayne farms.

The two families had travelled to Pemberton by P.G.E., their household goods, some animals, and farm machinery in freight cars. The Coopers spent their first winter on Lokken property, first in a cabin, then in the house. The second year, both husband and wife had jobs at Stricker's pole camp, Ernie "dragging the poles out" with his team, and Ruth cooking. By the third winter, Bob Taylor had completed a small three-room cabin for them on their own land. There they lived for a few years until Sandy and Gerald Ross built them a house, the one that now belongs to the David Valleaus.

When Jack Decker reached Pemberton in the fall of 1927 he left his wife travelling on to Vancouver with their two children. They did not return until after the birth of the third child. Meanwhile, Decker found a place to live, a cabin on land now belonging to the Cecil Helmers, one built by Bill Spetch, and there in the early spring of 1928, when snow was still covering Pemberton and its road, the Decker family was reunited. Frances remembers the generosity of close neighbours who seemed to be "trying to outdo each other" with such gifts as fresh butter, and even a quarter of beef. Decker and his father-in-law worked at building a home and when they had finished the roof, and walled in the kitchen and bedroom areas, the family moved up the road and into their new house.

More young single men came to work for families already established in the Valley. Bert Bish came from Vancouver to the Girling household, and on his days off found his greatest pleasure in roaming the hills. Cyril Keyes came to the Barbours; his younger brother, Leon, took a job with the Taillefers, working in the store. Taking advantage of the assisted passage available to war veterans, Eric Gethen immigrated from England, followed by his brother Harold. In coming to Canada, the brothers were returning to the land of their birth, which they had left when boys. For thirteen years Eric worked as a farm hand for Taylors and, later, for Girlings, before moving to his own land below Pemberton Station; working for the PX, Harold stayed a shorter time in the Valley. Living in a cabin on the present Henry Menzel property, Cecil Bucknell sometimes worked on the Lokken farm, but, after Indians built him the log house now belonging to the Kempters, he moved to the Creekside area.

In the late 'twenties and early 'thirties, jobs in the woods and the mills attracted men who later settled and farmed. In 1928 John Gronseth came to work as a sawyer at the mill belonging to Cy Keyes and Jim Dermody, but later built homes for settlers able to afford new and better housing, and for some just establishing themselves. The land he farmed at Mount Currie is now the site of the Commercial Timber Company's mill.

Like Lokken in earlier years, and Gronseth more recently, Magnus Urdal was an immigrant from Norway who arrived in 1929 to "subcontract poles" for Albert Bossy. Three years later, he bought land from Hartzell, then went away to work, and did not return to the farm for the seven years he spent working at Pioneer Mines, during which time he married. His friend, Kaare Instefjord, lived on that land and in 1933 became one of the early producers of certified seed potatoes. About the time Urdal had acquired his farm, Alfred Ridley, who had been a tie cutter, bought land adjoining.

In the late 'twenties, three men who had immigrated from Sweden arrived. In 1929 Thord "Slim" Fougberg came to work with Gronseth at the mill across the river on the Pat Dermody home property. Henry Erickson trapped for a living or worked at jobs in the woods. Erickson's wife says that during the depression her husband rode a freight car from eastern Canada into Vancouver, where he was on a starvation diet, and came on into Pemberton where he stayed because of food. For a time he lived with the Lokkens and worked only for his board; later, for wages. About 1930, when he acquired the Miller Creek trap line, he invited his cousin, Bert Lundgren, to come to Pemberton to trap with him. "It wasn't much of a trap line", Lundgren says. "If I'd had enough money to turn around, I would have turned around." But, in a few years the two were farming together on land now owned by Erickson. Later, Henry bought the adjoining farms of Jim Dermody and Jack Gronseth, in the area once referred to as the International Settlement.

William Germyn worked at pole cutting before he farmed the Count's land. From Philadelphia originally, James Bartow cut ties for a time, then farmed half of the old McLeod place, living in the house with his numerous cats, always leaving the windows partially open because, as he said, "When I say Scat! I mean Scat!" The Blattler family followed Germyn as renters of the Count's land. Five of their children entered the Pemberton Meadows School to fill any gaps in the range of grades from one to seven.

In 1929 Section Foreman Nicholson and his wife sent their children to the newly opened school at the station where they were valued members of the baseball team. Noble Prendergast's sons were their classmates and also members of the strongly competitive team. A later section foreman, Bill Elesko, had children who attended the same school in its early years. Joe Brown, another P.G.E. employee, lived with his wife in a cabin beyond the station.

Harold Wyatt-Purden was a 1930 newcomer. He farmed at first on the Baker place, where his wife joined him after a year, and five years later they moved to Donnybrook Farm, on the road to Mount Currie, land now cultivated by George Purden, the older son.

Earlier and later more families arrived. In Canada since 1925, Carl Gimse, a Norwegian lawyer, heard of money to be made hauling ties in Pemberton, and with a partner freighted his truck into the Valley and set to work. His son, Gunnar, immigrated in November 1927, and worked with his father; Gimse's wife, Sigrid, and his daughter, Sidsel, followed two years later. When he acquired his farm at Birken, Gimse had realized the dream with which he had left Norway. Living close to his son's home during the last years of his long life, he moved about his house in a wheelchair and, for entertainment, listened to classical recordings.

Having earlier visited the Valley, Milton and Stella Shantz decided in the fall of 1931 to walk into Pemberton. From Vancouver they hitch-hiked up the Fraser Canyon to Lillooet. Between Lillooet and D'Arcy they walked the ties, but when they arrived at the P.G..E. lodge at D'Arcy, operated by the Roy family, Stella could go no farther — her feet were too blistered. She worked for a time at the lodge while her husband worked on the railway to earn their fares to Pemberton. At Pemberton Station they bought a house in a woodsy area behind the hotel, close to James Duff's cabin. Seven years later they bought a farm from Jack Grady, and moved to the Agerton corner where they still found time for books, flowers, and music.

The Benjamin Kays, friends of Bill Germyn, came with four sons from North Vancouver to some land between the Cooper and Ross farms. Jack Fisher, with his wife and family, moved farther up the Valley, up to the Salmon Slough where they lived on land owned by his father-in-law, Racine. Several more families added to the school population. The Ridley's son and daughter attended the Upper Valley School. In 1935 Mabel Boeur's sister, Rose Collin, lived here for a short time, in which the eldest of her three children enrolled at the Pemberton Meadows School where, he remembers, the teacher was "a good shot with chalk".

In 1934 the widower Frederick Menzel brought his children to the Barbour place; the younger ones walked down to the Pemberton School. Menzel farmed for about four years. One of the oldest sons, Fred, bought the Baker place after the Purdens had moved to Creekside. At that time Sam Jim, an Indian who lived to be over one hundred, was a builder of barns who, in his old age, built for Fred.

More young Valley people married and established new homes. Sandy Ross married a girl from Norway; Gerald Ross, a girl from Wales. Morgan Miller and his bride lived the first winter of their marriage in a trapping cabin on McKenzie Lake, but the following year Jack Gronseth built them a house on land bought from the crown. Still later, when crossing the river with children by canoe or cable carriage became too onerous, they bought land from Carl Groat and moved the house to its present site.

From the Prairies, James Shier married the girl who had come west with him. Mary worked for more than two years at Port Alberni until they could afford to set up a home while Shier worked for the Lokkens, and then went trapping on Wilson land. Finally he could afford to rent the McKibbon land, now owned by Lex Ross. Alice Fowler married Jack McKay, then in charge of the Spetch store at Creekside. Slim Fougberg married and lived for a year on the Taylor farm. Kathleen Ronayne married Bert Lundgren and in 1940 the couple bought the Barbour place. Recently from Ireland, Phyllis Ronayne married Henry Erickson.

In the main, settlers were individualists from varied backgrounds. By no means did they always agree among themselves, but most of them did combine to help each other, not only in harvesting, and at building bees, but also, when necessary, in pressing for government attention to their major problems.

At Perkins' mill camp Provincial Archives, Victoria, B.C.

Salmon barbecue near the Birkenhead Provincial Archives, Victoria, B.C.

Artillery Farm, February 28, 1926 Provincial Archives, Victoria, B.C.

Stacking hay Provincial Archives, Victoria, B.C.

ABOUT FARMING, 1914 to 1940

By the end of May 1915, after steel rails had been laid between Pemberton and the coast, farmers had greatly increased their acreages of wheat, oats, and peas. Only the railway could have encouraged those men to expand as they had. But the percentage gains did not indicate many large farms. The local men starting off to join the Canadian Armed Forces travelled along a narrow road, and passed scattered little cleared patches used mainly for growing potatoes, turnips, and hay. The plots had been hewn, blasted, and grubbed out on higher spots among the cottonwoods and cedars of the Valley bottom, and were often invisible to travellers. For the men enlisting, memories of Pemberton would be memories of a few sizeable farms, but mostly of subsistence operations. Gradually, with the advantages of freighting by rail, and with increased population, acreages increased, and farming diversified. In the first year of passenger train service, government agricultural experts were visiting the Valley to give advice.

One came to investigate the continuing losses of young farm animals, losses for which no preventative would be found until 1917. Another, Beeman Todd, inspected bees. In June 1914 Will Miller had brought a hive into Pemberton; Jim Landsborough and Jack Ronayne soon started hives of their own. Production of milk and cream for a larger than local market was now possible and to advise in such new ventures, a dairy expert arrived in Pemberton from Vancouver.

According to Jack Ronayne, after the P.G.E. came, Pemberton farmers "started out . . . to do a little dairying. We did well as long as we could sell sweet cream, and, for some years, dairying was the sole means of revenue." George Groat was the first to ship cream from Pemberton, the first of many; Tom Craddox and Ernest Ward shipped from the Portage. Will Miller was the first to install a milking machine, with a gasoline motor to supply the electricity. Years afterwards, that motor operated George Walker's planer mill.

Settlers' activities, and their participation in agricultural organizations, show that, despite adverse conditions, they were working hard to increase their farming skills and to increase their incomes. In 1922 they held a fall fair in the Pemberton Meadows School, at which a professional from the Department of Agriculture judged the exhibits. After the judging he spoke to the fair goers about the growing of seed potatoes, explaining the seed certification program, and asking if the farmers would be willing to develop their potatoes for certification. The potatoes would be grown for two years under the supervision of the Federal Department of Agriculture Seed Protection Branch and if, after that time, they were free of disease, the Department would certify them.

Jack Ronayne gave further background to seed potato production in Pemberton: "Our sweet cream was ruled to be sour, and the price went down. So we had to get out of dairying. So we started in on commercial potatoes, and our conditions slightly improved. Well, then, certified seed came along and, through the guidance of the Seed Inspector, we learned how to produce our almost-free-from-disease potatoes." He explained the advantage to the seed industry of the Valley's isolation: high mountains make it very difficult for "the bugs to climb in".

Not long after the 1922 Fall Fair, W. C. Green secured from Lillooet one hundred pounds of Netted Gem potatoes and started the seed-growing program. In turn, he sold a ton of seed to Will Miller. In 1926, at the British Columbia Potato, Bulb, and Seed Show, Green won a prize for his entry of Early Rose seed potatoes. In 1930, under the supervision of the chief seed inspector for the province, Haddon S. MacLeod, Green and Miller grew a total of five acres of the Early Rose and Netted Gem varieties of certified seed potatoes. In 1932, at the annual meeting of the Pemberton Valley Farmers' Institute, vice-president J. O. Decker paid tribute to the pioneer efforts of W. M. Miller and W. C. Green, and to H. S. MacLeod and M. S. Bewell, "the latter being Dominion Seed Inspectors who had visited Pemberton in the Spring and had assured the growers of the excellence and increasing popularity of Pemberton certified seed potatoes."

By 1924, farmers had begun to organize. The Pemberton Valley Farmers' Institute had thirty members. In March 1925 President Lloyd Shore and Secretary John Peter van der Hoop had signed the by-laws of the organization. N. J. Baker, Sandy Fowler, and Pierre Souaillard, with Shore and van der Hoop, had been subscribers to the declaration for incorporation. V. E. Kiltz, Jack Ronayne, and W. C. Green, who for many years would be an Institute officer, witnessed the signatures. The aims and objectives of the Institute were "to promote conditions of rural life so that settlement may be permanent and prosperous; to promote the theory and practice of agriculture by lectures, essays, the circulation of information and other educational methods, and to stimulate interest by exhibitions, prizes and other means; to arrange on behalf of its members for the purchase, distribution or sale of commodities . . . ."

Immediately the Institute members set about to realize these objectives. The organization's report of the 1924 Fall Fair shows that award winners had received $52.50 in prizes. The next year, the newly organized Pemberton

"SOCIETIES ACT." (Chap. 83, 1920, Sec. 6.) No.

Declaration.

WE, the undersigned, hereby declare that we desire to form a society under the "Societies Act," and that :—

(1.) The name of the Society is " Pemberton Valley *Farmers' Institute."*

(2.) The objects of the Society are :—

(a.) To improve conditions of rural life, so that settlement may be permanent and prosperous:

(b.) To promote the theory and practice of agriculture by lectures, essays, the circulation of information and other educational methods, and to stimulate interest by exhibitions, prizes, and other means:

(c.) To arrange on behalf of its members for the purchase, distribution, or sale of commodities, supplies, or products, and generally to act on their behalf in all matters incidental to agricultural pursuits:

(d.) To promote social intercourse, mutual helpfulness, and the diffusion of knowledge, and to make new settlers welcome.

(3.) The operations of the Society are to be chiefly carried on in

PEMBERTON Valley.

Department of Agriculture VICTORIA, B.C. Rec'd JAN 27 1925

Dated this 24th *day of* January *, 192*5

Full names, addresses, and occupations of subscribers and witness(es).

FULL NAME.	ADDRESS.	OCCUPATION.
John Peter van der Hoop	Pemberton Meadows	Farmer
Nathaniel John Baker	Agerton	Farmer
Pierre Lonailland V.S.	Pemberton Meadows	Farmer
Lloyd Strong	Agerton	Farmer
Sandy Fowler	Pemberton Meadows	Farmer

[NOTE.—*See* overleaf for instructions.]

Strike out according to circumstances.

Witness (to all signatures) or ~~(the signature of)~~ W G Green as to all signatures

I hereby Certify ~~that a duplicate original~~ [illegible]
of this document has been filed with me
pursuant to the Societies Act.
Dated this 2nd day of Mar. 1925

H G Garrett
REGISTRAR OF COMPANIES

200-8-23-855

Meadows Athletic Club, known as the Boys' Club, decided "to have a stall at the Exhibition". In September 1929 an impressive display of trophies sat outside the school on a paper-wrapped plank set upon saw horses. Within the little building exhibitors had arranged displays of fine fruits, vegetables, and grains; heavy-headed stooks stood in the corners of the room. When judging was finished, those present — just about everybody living in the Upper Valley and others from lower down — gathered outside on the grass where E. C. Carson,

At Pemberton Meadows School, September 1929 Provincial Archives, Victoria, B.C.

the local MLA, gave out trophies. All were then invited to tea with Ernie Carson, and most of the fair goers trooped over to the Greens' house nearby, leaving the school doors wide open. Arriving at the school an hour later the young teacher found that a cow had wandered in and was munching on the sheaves. What a mess the teacher faced!

An early 'twenties photograph shows men, women, and children standing on a narrow strip of bare ground, their backs against van der Hoop's sunny barn wall, and all gazing at the side of an Ayrshire cow, her legs hidden from us by the depth of snow remaining in the barnyard. There to discuss the qualities of a good milk cow and to advise generally was Dr. Paul Axel Boving, the well-known Swede in the Faculty of Agriculture at the University of British Columbia. The Farmers' Institute had probably arranged the event.

In 1933, another important move to improve agricultural practices was the establishing of the first Illustration Station which for ten years Ernest Blakeway maintained on his farm, under the supervision of R. M. Hall of the Federal Government's Experimental Farm at Agassiz. A year later, in August 1934, several agricultural experts came to the first of the annual field days held under the sponsorship of the Farmers' Institute, and advised on a variety of topics: fodder crops and grasses, dairy stock, potatoes, turnips, and small fruits. When visitors walked over to the potato plot, Haddon S. MacLeod, a potato expert originally from Prince Edward Island, took command. To Pemberton's steadily increasing number of seed growers he stressed the need for relentless elimination of undesirable features for only in that way could anything like one hundred per cent good seed be produced.

Other things besides animals and crops then attracted attention. Against the background of towering mountains the Blakeways had developed very pleasant surroundings. The correspondent reporting the event noted that "the beautification of the home grounds is not neglected in the illustration work, and a fine lawn and flower border is coming along well . . . ." The field day came to a close with Irene Blakeway serving tea and "a more than generous supply of tasty refreshments under the welcome shade of a clump of trees." The report ended with a tribute to the Blakeways, "whose sustained and considerable effort" was needed "to keep a farm up to the requirements demanded by an illustration station." The vice-president of the Institute, W. C. Green, closed the afternoon with "a vote of thanks to the visiting speakers."

True to another Institute aim, the organization purchased and distributed a variety of goods needed by the farming community. In 1939 Chris Girling handled sales from his home. For many years the Farmers' Institute officers handled one popular item which none would think of storing in his house — blasting powder.

Until the late 'forties, fire, blasting powder, horsepower, and manpower were everywhere the land-clearing agents. With few exceptions, when the land was cleared, horses pulled the ploughs, harrows, cultivators, sprayers, mowers, and other equipment used in farming operations. Lloyd Shore and Alf Ridley were early farm tractor owners.

Some farms had varied production. The Joe Ronayne accounts for the late 'thirties show the sale of that great range: "Most of the produce was oats and wheat sold locally, also turnips, carrots and potatoes sold in small amounts, rarely large orders. Turnips sold then at $1 for 100 pounds and carrots at $1.25. Hay was sold [for as little as $15 a ton] by the carload lot as were cattle. The beef sold locally was evidently the extra meat when an animal was butchered for home consumption."

In 1931 men of the community formed a second organiztion which was to have an impact on farming: the Pemberton and District Board of Trade became active in the marketing of farm crops. At the organizational meeting held in the Pemberton Hotel, H. W. Purden was elected president, and later served for eighteen years as secretary-treasurer. J. W. Wilkinson was the first one. Others attending the first meeting included J. A. Taillefer, C. Wellington, H. Derrick, A. Spetch, T. Graham, G. Stack, W. Germyn, A. Johnson, G. Cowell, R. Dickey, and R. H. E. Taylor.

Some farmers diversified, yet Board of Trade records have recurring references to potatoes, and just a few to other products. Certainly some farmers devoted much of their time to potatoes. A great deal of work and care were needed to produce certified seed and, through many years, growers have competed in provincial and national potato exhibitions. To select and prepare exhibits of perfect or nearly perfect potatoes, perfectly matched, takes endless hours. No wonder farmers spent "most of the winter in the root houses."

Charles Wellington complained at a Board of Trade meeting that in spite of all the first prizes won in 1931 at a Vancouver potato show Vancouver dealers gave the potatoes "only second rating". Board members took action by asking their secretary to bring the matter to the attention of the Minister of Agriculture. In the following year growers were making significant progress with seed potatoes. The number of certified growers had trebled, and for the first time Valley farmers sold carload lots. In a large group of exhibitors at the Royal Winter Fair in Toronto, by winning both a first and a second prize John Decker proved the excellence of the Pemberton product.

In 1931, because its grower members wanted advice about marketing, the Board of Trade invited a potato broker as a speaker. Through the years the price received for a ton of commercial potatoes went up and down, but out of whatever was received, farmers had to pay all expenses, including freight, sacks, and agent's commission. The gross return for a ton of commercial potatoes was $17.50 in 1927, $53 in 1929, and $11.50 in 1931. In 1932 one beginning farmer hand-brushed eight tons, and cleared $23 for the lot. The following January, through the Board of Trade, a firm of brokers ordered a carload of seed potatoes, offering $17 a ton.

In spite of financial discouragements, vigorous efforts continued to improve marketing practices, storage facilities, and disease control. During the 'thirties outstanding awards came to the Valley. H. W. Purden submitted to the Board of Trade a "Snowflake Spud" design which was accepted and growers of commercial potatoes thereafter bought and filled sacks branded with the "Snowflake" design. To control quality of products the Board passed a motion that its stamp be on the labels of all root crops, "providing they were properly graded and inspected by one of the Board of Trade experts on Root Crops." Another motion appointed as the Board's inspector Harold Gethen, a fellow of the Royal Horticultural Society of England. Using old bridge timbers donated by the P.G.E., the Board combined with the Farmers' Institute to build a root house close to the railway tracks. About 1939, because potato blight was affecting potato crops, the group bought a community sprayer for which A. M. Ridley offered to supply a team and operate at a contract price of $1 an acre.

In 1934 increasing recognition of Pemberton potatoes came from the Federal Department of Agriculture which inquired about the Board of Trade's "marketing system for Snowflake Spuds", and for a sample of them. The Department had heard "reports of the Huge Success of this Board." Members prepared the report and sent it off along with a "large sample" of potatoes.

Squamish
17 March/25.

My dear Mamie

We live in a quick moving age. When I first struck Squamish it would have taken 2 months to get a letter into Pemberton & get a reply (at this time of the year) It might have been quicker in the summer when pack trains were on the Road.

Sorry to bother you but I read your first letter to quote 1.00 dollars per 100. f.o.b. Pemberton.

Today you mention a sale to Spencers at $55 per ton.

This is a way above $2 a sack and so I thought perhaps I had made a mistake?

When you have time to spare
tell me if you care the make
of Radio and cost - that you
listened in the other night.
I am always longing for one
in my Shack but the COST
kills the desire.
I almost forgot 500 I haven't
played for 2 years or more -
not since you were held up
by snow!
Well so long Best of
love to the Kiddies -
Hope Walter is keeping well
I believe farm work was
better for both of you, health
and happiness than
newspaper cropping.
Sincerely yours
John Madden
Health is miles ahead of
wealth!

Throughout the 'thirties Pemberton farmers won top honours in potatoes, turnips, and field peas. Winning awards against tough competition gave not only immense satisfaction to the individual winners, but also wide advertising of the area's agricultural products. In 1933, growers Decker, Ronayne Brothers, and Bob Taylor won five awards, including one first, at the Royal Winter Fair. The following year, Decker and Ronayne Brothers took seven. In the same year Ronayne Brothers won honours for field peas at Toronto and at the Hay and Grain Show of the Chicago International Livestock Exposition. Exhibiting potatoes in the Boys' and Girls' classes at Toronto, Eddie Ronayne won both early and late variety awards. The 1935 Toronto Royal also gave high honours to both Decker and Ross Brothers.

In 1937 the highest award for certified seed potatoes at Toronto, the American Potash Institute prize, came for the first time to British Columbia: J. O. Decker, the winner, received a gold watch at a dinner attended by the Minister of Agriculture; the President of the Pacific National Exhibition; the Dean of Agriculture at the University of British Columbia; H. S. MacLeod; and the Mayor of Vancouver, George C. Miller, himself once a farmer in Pemberton. In the same year, Decker was the first British Columbian to win the top prize for field peas at Chicago. He received the award so often that for a three-year period he was barred from competition, but at the end of the three years he re-entered, and once again won the championship.

At the 1937 Vancouver Winter Seed Fair, Decker, Green, and Ross Brothers won four first prizes, and one second. Similar successes continued. In 1938, at a Vancouver show, the Farmers' Institute won a challenge cup for the best potato display and individual growers — Decker, Cooper, and Ronayne Brothers — won eight awards, including five firsts, for certified potato seed, while Decker and Ross Brothers won two first prizes and a second for turnips. Also in 1938, at Toronto, the Rosses won a first and a second prize for one variety of seed potatoes, and Decker came first with another. Decker's winning entry was exhibited in Vancouver and other communities by the British Columbia Electric Railway Company for which he had worked for many years. The next year, at the B.C. Seed Growers' Fair, Decker, Cooper, Ronayne Brothers, and the Ross Brothers received a total of eighteen awards. Each success was the result of farming and exhibiting skills above the average, as well as of endless perseverance.

Looking back on the years of successful competition, during which she helped her husband, Frances Decker sums up some results of the many awards coming to the Valley: "Pemberton's enterprise in exhibiting led to a great interest in seed potatoes throughout B.C. Spuds were a show feature during the week ending November 1939 in the warehouse of F. R. Stewart on Water Street, Vancouver. The entire ground floor of the building was given over to the display, and sacks of 15 pounds were given away free (200 each day)."

All farmers were concerned with marketing. In 1934 Board of Trade members decided to send letters to the nearby mining communities soliciting orders. They did more than send letters: in the same year, three residents,

AT POTATO PARTY.

Perkins, Mahan, and Fred Oman, took loaded pack horses through Railroad Pass to the Bridge River towns. At the time, according to a news report, Pemberton people were keenly interested in "the recent medical discovery that raw turnip juice has all the beneficial properties of orange juice."

The packers therefore loaded their horses with turnips as well as potatoes, though the main purpose of the trip was to prove that a road could be built through the pass to connect Pemberton and Bridge River. Until about 1958 no road of any kind existed between the two communities, but residents of the mining towns who wanted a route to the coast shorter than that by way of Lillooet Town then started to build a jeep road towards the Lillooet River. Coastal markets remained the principal, though not the only, markets for Pemberton produce.

After 1934 the Board of Trade was less involved with production and marketing. In that year a resolution supported by all grower members asked for the formation of a separate growers' association which would use the "Snowflake" sacks to be obtained from the Board of Trade. Furthermore, the Board's inspector would inspect all potatoes and turnips shipped, charging 25c a ton for inspection. By July 1936, if not before, marketing of Pemberton turnips and commercial potatoes was under the control of the British Columbia Coast Vegetable Marketing Board. At that time Board of Trade members protested what they considered an unfair levy against Pemberton growers, and two years later those attending an open meeting elected Ed Ronayne and Purden to represent them at a court of revision concerning a quota system "to be imposed on the potato growers of the Pemberton district", a quota to be fixed by the Coast Vegetable Marketing Board. The farmers decided to ask Hudson Harvey, Limited, potato brokers, the Minister of Agriculture, and George Murray, MLA, to attend the court in support of the Pemberton delegation. When Ronayne and Purden returned they reported that Murray and the Minister had supported them well. By the solution reached, as long as Pemberton growers could "maintain a differential of not less than $4 a ton over the coast", the Board would impose no quotas.

Strenuous opposition to Coast Marketing Board actions continued. In 1938 growers did not want to be represented by anyone from Vancouver Island "who would not be conversant with conditions." The next year the Growers' Association asked the Interior Vegetable Marketing Board that Pemberton "be included in that Board's scheme." In 1944 each marketing board held a meeting with Pemberton farmers, but Pemberton eventually joined the Interior Board.

Through the years Pemberton growers met many times to discuss the growing and marketing of potatoes and sometimes of turnips, but these men were concerned about other commodities. In 1932 a cream cooler, a tank with One Mile Creek water piped in, was installed at the station, and Board of Trade members later sought "all possible information on the cost of establishing a creamery in the District." They wrote to the P.G.E. and pointed out the necessity of water in cattle pens "to prevent serious shrinkage in

Washing the cream separator

Tethering the bull

Working in heat and dust Provincial Archives, Victoria, B.C.

weight." In 1935 a letter to the railway requested "immediate action . . . in providing at Mile 1 hay racks, water and water troughs in the corrals." The year following, the railway not yet having acted on a promise made in 1934, the Board decided to write the Society for the Prevention of Cruelty to Animals about the appalling lack of facilities for animals in transit to Vancouver stockyards. At last the railway made the necessary installations.

Forty-year-old records give some idea of the concerns and triumphs of an earlier period, but do not give the day-to-day routine, of which both were an outgrowth, do not mention the regular seasonal work, sometimes in extreme heat or extreme cold, sometimes in deep snow, sometimes sloshing through flood waters. Viewed from the mountainside in the fall of 1939, the Valley seemed to be a series of interconnected lakes. Consider the almost general wetness of the land, the isolation, the marketing problems, and the mosquitoes: the spirit of the people and their accomplishments are amazing.

W. C. Green writing to his grandchildren

Dear Dorothy Anne and Dicky,

Dick and I were coming down the road the other day, when we saw something swimming in the slough. It made tiny little waves stretching out like a 'V' from a round black spot which was all we could see at the time. When it got close to the opposite side where the water was shallow, the little spot grew larger and pretty soon out crawled a little furry creature about the size of a partly grown kitten. You've heard of "Jimmy" Muskrat, who, by the way, is no relation to Honest John Muskrat. Well, he is the cutest little chubby fellow ever. Nearly as wide as he is long and a lot of ladies are in love with him. Some day your Mama will point him out to you on the street, but of course he won't look like the Jimmy Dick and I saw in our slough. There will be a little army of Jimmys all sewed together and dyed black and when you grow bigger and some of your girlfriends start strutting their "stuff" with a new Russian Seal coat, you can just stick up your nose and remind them they are only wearing a string of muskrat. However, if it is you who is wearing this shiny black fur coat, you can pretend it's real northern seal.

Well, Dick went on to the house because it was noon and as usual with him about this time of day, his stomach had started to holler, so he was going to pass the holler on to Mum, but I went down near the edge of the slough and watched the little fellow, for I was curious to know what he was going to do. He didn't pay the slightest attention to me and seemed to be just about as tame as Dopey, the squirrel. Jimmy, I saw, was hungry too. The water was a little too deep for him to wade so he seemed to keep paddling and hanging on to a branch. Every once in a while he would duck his head and up he would come with a long root in his mouth. His little jaws were working like a meat grinder and pretty soon the end of the root would give a little flip and disappear. Then down would go the head again for another helping. He was real polite and chewed with his mouth closed. So far as I could see, his was a one-course dinner and if he said grace I did not hear it or perhaps he didn't know one, just like a lot of us who should. He was still eating when Mum called me for dinner. He had finished and most likely was taking his after-dinner nap when Dick and I went up the road again, for we did not see him again that day.

There are a lot of Jimmy Muskrats in Pemberton and the trappers break up an awful lot of families with their traps every year. Jimmy and the Missus have the cutest little house built of sticks and mud with something soft like fine bark spread out for comfort on the parlour floor, which also serves as a sort of community bedroom. The house is built like a round beehive. It has two stories — the first one is underneath the water level with a little opening for a door. Jimmy and the kids have to come in that way and dry their feet before they come upstairs, for Mrs. Muskrat is very particular about keeping her parlour dry. I suppose if she had a vacuum cleaner she would use that as well. As I told you, the meals are mainly roots and these they can gather under the water — even under the ice. Very often Jimmy builds himself a little storage house close to the living quarters, where he can store a good food supply in case of a very cold winter, which freezes the ice down to the bottom of his root field. Old Man Winter sometimes can effect quite a blockade against the little animal folks when he turns on the freezer too much. When Jimmy and the family go to bed they all sleep in the same bed and snuggle up against each other. If you could peek in they would look like a one-piece fur blanket. Sometimes Jimmy and the Missus have little holes in the roof of their house, which acts like a sleeping porch in the summertime. There Mama Muskrat puts the babies to sleep. Sometimes the muskrats make the holes too large, and Hi-jacker, Blacky the Crow, glimpses the babies. Then this gangster swoops down and snatches the babies one at a time and flies them off to his nest to feed his babies high up in some tree. Poor Jimmy can't seem to do anything about it, and even the trapper gets sore, for he won't catch so many "rats" to sell for "seal" coats. But Mr. and Mrs. Muskrat usually have quite a few babies during the summer, and next time the babies arrive, usually six to eight, Mama Muskrat sees to it that they are hidden away from the sharp eyes of Blacky the Crow.

Lovingly,
Grandpa Green

New Settlers, the Green family — Provincial Archives, Victoria, B.C.

EARLY SCHOOLS

Before the construction of the P.G.E., for both parents and children schooling had been an extremely difficult problem. Some parents taught their children, and the children of the settlers seem to have become literate. Fifty years before rail service one family had solved the difficulty by sending a small daughter to her father's home in Scotland. Others, too, left the Valley. From 1904, when she was about seven until she was nearly thirteen and moved to Vancouver, Clara Ryan had lived and worked on the Ryan farm. Although she describes her "Pemberton education" as poor, she overcame her handicap, and later wrote exceedingly fine accounts of her early life. When he was eleven, Jim Dermody followed the Squamish-Pemberton Trail to the coast, and from Vancouver travelled by train to school at Phoenix, B.C., where he had lived as a young child.

A family on the Portage found still different ways to educate its children. For about two years before the first local public school opened its doors, the Spetch School at Owl Creek had been accommodating the younger daughters of the family, and a teacher employed by Samuel Spetch. Both Molly Garvin and Gladys Blakeway taught there. The second Spetch solution to the education problem came after mails were arriving by P.G.E. Through the four or five months he argued the need for lessons by mail, Spetch sent letter after letter to Victoria, the first going direct to the Premier, the Honourable John Oliver. At last the Superintendent of Education promised help. In 1919 Elizabeth, Muriel, and William Spetch became the first three students in the Correspondence Branch of the British Columbia Department of Education. The father's persistence in demanding education by mail finally persuaded the provincial government to set up what has been described as "the oldest and largest system of correspondence education in Canada."

When the first trains began to run, just a few Pemberton families within walking distance of the school site had children of school age. Among them were the Jack Ronayne family, the Punch family, and the Dermody family. Not until the arrival of the Ross children, in the spring of 1915, were numbers sufficient to establish a classroom. The first school trustees were George Thompson, Edwin Harris, and Jack Ronayne, who was secretary of the Board. Near the end of August, when the teacher was expected to arrive, the men of the community were still working on the school building, using lumber from Perkins' mill. Like most rural school boards the local trustees had chosen the teacher on the basis of her letter of application.

Pupils drilling, 1916 Provincial Archives, Victoria, B.C.

On August 21, Jack Ronayne drove his horse and vehicle about eleven miles to meet the new teacher, Christine Lanoville, who was arriving on the train. To the girl from Lulu Island, the trip with the Secretary of the Board must have been alarming. With the rivers and creeks high Ronayne had lots of trouble on "the floating corduroy", but horse and driver negotiated the hazards along the way and delivered Christine to her boarding house not far from the unfinished school building.

On August 25, 1915, Pemberton Meadows School opened in Hessions' house, but pupils were dismissed early that day because Jack Ronayne was putting their desks together. His later diary entries tell of continuing to work at the nearby schoolhouse and, on September 25, of "changing the desks into the new school". He set up the stove, hung blackboards and maps, and "split shakes for the school woodshed". Shortly before the Christmas holidays adults and children gathered for a "celebration at the school house", and all had "a very merry time".

Through the years the same men who had built the school looked after the necessary repairs, and made sure there was always a supply of good dry firewood. During the summer, mothers scrubbed and cleaned the building. None, or few, received payment for these contributions to the community.

The restoration of the Pemberton school will allow people to compare early and modern buildings and facilities. The lumber floors of the first schools soon became rough, adding to the difficulty of sweeping out the silt carried in on everyone's feet. Sometimes a sweeping compound was used to reduce the clouds of dust that rose every night after school, or to control the dust for a longer period an energetic adult might spend part of a weekend scrubbing and oiling the floor. Desks fastened to the floor made sweeping difficult, but only after years of this inconvenience did someone think of fastening desks to runners. Then desks could be shoved aside, not only to clean the floor, but also to make room for games during zero or stormy weather.

Each morning before school the teacher or a pupil carried in a pail of water. Colin Nicholson looked back forty years: "We had to go down to One Mile Creek to get a bucket of water. We'd find fish there, and we'd try to catch them. We were sopping wet when we got back to the school, and we'd tell our teacher, 'We fell down, and the water splashed all over us.' But we had caught a fish!" Then the pail of water would be set on a little shelf. Wanting a drink, or a bit of relaxation, pupils would take the dipper from its nail and drink their fill, then probably open the outside door to dispose of any surplus. Sanitation-conscious teachers tried to provide individual cups for the children, but years elapsed before paper cup dispensers were common.

Because funds were short, school boards could buy only limited supplies. They provided foolscap for examinations, multi-coloured construction paper, ink, glue, and chalk. Most schools had a set of wooden objects for standard drawing lessons and, often laboriously, pupils drew the sphere, the cylinder, and the pyramid, then shaded in the shadows they cast. Books other than texts were mainly for reference. Pemberton Meadows School had a strap, and John Ronayne claims the distinction of its being used first on him when Vivien Ross hit him with a snowball, and he said "Damn!"

No amount of restoration can restore the special smell of an early school. Chalk has a distinctive smell. Without duplicating machines, and with up to eight grades in one room, chalk was in constant use, and if you mix the smell of chalk with whiffs of wood smoke, with the smell of spilled ink, of wet wool drying, of frozen sandwiches toasting at noon on the flat-topped heater, and of some body odour and, through all, the smell of that sweeping compound, you arrive at an approximation of the cozy community smell.

As each year wore on daily cleaning of the school became an increasing problem. In September, if the teacher seemed reasonably human, eager children would volunteer for the necessary jobs: sweeping, cutting kindling, bringing in wood, cleaning boards and brushes — all to be done after school was dismissed. Often money was lacking to pay janitors, and eventually the tasks became tiresome. In March of one of the early school years in Pemberton, the trustees met "re: refusal of children to sweep floor".

Oct. 22 Mrs J. Decker.
Mrs E. Ronayne
Oct 27 A. Fowler
Beatrice Girling.
Nov 19 Mrs J M Ronayne
Nov 28 Sidsel Gimse
Dec 18 W. G. Blakeway.
Jan. 13 Betty Decker.
19. Mrs E. Ronayne.
Jan 21 The Bishop of Cariboo
" Rev. W. B. [illegible]
Ernest Blakeway
March 2nd Christopher Girling
" 16. Mrs Ronayne
" 23 Betty Decker
" 24. Gladys Ronayne.
" 25. Irene Ronayne
26 Mrs. E. Cooper
May 1/31 A. J. Paul Squamish.
June 9, 1931. Irene Blakeway.
June 10, 1931. Mrs J. M. Ronayne
Ernest Blakeway.
June 30, 1931. Margaret Ronayne.

From Pemberton Meadows School Visitors' Book, 1930-31

When it was needed, usually the teacher lit the fire. In winter months, if classes were to start on time, with ink thawed, and children at their desks, the fire would be lit well before school opening; if not, pupils would stand for an hour or more, books in hand, close to the stove. One inspector, as superintendents were then known, arrived one morning very early at Pemberton Meadows School, even before the teacher. No kindlings had been cut to start the fire and, even worse, the axe handle was broken. That teacher's rating would suffer.

When Harvey Derrick took charge of lighting the fire on cold mornings for a young woman teacher at Pemberton Station, adult janitor service started at local schools. Not only did Derrick light the fire, but he also saved the water system, probably the first in any school between Squamish and Lillooet. To protect the water intake against the frost he packed cow manure around the pipe running up the outer wall of the building and wrapped the insulated pipe in potato sacks.

The school at the station had opened in 1929, the year a new Pemberton Meadows School was being built on Ronayne land. May Taillefer was the first secretary-treasurer of the Pemberton School, and Bertha "Bussie" Green the first teacher. Like Upper Valley people in 1915, people at the station were greatly involved in financing and constructing the new building. Bill Fowler speaks of these good-hearted old-timers, including the two carpenters, Oscar Johnson and Andy Anderson: "This is about how that school got started: all these men volunteered their labour, the lumber was bought, and they built the school." They were hammering away the morning school began, and Bussie Pomeroy still remembers the pounding over her head as she tried to lead in the Lord's prayer. Another opening-day difficulty was the lack of outhouses, but fortunately the school was nearly surrounded by bushes and trees.

The two schools developed a keen rivalry in sports. Colin Nicholson still happily explains how it started: "Somebody talked Mr. Wellington into putting up a cup to see if we could win it. I was captain of the baseball team. So I went to our teacher and said, 'Look, we've got to win that baseball game, because Mr. Wellington put the cup up for us, and we can't let it get out of Pemberton. I want the kids out of school for four days so I can coach them. I want them to come to school and then we'll go to the ballfield. We'll take our lunches and eat them there.' She agreed. We practised and practised. It was just like a regular school day for four days. Then we hit the field. We beat them forty to one."

A member of the defeated Pemberton Meadows team, Bill Fowler, recalls the triumphs of his school: "We'd put boots out on One Mile Lake for goals and have hockey games there with the Pemberton School. Most of their skates were railroad spikes pounded out by Axel Johnson to fasten to the bottoms of their boots. But, in the Upper Valley, we had the Boys' Club; they bought us all skates. We beat Pemberton at hockey."

Bill speaks, too, about out-of-school fun. "In those days we were going to school, there was no problem in finding something to do on Saturday or Sunday, or any time. We would have to milk the cows. Then we could go fishing, or, in winter time, slide down the sidehill on a deer-hide. In the spring we might get on a chunk of ice, float down the river, and get off on the other side. We even built a club house. One building we put up, my brother and I, was a log cabin built out of cottonwoods. I think the door was about two feet high. We would make ice cream there, or boil some eggs — maybe got from a neighbour when he wasn't looking. Sometimes we would go up to Blackwater Lake or Tenquille. No one put on anything to entertain us. We had all kinds of things to do. Fred Ridley could play the mouth organ. Somebody would get some deer ribs and try to play like Red Mahan. The whole community could have a dance."

In 1922, seven years before Pemberton School classes started, men at Birken had held a "bee" and built a school. M. B. Pullinger was the first teacher at that school which continued in operation until 1944. Unlike many rural teachers most of those at Birken returned to their jobs for a second year, or for even a longer period. At one point the school closed and then re-opened for several years in a new building before closing again. Before the second opening, the first log building, which still stands near Birken Lake, had been remodelled as a teacher's residence.

In the 'thirties two more one-room schools were built, one at Mount Currie, and one at Alta Lake. For the Department of Indian Affairs, a Vancouver contractor constructed the first section of the Mount Currie School which was then called the Pemberton Indian Day School. For the first time parents could keep their families together instead of sending their children away to residential school. Until the 'fifties, when Indian Affairs increased facilities, that one classroom served the Reserve. Close to the main road, the building contained a teacher's residence in which the first to live were Joseph Barre and his wife.

After about twenty years the Mount Currie School gained a second building, this one containing classrooms and a residential section. In 1948 Sister Mary Immaculata and Sister Mary of the Redemption, missionary Sisters of Christ the King, joined two lay teachers, Preston McAskill and Mary Gronseth. A year later the Sisters took charge of all teaching duties at the Indian Affairs school and continued in charge through 1966 and later.

Among many pupils continuing from Mount Currie to secondary and post-secondary institutions, Mary Louise Williams, a scholarship winner, was the first to become a teacher, and after working in provincial schools returned home to teach. Even before her the Department of Indian Affairs had assigned native teachers to Mount Currie, two young women from the Interior.

In order to attend high school, until 1958 local Indian young people went off to study at such places as Mission, North Vancouver, and Williams Lake. Then in September 1958 four of these students, Delphine Peters, Normaline Ritchie, Rosaline Peters, and Billy Williams, enrolled at the Pemberton Secondary School, travelling from their homes by Howe Sound District bus. The number of Indian high school students increased year by year, to eight in 1959-60, twenty-three in 1960-61, and sixty-two in 1965-66. In the mid-'sixties the total number of Mount Currie students attending local provincial schools grew considerably. Because of lack of accommodation on the Reserve, pupils in grades six and seven registered at Signal Hill in Pemberton.

In November 1932, temporarily in an old hotel, a school opened on the west side of Alta Lake. The hotel had been built down at Cheakamus during railway construction and then, when rails reached Alta Lake, the building had been moved up there. Because few residents of the small community were land owners, few could qualify as school trustees, but the three elected, two old prospectors and Myrtle Philip, were people of great energy. With the help of their friends, they built a structure that would accommodate children during school hours and the whole community at social functions. Recently the Howe Sound School Board constructed a fine new building on the other side of Alta Lake, a building which will also serve as both school and community centre, and very fittingly the Board on which she served so well and for so long has named the school for Myrtle Philip.

Everyone who has lived in a rural area knows that the school Christmas concert can be a highlight of the year, and for many years Pemberton area people have enjoyed watching their children perform. Probably because the first Pemberton Meadows School was not very large, some concerts were held in the nearby log clubhouse of the Boys' Club, and Club minutes refer to members' plans for Christmas concerts. In 1926 the men planned that "Cy Keyes fill the role of Santa", and that "boxing be indulged in at concert". The 1928 program included "King's health, school items, recitations by children, prize giving, also items by Doc Souaillard, E. Gethen, and C. A. H. Johnston." In 1937, if not earlier, both Valley schools combined and presented their concerts in the same clubhouse.

Despite the limitations of the little schools, many children enjoyed and profited by their school days because teachers seemed to make up for lack of experience by interest, ability to improvise, and hard work, and their pupils usually went on to successful careers. What is more, teachers and schools were part of the community and many teachers formed lifelong friendships. Young women teachers coming into a population with a disproportionate number of young bachelors were instant objects of interest: men would wait at the station to appraise them as they descended from the train. Some rivalries developed. On the old road along the Rockslide, Battle Creek was allegedly the scene of a fight between two young men interested in the same schoolmarm. As might be expected, some of the female teachers married and became part of the permanent population. The schools were clearing houses for notices of coming events, and evening meeting places for adults. Each of these centres was a valued addition to the life of its community.

PEMBERTON MEADOWS SCHOOL CONCERT PROGRAM FALL OF 1921

1. Song, Misses Punch, Dermody and Green
2. Song, Mr. B. Markham
3. Recitation, Dr. Souaillard
4. Piano Solo, Mrs. Girling
5. Song, Mrs. Punch
6. Song, Mr. Bert Brennan
7. Action Song, Miss Bertha Green and Chorus
8. Song, Dr. Souaillard
9. Song, Mr. B. Brennan and Chorus

Pupils of Pemberton Meadows School, 1933-34 Provincial Archives, Victoria, B.C.

SCHOOL NEWS

PEMBERTON MEADOWS SCHOOL NOVEMBER FIFTH, 1934

Staff

Betty Ronayne — Editor-in-Chief
Elaine Waddell — Literary Editor
Anita Ronayne — School Reporter
Edith Fowler — Valley Reporter
Fred Ridley — Sports Reporter
Ann Fraser — Sixth Member
Business Manager — Billy Fowler

****

Editorial

This is the second issue of our paper. Every month we change our staff, and this time we have seven members. The new member is the business manager.

There will be quite a lot more in the paper this time, as we had a Hallowe'en party on Wednesday. We hope you like our paper.

****

School News

The rope of the ventilator came loose the other day. Don went up on a pole and fixed it. The rope goes through a pulley which should be fastened with a wire, but Don had to fasten it with a rope. When he was coming down he slipped on the wet roof. It made us laugh, but was not so funny for him.

The football went down a hole today, and was rather hard to recover. It was finally recovered.

Don went through the dividing fence today, by accident. He skinned his knee. The fence was repaired.

****

Valley News

Mr. Erickson, who was trapping on Mr. John Arn's trap line, was treed by a grizzly bear. He stayed up in the tree for about an hour, and then sneaked to his cabin, to get his pack and rifle.

There was a lot of excitement last Friday when the Pemberton Trading Company store was burnt. From all reports very little was saved.

The Women's Auxiliary gave a dance in the club house last Wednesday.

The Count and Countess spent a couple of days in the Valley. They took Mrs. Taillefer back with them to Chilliwack.

Looking up Barbour's Draw

WORK IN THE WOODS AND MOUNTAINS

Not all Pemberton settlers were farmers, and for one reason or other many people worked not on the land, but in the woods and mountains, those areas which were also the holiday haunts of Pemberton settlers. "Uncle Jack" Ronayne conducted more than one generation of children on climbs that took them to the surrounding peaks, and on rambles that led them to lakes ringed with jewel-like flowers and alpine evergreens. And the children grew and ranged at will through all the lovely mountain country. Their summer pleasure grounds, though, were also the haunts of trappers and prospectors.

For some men in the area, trapping wild animals has been a good way to earn extra cash. Edith Perkins says that in 1927, when she settled in the Valley, bachelors were prospectors in summer and trappers in winter. Outnumbering present-day trappers, former trappers often speak of life as it was up the rivers and creeks. Other men lived at home and trapped. Trap lines ran through such areas as McKibbon's Swamp, now an expanse of fields above Ryan Creek bridge, or through the swamp that, reclaimed, is Gilmores' farm, or through the McKenzie Basin. Farmers like Jake Lokken, John Arn, and Morgan Miller trapped in these former wet spots for muskrat and beaver.

Trappers going up the Lillooet in the fall would have supplies of canned and dried foods, sugar, tobacco, and matches packed by horses, maybe to the Headquarters cabin close to the junction of Meager Creek, the South Fork, and the main Lillooet, the North Fork. Once, two men made their way up to the Forks, confident that not many days behind a packer with his horses was following. While they waited one shot a deer and cut the meat into strips and left it hanging. When more than two weeks had passed they became alarmed about the packer and decided to look for him. To their astonishment — and displeasure — they found him still in Pemberton, not yet ready to leave. On their return with the pack train to Headquarters they had one source of satisfaction: the strips of venison were by then perfect jerky. Food packed up from the settlement was generally supplemented with venison, the occasional

Crossing Meager Creek

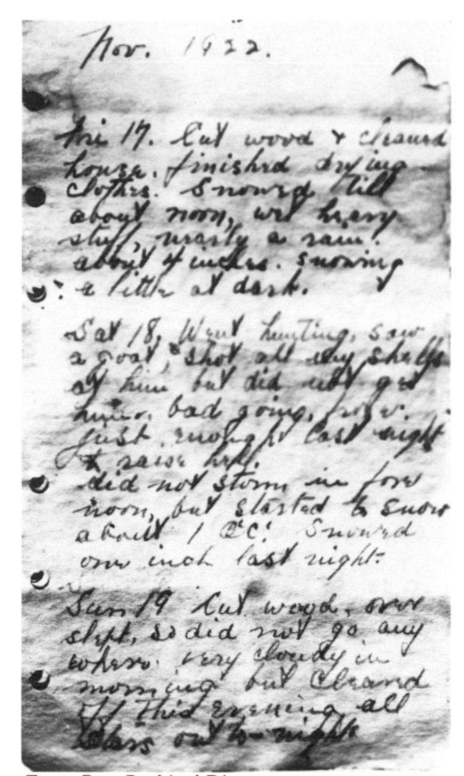

Nov. 1922.

Fri 17. Cut wood & cleaned house, finished drying clothes. Snowed till about noon, wet heavy stuff, nearly a rain. about 4 inches. snowing a little at dark.

Sat 18, Went hunting, saw a goat, shot all my shells at him but did not get him, bad going, snow. just enough last night to raise hell. did not storm in fore noon, but started to snow about 1 [illegible] Snowed one inch last night.

Sun 19 Cut wood, over slept, so did not go any where. very cloudy in morning but cleared off this evening all stars out to-night

From Bert Perkins' Diary

fish, and sometimes ice cream made by stirring snow into canned milk, then adding sugar and flavouring.

After establishing themselves for the trapping season the men would spend several weeks on their lines and then come down for a Christmas break. On snowshoes they might travel from Headquarters to Hamills', a distance of about twenty-five miles, in a little more than three hours. After selling the furs they had packed out with them, they would return to their cabins and stay until May.

Several women went with their husbands to the trap lines. One was Edith Perkins. At that time she usually wore riding breeches and high laced boots; she braided her red hair and wound it around her head. With her husband, more than once she summered at the Forks and, about 1928, planted a garden there. Beginning about 1940 both Kathleen Lundgren and Phyllis Erickson also went on what seemed daring expeditions into the wilds. After one Christmas holiday, when the Lundgrens were ready to return upriver there was so little snow that a friend was able to drive them in a truck as far as the deserted Hamill house. After they had lighted a fire and brewed coffee, they struck off on snowshoes, heading for their headquarters forty miles up the Lillooet. The river being low, they travelled for miles on sandbars and, without too much difficulty, forded when necessary.

Phyllis Erickson found the trapper's life to be a hard one. She did not mind crawling through brush or walking for seven or eight hours a day on snowshoes, but she did mind the monotonous, limited diet: "I never did like beans." Beans, macaroni, and rice were the staples. As the years went by, as the road became "just a little bit better", the Perkins family freighted in supplies for the Ericksons. Dried fruits were more varied, Phyllis Erickson says, and her husband built a small root house in which they stored vegetables from their farm. Each spring, green leaves brought hope, and the couple "cheered up".

Leaving the comparative isolation of Pemberton, with its twice-weekly trains, people like the Ericksons were almost completely isolating themselves. Seemingly no one died as a result of illnesses or accidents on the trap lines, although anticipating a severe attack of appendicitis one trapper carefully plotted the stages of the operation he would perform upon himself.

Edith Perkins describes an experience in October 1931 when she and her husband had summered at the Headquarters cabin. As in 1975, a huge section of mountain slid into Meager Creek. The river rose "Three feet in three minutes" and driftwood filled it "from bank to bank". This raging lasted "five minutes by my watch". Bert Perkins said it looked like an "old-time river drive", and though Edith had never seen an old-time river drive she did know "the scent of alpine timber . . . and the air was full of it".

"The river dropped to normal, but half an hour later rose higher than before. We could see the rise this time — two distinct elevations, like broad porch steps. It swept across the bar, jammed the creek near our cabin, and backed up all over.

"By this time we were out of doors, and my husband worked to clear the jam in our creek. I watched him from the bank. He was still working, but his back to the river, admiring his handiwork, when I saw the third wave coming. 'Get out!' I shouted. He showed his manly independence by dancing a jig on the footlog. I screamed and pointed. He looked behind him and he moved — rapidly. As his feet hit the bank, a rush of water carried the log away. My hair has never flattened!"

Usually trappers spaced their cabins about a day's hike apart. Some confusion overtook the men of one partnership when, after building a cabin, they sallied forth with their tools to build a second one. They followed a twisting track which at intervals almost turned back on itself. On and on they plodded, with the tools becoming heavier on their shoulders. Finally they found a likely site and built their second cabin. They realized later that, as the crow flies, they were only two miles from their first, but when they eventually quarrelled and decided to live apart they found uses for both structures.

The Hotsprings cabin on Meager Creek had the special advantage of naturally warm baths, but also a special problem. Because of the humidity and the warmth, articles left in that cabin would mould or rust, and before leaving in the spring, trappers always therefore hung all their gear and furnishings, including the stove, in the surrounding trees, so that air could circulate around everything.

One trapper had a surprising fear of being attacked at night by ferocious wild animals. To safeguard himself he drove spikes close together around the foot and the outer side of his bunk, and then filed the top off each spike to create rows of sharp, protruding barbs to impale any attacker. Men still talk about another trap-line oddity: big Red Mahan's tiny cabin. At night, well before bedtime, he let his fire die down until his stove was cool enough to handle. Then he moved it outside. Only then did he have room enough to go to bed.

The trapper's main interests were marten, weasel, muskrat, and beaver. Only after a mink rancher at Alta Lake gave up a losing proposition and turned his animals loose were there mink in any number. Winter after winter, never varying, one man's line yielded him sixty marten, and during the depression each pelt brought $12, about twice the price it would bring forty years later.

More than once potential emergencies developed. In a blizzard, working on the Elaho River, which has the same headwaters as Meager Creek, one man thought he turned back to the cabin which he shared with another trapper. Finally, realizing where he was, he headed towards the Hotsprings cabin. There, by midnight, he lighted a "bug" made of a jam can and a candle, with a wire attached to the can to form a handle, and "bug" in hand he started off on the twelve- or fifteen-mile hike to the Elaho cabin, which he reached before daybreak and where his partner was waiting until dawn before going to look for him.

At night in the cabins, besides cooking their meals, men had to skin and stretch their catch, maintain their rubber hip boots and their snowshoes in good condition, and wash and mend their clothes. Of course some of these jobs could be delayed until weather forced the trappers to stay in their homes, but one meticulous housekeeper among them had a regular routine for washing dish towels, of which he had twenty-three. At the end of three weeks, he would wash the towels, boil them in lye water, and then rinse them many times before hanging them to dry. No other man could be trusted with that job. Sometimes snow fell for days on end. Then trappers read by candlelight the well-worn magazines they had read the year before. They would play crib or poker. They might try to get reception on a crystal radio set, but so rarely with any results that batteries lasted a long time.

Year after year, the trappers returned to the upriver areas. Keirstead, Perkins, and Tom Greer trapped up there early. In 1929 Perkins' trap line extended along the main Lillooet from some distance below Meager Creek, and Oscar Johnson was on Meager Creek itself. In that year Anderson, who already had a line in the general area, and Slim Fougberg took over both the Perkins and Johnson lines. In 1931 Perkins returned to trap with Fougberg. Lundgren worked with Slim in 1938-39, when they travelled across to the

Elaho River, the waters of which flow into the Squamish. Cy Keyes trapped in the area of North and South Creeks, but not above them, and on Keirstead Creek, and part way up Railroad Pass. Henry Erickson took over his line. John Arn worked in the pass above Keyes, up Donelly Creek, and on the Hurley River.

Trapping was obviously of economic importance to the area. The Pemberton and District Board of Trade, whose members included some trappers, as well as loggers, prospectors, farmers, and business men, decided to investigate financial returns from trapping, and the records show that during one year in the 'thirties fur shipments brought $15,000 to the Valley.

In Pemberton summer is the only season for prospecting, and when summer came some trappers and others made their way into the mountains with specialized tools for investigating possible ore deposits. For many years, from the early days of settlement until the present, men have prospected in the mountains surrounding the Valley and in the general area. To date, though, no mine has produced anything of importance.

C. E. Cairnes, of the Geological Survey of Canada, spent much of September 1924 investigating the area. After P.G.E. construction most of the prospecting had concentrated in the Boulder, or Ure, Creek, and Margery groups of claims, both close to the head of Lillooet Lake, in claims on Owl Creek, and in properties near the head of Tenquille Creek. At the time of Cairnes' visit the copper content of local mineral deposits was of chief interest.

The geologist reached the Boulder Creek properties by wagon and by boat. First he followed the Pemberton Portage Road from Owl Creek to the head of Lillooet Lake, and then crossed the lake to its western shore. The properties there had already been discovered in 1915 when Harry McCulloch came from Saskatchewan, and hearing of a mining boom in Pemberton, travelled up to a prospectors' camp on Lillooet Lake. With Tim Charlton, he staked claims somewhere on the lake. Two men from New York offered the partners $50,000 for their claims, $5,000 down, and the balance after diamond drilling, but McCulloch and Charlton refused to sell.

In 1924, when Cairnes investigated Boulder Creek, prospectors had staked thirty-four claims on both sides of the stream, and had driven tunnels on one group of claims. Since Cairnes' survey, prospecting has continued near Lillooet Lake. Tim Charlton trapped the Duffy Lake area in winter, and prospected around Lillooet Lake in summer, and sold his claims to Britannia Mining and Smelting Company. One manager from Britannia travelled behind horses to reach the lake and investigate properties.

In the 'thirties, when he and Paul Dick set out to prospect in the hills beyond Tenas Lake, Bill Spetch rowed a boat for the first time. At two, one summer morning they started down Lillooet Lake, and to take Bill's mind off the misery of rowing with blistered hands, Dick entertained him with many legends of the country. After rowing about fifteen miles, the two walked across the portage, paddled six miles down Tenas Lake, walked a mile or more, climbed the hills, and staked some claims. Many years later, Spetch wondered why they had not just gone over the Red Bridge and staked claims there.

Like the country close to Lillooet Lake, the Birkenhead Lake area, formerly the Big Blackwater Lake area, was explored long years ago, and again in the 'thirties. With the promise of fifty dollars a claim, one man hired out to do assessment work, the work required annually of each claim holder. Every day for two weeks he climbed up from the lake shore and worked at his job, but for his efforts he got neither grubstake nor pay. A few years later, a mining company hired a man with a pack train to freight lumber and tons of food up the newly built Sockeye Creek trail. When his job was done, the packer left for his home in Ashcroft, expecting to receive a cheque in the mail. But no cheque came because the company had gone broke. After trapping all winter to earn money to feed his horses, the man returned the following year to pack out provisions from the vacant Sockeye Creek camp, and all summer, while prospecting near D'Arcy, he and his partner lived on the food that had been packed up Sockeye Creek and down again.

Few have prospected in the vicinity of the Lillooet Glacier. In 1932, three prospectors, Anderson, Oscar Johnson, and Fougberg, searched that area. They travelled the river and mountain country on horses, skirting Meager Mountain which, a member of the Geological Survey of Canada says, erupted violently about 2,000 years ago. Forty years ago the mountain's great pumice deposits were of little interest. The men rode the length of Polychrome Ridge, but staked no claims.

Some men have been loners questing for ore bodies. Pete Petersen spent so much time prospecting on what is now the Sun God that the mountain became known as Mount Petersen. For long years Felix Sam searched for a lost gold mine. Every summer until he was old, he used to work up the creeks and rivers with common headwaters: the Soo River, Rutherford Creek, the Ryan River, and Copper Creek.

For several years before Cairnes travelled into the Pemberton area, few reports of local mining activity reached departments of mines. Then came news of further developments around Tenquille Creek, and in reports of his investigations the geologist gives most space to those properties. In 1922 and 1923 several local men worked near Tenquille: Sandy Ross and Jake Lokken, at Codman's Mine on Crown Mountain; Sandy Fowler, on the trail to the mine. When the snow receded far enough, John Jack climbed up to Wolverine Creek to maintain his claims. Al and Nels Fraser prospected far and wide.

In 1924, as now, two routes led into Tenquille, one from the Pemberton Valley, and one from the old 72-Mile stop on the railway, near "No. 10 Downing Street". Cairnes travelled both routes, but preferred the second. His first entry into the mountains was from above Taylors' ranch, where he crossed the river by canoe, then "negotiated" the steep seven-mile trail to "the divide overlooking the headwaters of Tenquille Creek''. He had followed the John Jack Trail which Pemberton residents were climbing when summer work allowed. They crossed the river at Fowlers', or farther up, then on foot struck up the mountainside, crossed Gingerbread and Johnny Sandy Creeks, and, near timberline, Wolverine Creek. The second route into Tenquille, from old Mile 72, follows the Birkenhead River and Tenquille Creek. It is about twice as long as the John Jack Trail, but has a gentle grade.

The provincial government maintained the route into Tenquille. During the First World War local men had built the John Jack Trail, the government paying part of the cost. Bert Perkins' time book shows that in 1926 and 1927 he was in charge of building and improving various trails in the area, the Barbour, Tenquille, Green River, Fowler, and Blackwater Trails.

Spasmodic work on the trails continued. Some years later, in 1934, the Pemberton and District Board of Trade requested a $250 Department of Mines allocation to improve the trail to Tenquille Lake. In September 1926, rebuilding the Tenquille Trail, Perkins had employed eight men, Nels Fraser, Stanley Jordan, James Punch, William Tiegen, Oscar Johnson, Sandy Ross, Sandy Fowler, and Roy Legge. Four of Nels Fraser's horses worked at a rate of $2 a day; Big Nell continued after each of the other three put in two half days. From Mile 72 H. P. Stubbs packed in powder, fuses, and caps. With wages ranging from $7 a day for the foreman to $3.50 a day for the lowest paid man, total expenses for September amounted to $575. A camp meal at that time cost 35c; both Vivien Lokken and Sarah Greer cooked at the trail camps. Working from Mile 72 as late as the early 'sixties, Ab Gramson removed windfalls and fallen rocks from the Blackwater Trail leading into Birkenhead Lake. About five or six miles up the hill from the railway tracks, a branch from the Blackwater Trail crossed a bridge over the Birkenhead River. From there it continued to Tenquille Lake.

Because Mile 72 was a take-off point for Tenquille, prospectors and developers built cabins there. Angus McRae, one of the early engineers on the P.G.E., said that Phil White put up the first building. At one time his partner was Tom Lewis who, unlike other men, carried a pillow when he struck off into the wilds. Others associated with Tenquille mines had cabins there, between the Birkenhead and the railway: Tom Moffat, Jim Black, and McConnell.

Before Cairnes' investigation, another geologist had visited the Moffat and White camp north of Tenquille Creek, but in 1924 Cairnes concentrated his attention south of the creek. He discovered that ''although facilitated by the open nature of the country and abundance of rock exposures'', prospecting had been retarded ''by physical difficulties, the cost of getting in supplies, and by the quantity of snow that covers the country at this high elevation for the greater part of each year.'' Among the properties he investigated were those belonging to Thomas Simington, John Jack, and Tom Lewis, to all of whom Cairnes gave special thanks ''for many courtesies''. He found that the

Packing to the Crown Mine

Crown group of claims included the high summit of Crown (McLeod) Mountain. Near the summit, at about 7,000 feet, was a large cabin, and from it "excellent trails led to different showings on the property." Miners had sunk two shafts. The report gives less space to the Copper Dome group of claims, the Wonder claim, and the Silver Bell and Gold King groups.

By 1929 most of the Tenquille Creek country had been staked. To hold their mining properties, men usually completed the $100 worth of work required for each claim. In the 'thirties a company including Lloyd Shore secured an option on John Jack's claims and hired local packers to transport lumber up the steep, twisting trail so that a camp could be built, but until after the Second World War the considerable activity of earlier years did not revive.

Long before the first prospector in the Pemberton area started his search for ore bodies, logging had its beginnings here. Working with hand-made tools to fell the trees needed for various uses, the Lillooet Indians were this area's first loggers. During the Gold Rush, builders of the thirty-three bridges between Douglas and Tenas Lake went to the nearby woods for the timbers they required, as did the builders of boats. Similarly, when building bridges, men working on the cattle trail of the 1870's used available timber. And, when finally taking responsibility for roads and bridges, the Department of Public Works used local materials too.

When travel was by trail, forest product use could be only local. Farmers felled the trees they needed to build houses, root houses, and barns, and to supply themselves with fence posts, rails, and firewood. According to all reports, P. J. Dermody was the first in the Valley to mill lumber. In a second house, one built after the first had burned, Jack Ronayne used lumber from Dermody's mill and from the hatchery mill, both of which were water powered. After Perkins bought Dermody's mill he cut lumber for both

Millers' and Hamills' houses. In April 1914 Jack Ronayne noted that "Perkins sent down some log rafts, two men on each."

What must have been the first mill in the area operated in 1905 on the Portage. With a contract to provide lumber for the fish hatchery buildings, Duguid and Hurley of Lillooet brought in a "23,000 lb. sawmill outfit". When they had completed their contract, they took the mill back over the route they had come.

In 1891, if not earlier, the provincial government had already granted the first timber licence in the Pemberton area. Through the years, outside interest continued in local forests. Diary entries of 1909 and 1910 tell that "timber men went down river" and "timber cruisers here". In 1912 Parkhurst and Smith, a couple more, visited the Valley. On the Portage similar surveys were proceeding. Two years before the railway reached the area a reporter for the *British Columbian* commented on "the continuous forest of pine, cedar, hemlock, and fir" which bordered the road from Anderson Lake "to the Indian rancherie". All of "this great natural wealth" the reporter believed would soon be accessible.

By 1918 Samuel Spetch operated a water-powered mill at Owl Creek, and there Basil Taylor bought loads of lumber for several Valley homes, including his own. Assisted by the Soldiers' Settlement Board, war veterans were building those houses. Not far from Spetch Siding, from about 1917 to 1920 some Hindus produced lumber at still another mill on the Portage. When he built his house close to Owl Creek, Douglas Adie bought materials from those men. The railway had made forest products accessible to markets other than local, but until the mid-'twenties few exploited the timber resources.

About 1921, when the Pemberton logging industry was still in its very early stages, a man by the name of Gauthier bought cottonwood from several farmers throughout the Valley. He had the logs pushed into the river and floated down to Lillooet Lake where men gathered them into booms which a boat with an inboard motor pulled down the lake on the next stage of their journey to the coast. Some of the logs were badly mangled as they ran the Skookumchuck Rapids. Some sank. But Gerald Ross, a long-time resident, believes that most of them reached New Westminster. Whatever the fate of the cottonwood, Gauthier did not repeat the drive.

About the time the depression following the First Great War had been overcome, a number of men came to work in the woods. Some hewed ties; some operated or worked in pole camps; some, in tie mills. Significant commercial use of our forests began with the arrival of these men, some who were transient, some who were to settle and work at various jobs.

About 1924 tie cutting began. Albert Bossy let contracts for hewn ties, which were considered to be longer lasting than milled ties. Homer Stockwell cut ties at the far boundary of the Ross farm, walking in every night to stay with Sandy and Gerald. Alf Ridley was working at the same place with a partner and living in a tent back in the woods. With their team the Rosses pulled the ties, still in lengths, out to a landing, where men sawed them into units meeting railway specifications. Most of the hewers were Scandinavians, including Lundgren and Erickson. Some men still suffer from the heavy jarring of the hewing.

While some men were hewing ties, others were working in the mills which produced cedar and fir ties, the fir for export. Bossy had three such mills cutting timber on several farms, with a foreman at each mill. He established his first on Hartzell's place, and later set up two at the Salmon Slough. Two were powered by gasoline motors, the third by a tractor. Even after the Second World War Bossy's rusted old mill motors could be seen among the greenery of second growth. Stockwell stopped hewing ties, bought one of Bossy's mills and set it up near One Mile Lake. Across the Lillooet, Jim Dermody and Cy Keyes operated still another mill. Bill Spetch traded his furniture for a small mill, and began to cut ties for the railroad. He bought timber in the Valley, and during the winter farmers hauled the logs to sandbars in the Lillooet. When the river rose in March the logs floated. To catch them Spetch put a boom across the river, first opposite Mitchell's, later at Morgan Miller's and then pulled the logs out of the river and up to his mill with his team.

Men who gave pole contracts included Bossy, Ronald Lucas, Churchill, and Harry Thompson, who moved to the Valley after his Green River mill burned down. Owners rafted many of the poles down the Lillooet to Harvey Nelson Hill, old Mile 60 on the railway, where men dragged the poles out of the river and loaded them onto railway cars. Using trailers behind their trucks, Bob Taylor and others hauled all poles that were not rafted.

Over on the Portage, loggers and mill men were setting up tie mills and pole camps. Harry McCulloch cut ties and poles in winter, raised chickens, turkeys, and fruit in summer, and "never knew what it was to be hard up". For years, Roger Dickey and his brother shipped poles, some of them from Owl Creek Siding. Their brother-in-law, Jack Sowerby, was later a sawyer in one of their mills. One man who worked for them there, and later settled in the Valley, was J. C. Collins. At Poole Creek Station V. Lloyd-Owen's steam-powered sawmill was another producer.

Besides attracting new settlers, the woods industries made work for those already here. Ernest Cooper and Jack Decker worked in the Valley tie mills; Bill Harding and Cy Keyes cut poles; Jay Mighton pulled poles off the hillsides with his team. Frances McCulloch and Vivien Lokken cooked at the camps. A sixteen-year-old immigrant took a temporary job in one camp, and every morning rode her horse to a little shack in a clearing, and set to work. Her European parents had not prepared her to be a camp cook, but Sidsel (Gimse) Ross remembered with gratitude the kindness of the men like Keyes, Cherry, and Gronseth who brought her vegetables from the farms, and fresh meat which, she supposed, came once a week from Lillooet. One man showed her how to make an easy and popular dessert — jello.

In 1929, several men, including John Ronayne, the Ross Brothers, and Carl Gimse, whose son arrived from Norway that year, bought new flat-deck trucks to haul ties. Others, among them Bill Logan and Henderson, freighted their trucks into the Valley, and moved in to haul. The fairly frequent passing of trucks up and down the Valley served almost like a bus service for people unaccustomed to travelling any distance from their homes except with horses.

As might be expected, the Board of Trade was interested in the forest operations. In 1932 that organization hoped to bring into Pemberton "a shingle mill, or any other business". The following year it recorded that "for the first time in the history of Pemberton the area had received no tie contracts, nor had contracts been advertised." In 1937, the concern was over payments for "ties cut under contract, it being deemed a hardship for the said contractors to wait for settlement after ties have been accepted."

For years the British Columbia Forest Service rangers from Squamish, and briefly from Bowen Island, inspected forest operations in Pemberton. In 1938 a cabin was built close to the tracks in Pemberton for summer occupancy by an assistant ranger. Then as now, forest fires in summer were frequent possibilities, but since the 'thirties, methods of fire fighting have changed greatly. One resident remembers being "on a fire" beyond the Birkenhead bridge, close to the Cariboo Road: Perkins was the cook, wages were twenty-five cents an hour, and each man was credited with sixteen to twenty hours a day. After a fire guard had been completed, the fire fighters were told not to put the fire out, but to "just watch the fire guard". In two weeks the fire had either burned itself out, or rain had drenched it.

Going Prospecting

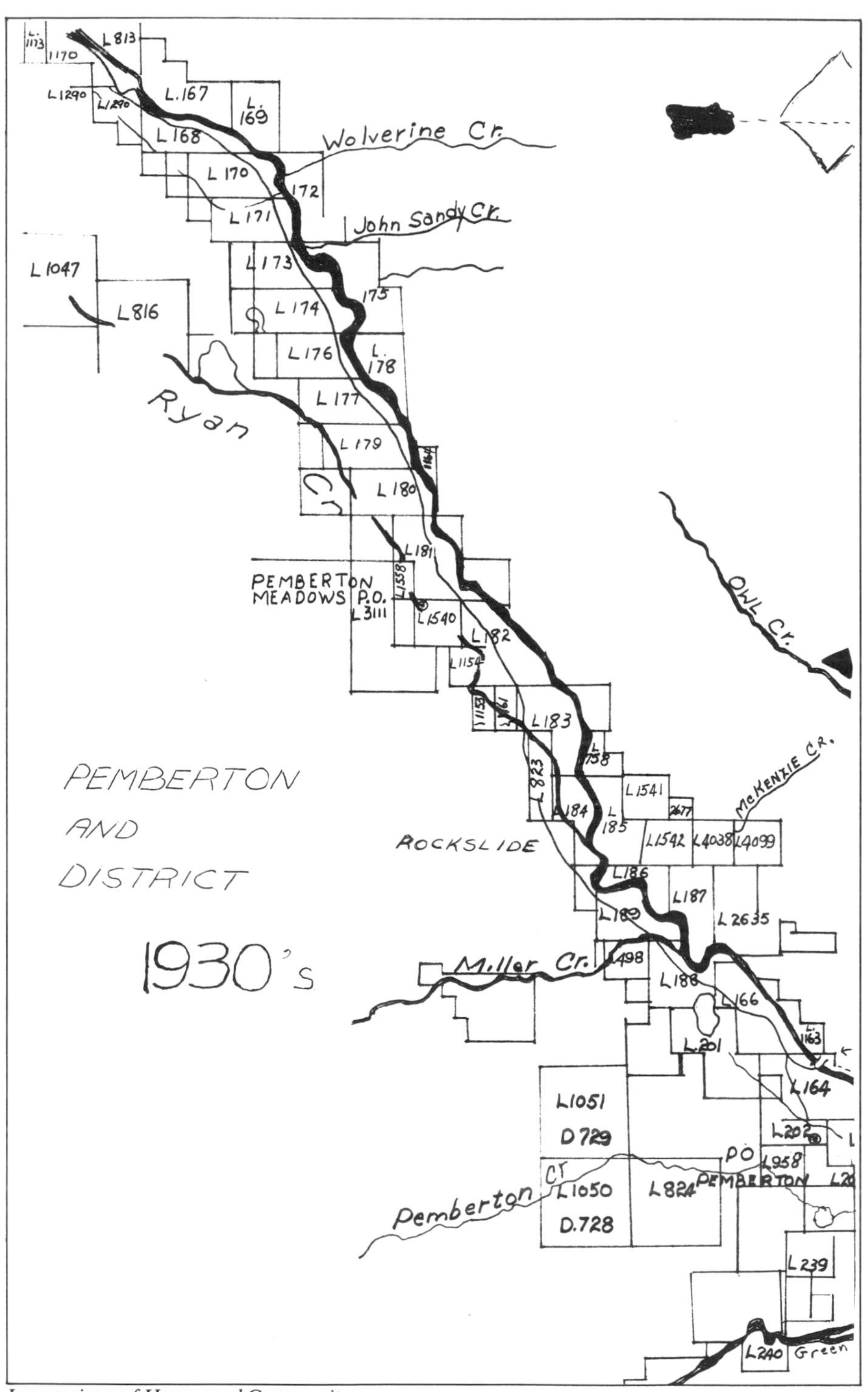
PEMBERTON
AND
DISTRICT
1930's
Wolverine Cr.
John Sandy Cr.
Ryan
Cr.
OWL Cr.
McKENZIE CR.
Miller Cr.
Pemberton CT
Green
PEMBERTON MEADOWS P.O.
L3111
ROCKSLIDE
PO
PEMBERTON
L813
L.167
L.169
L1290
L168
L170
172
L171
L1047
L173
175
L816
L174
L176
L.178
L177
L179
L180
L181
L1538
L1540
L182
L1154
L183
L823
L1541
L184
L185
L1542
L4038
L4099
L186
L187
L189
L2635
L498
L188
L166
L.1163
L201
L164
L1051
D729
L202
L958
L1050
D.728
L824
L239
L240

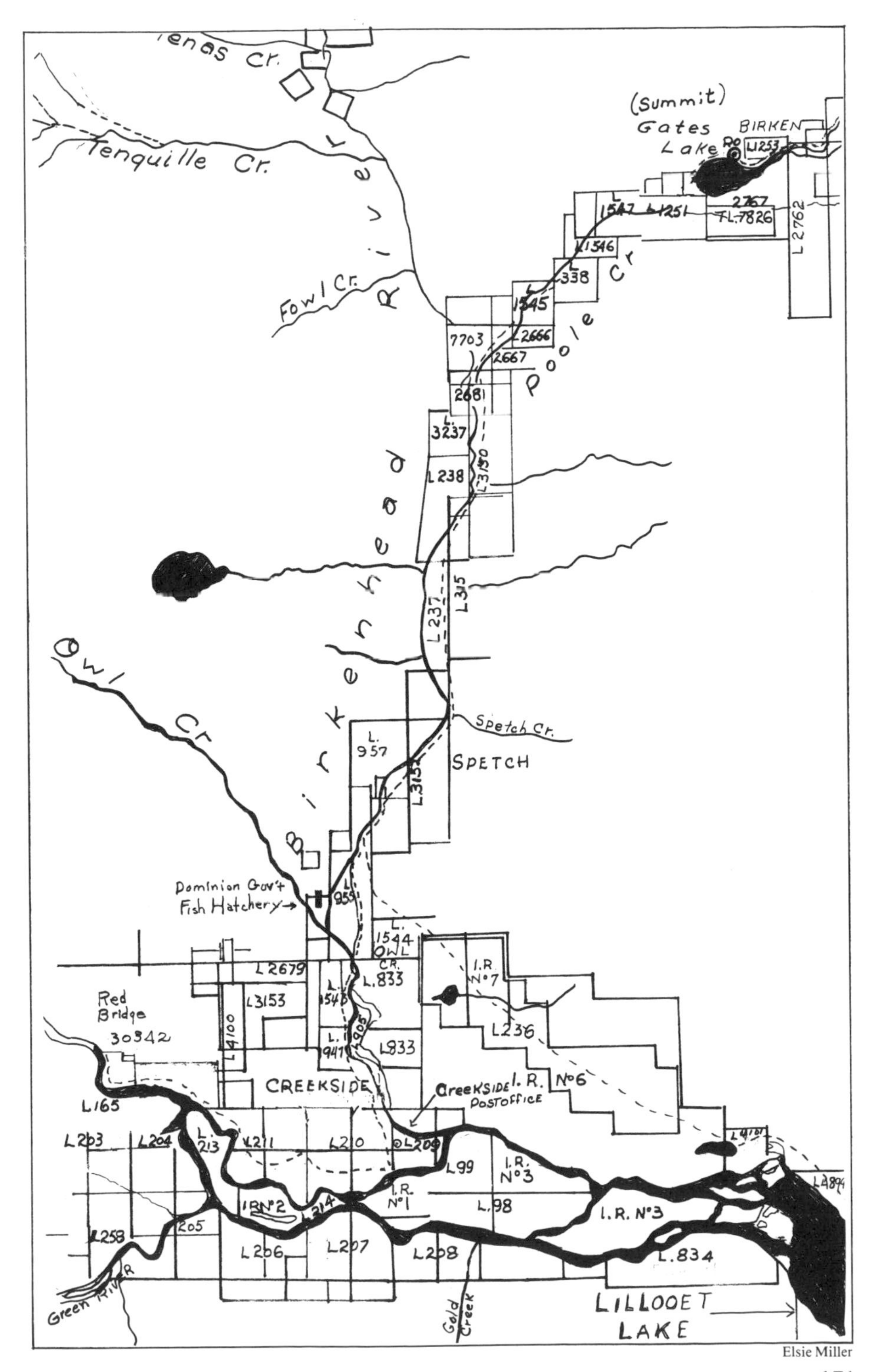

Elsie Miller

The Francis Joe family in June 1923

At Codman's mine, mid 'twenties: on horseback, from left — Anne Green, Rene Ronayne, Bussie Green, Lynn Green; others, from left, man from Lynn Valley, Roy Legge, Bob Taylor

IMPRESSIONS OF HOMES AND COMMUNITY

At almost any time in the early days Pemberton homes were prepared to receive as guests either friend or stranger, and in their warmth the hosts appeared to suggest that the visitor conferred the favour. The railway brought friends and relatives, even relatives of friends, more people than had ever travelled over the trail. In summer, if the number of visitors was too large for a home to accommodate, alternative sleeping arrangements could be made. Twenty-six years after a hike with friends from Port Douglas, a Vancouver woman wrote of "going on a milk truck to Pemberton Meadows and sleeping on the hay in a barn."

Frances McCulloch remembered fieldmen from the Soldiers' Settlement Board, muddy from tramping over Pemberton fields, arriving at her Owl Creek home. Above all, they wanted baths. She would offer to heat "a boiler of water" for them and her husband would bring water from the spring near the door. These guests would return evening after evening, and far into the night they and their hosts would play Five Hundred.

Two young men from Ontario spent the winter of 1923 in Pemberton. In 1967 one of them recalled some of their experiences: "Mr. Perkins, a former packer, at that time a successful hunter-trapper, used to invite us to lunch occasionally at his cabin in town. He was an excellent cook and I guess he thought we needed a good meal now and then. We stayed overnight with a couple named Fraser, who ranched successfully about a day's hike from town. The Frasers were the epitome of western hospitality, and I've never forgotten the few short hours that I enjoyed their acquaintance."

Beginning in 1915, the young people who came at the end of August to teach were usually strangers to the Valley and had to board with a family, and the farm women taking them in made their lives as pleasant and as comfortable as possible. In winter, in the early morning hours, though, when one studious teacher began to study, his room had lost any heat it had accumulated during the previous day from the heater in the living room across the hall, and he lay in bed, gloved hands clasping his book.

By 1929 the interiors of the homes were generally comfortable and attractive, the wooden exteriors usually unpainted because both time and money were scarce. The inside comfort was partly the result of settlers' ingenuity in making furniture, rugs, and bedding; partly the result of a much-improved freight service. Every kitchen had a black wood-burning stove, with a reservoir attached in which to heat water, and with two ovens, the baking oven below, and an upper warming oven heated by the stove pipe running through it. In the warming oven, cooks kept food hot for serving. Most kitchens had a long combined work and dining table, long because space was needed for family and guests and, sometimes, hired men. In general, families ate meals of varied and appealing foods. In summer, vegetables came from the garden; in winter, some from the root house. Women preserved vegetables, fruit, and meat in jars; and meat sometimes in brine.

At intervals families would still buy large supplies of staples. Every fall, Fowlers bought 800 pounds of flour, 150 of rolled oats, 200 of sugar, cases of dried apples, peaches, and prunes, a case of matches, and a case of 144 candles. The candle gave enough light for going to bed. Besides, in the days before flashlights were common, a candle was needed to make a "bug". With all their supplies stowed away, Bill Fowler says his family "didn't care if Bob Taylor of the PX never got up".

Until the late 'forties no Upper Valley home had a flush toilet, though the hotel and a few homes at the station did enjoy that, to most, unattainable luxury. Some homes without plumbing did have full-length bathtubs which were filled by hand with water taken from the pump at the kitchen sink, from the river, or from a well, and then heated. In having cold running water as early as 1918 the Spetch home was exceptional. Another source of water was melted snow: anyone who has depended on snow for a tubful of water has a little appreciation of the varying water content of different snowfalls. For most, taking a bath meant sitting in the round iron tub used for washing clothes. In winter people bathed close to the kitchen range, frequently at night, with the lamp blown, or turned, out. There, by the flickering light from the stove, the bather might enjoy a comfortable soak.

In the early 'thirties many homes had gasoline irons and women could, therefore, iron without a hot fire. Gasoline lamps and Aladdin coal-oil lamps were very common. With their mantles, both types gave brighter lights than earlier wick-model coal-oil lamps.

Even before the 'thirties some homes appear to have had dry-cell radios. In 1928, to raise funds for a Christmas treat for the children of the Valley, the Boys' Club raffled a radio, and planned a dance with music to be provided by a radio. Soon a number of Pemberton men were enjoying Saturday night hockey broadcasts. Some people like the Ed Ronaynes listened regularly to a weekly symphony concert, and invited friends to listen with them. While they listened, women would sit sewing, knitting, or darning. Hung from the centre of the ceiling, one lamp lighted the room.

When travel out of the Valley was infrequent, people were great visitors. In winter, after trails had been dug out, stock cared for, and roofs shovelled off, Doris van Beem recalls that "it was especially nice to bundle up well and take the team and sleigh down the valley to visit neighbours." For neighbours living above them, the twice-weekly mail days were visiting days at the van Beems'. To collect the mail bags in June and July, somebody in hip boots waded two miles down the road to where the mail truck turned, then waded back. Then all shared the news and, "yes, gossip, too!"

Living on the far side of the Lillooet River with two young children, Gladys Dermody had little opportunity of getting together with neighbours. Sometimes she would dress Jimmie and Joyce in their best and sit by the river bank while the children played in the sand and, with luck, they might see somebody passing on the road. On one Christmas Day, Gladys and Jim and Jim's sisters planned to cross the river and visit, but the ice was too thin to walk on, but so thick that it locked in the cable ferry.

Recently from Vancouver Sally Purden found life on a farm to be strange at first: "I thought that I would never get used to so few people around me because I had worked for five years in a large hospital. I never saw fewer than a thousand people a day, and when I came to Pemberton, if I saw two people a day, apart from the family, I was lucky. I was fortunate in making friends with the family who owned the hotel. One of the daughters [Rene Oman] was approximately my age, and used to come to visit me regularly. Two afternoons a week, when there were no trains, she could get away. That was what saved me from going completely 'wacky'.

"I looked after the chickens and I did some gardening, which was all new to me. I had to learn to make bread and make butter and all kinds of things. Prior to this time, I thought you just pushed a button and things happened. But I soon got used to it and didn't mind too much."

People without cars or trucks — most of the people — rode one of Bob Taylor's Pemberton Express trucks or a tie truck to visit the station. At the settlement they might visit, shop, or drink beer, or they might phone someone about some urgent matter.

In 1919 when Taylors needed a part for their car, one of the first in Pemberton, they used the P.G.E. phone at Pemberton Station. In 1939 the phone at Creekside was still at the siding, about one mile from the station. Eventually, using the railway's pole line, the provincial government provided a service, and by the 'forties Taillefer's store at Pemberton housed a government telephone though trying to use it could be a baffling experience. People to the north and the south might already be engaged in a long conversation, and then when the line was silent the first stage in reaching anybody was to crank persistently until the operator responded. If, finally, contact was made, whatever private matter was discussed was no longer private. Incoming calls were handled as well as possible. A chance car going in the right direction might take a note giving the message, or a P.G.E. employee might deliver the gist of the call. One husband had his shouted across the Lillooet: "Yer old lady's kicked the bucket."

When a football game or horse racing was to take place at Mount Currie, the population made communal use of obliging neighbours' trucks and cars. With a good proportion of the Valley's residents riding on the backs, the flat-deck trucks left early. All families brought large baskets or boxes of carefully prepared food — salads and meat, sandwiches, cakes, cookies, and pies — which was spread out on cloths on the grass and, with frequent urgings to try each specialty of each family, all shared the offerings. Especially for the men the football or baseball game between Indians and whites was the event of the day at Creekside. In 1955, years after he had left Pemberton for the last time, Father Victor Rohr wrote from Luxembourg about the "friendly Football games".

Ready to go Provincial Archives, Victoria, B.C.

Neighbours' cars or trucks, or sleighs in winter, took people to dances and card parties. Occasionally families like the Frasers, the Shantzes, and the Shores held dances in their own homes, but other parties took place in the log hall of the Boys' Club, built in 1925 on the upper boundary of the Green property. At the hall people played whist, the winning couple at each homemade table moving to the next, and people with top scores for the evening winning prizes, perhaps a knife and a handkerchief. One night when the card game was finished, in order to get warm everybody moved close to the big stove at the back of the hall. Thinking to make the fire burn hotter one man opened the stove lid and prepared to add a dash of coal oil. But he had grabbed an empty gasoline can. A loud explosion and a flash of flame! All but one player reached the door in record time and then looked back in embarrassment. The flames had disappeared, and a woman still sat beside the stove. The screw top of the four-gallon gasoline container had hit her on the chest and shocked her into immobility.

Bachelors, as well as families, invited friends to parties. In August 1934 the *Bridge River-Lillooet News* reported such an event: "Roy Legge entertained a supper party at his home . . . . The guests were Misses Tessie Ronayne, Kathleen Ronayne, Annie Green, Bertha Collins and Mr. Morgan Miller, Bert Lundgren and Leon Keyes. Among other things, Roy served his guests roast chicken, and beautifully cooked pie and hot biscuits. The rest of the evening was pleasantly spent at cards. . . ."

With an energetic orchestra dances in the hall could be nothing but lively. Ed Wilson plunked his banjo, Ernie Denver played the piano which was moved up from the station for the dance, and Bert Lundgren played his accordion. Another orchestra member was Red Mahan, maybe straight from the trap line, wearing hip boots folded down, a ribbed Stanfield undershirt, and heavy wool pants. As he vigorously kept time with a set of bones in each hand, his hair made a red halo around his head. Cornstarch sprinkled on the floor made it slippery, but rose as dust to whiten the men's dark shoes and pants as couples swirled and glided in waltzes, fox trots, and square dances. Small children lay sleeping on the benches while older people watched the dancers and talked. All were served later with sandwiches and cakes brought by the women, and with the coffee brewing on the big heater. Club rules banned liquor "or those under the influence".

Until about 1930 most gatherings took place at the Boys' Club, the only hall in the Valley. Then, using some of the lumber left over from the construction of the Kiltz store, volunteers built the Pemberton Community Hall next to the Pemberton Express office. Harvey Derrick, Lloyd Shore, and N. J. Baker were the first hall trustees. For its dance in April 1932 the Boys' Club planned to rent this building which, besides being larger than their own, had more facilities. It had a kitchen at the rear, and two cloakrooms, one on either side of the entrance hall. In addition, it had two benches built against the long walls of the main hall: with few exceptions, men occupied one bench; women, the other. In the fine new hall dancers could still swirl around, but here they had to avoid the big grayish cast iron stove in the centre of the floor, especially in winter when that stove was fiery red. Like other locals halls, this one had no plumbing. On dance nights, the Taylors next door good naturedly made their bathroom available to women and girls who came calling. The men were more independent.

In 1932 the Boys' Club began planning to replace their first hall. Known as the Upper Valley Hall, the new one was built on a corner of the Joe Ronayne farm. There the club had earlier established a skating rink and, in warmer weather, held various athletic events. Until the early 'seventies when it collapsed under a heavy weight of snow, this hall was the centre for Upper Valley meetings and dances, and in winter teachers took pupils there for a more active athletic program than was possible in the nearby school.

In 1955 Joe Taillefer summed up his recollections of earlier social life: "We had lots of good times. It was better than it is now. There was no booze." People had been particularly delighted when Ronnie Matthews, the blind pianist, had visited the Cowells, and had come to play at the first Boys' Club hall.

Many farm families and their friends enjoyed a special kind of recreation, the intense pleasure of summer-time trips above timber line. Jim Landsborough said that "The wild country was well explored every year between haymaking and harvest. Tenquille Lake (John Jack's cabin) became a summer resort." In the prospector's cabin or in a tent or under the sky, hikers slept well on carefully selected aromatic boughs. They got up early in the chilly air and ate breakfast, which might be porridge on an enamelled plate, coffee, homemade bread and jam. A 1923 photograph shows Gerald and Vivien Ross, Jack Ronayne and his daughters, Rene and Daisy, C. A. Hartzell and Jim and Norman Dermody. As some stood and others sat around a fire on a ridge above Railroad Pass, they were eating their breakfasts.

Adding to future mountain holidays Jack Ronayne started early to stock lakes with fish he brought in to Pemberton. From time to time renewing the water surrounding the fish, he would climb the mountains, following streams to the lakes. "In time," he said, "the lakes were stocked with Kamloops trout. Now Tenquille Lake and the Owl Lakes have an abundance of gamy trout for the angler and troller."

Going climbing

In *The Province* an account"In Memory of John Ronayne" summarized the experiences of generations of Pemberton residents: "John Ronayne acted as our guide, taking us up to 5600 feet in Wolverine Pass, with a drop on the other side of 400 feet to the campsite at the lake and for a week or two conducted us to Copper Mound, over Finch Ridge to Grizzly Pass and round the old mining trails to Silver Bell, Gold King and Li-li-kel.

"He entertained us all the way as he talked of birds and flowers, insects and fossils, interspersing his remarks with Irish wit and Shakespearian quotations.

"The children all loved Uncle Jack, for as soon as they could make the grade he took them up to Tenquille to catch the glory of the hills."

Exploring the mountains some people walked and climbed many miles. Returning through Railroad Pass from the Bridge River country, by mistake Robbie Miller and Ronald Ronayne followed the Hurley River instead of its tributary, Donelly Creek, and their mistake forced them to return to the Lillooet Valley by North Creek. Morgan Miller took a holiday hike from Bridge River into the Chilcotin country and returned by train from Clinton. Slim Fougberg and a companion followed the Bridge to its source, crossed the Bridge River Glacier, then branched down Salal Creek; next they climbed close to 8,000 feet in order to descend to Pebble Creek and Anderson's cabin. Reaching the Lillooet, they borrowed a boat from two prospectors, but the boat sank at a log jam, and left them to swim to the west bank. In 1932, with Perkins packing their supplies to timber line, Neal Carter, Alec Dalgleish, Tom Fyles, and Mills Winram, mountaineers from outside the Valley, thoroughly explored and photographed Meager Mountain. With his son John, his nephew Ronald, and with Landsborough and a friend from Vancouver, Jack Ronayne climbed Mount Samson, west of Railroad Pass. Later, cousins Clifford Ronayne, Ronie Miller, Eddie and Ethel Ronayne, and their friend, Jean Webster, climbed the same mountain shortly before Ronie enlisted to fight in the Second World War.

For many years the Boys' Club arranged out-of-door recreation in the Valley, the May 24 sports day being a highlight. For the first time, in 1930 the celebration included a baseball match between the two Valley schools. As usual, though, club members gave free treats to the children: peanuts, oranges, and ice cream. In 1932 the men bought vanilla, fifty pounds of coarse salt, and twenty pounds of sugar; somebody contributed cream. With four hundred empty cones to fill, the Fowlers took charge of making ice cream in Joe Ronayne's field. That day ended with a dance in the Lower Valley hall.

Some meetings, partly social, involved just a few women: Maria Punch, probably both Gladys and Annie Ronayne, and Teresa Miller. Each woman would hoist her small children into a wagon or a sleigh and drive off to meet at one of the homes. When the children were free of outer clothing and had settled down to play in an upstairs bedroom, and while dust sometimes drifted down from above through the floor where the children romped, the women

Going visiting

would start discussing the books they had been reading. Anyone who has visited the homes of these women will know that, besides fiction, their libraries covered a wide range of interests. Maria Punch's love of reading led her father-in-law to conclude that his first flashlight was useless — for three nights, Maria had taken it upstairs to finish reading an exciting book.

Several artists lived in the Valley and their special interests often took them out of doors to sketch or paint. Even on a raw fall day Pat Wilson sometimes sat and painted by the roadside. Rene Ronayne, who much later wrote *Beyond Garibaldi,* roamed the mountains sketching and photographing. Sigrid Gimse had painted scenery in several countries, but here she liked to paint portraits of her young dental patients and give the finished picture to the child subject.

In this generally harmonious community, some people, unfortunately, did break the law. Father Rohr wrote of Jack Ronayne, the Justice of the Peace who "administered justice" in the Valley, but who had "less to do than any of the J.P.'s in Lillooet town." Nevertheless, some problems among his neighbours demanded Jack Ronayne's attention. According to a Vancouver reporter, however, "Mr. Ronayne never accepted a fee for his justice of the peace work, which he carried on during his first forty years in the valley. He was known to walk many miles to hold court and would go out of his way on any occasion to perform his duties." Ronayne's diary tells of signing application papers for prospectors and land seekers, or for hunters wanting to collect a bounty on a wolf or a cougar. In May 1915 he went to bury a man at the Rockslide. Another time he heard a complaint from a man with a sore finger: a well-known farmer had allegedly bitten it.

Until about the time the hatchery stopped operations, Tom Graham served as justice of the peace at Owl Creek. He was replaced in 1936 by Harold

Wyatt-Purden, of Creekside, whose wife says that one of his greatest pleasures came from the fact that "his appointment took place under Edward VIII."

Workers in the woods incurred more serious injuries than did the man with the bitten finger. In the 'thirties, on a hill leading down to Ryan Creek, a runaway horse dragging a pole caught Stricker's leg and mangled it severely. Receiving a Workmen's Compensation Board settlement, the injured man returned to his native Switzerland. When another man broke his leg in a motorcycle accident, the Boys' Club arranged a benefit dance to "provide the Ridley family with the necessities of life in the way of food and light."

Even skilled and devoted nurses could not deal with all the medical needs. Dorothy Girling writes of "sickness or accidents which had to be dealt with without doctors within sixty miles. The hours of anxious waiting and watching when #2 had rheumatic fever — fortunately we didn't know it was that until the worst was over. The time Daddy came in from slashing on the back property across the slough as white as a sheet with a gash on the top of his head and no knowledge of what had happened . . . ."

Despite anxious ordeals of parents with sick children, and despite often low returns for what they sold, the bulk of the population appeared to lead serene lives full of interests and activities. During the widespread economic difficulties of the 'thirties, people lived off the land. During the depression, the ability to raise much of their own food, and the chance to pay land taxes by working on the roads insulated Pemberton people from the severe hardships many Canadians suffered. In that period Frances Decker's monthly grocery bill never exceeded $15.

Fun on Fowlers' Lake Provincial Archives, Victoria, B.C.

Flood aftermath at Girlings', about 1937

One of the cable ferries used to cross the Lillooet Provincial Archives, Victoria, B.C.

SERVICE INDUSTRIES AND ROADS 1914 to 1940

August 1933 Board of Trade Statistics

Width of Valley, 1 mile; length, 40 miles
Approximately 25,000 acres privately owned; 25,000 that could be settled

Population:	350 Indians, 700 Whites
Shipped in 1930:	2,000 poles
	26,500 ties
Shipped in 1932:	22,000 sacks root vegetables
	15 carloads of hay
Shipped yearly:	6,000 gallons of cream
	$15,000 furs
Stock in district:	2,000 head of cattle
	500 head of horses
Roads:	26 miles of local roads; 40 automobiles
Sawmills:	8
Mining properties:	7

Dominion Fish Hatchery
Hot Springs
Abundant water power

The 1933 Board of Trade statistics compiled for the purpose of promoting a highway to the coast outline the population and economy of the Pemberton area at that time, and any service industries had to draw revenue from those sources. For about twenty years the railway had been operating between Pemberton and Squamish, but Board of Trade members obviously believed that the P.G.E. had not sufficiently improved conditions. They wanted a road to the coast. Connecting with the P.G.E. rail link, the vital internal links were those few miles of local roads which meandered along with the river which itself meandered through the Valley and the inhabited parts of the district.

Without them industrial and commercial activity would have been impossible, for farms, mills, and stores depended on passable roads.

In 1919 G. M. Downton reported three good stores in the area: Wellington's, at Pemberton Station; the Pemberton Trading Company's, about one mile from the station; and Spetch's, at Owl Creek, near the Dominion Government Fish Hatchery. Operating there since 1908 the Spetch store continued to draw customers from the Portage and the Valley.

With experience in merchandising, Charles Wellington decided to go into business in Pemberton, and about the time the first trains began to run, George Stack and Oscar Johnson built a store for him. He lived upstairs, walking on creaking floorboards in the building that became part of the Pemberton Market. Wellington was "a guy with a big heart". For several weeks, until money arrived from the east, he let two young men from Ontario charge their food; for a playing field he donated "land in a pleasant cedar grove" across the tracks from the station. On June 3, 1933, community leaders celebrated his birthday by opening Wellington Park. His liking for people and his lack of suspicion probably led to the decline of his business for, according to the man who bought him out, "some people who worked for Wellington forgot to mark down their groceries."

In 1915 William C. Kiltz succeeded Frank Brokaw at the Pemberton Trading Company's store at Agerton. According to Bill Spetch, Kiltz erected the building there now, "plus the house and barn". The "building", the present Patenaude home, then housed both store and post office. About 1920, Kiltz asked Joseph Taillefer to work at the Agerton store. "Twice a week," Taillefer recalled, "I carried mail and groceries as far as Punch's, driving my own team." Taillefer later operated the store for Kiltz, and for so doing received a monthly pay cheque, a house rent free, and groceries wholesale. Then Taillefer extended the combined mail and grocery run to the Shaw place. Instead of going down to the Pemberton Meadows Post Office some people always found it more convenient to have their mail sorted at Agerton and delivered at their gates.

A cigar protruding jauntily from his lips, Taillefer himself usually presided over the store while his wife worked in the post office and in the boarding house they kept next door. At the back, farthest from the large front windows, the store was rather dark, but in winter, as Taillefer periodically flung back the hinged stove lid to throw in large chunks of fir wood, sparks lit up the shadows. And somewhere near the heater stood the cushioned swivel chair where the proprietor sat when business was slack. In the first month, when the store did only $90 worth of trade, business was at an all-time low.

Taillefer stacked the shelves behind the counter with canned and packaged foods. Boxes of dried prunes, apples, and fish stood on the counter, as did large jars of multi-coloured candies. Some glass cases held chocolate bars; others, cigarettes, cigars, packets of loose tobacco, plug tobacco, and snoose. Customers always stood at the counter to discuss what they wanted, and waited while the storekeeper assembled each order. Among essentials were tea, flour, and beans. Sacks of cattle feed set here and there made comfortable perches for the inevitable mail-night crowd waiting for the post office wicket to slide up.

A disadvantage of the Agerton store site was that Taillefer had to haul water to it. For that reason, about 1930 Kiltz told him to "pick out a lot at the station", and Taillefer chose the site now occupied by the drug store and its lawn. There G. O. McLeod, nephew of Alex McLeod, and a young prospector-trapper, built him a big new store with living quarters above.

A few years later, in October 1934, gasoline from a lamp dripped onto the newly waxed upstairs floors, and when May Taillefer lit a match "the lamp exploded". As Allan (Bud) Fraser reported in the *Pemberton Meadows School News,* "The stairs were burning so that she could not get down. She had to jump from the top window. Mr. Taillefer and Leon Keyes caught her when she dropped. The store was burning fiercely then. They saved all the tobacco and one of the show cases with candy in it. They also saved the safe, but they tried to pull it out when it was hot and warped it with the cable. One of the men turned the hose on it and the stamp books were all swollen. Mr. Taillefer had a carload of wheat and flour, which was also burned. They thought the community hall would burn down, too, because it was scorching. If the hall had caught fire the whole town would have gone."

Before many days May Taillefer was operating the post office in the community hall. Her husband bought Wellington's store and added to the building to make room for living quarters and a post office. Years later, in order to spend more time gardening at home and fishing at Blackwater Lake, Taillefer retired. His younger son, Warren, carried on the business.

A few years after Taillefer started working at the Agerton store, his employer, Kiltz, expanded by opening a business at present-day Mount Currie, then called Chilsampton and, later, Creekside. About 1922 he built his log cabin store across the road from the present church. Bill Spetch says that Brooks, the man put in charge of this business, was a former Hudson's Bay trader and was the first white man to live in Mount Currie. Joe Taillefer recalled that Brooks left Mount Currie to operate still another Kiltz store, this one at Bridge Lake, to which Taillefer sent groceries from Pemberton. The first Mount Currie store burned down, and after the fire Kiltz built near the Mount Currie Station. After Brooks left, Gerry Cowell ran that operation and would return to it twice. During his absences Fred Edwards, Bill Simpson, George Simpson, Fred Sweet and Walter Spetch operated the business.

At Owl Creek William Spetch took over his father's business and the post office in 1929 when Samuel Spetch returned to Birken to open a store. Bill Spetch says that trade at Owl Creek was good, with both hatchery and Valley people among his customers. In 1934 the *Bridge River-Lillooet News* called him the "Charles Woodward of Owl Creek". By trading beef for lumber,

Spetch was able to build a store which he expanded after the Second World War and which is now Mount Currie Foods. A few years after he had opened his business in Mount Currie, Spetch closed the Owl Creek business and moved the post office down to the new store.

In the 'thirties a store opened on the W. C. Green farm. In August 1934 a local reporter welcomed the news that "Mr. Cowell of the Lillooet Lake Trading Company's store at Creekside contemplates in the near future moving his family into the Upper Pemberton Valley and going into business for himself. Besides Mr. Cowell, there is Mrs. Cowell and bright little Master Roy Cowell. Mrs. Cowell's eldest son is Ronnie Matthews, the talented blind musician." Ronnie's younger brother, Jack, lived with the Cowells and in 1930 completed Grade 8 at the Pemberton School. Gerry Cowell set up business in a log building later moved up the road to form the first section of the present W. C. Green home.

The barbershop

Another store established in the 'thirties was the Log Cabin Store built on the corner now occupied by the south end of the Pemberton Hotel. Mr. and Mrs. Joseph Prendergast were the owners of this store with its unique feature — a barber's chair. Prendergast was the area's first licenced barber. Previously everybody had relied for haircuts on relatives or friends.

To storekeepers, in fact to all residents, the sometimes uncertain condition of the roads was a constant concern. "In the old days before tractors," explained Jack Ronayne, "the principal subject of discussion at a public meeting was how to keep the roads open, and no plan seemed effective." In 1958, when Bob Taylor wrote about the trials of operating a Model T on our early roads, as the owner of the first express service in the Valley he looked back nearly forty years: "It was not until 1919 that our Model T appeared, brought in to expedite transportation from Pemberton to a point some fifteen miles up the valley, where we had purchased a farm. The winter of 1919 was an open winter insofar as snow was concerned, but it was a cold one, with resultant frost in the ground to a depth of two feet. This made sleighing bad and wagoning bumpy. The old Model T took quite a beating, but kept going in spite of roads and terrified horses and oxen."

In each of two places a gate closed off the Valley road because there were no fences to keep in cattle which were let loose on the roads. Two cattle gates restricted the cattle to certain areas, but anyone driving between Upper and Lower Valley had to open and close the gates.

Taylor describes more driving difficulties of earlier years: "Twelve bridges to navigate, one mile of straight corduroy, and one lengthy 'bridge' about three hundred feet long that had a habit of moving up and down or leaning sideways, depending on frost heave in winter and high water in summer. The road itself was, on average, about ten feet wide, and the brush in winter, with an icy rain, formed a barrier clean across in places that had to be parted with the windshield. As we did not have a windshield, it was sometimes parted with heads. We had no antifreeze, electric headlights, self starters, or anything that helped in the least. If you got stuck, you emptied the radiator before it froze, and after you got going you risked your life on Ryan Creek ice, or chopped a hole some place to get filled again. Every time you stalled, you got out and cranked. You hung a lantern on the radiator cap, if you were foolish enough to try a night trip. In those days the P.G.E. trains met at Pemberton at 2 a.m., so there was not much choice about night trips. I would suggest that the reader . . . picture himself ten miles from Pemberton in the dark, the temperature ten below zero, in this vehicle with a flat tire.

Pemberton Express, 1920 — Provincial Archives, Victoria, B.C.

"I would at this point note that to change a tire you took a jack and lifted the car, then pried off the tire, after which you thawed out the rubber patch, so it would stick to the tube. If you were lucky, you pried the tire back on again, and then got the hand pump going. This operation, in favorable conditions, took approximately one hour, so of course you drained the radiator. This, in turn, let the motor get cold, so in order to get mobile, you warmed up cranking Lizzie.

"Now Summer was a cinch, compared to Winter; all you had to worry about was high water and mosquitoes. The bridges floated up and sometimes settled back in the right place, or sometimes they floated clean away. But most of them went down a foot when your front wheels hit them, and went up a foot when your back wheels left the other end. If you travelled at less than ten miles an hour, the mosquitoes could keep up with you, and if you went over ten miles an hour, anything could happen . . . . From the middle of July to the end of August, water on the Pemberton road from Miller Creek to Miller's farm, a distance of about seven miles, varied in depth from six inches to thirty inches. In these periods you travelled in a six-inch deposit of gooey silt, which did not firm up until the water receded. If you stopped for a few minutes, all your wheels became firmly rooted to the ground. The horsepower and the gearbox of the Model T were not built to handle this situation. A shovel and gum boots was the answer. If you got a flat tire, you just kept going until you got to dry land. The road from Pemberton to Mount Currie was impassable from July first to October, because low places collected water that was too deep to navigate. If you wished to drive to D'Arcy you got pulled through with a team of horses, then drained everything on the other side."

That Model T became a multi-purpose vehicle: "It was ambulance, hearse, and general transport. In 1920 it became a commercial vehicle and was the first service of its kind to the farmers. It carried mail free both ways for many years. It took many years to become popular, and the first was the worst, because the horses simply took to the bush on sight of the car, and some hard feelings followed. The modern public should try to control a team of oxen with a G-rope and a prod, when it meets a Model T on a narrow road bordered on one side by brush and on the other by a deep river."

Taylor's PX service continued for many years. Through most of those years, two mornings a week, a flat-deck truck drove away from the Taylor farm to collect cans of cream for shipment to Vancouver. As he proceeded the driver stopped for the cream, sometimes brought out of ice houses, sometimes carried up from rafts where the cans had been suspended in the chilly river waters. At many farm gates the owners had left mail bags in shelters built to hold mail and groceries. And along the route passengers hopped aboard, some on their way to Vancouver, others going just to the station. The two picked up first rode in the cab, others sat on the truck deck — in winter as close as possible to the back of the cab.

Twice a week, just as soon as mail from the evening train had been sorted, the PX truck returned up the Valley as a mail truck. Again it usually carried passengers, as well as mail and groceries and returned cream cans. North bound and south bound the driver stopped regularly at the Pemberton Meadows Post Office.

"Sonny" Taylor remembers his difficulties in reaching that post office during high water. Making his way in from the first Pemberton Meadows school house, he had to follow a winding route. When he arrived, Maria Fraser, the postmistress, would say, "Never mind, we'll soon be in our new house on higher ground." Once, trying to drive a mail truck through, another man spent four hours in the spring mud of Hartzell's grade. Finally, late at night, he shouldered the settlers' individual mail sacks and delivered them on foot for two or three miles. The PX cream and mail trips were the regularly scheduled trips up and down the Valley but Taylor trucks and others also hauled vegetables, hay, ties, and poles.

Probably local weather and soil conditions made road maintenance more difficult than on the coast. The man in charge was the road foreman, and like his superior, the general foreman, he was sometimes criticized, and sometimes praised for his performance. During long-ago winters, when roads were unplowed, maybe he had respite from worry. Then, towards spring Miller Creek could be a dividing line between bare and snow-covered roads; above the Ronayne farms, too, roads might be bare: at such times, before starting on a trip through the Valley, drivers would arrange to use both sleighs and wagons. In 1939 when crews regularly plowed snow off the roads, the Board of Trade asked the men to leave about six inches of snow "to give both sleighs and cars a surface on which to travel".

Until the recent paving of roads, at spring breakup several seas of mud developed and car or truck travel through each was either a long, slow grind, or completely impossible. People might leave a vehicle at one end, navigate the muddy stretch on foot, and then borrow a vehicle at the other end. Fortunately one stretch always remained firm, the narrow road between the Rockslide and the Lillooet River. After $1100 was spent filling a muddy section with rocks the road bordering the Lokken (Summerskill) farm stayed passable in all weathers.

When road conditions were poor, people protested. In 1932 the state of the road between Owl Creek and Pemberton was so unsatisfactory that the settlers lost patience: if the Department of Public Works would not make the necessary improvements, the residents themselves would get the job done. The following year they wanted a log jam removed from the Lillooet, a potential flood threat to road, farms, and homes. In 1934 some people lost confidence in road officials. The Board of Trade proposed to the Department of Public Works that "five competent local persons take charge of all the road work in this area", and then the work "would be better managed than it is . . . under a District Foreman Engineer and would result in a big saving." At the same time

Board members urged that "horses be used for road work whenever possible and advantageous" and discussed "poor road conditions created by logging at Birken." In 1936 these men asked for a district tractor to be used where horses "would be inappropriate and inadequate", and requested repairs to the Fowler family's link with the settled side of the river, a cable ferry. At a March 1937 meeting, Board of Trade members heard protests about paying a car licence fee for the period "after the first of December in each year, after which date motor travel is invariably impossible."

At the same meeting they passed a resolution expressing their appreciation of the work of Sandy Fowler, the road foreman. Since the day in 1922 when his wife climbed to Codman's Mine to take him news of his appointment, Fowler had held the job, and was to serve in Pemberton until 1945 when he was made road foreman in Squamish.

Ben Cherry remembers contributions of an even earlier road foreman. About 1920, after the Red Bridge was rebuilt, the Public Works Department put Olus Lee in charge of roads throughout the Valley and Lee, according to Cherry, was a practical man who had been an engineer in the First World War: "When the Public Works engineer would come from Vancouver to get his spring estimates, Lee would say, 'Well, there should be a bridge here,' or whatever it might be. The engineer would say, 'O.K., how much money do you want?' 'Well, I can build that bridge for $500.' 'You can't build the bridge for $500; we'll put in $1,500.' The result was that Lee built his bridges for $500, but he also put an approach on each side, and usually these approaches were up to two miles in length. That is how most of the original muddy roads developed into good roads."

Few know that besides building and maintaining roads, earlier road foremen had another responsibility. River control. "Perhaps a little later than '20 or '21," says Cherry, "the Public Works did a lot of river bank protection work. They had one old one-lung Fairbanks Morse engine, I suppose about 12-, 14-, or 16-horsepower. In the present twelve miles of drainage area, using that engine, the road crews must have driven hundreds of piles. Some of these piles formed piers going out into the river to try to direct it into its old channel; some protected the banks. Then, I suppose thousands of tons of brush and rock were dumped behind the piles lining the Lillooet, all up the valley. The protection work was mostly on the west side, of course, because the men were trying to force the river back against the mountains on the east."

Until the 'fifties little improvement occurred on the road between one-time Agerton and Pemberton Station. In 1939 the Board of Trade requested an "immediate course of action" on that section of road described as being "constantly under water". When it was flooded, cars proceeded very slowly throughout that stretch; school children and other walkers removed their shoes and rolled up their pants. At a 1937 meeting, residents had prophetically expressed resentment at what they considered unfair diversion of district road funds to the Bridge River communities: "During the last three or four years necessary road maintenance has been sacrificed in favour of other areas in the district . . . . This community will be growing and paying taxes when the mining areas are dead.''

Dorothy Girling describes winter travel conditions in the 'thirties. A month before her first child was born she drove to the station in an open box sleigh: ''It took four hours to do the fourteen mile drive and the thermometer registered ten degrees below zero [Fahrenheit] when we reached the hamlet . . . .

''Homecoming with child #3 was one of THE events. She was eight weeks old and it was New Year's Day when we left Grannie and Grampa's in North Vancouver and set out. It snowed all the way up Howe Sound — it snowed all the way up the P.G.E., and when we arrived at the little station we had to put up at the small hotel. Next morning we started off bravely in the freight truck for the drive through the snow. Half an hour and half a mile later I cried out for a halt: #1 was car sick, #2 was weeping, #3 was cradled in one arm, while with the other I tried to keep the stacked up freight from descending at each lurch of the truck. So each carrying a child, we [husband and wife] trudged back to the hotel, undressed, and started to dry out our clothes, hoping to drive up by sleigh. This plan fell through, and we had to spend another night as before. Next day, the snow plough started out ahead of us, and as the freight had gone through, we had the back of the truck to ourselves. We left at ten a.m. To make a long story short, it was seven p.m. when we finally reached home, having had an hour's break en route.'' Nine hours! Longer than by sleigh!

About 1914 Bob McLauchlan had started construction of the hotel where the Girlings spent two nights, the Pemberton Hotel, and what he built eventually became the first unit of the present Pemberton Motor Hotel. In 1918, when the Taillefers came to the Valley they could not move into the house they had been promised, the present Shantz home, because the occupant refused to vacate. Then, for a rental of $5 a month, McLauchlan offered them the two-storey unfinished hotel. This fair-sized shell of a building had no partitions, and only a pot-bellied stove to keep it warm. Although the Taillefers nearly froze during their first winter, they did plan to buy the hotel and, for probably a year or more, did operate it.

When a meal was ready Taillefer stood outside the building and rang a cowbell to summon guests until Wellington gave him a triangle to beat. Two of the fine dishes served were pancakes, with a dash of cornmeal to give them grittiness, and wild ducks. In those early years, before leaving Vancouver one prospective settler would send a wire: ''Reserve me a suite of rooms''. ''The funny thing,'' Taillefer said, ''was that there was no room. We gave him all the attic.''

Before long the couple sold their interest in the hotel and moved up to Agerton where Taillefer worked at the Pemberton Trading store and the family lived nearby in the big house with its six bedrooms upstairs. To earn a few extra dollars they decided to take in boarders, and the next year when the Red

Bridge was being rebuilt they had fourteen bridge workers from other areas boarding with them, each paying $14 a week. Local men ate their noon meal at the boarding house. "We fed them well," Taillefer said; "even gave them fruit and nuts — at first." Altogether the Taillefers cleared $500 as a result of the bridge rebuilding. Hiring out their team at $8 a day to haul timbers helped build up those earnings.

Meanwhile, William Tuck, a P.G.E. roadmaster, was improving the hotel which Frank Buckley remembers as "pretty tough looking", and was expanding the operation. In 1929 the hotel had some plumbing fixtures, but the only bathroom was at the bottom of the stairs leading up to the bedrooms. A "fine, hospitable lady", Tuck's wife ran the business, which included providing meals for train passengers. When meals were ready, guests sat down together at a long table covered with a white cloth. Breakfast could be hearty: prunes, porridge, bacon and eggs, toast and coffee. Tuck built the first partitions in the hotel and lined his rooms with beaver board.

Later, to mixed community reaction, Tuck acquired a beer licence. "When he made his trips up to Lillooet or down to Squamish," Ben Cherry recalls, "anybody that wanted beer — that is, the local people — would walk in and help themselves and put the money on the till. When Bill came back in a day or two he counted the money and, generally, he had been paid in full."

For their private enjoyment, one Saturday night two drinkers took over the beer parlour. Expecting his customers to leave as eleven o'clock neared, Tuck called out "Closing time", and all left except two men from the P.G.E. work train stationed on the Pemberton siding. These two shoved Tuck out, bolted the door, and stayed on until Monday morning. From time to time, when the hotel owner had knocked on the door, they had answered that they were "doing fine".

By 1929 Tuck had sold out, and after a few months the new owner sold to the J. W. Wilkinsons. With the Wilkinsons, and helping them in their business, were their daughters, Elsie Lund and Rene Oman, as well as Rene's husband, Fred, who worked in the beer parlour. Board of Trade minutes show that up to 1940 hotel owners succeeding the Wilkinsons were William Harris and then Fred Kershaw.

By 1940 roads were plowed in winter, but each spring, for many years, long, muddy, sometimes impassable stretches developed. The few businesses existed to serve the farmers, trappers, prospectors, loggers, and mill workers. The PX continued its regular deliveries of mail, groceries, and freight. The McKenzie store business had changed hands several times, finally disappearing in the 1934 destruction by fire of the Kiltz building. After the railway arrived, Wellington's, later Taillefer's, store opened. Axel Johnson continued to shoe horses and bend wagon tire irons and, like the mechanic in the PX garage, he did car and truck repairs.

THE RAILWAY, 1914 to 1940

With the Pacific Great Eastern Railway serving them, in many ways life for Pemberton area settlers became easier. Still, as the years went by dissatisfaction developed. A railway that ended at Squamish and barged most of its freight to Vancouver was not a complete answer to transportation problems.

The earliest available timetable took effect on October 11, 1914 and shows fourteen stations: Squamish Dock, Squamish, Mamquam, Brackendale, Cheekye, Cheakamus, Watson, Water Tank, Brew, McGuire, Mons, Rethel, Tisdale, and Pemberton. Of these, only five were regular stops. Trains were scheduled to leave Pemberton every morning except Sunday at 8 a.m. and to reach Squamish Dock at 1:45 p.m. After transfer of passengers, baggage, and express from the Terminal Steamship boat, northbound trains were scheduled to pull out from Squamish Dock at 2:15 p.m. and reach Pemberton at 7 p.m., having covered a distance of 56.9 miles. At no time was speed to exceed twenty-five miles an hour, and between Cheakamus and Pemberton the limit was fifteen miles an hour. Rules also required that "all trains must be handled under absolute control and without regard to making schedule time at all points where track becomes rough."

Trains were pulled by steam engines which at intervals stopped at water tanks. Until recently foundations of an early Pemberton water tank remained near the firehall, and a later tank stood close to the present railway crossing. The railway's need for water led to the damming of One Mile Creek, but the water system constructed by the P.G.E. did serve not only the railway, but also part of the community at the station.

One railway official believes that the first station at Pemberton was built in 1914. At an early date, on a slope above the tracks, the company erected a little building that provided living quarters for the station agent. In 1923, when transferred to Pemberton, Agent G. C. Sidsworth lived there with his family. Some time later Charles Wellington and Harvey Derrick looked after the railway business, including the telephone, and in the early 'thirties when Wellington sold his store he and Derrick moved into the railway house in which Derrick continued on the job after Wellington's death.

Probably early in 1915 the tracks reached Mount Currie Station, then Chilsampton, the name by which even in 1939, years after the community had become Creekside, the railway company called that station. Rosie Joseph tells of her mother's excitement when the first train reached there: without stopping to put on her shoes, the young girl rushed out from her home to see what for everybody along the line was a strange sight — an iron creature snaking and steaming through the wilderness.

In 1915 when regular service began, on Monday and Thursday the passenger train ran north to Lillooet. On Wednesday and Saturday, it made the return trip to Squamish. In the third week of January 1916, however, very deep snow interrupted regular service and, after one night when three feet fell on the previous accumulation, all service stopped.

In fact, winter travel on the early trains was often irregular. Coming home to spend the 1914 Christmas with the Barbours, Bebee Fowles had to travel north on a work train. Deep snow delayed the train at Alta Lake, but the engine finally pulled the cars through to the end of the tracks at Pemberton. The snow stalled one train in or near Pemberton itself in 1916. On skis made from boards the crew made their way to Alta Lake and Rainbow Lodge which had been in operation since the preceding April. Because the oldest man among them had found the trip very hard going, the men rested there for three days. On regular skis and carrying a supply of hard-boiled eggs, Myrtle Philip then travelled south with the group. Their lunch stop was Water Tank where one of the crew phoned Squamish and arranged to have an engine meet them on the trestle over the Cheakamus.

During the same period without train service, Annie Ronayne was waiting to bring home her second daughter, Kathleen, born during January. Annie kept phoning from a public phone to obtain a message which Margaret Green in North Vancouver was to receive from Joe Ronayne, a message which would tell his wife when he and E. Sampson would be leaving Pemberton to walk to Squamish to pick up his family. Joe was going to bring a hand-sleigh with him.

Annie Ronayne described the trip home: "The first day, starting from Squamish with $7 worth of provisions, I travelled on a pump car, sitting on my suitcase, with baby on my lap. Four men pumped. At Mile 16, because of the depth of snow, we had to abandon the pump car. We stopped there for the night in an abandoned railway shack, as we did farther along the way. Daddy attached the steel runners he had bought in Vancouver to the sleigh. A man gave me a pair of mackinaw pants to wear, which was a great help.

"The second day, we set out for Brandywine Falls. I was carried pickaback across trestles. I tried snowshoes, but got too tired. We slept at Brandywine in a large cabin with rats scurrying around. On the third morning, we left for Green Lake. Finally we could see Rouger's log house across the ice. Sampson was in the lead, Daddy behind, and I astride the sleigh, with the baby under blankets between my legs. When the ice started cracking, Daddy shouted to Sampson to swing off, but it was too late. The sleigh went down into a few inches of slush. I got a real fright, thinking the baby was drowning. The next morning, the fourth day, we started off to where the train was snowed in. We ate in the caboose, and Sampson slept there. We went into a cabin with an ice-covered floor. But we kept warm on a bed of fir branches, with our goat skin robes wrapped around us.

"Next morning, on the fifth day, we reached Pemberton. When we ate dinner at the hotel, my appetite was low due to lack of sleep. We travelled on up the valley as far as Millers'. Daddy went home and returned to fetch me. We had to follow a narrow cow trail, too narrow for the hand-sleigh. Travelling on foot was tiring, so I was carried now and then. By noon on the sixth day, we reached home. Mrs. Sampson had dinner ready. Margaret did not recognize me." The Joe Ronayne's baby girl had been born early in January. Her father had left for Vancouver on March 2 and returned with his family on March 15.

Party at a new house

At a neighbour's house, on February 23, the Edmond Ronaynes' first child had been born. Because the snowfall had increased by four feet shortly before Tessie's birth, Joseph Ronayne drove his big-footed Clydesdales up the road and around the Ed Ronayne house, then back down the road again. Jack Ronayne made an entry in his diary for February 23, 1916: "Went with horse and sleigh for Mrs. Harris. Ed's wife had baby girl at Mrs. Ryan's."

Somehow on February 10 letters had come through, and with them news of the destruction of the Parliament Buildings in Ottawa. On February 25 the first newspaper since January 21 arrived, and Jack Ronayne read until his eyes were sore. On February 26 he recorded "no flour, sugar, or coal oil at store." Some time after mid-March the P.G.E. resumed operations.

An early settler wrote that "the P.G.E. is more free from slides than the Fraser Canyon", but from time to time, such occurrences did cause delays. One happened in 1929 when an immense rock rolled onto the track between Pemberton and Green River Crossing. Bill Spetch says that the rock never was removed; instead, the track was built around it. The stalling of the train by that mammoth rock resulted in an alleged lawbreaker having a warning of a pending investigation. The provincial policeman coming to do some investigating had to walk from the train to Pemberton, and on reaching the station, but before proceeding to the house he had come to search, he stopped to report the big rock. His stop was just long enough for the bootlegger to dismantle his still and hide it.

Another cause of minor delays was the straying of cattle onto the tracks. A 1919 bulletin requested that all engineers "please keep careful look out for cattle on Pemberton Portage." So suddenly did one cow appear before a roadmaster's speeder that he was unable to avoid hitting her, and for some distance travelled with the terrified cow on his lap. At the first opportunity he bathed and changed his clothes.

By 1919 the tracks extended as far as Clinton. In June of that year, from all stations, Squamish to Clinton, the railway advertised special fares — war tax included — to Lillooet where the attraction was the long-established Dominion Day celebration.

Along the line near Pemberton, and between Pemberton and Squamish, over the years various changes took place. John Buchanan, a P.G.E. conductor, said that about 1928 the railway filled in a great portion of the space spanned by the old wooden trestle which had started not far beyond Pemberton Station. Then about 1932 bridge builders erected a steel trestle over the Lillooet River.

After the opening of Rainbow Lodge, more lodges opened for business.

Pemberton Station, early 1930's

The Nyes, Mary Taylor's parents, built Daisy Lake Lodge at Garibaldi and, according to Myrtle Philip, made their operation pay. Later, she says, the Cranes built Alpine Lodge. But because for many years Rainbow was the meal stop at Alta Lake it was known to all travellers. Long tables set with steaming platters and bowls of food were ready when train passengers trooped through the wide door of the lodge. Genial and efficient, Alex and Myrtle Philip were always there, moving around and supervising every detail.

To their meal-time guests the Philips were best known as the owners of Rainbow Lodge, but husband and wife were far more than excellent hosts. In several ways each contributed to the larger community. In October 1974, more than two years before the building burned to the ground, Joan Saxton, Rainbow's last owner, organized a "Myrtle Philip Day", when dozens of former lodge guests and other friends from Vancouver to Mount Currie and beyond came to spend a day reminiscing at the lodge. Besides looking after the housekeeping and cooking at Rainbow, Myrtle used to supervise the horses and arrange and lead trail rides. She and Alex were in charge of the post office and operated their own store; she was midwife and first aid attendant to all who needed her; she was first secretary-treasurer of the Alta Lake School Board, and served with that board as long as it existed, and then served for many years on the larger Howe Sound School Board. Besides all of her other involvements she was a principal organizer of Alta Lake social events, including the annual Christmas and New Year's parties which are now remembered so nostalgically.

Forty years ago Alex was the well-known writer of such novels as *Whispering Leaves, The Painted Cliff,* and *The Crimson West.* Myrtle recalls Alex nearing the end of one novel and asking her what he should "do" with one character. "Make him jump over a cliff," she replied. And in that way Alex did dispose of him. Canada's "first all-talking motion picture" was based on

Programme

1. Overture - - - - - - - - - Bert Zala at the Console
2. Reception of the Premier of British Columbia
3. "O CANADA"
4. Speech by the Honourable T. D. Pattullo
   Premier of British Columbia
5. Speech by His Worship, Mayor D. Leeming of Victoria
6. Address by Kenneth J. Bishop, President of Commonwealth Productions Ltd.
7. Introduction of the Author, Alex Philip, also Miss Lucille Browne and Nick Stuart, principals of the Cast
8. Mr. Fred Wright, Solo
9. Presenting Canada's First All Talking Motion Picture
   "THE CRIMSON PARADISE"

GOD SAVE THE KING

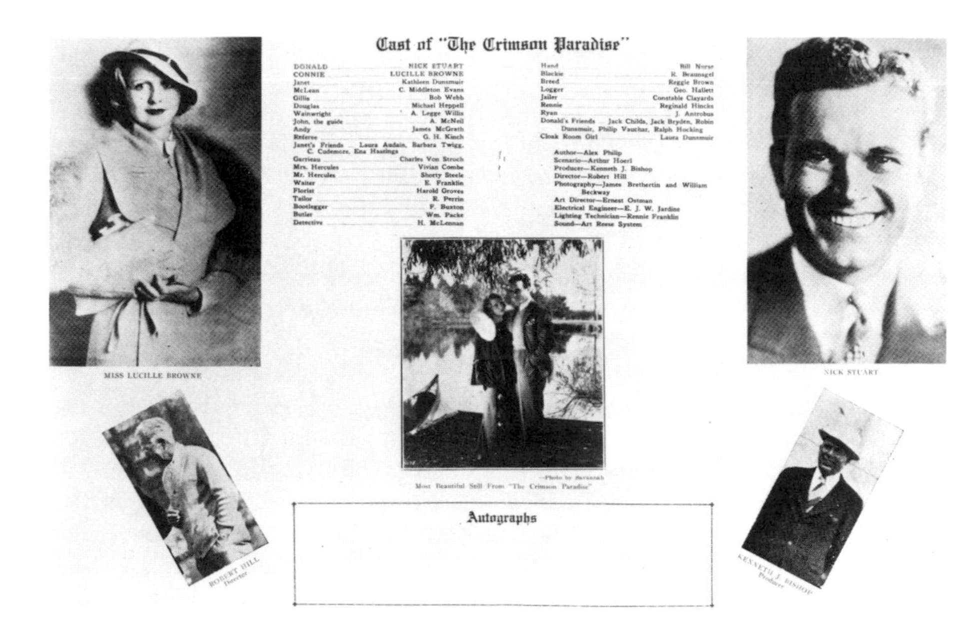

Cast of "The Crimson Paradise"

DONALD	NICK STUART
CONNIE	LUCILLE BROWNE
Janet	Kathleen Dunsmuir
McLean	C. Middleton Evans
Gillis	Bob Webb
Douglas	Michael Heppell
Wainwright	A. Legge Willis
John, the guide	A. McNeil
Andy	James McGrath
Referee	G. H. Kinch
Janet's Friends	Laura Audain, Barbara Twigg, C. Cudemore, Ena Hastings
Garrieau	Charles Von Stroch
Mrs. Hercules	Vivian Combe
Mr. Hercules	Shorty Steele
Waiter	E. Franklin
Florist	Harold Groves
Tailor	R. Perrin
Bootlegger	F. Buxton
Butler	Wm. Packe
Detective	H. McLennan
Hand	Bill Nurse
Blackie	R. Braunagel
Breed	Reggie Brown
Logger	Geo. Hallett
Jailer	Constable Clayards
Rennie	Reginald Hincks
Ryan	J. Antrobus
Donald's Friends	Jack Childs, Jack Bryden, Robin Dunsmuir, Philip Vauchar, Ralph Hocking
Cloak Room Girl	Laura Dunsmuir

Author—Alex Philip
Scenario—Arthur Hoerl
Producer—Kenneth J. Bishop
Director—Robert Hill
Photography—James Brethertin and William Beckway
Art Director—Ernest Ostman
Electrical Engineer—E. J. W. Jardine
Lighting Technician—Rennie Franklin
Sound—Art Reese System

MISS LUCILLE BROWNE

NICK STUART

—Photo by Savannah
Most Beautiful Still From "The Crimson Paradise"

Autographs

ROBERT HILL
Director

KENNETH J. BISHOP
Producer

The Crimson West. "Produced and filmed at Victoria, British Columbia, by the Commonwealth Productions Limited" the "world's premiere presentation" of *The Crimson Paradise* was made at Victoria's Capitol Theatre. There in December 1933 for the noteworthy event was the Premier of the province, the Honourable T. D. Pattullo; the Mayor of Victoria; the president of Commonwealth Productions, makers of the film; Myrtle Philip; and Alex Philip, the author.

Those who have never lived under pioneer conditions may have difficulty in imagining either the preparations before travellers set foot on the trains — and became passengers — or the leisurely trip. First, everybody wanted to appear suitably dressed in the big city, but few had many changes of "best" clothes, and in winter those were woollen. Because the woollens could be washed only at the risk of shrinking, they were aired, brushed, sponged, and pressed. In winter the unexpected need to travel always seemed to come when father's other suit of heavy underwear was unwashed. Travelling to the station in an unheated sleigh or truck necessitated warm underwear, and mother would therefore start the water heating, get out the wash tub, place it on facing chairs or on a bench, then go to work on the scrub board. Her knuckles had hardened long before, and would not skin. Drying clothes in a hurry was a greater problem. Probably by hand she would wring the garment as dry as possible, then hang it on a line or rack over the cookstove, and turn it from time to time. Meanwhile, steam on the cold windows increased, condensed, and ran down in streams. If mother was leaving her family for days or weeks she would work extra hard to leave house and clothing clean, and to bake bread, cakes, and cookies to last during her absence. If her children were very young she might make arrangements to leave them with neighbour women.

But the train was often late. Edith Perkins has said, in fact "in those days the train was on time when it was fourteen hours late." Often passengers waited weary hours in the only possible waiting places: the store, the hotel, or the PX office. In the station building itself heat and lights were the only concessions to comfort. Finally when somebody shouted that the train was coming, travellers and all the population who happened to be in the vicinity poured out of doors and flocked down to the station platform. Some passengers on the incoming train descended for the brief stop, a number to rush up to the beer parlour and run back with a case, others to look for friends among the onlookers.

Some time after 10 a.m. south-bound passengers just boarding could at last relax with cronies in the smoky train atmosphere. Some talked; in those days before phones the people caught up on local news or did business. Others played cards, drank beer, knitted, or read. A veteran of the Yukon Gold Rush and with gold nuggets suspended from the watch chain spread across his vest, Gold Nugget Charlie paraded up and down the passenger cars selling magazines and sandwiches, but he advertised most loudly his fresh roasted pea*nuts*. In winter, though reeking fumes were already spreading down the corridors, from time to time a crewman replenished the coal heater in each passenger coach. When dusk began to fall a man lighted the dim coal-oil lamps swaying back and forth above the aisles. Crews were courteous and considerate, often accommodating passengers by making unscheduled stops. On winter nights, the brakeman swinging a lantern and striding down the corridor and then a sudden rush of cold air were certain signals that a stop was ahead.

Reaching Squamish, some carrying luggage, some carrying babies, all walked or struggled off the train and made their way to the waiting steamer. Leaving suitcases near the purser's office travellers continued through a long passage bordered on one side by a series of hardwood seats built against the exterior walls of staterooms, and finally reached the saloon, with its upholstered seats and sat there, or went down immediately to the dining room with its white linen cloths, its shining silver, and its attentive white-coated waiters.

The trips by train and boat were usually happy social occasions which lasted until usually close to 6 p.m. when the Vancouver skyline appeared. As soon as country people emerged onto the deck of the steamer they sensed the heavy, acrid city smell, but for a few days they would enjoy, among other things, a bathroom, big stores, and movies.

Travel by train and the obvious advantages of shipping by rail were only some of the benefits of a railway. Settlers were certainly closer to absent relatives and to goods they needed and desired. Those twice-weekly mails, with letters, newspapers, magazines, parcels, and catalogues made additional links with the "outside".

Those catalogues had various uses. They offered a shopping wonderland, and new goods reached Pemberton customers much faster by rail than before: exciting new clothes in long boxes, gleaming dishes emerging from yellow straw — many, many delights. Children spent endless hours poring over pages almost tissue thin showing rows of dolls with outstretched arms; all kinds of toys, wooden, celluloid, and rubber; tantalizing book covers; sports equipment; harness on handsome prancing horses. In early railway days women had wide choices of nipped-in, laced corsets, and men had a broad range of underwear to choose from, heavy ribbed wool to light cotton, all modelled on heavy-muscled men, often shown in athletic poses. When coloured catalogue pages first appeared at the front of the book they showed mainly suits, coats, and dresses, their colours chosen to have maximum eye appeal. Each catalogue gave delight and instruction until replaced by a new one, and then it might be used as a cut-out book, or relegated to the privy, either at home or at school.

In spite of all the advantages the railway offered, Board of Trade members were convinced that still further improvements could be made. They decided to write E. C. Carson, MLA, asking his help in placing before "the powers that be" a request that any new P.G.E. director should be appointed from "persons who live along the line and know the wants and requirements of the settlers of the District." They were alarmed that a loading ramp might be removed and asked that a "permanent boarding place" be provided, "with access thereto," on the "Y" at the southern end of Pemberton Station. In 1930 a railway official agreed to that request. Board of Trade members were dissatisfied with published reports of freight movements: tonnage moved to and from Pemberton was omitted. After the Pemberton Hatchery was abandoned, the Board requested that Owl Creek remain a flag station. But in 1932 members expressed their greatest dissatisfaction. Unhappy with having their products barged down Howe Sound, they demanded that if the government "did not finish the P.G.E. or sell it", that the government "consider turning it into a motor road."

D'Arcy Station and Lodge

INTO THE MODERN ERA

THE GREAT FLOOD

The Lillooet River and its tributaries are quiet and shallow in the wintertime, but turn into raging torrents when fed by melting snows and glaciers during summer months. Flooding had always been a problem in the Pemberton area, some years much more so than others. By 1940 some rather inadequate dykes helped to keep the river within its boundaries, especially where there was a sharp bend. Seepage from the river helped to supply underground irrigation for the growing crops, and therefore any slight flooding was a curse on the low ground, though it actually improved the harvest on the higher fields.

In the fall of 1940 early cool weather in September had whitened the mountaintops with the first of the winter snow. In the bright sunshine of the first two weeks of October, the potatoes were harvested and on many farms already pitted or in roothouses ready for the winter. Then on October 15th the weather unaccountably warmed up. It started to rain and rain and rain — five inches in twenty-four hours. The warm rain on the mountains brought the melting snow rushing down the Lillooet River and its tributaries, notably Ryan Creek which emerges from the mountains back of the Ross farm and runs down the west side of the valley to join the Lillooet north of Morgan Miller's farm.

At the north end of the valley on a partially cleared farm lived Lucien Van Beem and his wife Doris. A Dutchman raised in Java, Lukie had come to Pemberton in 1924. Doris, a native-born Canadian, who spent her early years in Vancouver, recalls her experiences during the flood:

"Having never been near a farm in my life, I came to Pemberton on March 21st, 1940 to visit my friends the Gerald Rosses. Little did I realize that day, that not only would I marry and settle here, but that I would go through a period of initiation that would strengthen my love for the valley and cause me to be ever thankful for the little place I fill today.

"During the next few months, a brother of mine also came to Pemberton with his wife and wee daughter to see if this climate would help his asthma.

They were living in a two-storey house half-way down the valley, by the Greens' farm. This particular October afternoon, Tom rode up to visit us in our one-and-a-half-room cabin, which was less than a foot off the ground; our first home, surrounded by tall trees, woodshed, barn and chicken house close by. Lukie had one cow and calf, a team of horses and about 15 chickens. The remains of a slough in the low area between house and barn filled up during the summer high waters, I was told, and so a log was resting across it at one place, suitable to come and go to the barn. That log was to prove very useful.

"When my brother arrived it was raining. The day was warm for mid-October. It had been raining most of the day. Around 3 o'clock, Tom remarked that there were a lot of puddles to dodge, so he'd better get back, as it did not appear that the rain would soon quit. As he left he asked, 'Ever had a flood here?' 'No,' Lukie replied, 'Only high water'. Away Tom went. Lukie noticed a squirrel going somewhere on low land, gathering nuts and bringing them to the high place on the knoll where our house stood. The warm rain continued to fall. Noticeable was a stream of water down at the gate entrance. Seems to me, my husband mentioned that it was good that the log was there, because the slough would fill up, and he needn't get wet going to milk.

"We went to bed listening to the rain pouring steadily on the shake roof, and drifted off to sleep. Some time later, I awoke with a start at the noise of something hitting the side of the house, and heard a steady sound of water running. We both arose quickly, and, even in the pitch black, we saw the water was all around us and roaring through the slough. A fallen tree was riding the water and had bumped into the chicken house behind our cabin, and over the edge of the slough.

"Still the rain poured down, and I could see Lukie's concern. He dressed as best he could against the elements, and went to investigate. Imagine my fear when he went across that log. All, so far, was dry at the barn; it was as high as the house, but he could determine that before long everything might be inundated. I was glad to see him back. He decided, since we had no boat and might have to leave, that he should make a raft. I managed to give him a little something to eat while it was still dark, and then he found enough odds and ends to start building. By now, it was around six in the morning, and the water was coming up on to the knoll. Lukie went back to the barn and put a plank up to the mow, so that the cow and calf could be driven up there. He also put a board up in the henhouse, and, last of all, turned the horses loose. By this time the log was almost under water, so I was relieved to see him back at the cabin. I had just put what I could up off the floor. When my husband had finished the raft, he took a fencing tool in his pocket and, as the water was coming close to the floor of the house, said, 'I think we had better head down to Wilsons'.

"Betty Wilson too had first come to the valley as a visitor. She came to the Deckers' in May and married Ed Wilson that same summer. Their house was on fairly high ground about two miles away. We 'set sail'. My heart was beating loudly I'm sure — I'm not a courageous person — but I calmed a little when we seemed to be floating quite well, and every time Lukie came to a fence he snipped the wire with his fencing tool, holding us at the fencepost while he did so. We finally came to Jim Bartow's place; he also was high and dry. When he invited us in there, I was hesitant. About fifty cats and chickens were running in and out of the house, so Lukie declined his offer. It wasn't too far to Wilson's farm from there, and we were getting close to the road. We kept on and soon reached it.

"We thought we were doing very well, when suddenly we came to a place where the river dyke had broken, and the water pouring in from two directions caused a strong whirling current. The raft rammed a fence post and we upended. Down I went. The water was icy cold and I couldn't seem to hit bottom or rise up. Suddenly I was being pulled up and held by my dear husband. He swam with me to a shallower spot, and I was very thankful to be able to walk in water waist high. We knew it was the road we were walking on and kept on towards Wilsons'. At times a hole gouged by the water would be too deep for me, so Lukie swam with me, then it would be shallower again. At last we came to Ed Wilson's gate, and there they were on the porch looking for us. They felt that we would try to come.

"Ed called to Lukie to bring me to a certain place, where it was deep, but he had a rope strung across so that we could work ourselves hand over hand towards the house. Lukie put me in front and we began. Yes, the rope did break and down I went again. This time I was caught in a snag and just when blackness seemed to be closing in, something got a hold and I was pulled up. Yes, Lukie again, and we were both on the other side. Ed and Betty took me. Lukie was exhausted because he had been in the water a long time.

"The Wilsons already had John Jack with them, an oldtimer who lived in a shack nearby, and we all enjoyed very hot coffee and pancakes together and thanksgiving for our blessings. As I helped Betty to flip the pancakes, I almost fainted. I was pregnant. After my daughter was born, from the first she screamed when I tried to bathe her. I wonder what grandmother would say to that!

"That same evening the rain let up some, but continued through the night. The next morning the sun was shining and casting pictures on the still-flowing water. The water went down very quickly, and by the afternoon Lukie insisted that he go home to see the situation there. He had to pick his way as he walked off, and I worried all the time he was gone. He found the cow and calf safely in the mow, the chickens all on top of their house. He cleaned the silt from our house as best he could, and then came back to Wilsons'. The next day Ed loaned us a horse and we rode home on it together, everything being still very mucky. Luckily, none of our belongings were ruined, but some other people were not so fortunate. Of course, I was anxious about my brother and family, but found they had a ringside seat from a high vantage point and remained high and safe as the flood waters whirled by. We could smile later about the pumpkin floating by with a rooster on it, and the way the family managed to hook it in, but the more serious losses of crops and animals were no laughing matter. But with the effort of all pitching in, things began to move and to grow and out from the flood-silt the more fertile land brought forth bounty.

"I have never forgotten that I owe my life to my husband, as I do my soul to God; nor have I ever forgotten the closeness of a few neighbours who shared our experiences."

About one mile down the road from the Wilsons lived the Girlings, father and two married sons. The farm was known as Artillery Ranch, both Chris and Barry having served in the British army in World War I. Dorothy Girling, farmer's wife and mother of three small daughters, describes her experiences:

"We had floods in some degree every year for 10 years, floods when the menfolk and the womenfolk, too, worked all night and day trying to hold back the water. How they laboured — cutting brush, digging sod, filling sandbags. One night a young schoolgirl spent half the night sitting on one spot where the water had begun to seep through. Well I remember the helpless anxiety of sitting at the back window all night, watching the lanterns moving back and forth, sometimes a group together as if in consultation, and sometines in sudden rushing. One week, my husband slept six hours in sixty before giving up and seeing the dyke broken beyond repair.

"Finally in 1940, just as we had one quarter of our best-ever potatoes dug and in sacks in the fields, there were four days of torrential rains. Some years previously, the Provincial Government had built dykes all along the riverbanks. We could walk along the road and see the water flowing level with our heads. Just above our farm, where the river took a big curve out and around the point, a huge cedar swept down on the flood-waters, jammed its point onto the curve of the dyke, swung around and pried an opening in the dyke. Not much of an opening was needed for the full force of the swollen river to rush in, and find an easier way than sweeping out and round the point. In no time, the river had found its way into our farm land, and spread wider and wider. Back at our house, we had already felt the oncoming deluge when the slough, which joined the river lower down, had backed up and inundated our fields. Our house, the same house we had put our dreams into just twelve years previously, was on a slight rise in the land, and never, at the highest waters, had floods come within thirty feet. However, at two in the morning, we heard an ominous trickle which soon turned into many streams, as the water started pouring into our basement. We were lucky, being one of the few families who had a basement; most of the homes had three to four feet of water on the main floor. The men who had been digging our potatoes before the rain started had left their horses in the front pasture. On that first afternoon, when the slough water was backing up, the horses, Major and Queenie, had come to the 'prairie' gate which opened onto the land around the house and the water there was then a foot deep. The girls wanted to go and let them through, but knowing how cold the water was, I said, 'No, Daddy will be home soon and see to it'. By the time he came the same spot was waist deep, and the horses had gone off. The girls and I had taken the wheelbarrow and pulled all our carrots and beets from the garden, and left them in the wheelbarrow to be 'out of the water'.

"The next morning the water filled the basement to five feet, and the wheelbarrow showed the tops of its feet as it lay upside-down. By now the whole valley was one roaring surging mass of murky grey ice-cold water. We couldn't see the home farm or barns for the swirling mist that lay over all. We were completely isolated, and with no knowledge of the fate of our neighbours, nor of our stock which were tied up in the barn right in the path of the stream of water. We had worked all night salvaging what we could from the basement — wood, jars of preserves, fruit, vegetables and meat. We used to can half or three-quarters of a beef at a time. I always remember the irony of it, when I thought I was smart hanging the axe on a nail, only to look at it longingly for days, across a sea of muddy sludgy water.

"Having done all we could, I tried to occupy the girls in their playroom, making a pretense of doing some school lessons and playing games. We tried to keep their attention from the chickens which every now and then were swept past us, valiantly trying to swim against the current.

"It was amazing how long they kept afloat, but inevitably becoming waterlogged and giving up one after the other. Daddy was at the end of his tether with anxiety as to the fate, not only of men and beasts, but our whole livelihood. One of our morning distractions was a flock of stubby field mice which collected on our front steps. We counted twenty of them and the girls fed them out of their hands, and they came right indoors to get out of the wet.

"All the while I was watching the debris sweeping by: whole fir trees, logs, outhouses, fence rails from farther up the valley. My great fear was for an Indian family — father, mother and two children — who were camping in a shack while helping with the potato digging, a shack that was right in the path of the break in the dyke. Suddenly out of the mist came voices and, looking out we saw two men, one in a canoe trying to open the barbed wire gate below the water level, the other riding the swimming horse Major, while Queenie followed behind. For a few desperate minutes time stood still as they wrestled with the gate, gradually lost the struggle and vanished in the mist, carried away with the current. A sinking fear seized us all, the children cried and we strained our ears and peered out into the fog, but could hear nothing above the waters' roar. We went back to try to think of other things.

"Then, joy of joys, voices much nearer, and there were the two in the canoe, with Major swimming behind on a lead rope. They got him to the top of the haystack in the barn, and came to the house, tying up the canoe to the top step. We plied them with coffee and rum and fitted them out with dry clothing. They had been in and out of the water since early in the day, rescuing stock, pigs, horses and cows. Queenie had been swept away, but we found her later caught in a barbed-wire fence. As the men talked to us, we heard two shots ring out across the valley. 'Guess that's Mum,' said Bill Fowler, one of the men, 'she's alone with the kids. Dad is down the valley, and she'll be wondering if I'm alive'.

"As the water went down, in a day we were able to get to a spot where we could shout across to those on the home farm, and get reassuring answers as to the safety of the stock. Later we learned how Grandfather and Uncle Chris had struggled out in water chest high and relieved the cows of their milk. And what of the Indian family? As the water subsided, the man appeared in a canoe across the fields to see if we had anywhere we could put them. The mother and two children had spent two days and nights sitting on the bunk in their shack, and their horse and dog had shared their shelter. Our granary, standing three feet off the ground still had a thick layer of silt left in it. My husband cleaned it out for them and installed an airtight heater. The girls and I collected dry clothing and cooked a big pot of stew. We had two anxious days with the baby; she developed a bad case of bronchitis, but pulled through. I remember worrying about what we would do if the baby died, as we were completely cut off from the rest of the world for days to come. Bridges and parts of the road were washed out, and travel was impossible.

"The aftermath was beyond description: silt, wet, slimy, smelly silt, covered the face of the land and every house, every crack, every cupboard, under linoleum, plastering furniture, corrupting books and papers everywhere. Wandering over fields we would find ourselves in a foot-deep quagmire of silt, like a shallow quicksand. Farm equipment, tractors and all machinery covered with it. We walked through bushland and saw cucumber vines and vegetable marrows hung up in trees feet above our heads . . . ."

Two miles farther downstream lived Jack Ronayne, his son John and John's wife Maud. Their house of logs sat low on the ground. Maud had come to the valley as a bride in September 1940 and had barely had time to settle in when she received a rather drastic initiation to life on a pioneer farm. Because the river had been rising steadily for two days, Jack and John were out working on the dykes every day. Because the house was oppressively warm, Maud had the back door open to cool the kitchen when Jack's brother Joe and his wife Annie, neighbours on the south side, called in to see her. "Are you coming to see the flood?" asked Annie. "Why don't you leave the bread rising and come with us?" But father-in-law Jack said, "Don't go. Come and help me get in the carrots and onions." So she stayed and helped Jack dig the vegetables from the garden patch and lay them out to dry on the open porch at the back of the house. By mid-afternoon the water was in the fields, but Jack told her not to worry: "We are high here. The water never has come into our house." After the vegetables were all brought to the porch Jack decided to take some coal-oil to his brother Edmond because he knew that the family were short of it. On the way home he fell on the slimy mud and found later that he had broken two ribs. Soon after his father returned John went away to work on the dykes and did not come back until midnight.

Maud watched the flood waters rise on to the back porch and because the water was flowing from the north she expected it to start coming in through the back door. Around 5 o'clock she heard the swishing of the water not through there but through the logs on the south wall of the house and hastened to lift the sacks of sugar and flour from the floor on to the kitchen table. In the living room where the water was pouring through the wall she added all the leaves to the big table and piled everything on it. She emptied the low drawers and lifted goods of all sorts to the only high shelf. She was wading up to her knees when John came home. By lamplight they put the highboy in the bathtub and carried their bedroom suite upstairs. There they retreated too, with the cushions off the chairs and the loaves of freshly baked bread, to await morning.

At the first light John left on a raft to see what had happened to the cattle. Soon after Joe paddled through the kitchen in his canoe and called to his brother: "Jack, Jack, are you alright? Come on over to our house. We are not near as wet as you." So Maud took a clean dress and climbed into the canoe with the two brothers who paddled their way across the fields to Joe's house where Annie urged them to stay for both lunch and supper.

By evening the water had started to subside and they returned home, getting into their house by a window in the staircase. By next morning the water was down, but oh, what a sight! Everything up to a two-foot level was plastered with silt. The pots and pans, the rubbing board, the eggs in waterglass, the carrots and onions so carefully collected the day before, all had floated away on the flood waters. The newly harvested potatoes in the roothouse were covered with silt and as they dried had to be cleaned before shipment to Vancouver wholesalers. Most of the chickens were drowned, having flown from their roosts onto the debris-laden water, thinking it to be solid ground.

Eddie Blakeway came up with the news that the cable ferry that was used to cross the Lillooet river was hooked up on a tree on the far side. Jack and John had pasture lands on the east side of the river. Eddie and John and Jack set off in a canoe to cross over to free the ferry. Unfortunately the dog decided to join them. He jumped from the high bank into the canoe, tipped it over, and all three men were in the river. Eddie caught hold of the canoe, and Joe Ronayne, hearing the yells, rushed to the bank and pushed out a log to which the other two men clung.

Meanwhile at the house Maud found it impossible to build a fire because the fire box, ash trap and oven were full of silt which had dried there like cement. The men's workboots kept under the staircase appeared as though a gang of children had been playing mudpies. Maud pumped bucket after bucket of water, but nothing seemed to make much impression. Kathleen Lundgren came in the next day to help and as one pumped, the other swished, and after a long, hard day they at last could see the floor. It took two weeks of washing before the house could be said to be clean. Two years later the lino that John

Flooded fields

had put down fresh the September just before the flood was rotten, and when he pulled it up he found silt underneath.

Another family, the Morgan Millers, after a summer's work had moved their house from the north-east side of the river to that part of their property which bordered on the road. Because the house was still on logs and not set in position Morgan, his wife Bertha, their two little girls Jean 4 and Laurie 3, together with Morgan's brother Ronie, were spending the night in a small cabin. In the early hours of the morning little Laura piped up "Someone's spilt a lot of water on the floor, Mommy." The adults found that there was indeed water on the floor. The river having broken its banks at the bend had washed out the road and was flowing across the field. Carrying the children, they set out without delay across the flooded fields to Lokkens, whose house was slightly higher and had an upstairs to which they and the Lokken family soon retreated.

The next morning Ronie Miller set off by canoe for his father's house farther north and found that the little cabin of the night before had been swept to the corner of Morgan's property. The Miller family moved back into their house which was still on stringers and unmoved by the flood, but they had no opportunity to build a proper foundation that year nor to board in the bottom of the house. They spent the winter with the house high off the ground and the cold air underneath making the floor more than a little chilly. The following spring their third daughter, Mary, was born.

Morgan's father, William Miller, wrote to his sister Nell on November 11, 1940:

"We had a very fine summer in Pemberton. The best crops we ever had, no overflow from the river, a coyote took a few of our chickens and the climbing cutworms did a little damage to our potatoes. That was all the trouble we had until the 18th October, then it rained for about 3 days. The water came up 4 foot higher than we have ever seen it. It got so deep and swift that 11 head of our cattle drowned, also 9 hogs and 10 colonies of bees. Some people up the valley nearly got drowned. Our hay got wet as there was about 3 feet of water in the hay mows. Robbie and I had about half our turnips pulled, piled and covered with their tops; they all went. Our potatoes are here yet in roothouses but so muddy that they are starting to rot in the bottom of the pile. The flood set us back at least $1,000. I only mention our loss, but some people are probably worse off. Morgan's muskrat crop is gone. He will lose $1,000 worth of rats as well as potatoes and hay and maybe some turnips. Alf Ridley, who lives a mile and a half above us, lost 8 of his 11 cows and all his hogs. The Indians must have lost most of their cattle, hogs and potatoes . . . . We left a boat tied to the house, as it might easily have kept on raining for a week instead of three days. Our four horses came through alright; they stood on the highest land until the water went down. If the cattle had done that none would have drowned. Instead, they kept running up and down the road, getting into deep holes and getting stuck on the barbed wire fences. Our troubles are not over yet; we have clear zero weather now, so our potatoes and turnips may freeze . . . ."

In 1940 most of the population lived in the Upper Valley or Pemberton Meadows, but there were a few farms below Miller Creek. The Gimses at the

Canoe in the home pasture

Barbour place about two miles south of Miller Creek had just finished harvesting a record crop of potatoes, about 60 tons says Gunnar Gimse, now a resident of Birken. The potatoes were lying in piles around the field ready to be covered in preparation for the winter's cold. Very little of that fine crop was every recovered. As the flood receded the story was the same everywhere: cows, calves, pigs and chickens found drowned, farm machinery covered in silt, crops ruined.

The next year the grass was very poor, huge logs had to be removed from the fields, and livestock losses were heavy. And the people had received no flood relief, little publicity, and only a little seed grain supplied by the government. All the housewives mentioned the terrible cleanup job, but one bachelor solved the problem quite happily: he made trails through the dirt for all the world like trails through a snow-laden field.

The van Beem family and Edith Perkins

NEW ARRIVALS

After the flooding the Pemberton farmers struggled to get on their feet again. The only government help offered was seed to plant the following year; nothing for ruined homes, drowned stock, spoiled machinery and lost tools, nothing even for stored crops ruined and unsaleable. Farmers and businessmen all realised that some effort had to be made to prevent the recurrence of such a disaster. The Pemberton Drainage and Reclamation Committee formed by the Board of Trade and supported by the Farmers' Institute consisted of Bob Taylor, Joe Taillefer and Harold Wyatt-Purden, and their main purpose was to prepare a brief to be presented to the Post-War Rehabilitation Council. The brief called for the dyking and straightening of the Lillooet River and its tributaries, Ryan Creek and Miller Creek, and the lowering of Lillooet Lake. The chairman of the Post-War Rehabilitation Council, the Hon. H. G.T. Perry, was present at a hearing on flood control held in Pemberton on October 2nd, 1942 and the Farmers' Institute sent Nels Fraser and Ernest Cooper as its representatives.

Apart from appealing to every branch of the Provincial and Federal Governments which might conceivably be willing to help, the Drainage Committee was active in the field. The committee by this time also included Sandy Ross, Morgan Miller, Ron Ronayne, Eddie Ronayne and Walter Green. They completed the Miller Cut, thanks to $275 subscribed locally and to a donation of powder from the Provincial Government. Most of the labour for this project was donated.

Finally, in 1946, the efforts of the committee were rewarded and the federal government agreed to carry out the reclamation project under the Prairie Farm Rehabilitation Act — ironically passed to deal with drought conditions. Besides dyking and straightening of the rivers and making certain alterations to the channel between Lillooet Lake and Tenas Lake, the project had the eventual effect of lowering the water of the Lillooet River by some 15 feet, and ditches constructed in strategic areas to run off surplus water brought large blocks of former swamp land into production. At a meeting held

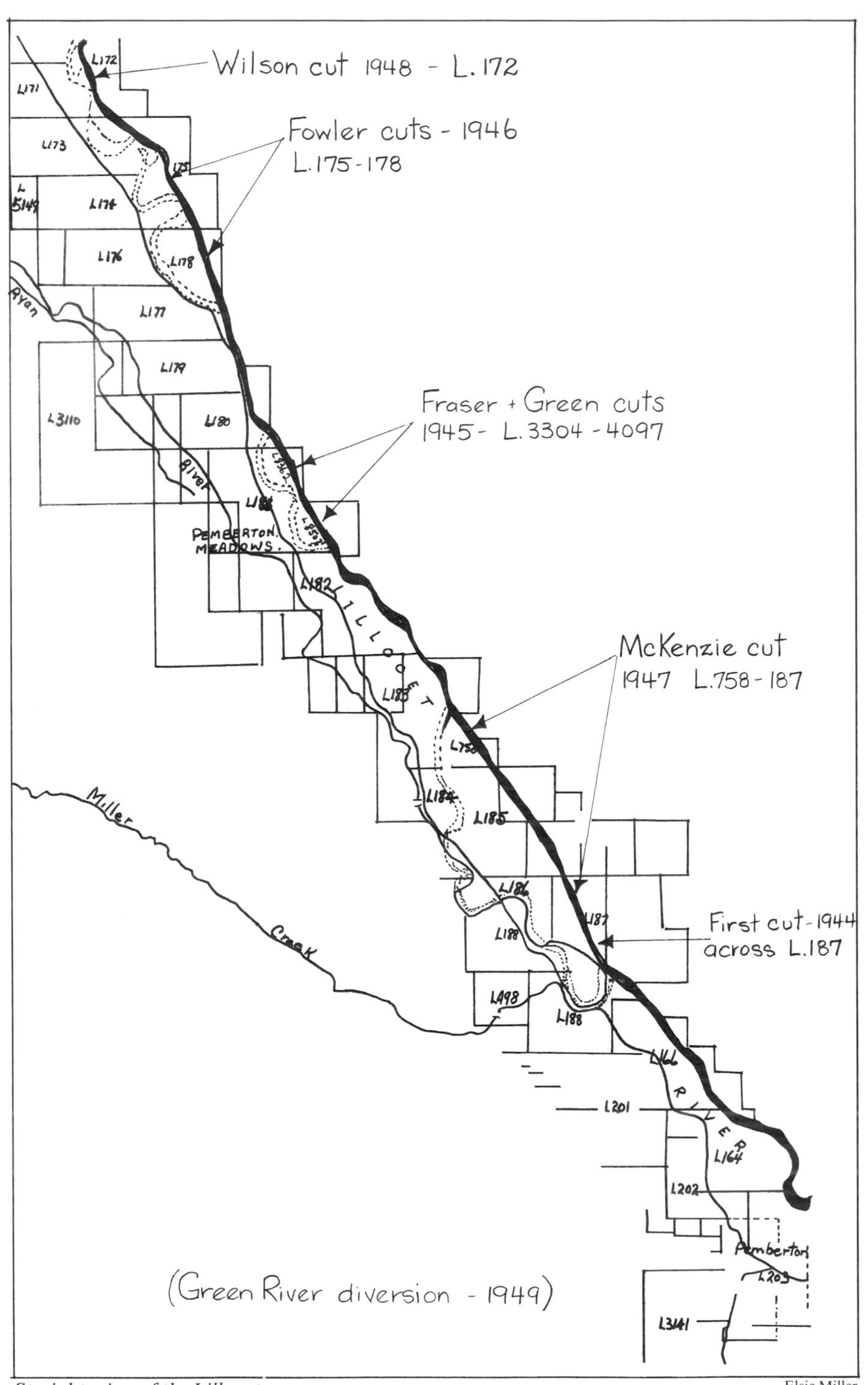

Straightening of the Lillooet Elsie Miller

at Pemberton Hotel that same year the committee met with government representatives: J. Gillett of New Westminster; J. McGuigan, also of New Westminster, the engineer of the project; J. D. McLeod of Vancouver; George Spence and G. I. MacKenzie of Regina; and J. C. Moore of Calgary. This group commenced the preliminary work of verifying previous reports and of securing profiles of the Lillooet Lake outlet, rough topography, and levels of the Pemberton Valley. Throughout the procedure the Drainage Committee men were active in the field, hacking out survey lines, digging shafts, swinging on cables over rapids to get soundings, sleeping out in the rain and mosquitoes, and trying not to get in the hair of the engineers. The Pemberton and District Dyking Commission was officially formed in 1947 and the letters patent show the first committee as Sandy Ross, Morgan Miller, Bob Taylor, Harold Wyatt-Purden and Ronald Ronayne; Joseph Taillefer acted as the first returning officer. Not only were existing land holdings improved, but much reclaimed crown land became available for settlement, notably the area between Pemberton and Mount Currie, a large section above Miller Creek, and a block of land in the northern part of the valley near the Wolverine Cut.

All this was not accomplished without some tribulations: land for ditches was at times taken from those who stood little to gain from the works; residents were awakened at early hours by the window-rattling blasts set by Sandy Ross; local men and government engineers did not always agree on methods; taxes were levied before completion, with predictable protests. Worst of all, in July 1948 high water caused flooding when the drainage project was but half completed. The farms in the Upper Valley were safe behind dykes, but the flood waters swept on to inundate the Lower Valley farms of Bert Lundgren, Morgan Miller, Slim Fougberg, Andy Anderson, Henry Menzel, Fred Menzel and Vivien Lokken. The project was finally completed,

P.F.R.A. Camp Provincial Archives, Victoria, B.C.

Lowering Lillooet Lake Provincial Archives, Victoria, B.C.

however, and taken over by the local committee with power to levy taxes and generally maintain the dykes. Under the Tri-Partite Agreement signed in 1948 the Federal government did the construction, the Provincial government provided access roads and rights-of-way and the local committee accepted responsibility for general maintenance. A dragline was purchased for ditchclearing and Morgan Miller became foreman of works.

A serious flood threat developed in the summer of 1950 and the dykes at several points had to be reinforced with sandbags, but nowhere did the river break through. Over the next ten years the water level of the Lillooet River gradually dropped and some farmers who in the pre-drainage era had been safe on the high land were faced with the necessity of buying irrigation equipment. Drying out became more of a problem than flooding, and higher taxes forced farmers to press all their land into production. By the mid-'sixties irrigation pipes were a standard feature on most potato producing farms.

The new land made available by the drainage project brought a rush of new settlers in the late 'forties and early 'fifties. New modern services also encouraged the purchase of both old run-down farms and the new government land.

As early as 1912, the potential for electrical power from the Bridge River had been noted by the land surveyor Geoffrey Downton whose daughter Marjorie Gimse lives in Birken today. From Mission Mountain he was able to see that the river at a much higher elevation was separated from Seton Lake by a relatively narrow mountain barrier. In late 1947 work began on the 12,200 foot tunnel under Mission Mountain to divert Bridge River water through the mountain, dropping 1,200 feet in large steel pipes or penstocks. By the winter of 1931 the tunnel was completed, but the depression and the war years halted further development until 1946. Pemberton residents chugging up Howe

Sound on the old Union Steamships observed the progress of the power line and began to hope that at long last electrical power would reach Pemberton Valley. By October 1948 Powerhouse No. 1 was completed and the village residents could see the power grids running across the flats to the south, but when the power was turned on at Bridge River there was no branch to Pemberton Valley. Local organizations appealed this decision, notably the Board of Trade. The Women's Institute even asked support from the Fraser Valley in an effort to have a representative of the power company to meet with Pemberton residents. By 1950 rumours were rife: the power was coming; the B.C. Electric thought the district too small to justify a transformer. Local residents still purchased power plants, but made sure that wiring was up to standard. Only when tenders were invited for pole cutting, did the Valley finally believe!

In 1951 electricity came to Pemberton! First to the village, in March. Then the line was strung along the Valley road to connect most of the residents by the fall. Mount Currie had to wait three more years.

The summer of 1951 was a busy and harassing one for the Valley's only electrician and plumber, Jack Taillefer. Every family wanted wiring and many wanted plumbing too. Each woman felt that she had most need of power and "would he please come tomorrow!" Every farm household wanted a water pump, at last to be rid of hand pumps and buckets, of trips to the river, and of the need for melting snow. At last to say goodbye to the outhouse, freezing in winter and flyridden in summer. Many households already owned washers, temperamental gasoline washers cranked like a powersaw and just about as noisy, with the exhaust pipe through a window or the open back door, but these their owners soon traded in for quieter and more reliable electric models. Those nice clean electric lights shone out brightly from the windows, and gasoline and coal-oil lamps were set aside for emergencies. No more pumping gas lamps with the flames leaping round the mantle, no more sad irons. The family who could not afford a refrigerator this year, or an electric stove, would surely have their gleaming convenience next year or the year after.

One single appliance, the electric freezer, revolutionized the eating habits of the settlers. No more canned meat which, whether rump or flap, managed always to taste the same; no more canned peas, their fine flavour completely destroyed by long boiling. Now strawberries retained their flavour, butter kept fresh through the long winter months, bread did not need to go stale and best of all, a variety of meat and poultry made meal planning easy.

With the electrical power came, inevitably, the telephone, for beneath the powerline, on the same pole, telephone wires could surely be strung. Two years of harassment by local organizations resulted in the first few telephones being installed in 1953. All on one party line operated by the crank system, each caller had a distinctive ring and all calls went through the Squamish exchange.

The first listing for Pemberton included the following numbers:

Private		Business	
2E	Van Beem	2D	P.G.E. Railway
2W	Fowler	2G	Pemberton Co-op
2H	Decker	2T	Pemberton Express
2Q	John Ronayne	2K	Warren's Store
2X	Green	2P	Fleetwood Logging
2Y	Robert Miller	2G	Walker
2F	Fougberg		
2B	Taylor		

As the years went on more phones were added until eighteen families shared the same line. The phones were frequently "out" for days at a time: long distance calls were particularly trying because if another subscriber lifted a phone the voices died away in the distance. In 1957 the contract to build a separate exchange at Pemberton was awarded to a local contractor, Zurbrugg and Son, and at 8 a.m. on September 17, 1958 Pemberton's $125,800 dial telephone system went into service with approximately 100 subscribers. At that time, two-letter, five-figure numbering was used throughout B.C. Telephone's operating area, and Pemberton's designation was TWINOAKS 4, a very appropriate designation because oak trees do not grow in Pemberton! Although years later in having telephone service, Pemberton joined the automatic system ahead of both Lillooet and Squamish. By 1966 the number of phones had grown to 270 and were a routine feature of every home.

Conditions on the farms in the war years changed very little from the 'thirties because the Wartime Prices and Trade Board controlled the prices of produce sold on the commercial market and therefore, indirectly, the seed market. Heavy demand for potato seed in the first three post-war years, however, encouraged an increase in production: by 1949, 203 acres grown by some 40 farmers passed government inspection for seed. That same year a Seed Potato Control Area was formed in Pemberton, which meant that only local seed could be planted.

Pemberton's isolation was now an advantage because diseases prevalent in the Fraser Valley and elsewhere would be kept out. A local committee ensured that the rules were abided by — its first members were Sandy Ross, Morgan Miller, Slim Fougberg, and Jack Decker. The Netted Gem continued as the principal variety because it was a good keeper that sold readily on the commercial market if seed sales collapsed, as they often did. Ernest Cooper introduced the White Rose in 1941 and other farmers grew small quantities of Early Rose, Epicure, and Green Mountain. Growers like Ross Brothers and Jack Decker continued to win prizes for their potatoes, and for three years in succession Decker also won the grand championship for peas at the Chicago International Fair. Post-war demands for flower seeds encouraged Jack

Potatoes in Flower

Decker to enter this market too for a few short years, and now lupines seeding themselves year after year make a fine showing along the fences of the old Decker farm every summer.

On the outbreak of World War II many of the young men left the valley to join the armed forces, two of their number, Ronie Miller and Pat Wilson, never to return. The young men left behind to run the farms formed a platoon of the Pacific Coast Militia Rangers, drilling under the leadership of Sergeant Arthur Mawbey, veteran of World War I and his assistant Lance-Corporal

Old Iron Wheels

Morgan Miller. At the end of the war and during the late 'forties and early 'fifties Pemberton had changed and was changing in a variety of ways.

The good years following the war started the transition from horse power to machine power. Teams of horses were still used, but iron-wheeled tractors were making their appearance; shortage of labour hastened the changeover. Cream still represented a steady if small income to many of the farms, though as it only sold for butter-making the price proved low, so low, in fact, that many of the former dairy operators had converted to beef production, often

1948 Show at New Westminster

by the simple and cheap process of purchasing a series of beef bulls and gradually weeding out the dairy types. Most farms grew turnips for which only a limited market existed, but farmers could pit the turnips and use them for cattle feed if the market evaporated. A few carrots were grown mainly for local sale. Grain still planted by hand biblical style was cut green for hay or bound and threshed in the winter, though by 1949 no working thresher existed and only a couple of beat-up binders.

The Potato Planters

Hay, that great lifesaver of the 'thirties, could still command a market, but haying crews in the post-war boom of the cities became first difficult and then impossible to find. The hay loader introduced into Pemberton in the late 'thirties did, though, eliminate the need for gang labour. With the assistance of a driver, often wife or young son, the farmer could put up his hay virtually alone, but by the time he had loaded all the hay and forked it up into the high steep-roofed barns he usually felt that the forty to fifty tons he needed to keep a herd of cattle through Pemberton's six months of winter had taken enough of his time and energy. Sandy and Gerald Ross still put up hay for sale, baling in the winter months with an old-fashioned baler converted from horse to tractor power and putting out huge bales weighing up to 140 pounds.

Beef production offered a steady income, but several years were required to build up a herd, and prices, apart from the bonanza year of 1951, were to remain low for many years. The discovery of the need for iodine did not end the problems of Pemberton's livestock industry. In the late 'thirties a virulent strain of calf pneumonia appeared in the herds of Pemberton Meadows, and spreading from farm to farm the disease decimated the calf crops, killing half to two-thirds of the calves in the affected herds. Appearing in calves between two weeks and two months of age the disease struck quickly: a calf running around in good health in the early morning could be dead by nightfall, grunting out its last breath with stiffening limbs. The government veterinarians blamed the springtime dirt of the barnyards and poor management, but most farmers were convinced that a bug was involved because some farms seemed immune though their barnyards were no better than average. Sally Purden, the Indian Department nurse, decided to try experimental shots of penicillin on

The Man Killer

The Back Breaker

her husband's ailing calves and managed to cure a few. Other farmers followed suit and saved at least some of the stricken animals. Gradually partial immunity was built up in the herds and the disease became less severe while farmers avoided the early spring for calving and used selenium shots to give the animals some added resistance. In time the disease slowly died out.

In 1962 five farmers — Morgan and Don Miller, Lexi Ross together with Swiss-born Gus Zurcher and Al Staehli — formed the Miller Creek Livestock Association for the purpose of obtaining permission from the B.C. Forest Service to graze cattle on alpine meadows during summer months and thereby supplement their limited home pasture. Gus Zurcher's early life in Switzerland had given him training and experience in alpine grazing and the meadows they planned to go to on the west side of the valley at elevations of four to six thousand feet were well known since boyhood to the Miller brothers.

Supported by local Forest Ranger Don Gill the group obtained their permit and at once set to work. They slashed out a trail from Miller Creek up the steep mountainside to the meadows, bridging a roaring canyon stream on the way. Finally herds of cattle born and bred on flat valley land were persuaded to climb the steep, rocky trails. Families and friends pitched in to help with the drive. Once well-started the cows did not plod on stolidly; young and old frequently tried to dodge back. The first animals arrived at the meadows on July 10th, 1963. The Association then built a cabin to shelter the workers while they engaged in the yearly tasks of clearing and re-locating trails, checking, salting and treating cattle, even rescuing them in early snow falls. The grazing season on this range is short, but the cattle thrived on the mountain forage and air. The owners with their families share the work of patrolling the herds and keen horseriders as most of them are they enjoy a holiday in the mountains.

Settlers in the early 'fifties did not face the physical hardships of those who came earlier. The advent of machinery helped the farm operator, while his wife's life was considerably eased by the coming of electricity and with water being pumped to the house. But all these conveniences had to be paid for. Most new settlers started with heavy land payments as well as with machinery to buy and buildings to construct. Often the farmer worked away from home for cash, putting in an extra shift on the farm in the evenings. Wives could be seen out on the tractors cultivating the land, slashing out saplings with a brushhook, working on the sorting crews, picking up potatoes, topping turnips, and milking the cows with the baby in a buggy outside the barn. The more easily cleared land had, in the main, been taken up by the earlier settlers, and newcomers therefore faced heavy costs for bulldozing, but early in the 'fifties a government-sponsored land-clearing scheme went into

Building the Barn

operation with low interest loans for those anxious to bring brush land into production. After the bulldozing came the stick-picking when whole families spent evenings and weekends picking up the small sticks left behind after clearing. In addition, bulldozed land has lost a good part of its topsoil, and as a consequence several years must pass before the land can be brought into full production. Meanwhile, father worked out and mother made do with an old shack for a home, patched clothes, grew and canned a big garden, helped on the farm, sometimes worked out too while waiting for the prosperity which in the 'fifties was supposed to be around the corner. Many of those who came left for jobs and better opportunities elsewhere, but those who stayed gradually cleared the bushland and turned it into a farm. Finally they built a modern house and their friends then envied them their luck for having managed to get hold of property that by 1966 had increased in value by leaps and bounds.

Settler's Cabin Provincial Archives, Victoria, B.C.

As the drainage programme progressed new settlers came to the valley, buying up old and abandoned farms and filling up the new lands drained from old swamps. From Quebec, the prairies, and from all parts of British Columbia, they came to take up land, to run mills and to start businesses. Many were

New Canadians, recent immigrants from all over Europe: Finns, Swedes, Norwegians, Dutch, Swiss, Hungarians, and British as well as Chinese from Hong Kong, and Americans. They enriched the already homogeneous Valley population with their varying cultures and brought a fresh outlook and energies to old problems.

The Austins came from the prairies in the early 'fifties to run a small sawmill on the island lots created by the changing of the river channel at the north end of the Valley. Their stay was abruptly terminated by the death of their son Eddie, a young man in his early twenties recently married to a local girl, Noreen Shier. After a day's work in the bush Eddie was crossing the Lillooet on a cable car with Bert Bushagger and Gus Zurcher. One corner of the raft slipped underwater, then upended, and the cable snapped. The three young men were swept into the swift-flowing river swollen with the summer run-off. A strong swimmer, Gus Zurcher made it to the shore, looked back to see only Eddie Austin still clinging to the raft and, stopping only to remove his boots, plunged back into the river. He fought his way through the icy waters and when only eight feet separated them Eddie disappeared. Neither he nor Bert was ever found.

Also from the prairies were Howie and Marion Ayers who bought the old Harvey Nelson land in the 'fifties and added several lots to the original title. A refugee from the city Howie worked as a truck driver and machine operator. Warner and Audrey Oberson who purchased Milton Shantz's land were also part-time farmers, Warner working for the railroad and Audrey at office bookkeeping. Much later in the 'seventies there were to be many families with small holdings who were raising a few animals and growing fruit and vegetables, but dependent for their main income elsewhere.

Three Dutch couples followed Austins in the mid-'fifties: Tony and Nell Van Loon, Bill and Ann Van Geel, and Cor and Lennie Durvin. Durvins purchased the old Blakeway log house, dragging it five miles up the valley road to a sandy place near Salmon Slough. They sold out to Bert Praat, another Dutchman in 1959, and the old house endured a second move. Ann Van Geel's first son John was born in the Valley with neighbours Doris Van Beem and Elsie Miller on hand to assist. When the Van Geels left in the early 'sixties the holding was divided between the Van Loons and Bert Praat. Though still retaining Pemberton holdings Praat now farms on the lower mainland, but the Van Loons stayed to develop the virgin bushland into a fine prosperous farm through their united hard work and thrift. Over the early years Tony worked out and spend his evenings and weekends on the farm. Working as a bulldozer operator, he obtained the weekend use of the machine in lieu of part of his wages and was able to clear the bushland at minimum cost. In a few years broad fertile fields stretched from Salmon Slough to the Lillooet River. The old Austin cabin was replaced, first with a small house and much later by a modern home large enough to accommodate their family of five who were raised in the same hardworking tradition. Another Dutch couple, Martin and Catharine Beks, settled rather later on part of the old Girling land where Martin operated a shingle mill for some years before turning to full-time farming. They too replaced the old log house which had served the Barry Girlings during the flood. Other Dutch families included the Harmsens who rented both the Lokken farm and the Van Rechteren land for a short period before settling in the Fraser Valley, and the Van Gools on the Cooper land in the upper vallcy.

The Swiss families developed their farms as part-time enterprises, working full-time at other occupations. Al and Marti Staehli bought their land from bachelor John Arn, a fellow countryman. Al worked for the forestry and later, as their family grew old enough to take care of the farm chores, Marti joined him during the summer months to cook for the fire suppression crews at the camp above Pemberton. Fotsches took over Toni Bikadi's farm on the Mount Currie road in the early 'fifties when Hungarian-born Toni went logging. Roger Fotsch worked part-time at many jobs, moving to Vancouver for a period, but later returning to work for the Parks Board and to develop a small sheep enterprise.

Zurbruggs and Zurchers settled on former swamp land to replace swamp willow and rushes with pasture for cattle and sheep. Gus Zurcher worked for the Highways Department, developing his farmland at the weekends, and being ably assisted by his wife Leny. Raised on a mountain farm in Switzerland Leny tackled the farm work with energy and skill. Gus built his home in the Swiss style with covered porch and wide overhanging eaves and his farm is noted for the exotic breeds that he has developed by a program of artificial insemination. Fred Zurbrugg became a contract carpenter in partnership with his son and built many chalets at Whistler Mountain as well as many buildings in Pemberton, the telephone exchange in 1958 for instance.

German Harry Hormes farmed just south of them, starting improvements that his widow continues today. A woman of many talents Senta Hormes paints pictures, remodels furniture and embroiders with exceptional skill. German, too, were the Saefkows who rented the old Cooper farm and are chiefly remembered for their skill in sausage making and for Mrs. Saefkow's talent as a pastry cook. After they moved to northern British Columbia, Charlie Woldersdorf, also German-born, ran the farm as a part-time addition to his principal occupation of electrician. The Woldersdorfs left after a few years for the wider opportunities of the lower mainland.

Two Finnish families, the Hjelts and the Kuurnes, left the Bralorne mines to purchase small farms, the old Hartzell place and the Punch land. Like the Swiss, they worked their farms part-time, Purti Hjelt working for the Highways and Petter Kuurne as a carpenter. Purti and Liisa Hjelt left for Vancouver in the early 'sixties, but Petter and Aino Kuurne stayed on to develop a neat small farm where in the season they dried their hay on spiked poles in the style of northern Scandinavia.

Another Scandinavian, Swedish-born Fred Ostman, settled just north of the Lillooet River bridge on the new Mount Currie road on land that had been subject to severe flooding before drainage. Fred owned and operated a bulldozer, clearing and road-making, gradually clearing off the heavy timber from his own land at the same time, eventually growing potatoes and raising beef cattle. Another Swede, Verne Lundstrom, purchased land from Bert Lundgren, but Verne's principal interest in the property was the timber available and after working for several years in Pemberton both pole cutting and logging he and his family left for greener pastures. Returning veteran Slim Fougberg, a former Valley resident and originally from Sweden, started farming right after the war on land which was largely swamp, only a small fringe near the road being suitable for crops. Slim brought the first chain digger into the valley and organized large crews of workers to dig a good proportion of the valley's potato crop in the early 'fifties.

Sam and Dorothy Gilmore who bought Slim's land were among the many couples lured from the lower mainland by cheaper land and lower taxes. The Gilmores rather than Slim reaped the benefit of the drainage. As the years went on the river level went down and with the aid of ditches the back swamp-land was brought into production. Gilmores brought a dairy herd with them, but soon changed to beef and potatoes as their source of income. Sam and his sons ended by bringing all the land into use: though often wet in the heavy fall rains, and needing ditching, this area never again had the disastrous floods of the past. Behind Gilmores, Jack and Gay Guthrie also settled on former swamp-land and tried their hands at dairying. Jack had a milk run for a while and delivered milk to the village residents, but later moved into beef production and worked for several years for the Highways. His wife Gay still teaches at Signal Hill Elementary School. Another couple who tried dairying, Gunnar and Margaret Nielsen, purchased the Van Rechteren land. Arriving in the early spring Danish-born Gunnar drove his pure-bred milk herd ten miles up the muddy Valley road. Knee-deep in places, the mud made hauling the cows by truck impossible and by the time the cows reached the farm they were exhausted and covered with muck. The Nielsens ran a milk delivery business for a time and grew potatoes, but left after a few years to return to the lower mainland.

Another who stayed but a few years in Pemberton was Hector Harwood who rented the Barry Girling farm in the late 'forties. Hector, who was originally from New Zealand, butchered for other farmers as a side-line and hawked the meat up and down the Valley, but later moved to Mount Currie where he ran a small cafe by the railroad. After having left the area for many years Hector and Adele returned to Pemberton to retire.

Len and Marion McNolty who followed Harwoods on the Girling farm also moved on to northern B.C. Len tried every aspect of farming, dairying, raising pigs, selling eggs, growing potatoes, whatever had a possibility of making money, and as a consequence his lively family of boys was always busy. Len's brother Merv bought the Blakeway farm and during most of his stay in

Pemberton worked at other jobs, farming at the weekends. He moved with wife Pat and family to Ontario in the early 'sixties, but his son Stewart returned to Pemberton to marry Judy Taylor and become a permanent resident.

To Kel and Peg Harris who came from North Vancouver in the early 'fifties, the small holding they purchased from Frank Smith's heirs offered a chance for an extensive garden and room for their growing family rather than a source of income. Kel worked first in Taylor's garage and later for the school board as a bus driver.

In the upper valley Kirkland and McCubbin purchased land from Dunc Morrison, for a few years combining their Pemberton farming with their main interests in the lower mainland. Soon this proved unprofitable and Kirkland sold out to Elmer and Ruth Hellevang from Ladner. Starting out in the early 'fifties in a small, very basic cabin Ruth coped with carrying water from the slough, a wood stove, and generally primitive conditions, while Elmer worked out as a carpenter. But from that wood stove in that tiny cabin came well-cooked meals and feather-light cakes for Ruth had quite a reputation as a cook. Later, as her family grew, Ruth too worked out, teaching at the elementary school. Over the years the bushland was cleared and farming took more of Elmer's time. The little cabin was added to again and again until further improvement became uneconomic and Elmer built a modern home. During his years as a carpenter Elmer built the Health Centre on contract and was involved in the remodelling of the Pemberton Hotel.

Building the Health Centre Provincial Archives, Victoria, B.C.

From the same area of the lower mainland came Bob and Elsie Spetifore. In partnership with Fred Collister, Bob purchased the Chris Girling farm in the early 'fifties. Fred and his wife Eleanor moved to Mount Currie in 1957 to take over a hardware store and post office, while Bob remained with the farm, though for many years he worked out trucking and driving machines for logging companies to supplement his farm income. Later Bob's two sons, Bob and David, joined him in the operation of the farm. The old Chris Girling house burned in the early 'sixties and in time modern homes were built.

George and Frieda Mitchell came from Chilliwack to settle on Alf Ridley's old farm in 1953 and proved themselves to be true farmers by first building barn, roothouse and machine-shed, before replacing the old log house. A plumber by trade George found plenty of opportunities to work out during the early years, and Frieda, a farmer's daughter, kept the home farm going. She was often to be seen out cultivating the fields, her younger children riding on a board behind her. Though Alf Ridley had farmed on the property for more than twenty years, much of the land had been subject to flooding, and the Mitchells were faced with considerable clearing before George could settle to full-time farming and gradually replace Alf Ridley's old dairy herd with beef cattle to supplement their income from potatoes.

To the low-lying land below Henry Erickson's, Jim Shier brought his wife Nell in the 'forties. Jim first trapped the swamp and later when it was drained went into farming. This land Lex Ross purchased from widowed Nell in the early 'sixties. Below this property was a large expanse of heavily timbered land accessible only by cable car across Ryan Creek. Harry McCulloch had started earlier below Joffre Creek on Lillooet Lake and here farmed a small clearing in the late 'forties and early 'fifties. A new bridge over Ryan Creek and the rerouting of the road encouraged Harry to sell his land to Dr. Dwight Dill, a wealthy Texan, who acquired all the land between Lex Ross' and the Ryan Creek bridge in addition to the Van Rechteren farm in the Pemberton Meadows and James Landsborough's farm farther north. Dr. Dill and his wife lived in Pemberton on a full-time basis only briefly, for the most part leaving the clearing and cultivating of the land to managers and the broad fields above Ryan Creek show how a landscape can be transformed by heavy equipment and money to carry out the seeding down of the new land. Ploughing in crop after crop of clover and buckwheat to build up the soil, the managers later grew a wide variety of crops from strawberries to wheat. Also from Texas was Jay Moore who settled on the Mount Currie road in the 'fifties and built a large barn and neat home on his holdings where he raised both sheep and pigs until ill-health forced his retirement from active farming.

And the older settlers had not disappeared. Don Miller returned from the army to join his father and brother Robbie on the home farm. The drainage scheme had greatly increased the usable acres and, as in other places, fields replaced swamps and the black old spears of water-killed cedars were finally cleared away. Later when sole owner, Don replaced the sagging old house and built up the largest herd of beef cattle in the Valley. Alf Ridley's son Fred, also a veteran, returned with wife Billy to rent the Van Rechteren land for a few years before moving to Ontario. The Fowler brothers, Bill and Leonard, each took over part of the family farm when their parents moved to Squamish in the 'forties. Both farmed at different times, mostly part-time, but the drainage that helped many dried out much of the Fowler land, and the farm was virtually unused for many years: Bill followed his father as road foreman in Pemberton and later moved to Lillooet, while Leonard turned to full-time work in the woods. Ronald Ronayne, another veteran, settled on part of the Landsborough land, farming there until the mid-'sixties. His brother Clifford and two cousins John and Eddie followed their fathers on the home farms. Bert and Kathleen Lundgren purchased the Barbour farm in the early 'forties, like others clearing and bringing into production the bush and swamp. Starting with a newly built log house which they later sold to Lundstroms, the Lundgrens lived in the old Barbour house until Bert built a fully modern home in the early 'fifties. A good carpenter like most Scandinavians, Bert worked out on many construction projects.

The Menzel brothers who had spent much of their youth in the valley also returned to farm. Fred farmed the old Currie ranch for several years before selling out to Jim Collins. Henry, a veteran returning with his Scottish-born wife Phemie, bought a lot north of Lundgren's property, but high clearing costs and the increasing dryness of the land forced him into full-time employment on the road, and he kept the farm as a part-time venture. Max Menzel, who married locally raised May Taylor, purchased a farm nearby and worked part-time for the fisheries in the summer, and assisted by May he raised a few cattle and grew a small acreage of crops.

Norwegian-born Magnus Urdal returned to his farm with his wife Clarice after spending most of the war years working for the U.S. Army. A hard worker skilled at a variety of trades Magnus worked for the P.F.R.A. and in many construction jobs while farming. He sold his farm to John and Edna Leach in 1958 and worked full-time for Jack Nelson and also under contract for the school board. Magnus worked too at Franks' Mill both as a millwright and carpenter.

George Purden continued on the home farm after his father's death while his mother continued her work for the Indian department. Many of the sons of the original settlers like the Frasers, the Fowlers, the Rosses turned to logging as their occupation but continued to hold their land. Michael Ross later worked on his father's farm, but the Wilson family left in the 'fifties, their property being sold to a Vancouver doctor. Harry Kenyon managed the farm for Dr. Arbour for several years, and his skill as an amateur veterinarian was much appreciated by his neighbours. Frank Tierney rented the old Landsborough farm for a while before it was sold to Dr. Dill. In fact there was much coming and going during the developing years, particularly among the renters.

With all the newly drained land, a fresh crop of settlers, more machinery, the coming of the power, the telephone and the train through to Vancouver, the 'fifties should have been a time of great prosperity for Pemberton farmers. Unfortunately prices during these years for both potatoes and cattle were very depressed. Two good years for potatoes and one good year for beef between 1948 and 1965 were not enough, and though seed potatoes commanded a better price the supply of seed potatoes far exceeded the demand. Farmers with orders not unnaturally held onto their customers, and the late comers had only the fringe of the market. For most, therefore, the commercial market held the key to prosperity — or otherwise.

Early in 1941 a group of farmers and businessmen formed the Pemberton and District Co-operative Association with the object of obtaining feed and supplies more cheaply. Edmond Ronayne, John Ronayne, Ernest Blakeway, Frank Kershaw, Gunnar Gimse and Harold Wyatt-Purden attended the first meeting on July 25th of that year. Starting in a very small way with a working capital of $500 borrowed from its members, the Co-op opened a small store run by Mrs. Prendergast, but its main business centered on the warehouse built near the railroad tracks. The first manager, Mr. Pope, was paid the princely sum of $5.00 a week for two eight-hour days; the following year Harvey Derrick, for many years part-time station agent, was offered $10.00 a month for looking after the warehouse. Soon phasing itself out of the grocery part of the business, the Co-op took over the "Snowflake" brand from the Board of Trade, and became actively involved in the shipment of both potatoes and turnips through the Interior Vegetable Marketing Board. The "Snowflake" was registered by the Board of Trade and printed on the sacks to identify Pemberton potatoes — no other area could use this brand. Arthur Mawbey became manager and shipper in 1945, followed in 1950 by Eric Gethen who became the first full-time manager and was also responsible for the bookkeeping formerly done by the members of the committee. Harry Erickson took over from Eric Gethen in 1957 and he was followed by John Cosulich in 1959.

By 1954 the demands of the Vancouver wholesalers for washed potatoes provided the incentive for the Pemberton Co-op to approach the government for assistance in building a packing house which, with considerable government help, was eventually completed in the fall of 1956. Jack Nelson won the contract and paid his workers $1.75 an hour, among whom were Magnus Urdal, Bert Lundgren, Morgan Miller and Henry Erickson, the first three serving as the building committee.

That first winter of potato washing in the new warehouse was a year of rock-bottom prices. None of the farmers could afford to hire a crew for washing at the station, and therefore agreed to trade labour to get the work done. First the potatoes were rough-graded in the farm roothouses and then hauled down to the Co-op warehouse for washing and re-sorting. The washing crew worked from 8 a.m. to 6 p.m., with farmers feeding their animals in the winter darkness, having a quick breakfast, and driving down to the village. After a full day at the warehouse they returned home to face another round of chores. Most of them worked at the warehouse from four to six weeks and in addition traded labour at their farm root-houses. To calculate wages per hour out of the profits proved to be very depressing. Through the years strenuous efforts were made to include seed potatoes in the Co-op business, but this was never completely successful because many buyers preferred to deal directly with the farmers or through the Northern Seed Company run by Charlie Bradbury. The Co-op was destined throughout its life to skate on the very thin ice of one financial crisis after another, but it nevertheless served a useful purpose as shipping agent and supplier at a time when transportation was difficult and phone service was unreliable or, as in its early days, nonexistent. The road to Vancouver finally put an end to the Co-op: produce could be shipped direct, and sacks, feed, fertilizer and other farm needs delivered to the farmer's gate from mainland suppliers.

Prices for commercial potatoes in the spring of 1965 reached a record high level and there was a shortage of seed stock: Pemberton started the season in a glow of optimism. At the University of British Columbia that same summer a research team managed to isolate two viruses which affect the growth and tonnage of seed potatoes, and researchers needed to try out these virus-free cuttings which had been grown in the greenhouses of the University. Because isolation was essential, Pemberton and part of the Cariboo were chosen as the testing grounds. Cuttings were planted at Clifford Ronayne's farm in 1966, and at George Mitchell's the following year, and from this small beginning the project was eventually expanded to include most of the Valley farms. The yields from this virus-tested stock proved significantly heavier, and the publicity put out by the Department of Agriculture was to bring buyers from other areas of British Columbia and most of the western potato-producing States, even Idaho. Shipments to such far away places as Holland meant that Pemberton potatoes had "arrived" and that the isolation which had been so long a disadvantage now offered dividends of greatly increased prosperity and stability of income. The trend of farmers' sons away from the farm was halted, and farming was again a viable occupation for young men.

The Farmers' Institute continued through the early 'forties, but was fairly inactive from 1945-53 because its function was taken over by the seed growers association and the same men were members of both groups. With the decline of the seed market of the 'fifties, the Farmers' Institute became revitalized and supported the Co-op in its drive for a warehouse for the marketing of commercial potatoes and bringing in speakers to talk on the possibility of other crops for the area.

Apart from their control of the seed potato growing, the Pemberton and District Seed Growers Association also agreed each year on the selling price for their produce, a price which often dropped as the season wore on! Every year they held a field day in late July or early August and invited buyers to view the fields. In the early 'fifties prizes were given for the best fields judged on freedom from disease, cultivation and appearance. Lunch for the visitors was served by the farmers' wives in the Upper Valley hall and a dance was held in the evening after the visitors had left. Interest flagged when machinery and fertilizer salesmen outnumbered the buyers, and the buyers who did come kept a low profile on price and emphasized instead "the great way of life you have here". Abandoned for several years when the potato market suffered a depression, the virus-free program saw the revival of the field days in the late 'sixties and plenty of interest from buyers.

Digging potatoes

Provincial Archives, Victoria, B.C.

Loading potatoes in the 'sixties

NEW SERVICES

The advent of machinery in the 'forties made a great difference to potato production too in Pemberton. Instead of a man planting the seed by hand in a plough furrow, the mechanical planter both made the furrow and covered the seed; it had added the fertilizer from a separate spout, the potatoes either being pre-cut or cut on the machine to help prevent the spreading of disease. Machines made cultivation and spraying quicker and easier than working with stubborn cayuses which resisted catching and indeed resisted any kind of discipline. In earlier days Indian workers from Creekside hired for the potato digging stayed on the farms in old cabins, and The Wacker, an early type of digger which threw the potatoes out sideways, made picking slow and often left much of the produce in the ground.

With the introduction of tractors and chain diggers in the 'thirties, larger crews became necessary. Hired by the day these crews had to be transported from Mount Currie (Creekside) by the old narrow winding dirt road which crossed the railroad three times at blind, unguarded crossings at which a careful driver cut off the motor to listen for the trains. Slim Fougberg, owner of a chain digger, organized crews, and arranged for their transportation. Later as more farmers purchased diggers a keen competition developed for workers. The lack of phones in Mount Currie in the early years, coupled with the always uncertain fall weather, added complications: if it rained in Pemberton and not in Mount Currie, the workers would wait in vain; and if the reverse, the farmer would arrive in the rain to find all his workers still sleeping. The building of the new road in 1954 halved the time spent driving; in fact, the good surface, and the more direct route without the dangerous crossings, made the driving so easy that more wives were pressed into service for this job.

With the electricity came the sorting machine, and no longer did the farmers spend long hours alone in dark dank log roothouses painstakingly taking out the culls one by one. The new machinery sparked the building of larger

Road Improvements

Spring Break-Up

roothouses and the sorting by a crew of seven or eight went on at the rate of twenty ton or more a day.

Lack of transportation kept Pemberton from the mainstream of provincial life in the 'forties and early 'fifties. Approximately 75 miles of roadway was available to local car and truck owners, and for these few miles the people paid the same insurance rates as people on the lower mainland. These local

Spring Shopping Trip

roads presented many problems. The Valley dirt road was narrow, little more than a single track in places, dusty in summer, snow-covered in winter, like a washboard in the fall rains, and a quagmire of mud during the spring breakup. The severe winter of 1949-50 pointed up the lack of effective snow-clearing equipment. In December 1949, a total of five and a half feet of snow fell in one thirty-six-hour period and left the Upper Valley to horses and sleighs as the only possible transportation. The road crew could do nothing with the equipment available and nothing resulted from appeals by the Board of Trade to the Public Works Department at Victoria. Sandy Ross and John Ronayne both made sleigh trips to collect mail and much-needed lamp-gas and groceries for the Upper Valley residents, and made those trips in that severe January of 1950 when the temperature plummeted to -40F at night and rose little above -20F during the day. After nearly a month of these conditions Public Works Foreman Bill Fowler decided to commandeer a B.C. Electric bulldozer left behind in Pemberton at the end of the summer's work. Assisted by several other young men, Bill succeeded in digging out the machine and managed to start the motor, whereupon Dan Fraser drove it up the valley road, clearing a track as he went. The clearing occupied all day as householders from every road side home rushed out with offers of refreshment. Far from being pleased with the "initiative" of the local men, the Public Works Department was more concerned with the illegal commandeering of the bulldozer.

In the early 'fifties, however, gravelling and ditching of the Valley road had started, bit by bit abolishing the worst of the mudholes. By 1953 the old narrow dirt road to Mount Currie with its three unguarded crossings had been replaced by a fine new gravel road taking a more direct route across former swamp land. The new wide bridge over the Lillooet was opened that year by the MLA Gordon Gibson. Walter Bergman, principal of Pemberton Superior School, had all his senior pupils there for the occasion. By the 'sixties heavy logging trucks were straining the ability of the Public Works to keep the gravel road graded and smooth. The clouds of dust thrown up by every vehicle, in particular the heavy trucks, became a safety hazard: no one could pass the trucks and, indeed, to be passed by one meant having to slow down almost to a stop for the minute required for the clouds of dust to clear away. After many appeals from local organizations the Public Works did supply old engine oil for spraying the roads, but usually too little and too late.

Meanwhile the one-track dirt road to Birken and D'Arcy was widened and some of the worst hills eliminated. Logging operations in the Upper Valley extended the road several more miles up the river. The increase in the work crew, the coming of more efficient graders and, most important, the school bus routes, meant that the local roads were well cleared and graded in the winter. Three-foot snow falls were cleared overnight and farmers could have their driveways ploughed for a modest sum.

Rail conditions too had changed little from the 'thirties. Travellers to Pemberton still caught the Union Steamship *Lady Cynthia* or *Lady Alexandra* from the foot of Carrall Street at eight in the morning. Late-comers raced across the railroad yards while the good-natured crew kept the gang plank down. The boat took more than five hours to reach Squamish with stops at Bowen Island, Britannia Beach, and Woodfibre on the way. They were friendly boats, the lifelines of the coastal communities as well as of the P.G.E. passengers travelling farther north. In the big lounge with its long leather-covered seats, passengers to the various hamlets gathered in groups, gossiping to while away the time on the rather tedious journey: new babies were duly admired, results of visits to doctors and dentists discussed, and often parcels undone and contents displayed. The few private rooms were usually rented by parties of men who wished to enjoy a few drinks, or by parents of new babies wanting peace and privacy. By 1956 the "Ladies" had been replaced by the tiny *Bonabelle,* an ancient tub that rolled and pitched in the slightest sea.

Travellers on the boats watched with interest the progress of railroad construction along the edge of Howe Sound, and finally the great day arrived when the track was complete! The inaugural train was filled with dignitaries: Premier W. A. C. Bennett; President of the P.G.E. railroad, Joseph Broadbent; representatives from a wide selection of North American railroads; the press in full force; and parties of pioneers from every whistle stop on the line. This inaugural run left Vancouver on August 28, 1956 and expected to reach Quesnel the same day, but the little mountain line remained true to its unpredictable tradition when a fall of rock on the line along Howe Sound took all night to clear and not until early afternoon on the following day did Pemberton's Walter and Margaret Green, Bob Taylor, Maria Fraser, Annie Ronayne and Chief Bill Pascal of Mount Currie step off the train. All of Pemberton

Pemberton Station 1949

turned out to admire the new Budd cars and to take pictures of the Premier on his first visit to Pemberton, while a party of local women gathered on the hotel porch and led by author Gay Guthrie sang a song to the tune of "Clementine".

Honoured Guests and Fellow Workers, gathered here on this great day,
Welcome to our little village on this newly made railway.
Here's the story of this railway which now goes right through to town,
It's a story filled with laughter, filled with tears and smiles and frowns.
Once in history it appears that there was a company
Form'd to build a provincial railway to be called the P.G.E.

Pacific Great Eastern, Pacific Great Eastern,
Pacific Great Eastern chugging along
Knowing you came right from Vancouver
Makes your every chug, a song.

In the files at Victoria there were plans for this railway,
But the years slipped by unheeded and the plans went mouldy gray.
From 1912 to '56 is only forty-four long years
But it made it here today and so we offer up our cheers.
Thus it was that while the wheat crops in North-er-en B.C.
Spoiled in granaries for lack of storage, West Van. gardeners pruned their trees.

The landscaped gardens, oh so lovely, were the finest to be seen,
And the Right-of-Way for railroads was covered with lawns green.
Then the Government grabbed their courage and they took the fatal stand:
"The P.G.E. must finish up and unite this B.C. land".
In the building in Victoria where the Parliament does meet
Oh the silence and the wonder as every M.P. took his seat.

For the rumour runs the house round that the P.G.E. will run
Through West Vancouver, over gardens, and, of course, that can't be done.
Oh but somehow in the working it has turned out very well,
For those gardens make the scenery much more grand than I can tell.
In the building of this railway there have been some strong complaints
But it's finished and this knowledge keeps our joy beyond restraints.

There was a lot of blasting to knock all the rock away
And make a nice, wide, even roadbed for the P.G.E. Railway.
When the path was nice and clear and the tracks were laid down straight
The highway blasting scattered rocks and the tracks were thus made late.
There are other things to tell you, but my story grows too long,
So we finish as we say again, "PRAISE THE P.G.E. IN SONG".

The rail service was greatly improved by the Budd cars which gave a much faster service, only three and a half hours to Vancouver. For a short while a summer service of two trains a day operated, but it did not prove profitable.

The Wedding Party

Various experiments were made with the time table, one of which involved a 3 a.m. departure for Vancouver, but finally the service settled down to a daily up train arriving just after 11 a.m. and a down train leaving just after 6 p.m. The farmers and businessmen expected that freight rates would be reduced with the completion of the railroad, but instead the rates increased, and the removal of the old mail-sorting car from the train caused a deterioration in the speed of mail delivery. For reasons known only to Ottawa the mail was shipped up the line to Lillooet and trucked by way of Lytton to Vancouver where it was finally sorted. As a result, mail for D'Arcy, which once had a swift delivery, by way-mail, now went all the way to Vancouver and back — more than two hundred miles to travel thirty. After vigorous local protest, the government instituted a separate bag for Squamish, but more than twenty years were to pass before any major improvements took place.

During the years when the railroad was the only means of transportation, on many occasions both freight and passenger trains were delayed to accommodate the passage of sick people to hospital, the crews proving solicitous and helpful. Early in the 'sixties, Thelma Hamilton, a nurse living in Pemberton, offered to accompany a young Indian woman who was already in labour and who was travelling out to Squamish hospital. A young student working the coffee and sandwich concession was very alarmed and nervously knocked on the door of the compartment where the young mother-to-be was lying, but hesitated to enter at all and heaved a real sigh of relief when the train reached Squamish without mishap. A few weeks later Indian Department nurse Marg

Stokes was called hastily to accompany another woman in the same condition and found herself with very little equipment presiding over a delivery on the train and the same young student assisting her by boiling water, and fetching and carrying. When he next saw Thelma Hamilton he described his experiences with the aplomb of an experienced obstetrician!

The building of the Station Agent's house at Pemberton in 1958 and the opening of the new station in 1962 completed the modernizing of the railroad in Pemberton. The station was the occasion of a local celebration, the Premier stopping off to attend a Board of Trade luncheon and to visit three local schools. This station was built by a local contractor, J. Marchbank, and the agent at that time was Sean Kelly. Premier Bennett presented Ada Taylor, Pemberton's oldest resident, with a lifetime pass.

But Pemberton still had no road to Vancouver. That energetic band of Pemberton boosters, the Board of Trade, fresh from their triumph of Dykes and Drainage, set their sights on a road to Vancouver. Over the years they had harassed the Minister of Highways about the poor maintenance of local roads and the dangerous crossings on the route to Mount Currie. In 1956 they voted three extra members to their Squamish-Pemberton road committee which now consisted of Slim Fougberg as President, Bob Taylor, Bill Spetch, Chief Bill Pascal and A. Anderson, the Indian agent. Together with other interested branches of the organization, they tried to arrange a cavalcade driving up Harrison Lake, Tenas Lake and Lillooet Lake and through to Pemberton, in order to point up the need for a through road so that this scenic route could become a round trip. When Squamish celebrated its road link to Vancouver in August 1958, the Pemberton Board of Trade planned to take a jeep caravan over the B.C. Electric "tote road" and various logging roads to join the ceremonies at Squamish, and in spite of forest fires and woods closures the men did make the trip.

One may be sure that they did not miss the opportunity to press the Highways Minister for a start of the Pemberton road, the road they felt necessary to develop the area to its full potential.

But the opening of Whistler as a ski resort rather than the efforts of any Pemberton organization provided the impetus to the Highways Department. The narrow gravel road built from Squamish to Whistler in the early 'sixties was soon extended the final 25 miles to Pemberton. By the early summer of 1964 the first venturesome souls were dodging the highway crews with their rock-blasts, winding round the detours, and crossing temporary log bridges to break the isolation finally and to drive out to the coast.

In July of that year Langley Freight Lines brought in the first commercial freight load — furniture for Pemberton's first druggist, Bob Priest. In October of the same year the first prefabricated house to travel the new road came in on a semi-trailer driven by Doug Clarke of Surrey and John Redmond of Port Kells who reported that "the road is a little scary in places. The detours were a little too narrow and the dual wheels were riding over the edge. We were very glad to see Pemberton."

Pemberton Needs a Road

But improvements came quickly and the worst of the detours removed. Two years later the first load of Pemberton logs was shipped by road to the coast. The road never was officially opened: the residents of Pemberton and all points north to D'Arcy used it just as soon as they discovered a negotiable track, christened the steep winding hill a few miles from the village "Suicide Hill", and very quickly knew every twist and turn of it. Over the next few years some of the log bridges were eliminated in favour of more modern structures, but it was to be 1969 before the new road was blacktopped to Mount Currie. Work crews continue smoothing, straightening, widening and

The load that didn't make it

bridge building, but the road is there and Pemberton people wonder how they ever managed without it.

The coming of the road also brought the large trucking outfits like Squamish Transfer into Pemberton with goods for the hotel and stores. In season they used the back trip to take farm produce to the lower mainland and beyond. Log hauling expanded with the completion and later improvement and expansion of the local roads.

The most serious effect of Pemberton's isolation had been the lack of medical services. In the early days sick or injured settlers either doctored themselves or made the long, cold ride on a P.G.E. speeder to Squamish where there was a doctor but no hospital. Babies were delivered by Indian mid-wives trained in their own traditional herb medicines, or by neighbours such as Mrs. Neill. The more prosperous or more nervous preferred to travel to Vancouver several weeks ahead of time to await the new arrival; this holiday was often the only one had, if it could be regarded as such.

In the spring of 1920 Ada Taylor settled in the upper valley on her son Bob's farm. Granny, as she became known in later years, was an English state registered nurse who had taken her midwifery certification at Queen Charlotte's Hospital in London. Ada Taylor had nursed in London, in Australia, on the Cunard boats, and she had run a Maternity Home in Kerrisdale in World War I, but she regarded her services in Pemberton as the highlight of her life. Soon after her arrival in Pemberton, she was operating a Red Cross outpost first aid station, handling surgical and midwifery duties in literally hundreds of major and minor cases.

Granny was a notable midwife and monthly nurse with a special affection for the very tiny or premature babies, many of whom would not have survived without her care. Picture her bundled in coats and blankets, riding a heavy farm sleigh on a freezing winter's night, spelling her son Bob in the driving seat when his hands became too cold to handle the reins; or, in summer bumping along puncheon roads seated on the gas tank of a Model T Ford which had no windshield to protect her from the dust, and climbing out every few miles to open and close gates for her driver son. On arrival at her destination she would find few conveniences, but would immediately set to work improvising what was needed. Many a tiny baby started its new life, not in a hospital incubator but in a dresser drawer lined with blankets and heated with hot water bottles.

Granny never refused a call for help, and typical of her devotion to her nursing duties was her attendance at the birth of Harold and Sally Purden's first child. Herself a nurse, Sally had planned to have her baby in a Vancouver hospital with all the advantages of modern medicine, but the baby decided otherwise. Because the Purdens had no near neighbours, Harold set off post-haste to Pemberton to get help. Stopping only long enough to rouse Granny, he hurried back to his wife who was quite alone. Unable to find transportation and though a tiny woman then in her sixties, the undaunted Granny set out on foot in the deep snow and 25 below zero cold of that winter's night to walk a "country mile". She arrived in time to deliver Betty Purden who was born between three and four in the morning. In all she was to deliver thirty-three babies, including many of her own grandchildren. As late at 1948 and well in her seventies, she was on hand to attend the birth of Larry Cowell whose mother was one of Granny's "own" earlier babies. In 1950 she was called out when the thermometer had plummeted to 35 below zero to deliver Freddy Menzel.

In 1936 Sally Purden was herself appointed part-time resident nurse by the Department of Indian Affairs, a position in which she continued until 1971. Sally wrote of her experiences:

"In the beginning I held monthly clinic and attended emergencies, which occurred quite frequently. One of the first cases I remember attending was a young boy who had been kicked by a horse, a glancing blow to the lad's forehead, but a four-inch laceration over the right eye. At that time I had been given no supplies of any sort by the Department to carry on my work, so I used a straight three-edged needle that the Indian women used to sew buckskin, and a fishing line in place of catgut. However, all went well, and no scar shows today, and, of course, this was years before anti-biotics. There have been many tragic events in the many years I worked. The most heartbreaking to me was the death of Minnie Joe (Mrs. Dick Joe) and five of her children in a house fire. One little girl lived till 5 a.m. and kept asking if her mother was okay. Another event I shall never forget was the death of Mary Ann Billy. Just as I was basting the turkey for the last time on Christmas morning three Indian Councillors arrived to tell my husband (Harold Wyatt-Purden, J.P.) that Mary Anne Billy was dead and it looked like foul play. In the end I was the one to go to investigate the conditions and had to phone by copperwire (railroad phone) from Creekside station to the Provincial Police in Squamish and Constable Malins had to leave his Christmas dinner to come and investigate the crime. When I arrived home I put the meal on the table, but couldn't eat anything.

"Fortunately not all of the accident cases died. While working in the woods under contract to Fleetwood Logging, George Felix Leo overturned on a side hill, and was pinned underneath the tractor he was operating. The tractor ignited and he was badly burned. I will never know how Adolph Leo got him out from under that burning machine. Dewey Anderson sent in his private plane and pilot to take George out to Vancouver, and the Fleetwood Manager insisted I accompany him. It was a seaplane, of course, and we took off from Lillooet Lake and landed in the water at the foot of Burrard Street. George was only in fair condition on arrival at St. Paul's Hospital, but recovered after very good treatment there.

"The time that Alex Dan lost his leg makes quite a story too; it was after a dance at Pemberton and the south-bound freight train was standing in the station. At about 2 a.m. Alex decided he must get to the other side of the tracks and started to climb through between the cars. Just at that point the train

The Nurses

Ada Taylor *Sally Purden with Betty*

started up and Alex's leg was severed just below the knee. When I arrived on the scene, about 2:30 a.m. (no telephone then) he was still lying in the ditch where he had fallen and the open wound was covered with chips of wood . . . but fortunately no excessive bleeding. It took us until 6 a.m. to arrive in Squamish by freight, where Dr. D'Appolonia cleaned the wound as best he could and started an intravenous. At 8 a.m. we boarded the Budd car heading for Vancouver and St. Paul's. We arrived at North Vancouver with the I.V. still running and there an ambulance was waiting. From there we travelled about 70 m.p.h. with flashers and sirens across the bridge, through the Park and on to the hospital. It almost seemed like an anti-climax after the slow trip we had coming down from Pemberton. After some months and one or two operations, Alex was able to come home. I must say that I enjoyed my work with the Indians; certainly I can say I did not have many dull moments. My family never knew when they would come home and find a note from me saying I had gone to Squamish or Lillooet and would be back the next day."

Sally Purden was followed by Margaret Stokes who was employed full-time and occupied the first official nurses' residence in Pemberton. After Margaret Stokes came Mr. G. Urquhart, who was followed in turn by Miss M. I. Fraser. These nurses were often also called to assist white settlers in emergencies.

In 1940 the Public Health Service began sending nurses to Pemberton for one or two days each month to look in on the old people and visit the mothers with young babies. Lorraine Carruthers, the first of these, was called to help a sick man in the Upper Valley when part of the road was under water and she agreed to make the journey on horseback, though she had never ridden a horse before. Local residents speculated on how much sitting down she would do the next day after that twenty-mile trip. These nurses also visited the schools and advised parents of children needing glasses or having other health problems. By 1960 Leone Cosulich, wife of the Co-op manager, was established part-time as resident Public Health Nurse. Though only paid for a few days a month, like all other Pemberton nurses Leone was often called for advice and help. Just before Christmas of that same year Thelma Hamilton, a former army nurse of wide experience, came to Pemberton with her husband Bill at that time working for Texas Farms though later employed by Weldwood Logging. These two nurses became great friends and worked together on emergency cases.

Early one morning Thelma was aroused by the phone ringing: Leone had news that Mrs. Sandoff of Mount Currie was in labour. Both were aware that Mrs. Sandoff had serious medical problems and Thelma agreed to meet Leone at the Sandoff home. Bill drove Thelma over in their panel truck to Sandoff's small panabode house just outside the Indian reserve. When they opened the door the living room seemed full of sleeping children for this was Mrs. Sandoff's eleventh pregnancy. On examining their patient the two nurses agreed that twins were to be expected and Leone alerted Corporal Nelson of the R.C.M.P. to bring the Air-Sea Rescue unit to Lillooet Lake. As Sandoff's home was some six miles from the lake, they decided to move their patient immediately so that she would be at the lake when the plane arrived. Bill Hamilton and Mr. Sandoff carried Mrs. Sandoff out to the panel van on a bedspring and mattress while the eldest daughter, just sixteen, took charge of the awakening youngsters. Her mother's main concern was her daughter's smoking while the mother was away, no doubt worrying about the possibility of fire.

The nurses decided to take Mrs. Sandoff to Roy Penrose's summer cabin near Joffre Creek, over a rough gravel road which went across the flatlands to Lillooet Lake, over a narrow trestle bridge, then up and over an alarmingly steep hill. Roy Penrose heard the vehicle coming, and looked out of his window and was startled to see a party headed for his cabin carrying a patient on a mattress. When he understood that they were expecting a plane, he pointed out that the mist then rolling down on the lake from the mountains would prevent the plane from landing. He was right, and Air Sea Rescue had to land on Anderson Lake some 25 miles the other side of Mount Currie. The doctor and the nurse travelled by police car to their patient. The plane took off immediately because mist was threatening to close in that lake also. After a long labour Mrs. Sandoff was delivered of small but healthy twin baby girls at 7 p.m. that evening. The Air-Sea Rescue nurse and doctor were unable to return to Vancouver because the fog had closed in both lakes, but eventually left at noon the next day.

Doctors were important to the community too, but fifty miles away at Squamish or Lillooet they were necessarily less part of the lives of the settlers than the nurses. Early references are to Dr. Newcomb of the P.G.E. and Dr. Paul of Squamish, the latter acting as school doctor and appearing at the schools about once a year to examine the children. Dr. Paul would also, if his Squamish duties permitted, travel by speeder to Pemberton to deliver babies, but if he did not arrive in time there was always Ada Taylor. In 1948 Dr. Laverne Kindree started his practice in Squamish and began regular monthly visits to Mount Currie as part of his duties as Public Health Officer. Pemberton residents wishing to consult him had to hang around the hotel, hoping to catch him before he went south on the train. The much improved service brought by the completion of the railroad to Vancouver allowed Doctors Woods and Olivier of Lillooet to travel down on the morning train and return the same night, and they started regular fortnightly and later weekly visits, attending their patients in a hotel room, using an examining table supplied by the Women's Institute. This table kept at the hotel had been commandeered on one occasion by a party of surveyors who were using it for drafting maps and who were very annoyed when asked to relinquish it to the doctor.

The building of the Health Centre as a centennial project provided a doctor's office, and a change in railroad timetable had Doctor Kindree and his partners from Squamish making regular weekly visits. In the early 'sixties Dr. Van Geyn became Pemberton's first resident doctor, living in a trailer near to the Health Centre which he used as part-office and part living quarters. He was assisted by his wife, a registered nurse with mid-wifery qualifications. The Van Geyns were both trained in Holland and stayed in Pemberton only a little over a year. During his stay Dr. Van Geyn delivered the first baby born in the new Health Centre, a baby girl born to Muriel Newman. It was to be 1969 before another resident doctor came to Pemberton, Dr. Art Moody who today provides medical services for Pemberton, Mount Currie and Whistler.

The police service in the 'forties consisted of a B.C. Provincial Police officer sent up to Pemberton eight or ten times a year from Squamish. As of necessity he came on the train and word of his arrival soon spread through the village. At dances when the policeman was conveniently in Squamish it was not uncommon to see bottles carried fairly openly. Though the hall committee frowned on drinking on the premises most of the men stepped outside for a "quick one" in the course of the evening. As the community hall had no public conveniences, not only drinks drew people outside. Thieves were rare and no one even in the village locked doors; in fact, most doors had no keys and anyone wanting privacy, to take a bath for example, would stick a knife in the door jamb. Crime was not a community problem nor were spies, in spite of the Board of Trade resolution of 1940 to ask the assurance of the R.C.M.P. that the activities of any local "fifth column" and Canadian Communists had been thoroughly investigated and were under continual surveillance. Local justices of the peace John Ronayne and Harold Wyatt-Purden drew on their considerable local knowledge to administer justice with impartiality and good sense. Jim Collins, Jack Decker and Jack Graham who followed them in the 'fifties and 'sixties were to have a busier life.

Of course illegalities existed. Sitting in the section house, one could see men leaving the extra gang's work train to walk over to the beer parlour, and later emerge carrying cases of beer which they carried across the tracks to sell to other men who stood in the shadow of a large cedar tree in the area where Talbot's log yard stands today. The bootleggers would return to the beer parlour and repeat the transaction as many as six times in one evening. Selling alcoholic beverages to Native Indians was illegal in the 'forties, and brought quick profits, but naturally no local resident would ever admit to being involved in this trade. Unless brought home after a trip to town, liquor was ordered from the Lillooet liquor store and arrived by registered mail; the postmaster knew well who drank and how much. At times desperate drinkers resorted to vanilla essence or shaving lotion. When workers of a construction gang, heading home for Christmas holidays, were held overnight at the hotel because of heavy snow, they cleaned out the cook's supply of essences, and two of the men who became quite violent were banished by hotel-keeper Frank Carrachelo to a log cabin down the tracks to "cool off". On another occasion the Green River section gang purchased a pile of groceries, including raisins, sugar and yeast. A few days later the "boys" started in on their brew, enlightened the foreman of their opinion of him and his ancestors, and jumped a freight bound for Quesnel. Summoned by foreman Gimondi Bruno, Constable Edward Malins rode up from Squamish by the next train and found one old man at the Green River bunkhouse still with a large washtub of brew strong enough to be smelled from the track some 200 yards away. The trembling old man denied all knowledge of the contents of the tub, but could not walk straight enough to help Constable Malins dump the brew. The trouble was that because most makers of home brew were thirsty people they could not wait for it to "ripen" and therefore drank their brew in a very raw state.

In August 1950 the R.C.M.P. took over from the provincial police. Constable Malins was on duty as before but in a different uniform. Before long the increase in population made more frequent and longer visits necessary. The policeman would rent the top floor of the hotel for several days, using it as his office and covering the area in a hired car. Anyone he arrested was confined overnight behind the hotel in a small building which doubled as an office and meeting place for the Pemberton Valley Dyking District. The duties of the part-time guard included opening the small cell to allow the prisoner to use the toilet, and when one "criminal" decided that he had enough confinement he simply walked out of the door while the guard, an ex-soldier from World War One gave chase and yelled "Halt, in the name of the Queen!"

The Pemberton detachment of the R.C.M.P. was formed in 1961 when the present residence and office were built. As the area expanded, so unfortunately did the crime. People locked up their houses and vehicles, and the magistrates became concerned with juvenile delinquents: the old easy-going days were gone.

Riding to School Provincial Archives

First pupils of Signal Hill School

EXPANDED SERVICES

At the time of the consolidation of British Columbia's school boards in 1948, this area had three schools, Pemberton, Pemberton Meadows and a log school at Birken, each with a separate school board. That year Pemberton Meadows secretary Frances Decker turned over to the Howe Sound School Board $128.73 in cash and inventory: One-room wooden frame school, painted red at $1,800; Land at $100; Furniture at $300; Firewood on hand at $10; Insurance (still to run) at $17.25; Shingle Stain at $32.57; Office Supplies at $7. Records of the 'forties show the janitor being paid the princely sum of $1.50 a month! In 1950 under Mercy McPhee the Pemberton School in the village had ten pupils and Pemberton Meadows under Violet Crane had twelve. The building of a new high school in Squamish shortly afterwards caused a large increase in the school tax for which the Pemberton residents could see little advantage, because only a few could afford to board their children in Squamish. Margaret Fougberg, who served as the area's first member on the Howe Sound School Board (1946-1959), therefore travelled many miles circulating a petition requesting a local high school. As a direct result of her efforts Pemberton Superior School came into being in 1951 — a two-roomed Quonset building serving grades one to ten. The first principal was Art Nicholson and his assistant Bob Cherry. Two years later the first school bus started its run from Pemberton Meadows with Jack Nelson as part-time driver who was paid at the high rate of $5.00 a day. The size of a standard van, this minibus had windows all round, none of which opened, and seats on either side facing a centre aisle. During the summer months the students "sat and looked at each other and sweated".

By the fall of 1956 the school had outgrown its accommodation and the drainage building was pressed into use for the elementary pupils under substitute teacher Gay Guthrie, whose daughter Donna toddled up and down the aisles between the desks whenever her mother was unable to round up a babysitter. Later in the year when replaced by Jessie Tucker, a teacher from England, Gay was able to go back to her home duties for a few years before

First High School Provincial Archives, Victoria, B.C.

returning to the classroom. Teaching in '56-'57 were Principal E. L. Anderson and Miss L. L. Taylor at the High School, Mrs. Piggott at Pemberton Meadows, and Miss Peterson had followed Lorna Hamilton at the newly constructed school at Creekside serving the non-Indian children of that area.

The rapid increase of the population of the 'fifties soon required a much larger school at Pemberton, one which, when completed in the fall of 1957, included new washrooms, additional classrooms and a gymnasium. The school now rated as an Elementary-High School because for the first time all grades through to grade twelve were taught. The first graduating class consisted of only two pupils, Michael Ross and Mary Miller, both grandchildren of pioneer

The School Treat Provincial Archives, Victoria, B.C.

resident Teresa Miller. Mary returned in the fall of 1958 as the first school secretary though only part time. That same fall the school bus service was expanded to include Mount Currie, and for the first time Native Indian pupils attended a local high school rather than travelling to the Indian boarding school at Mission under the auspicies of the Catholic Church. Art Tinney, Principal at this period, has some comments to make:

"The children were notable for their simple straightforwardness, willingness to submit to discipline, and their happy dispositions. The big city hadn't brought its worst attributes to Pemberton. My salary was $4000 a year. One summer day, I was upset by the disappearance of all the Indian children and went to find out where they were. What a sight met my eyes on that sunny June day in Mount Currie. There were the young folks on horses all over those beautiful pastures, galloping their joys up and down the countryside. I resolved that this form of 'Kidnapping' had to stop. We hired two young Catholic teachers especially to assist in this integration — Sam Frketich and Chuck Curteis. The key was basketball."

With the fine new gymnasium the basketball teams soon became a very popular part of school life: restricted by five months of snow every winter Pemberton and Mount Currie responded eagerly to a sport which offered both winter exercise and a chance to travel to other schools in competition. From the start the Red Devils gave a good account of themselves, often managing to beat schools with twice or three times as many pupils. Visitors were given supper at the high school with school pupils cooking the food under the supervision of the mothers of the Pemberton team members. After the games the visitors were given overnight hospitality and put on the train the next morning. In those early days when the school was small the impossibility of raising two teams meant that frequently the stars of the junior team also played on the senior team. Early coaches of the teams include Gay Guthrie and Don Gill the forest warden. Over the next few years the school was added to twice more so that by 1965 it boasted an expanded gym, office, staffroom, home economics kitchen, science laboratory, library, machine shop for industrial arts, and lunchroom with small kitchen.

Meanwhile the elementary pupils were fast outgrowing their classrooms and Signal Hill Elementary was built by local contractor Magnus Urdal in 1963. The new school was situated just south of Pemberton on the south side of the P.G.E. railroad and the name refers to the small mountain hump right there from which the Indians in the old days signalled the arrival of the dreaded Chilcotins from the north. Starting with two classrooms, office, and covered play area, the first principal, Brian Edwards, taught grades six and seven while his assistant Marjorie Vaughan-Jones took grades one and two. Also under his principalship were the elementary pupils still housed at the high school, a situation which continued until further expansion of the elementary school finally brought all the pupils under one roof.

That popular entertainment of the one-room school, the Christmas concert, was retained by Brian Edwards and as the years went by it became quite sophisticated. Still a very large proportion of the valley residents attended to fill the school auditorium to overflowing and somehow the flavour of earlier years was retained. Children sat in front; parents, friends and grandparents in the main body of the hall; and crowded in the back seats and standing against the wall were the young adults who were still near enough their own school-days to remember the school concert with affection.

During the fall months before the snow Signal Hill pupils played soccer, and later when they could be taken out by road they travelled to compete with other teams. In the earlier years they played against the Mount Currie Indian Day School with whom they also competed at the annual Sports Day in June. This event started with the building of Signal Hill and brought together all the elementary pupils from Signal Hill, Pemberton Meadows, Creekside, Birken, those still taught in the High School building, and the Indian Day School pupils. The sun always seemed to shine at the elementary school Sports Day and interschool rivalry was keen.

Pemberton Meadows expanded to a two-room school in 1956, but the second room was only used for two years because the main population base had shifted from the Upper Valley farms to the village and surrounding area. At times the extra room was used to house overflow from Signal Hill, but difficulties with the bus schedule and the push to start all pupils on the same basis forced the closure of this school in 1969. In the 'seventies , though, it reopened as the Coast Mountain Outdoor School dormitory, the first of its kind in B.C.

During this period of rapid expansion both the lack of a road to Vancouver and the near-impossibility of obtaining rental accommodation forced the Howe Sound School Board to embark on a program of building teacherages, so that married teachers would be encouraged to come and stay in the area. Duplexes were built at Pemberton Meadows, at the High School, at Signal Hill, and at Creekside where the original small teacherage included in the school building became a play area. The school bus service was soon expanded to include a second run to Mount Currie and buses to D'Arcy and Whistler Mountain. The staff of one employed at each school at a very minimum wage to sweep up and light fires was expanded to include custodians, busdrivers, maintenance workers, and lunch room help, all at a very considerable budget. First maintenance foreman in Pemberton was Fred Meen who holds the same position today.

The Pemberton branch of the Parent-Teacher Association started in 1956 under the presidency of Doris Van Beem flourished briefly, but never attracted enough members to accomplish its true aims. At one annual meeting the committee gathered to be sworn in at one end of the schoolroom faced an audience of one! In time, the parent-teacher meetings held at each report time came to replace the more formal organization.

Early diaries mention the visits of "preachers" without stating their denomination, and not until 1920 did official records show that Anglican ministers travelled down from Lillooet by train to hold services in the homes of the settlers, usually during the summer months. Rev. G. C. Gardner, Rev. W. B. Irwin and Rev. J. J. Cowan are among those who served the area in those early years.

In June 1932 the Anglicans of Pemberton decided to form a church, its first officers being Bob Taylor as Church Warden and Pat Wilson as Clerk of the Vestry. By the end of that year, as a result of collections and fund-raising dances, the little church community had some $44.20 in its treasury. The building of a new school at Pemberton Meadows in 1929 enabled the Church Committee in 1933 to purchase the old school building which was situated between the Green and Punch properties. Unfortunately some confusion about the ownership of the lot prevented the church from gaining legal control of the land on which the church building stood.

The Taylor and Girling families, with some help from relatives and friends in England, secured vestments and altar furnishings. Harold Gethen made the altar rail and pews from local wood obtained from Bossy's mill. The carving on the front of the altar represented a mower section knife — as befitting in a farming community — and as well showed the three points of the Trinity. The wood in the cross came from odd bits of firewood and contains the four most common local woods: cottonwood, fir, cedar and pine. The first organ and the communion service were donated by the Diocesan Women's Auxiliary. Margaret Green and Maria Fraser were the first caretakers of the church and Stella Shantz its first organist. The church was dedicated by Bishop Adams on November 22nd, 1933.

By 1936 the parish had been transferred to the New Westminster diocese and Rev. T. L. Rimmer travelled up from Squamish during the summer months, continuing until the end of 1938. For the next eight years services were very irregular until the Rev. James was appointed in 1946, followed by Rev. J. S. Twining and in 1948 by Rev. Charles Gibbs who provided real continuity of service because his eight or nine visits a year during the warmer months continued until 1962 when the parish was returned to the Cariboo diocese and served from Lillooet.

By 1961, with more than 100 adherents and 13 candidates for confirmation, the Anglican church members felt that the little church was no longer large enough for its needs and was too far from the centre of the population. The following year, under the ministry of Rev. B. M. Gamble from Lillooet the congregation appointed Bob Taylor, Joe Antonelli and W. Vaughan-Jones as building committee to plan a new church capable of seating 100 people. The site was to be on a lot donated by Bob Taylor about a mile north of Pemberton on the Valley road. A very practical T-shaped design was finally adopted, the smaller portion completed first and used for services while the larger hall planned for suppers and meetings was being finished. In the meantime services were held in the Pemberton Community Hall. By 1964 the Rev. A. Jenner was serving the congregation and first service was held by Bishop Godfrey Gower in the partially completed church on July 25, 1965.

Though the Anglicans established the first church in Pemberton, the first recorded missionary to visit the area was Mr. Bromich of the Methodist Church. He came before World War I and conducted services "on Pastures Green with Quiet Waters by", meaning the Ronayne ranch. From then on occasional Methodist services were held in the settlers' homes. The Rev. William Rickaby was one of the ministers:

"While at Lillooet June 1921 to June 1925, I went down to Pemberton once a month and usually held services at the school house half-way up the valley [later purchased by the Anglican Church]. However, as I visited every home in the valley there were times when services were held in private residences. I believe I have held services at the station, at the boarding house of Mr. and Mrs. Tuck, at Bakers', and at the home of an English family who lived at the bend of the river about 12 miles or more from the station. They had two grown sons at home and were Church of England people originally [probably Girlings]. On my monthly trip, besides Pemberton I visited Portage, McGillivray Falls, D'Arcy, Birken and Owl Creek Hatchery and surrounding homes."

Mr. Rickaby was followed by a Rev. John Gibson who came up the line from Squamish, and by Rev. Allen Pound stationed at Lillooet. In the tightening financial conditions of 1929 Rev. Evan Baker took over the whole area from Squamish to Lillooet. He describes an early visit to Pemberton:

"I began to make inquiries from Mother Taylor [Mrs. A. C. Taylor]. . . . She gave me a good suggestion that as no one held services in the village of Pemberton (the Anglican services being held in the upper valley) I shouldn't be treading on anyone's corns, and there was the hotel. I took the hint and the hotel owners (Anderson, I think) allowed me the use of the dining hall for the evening service. I put up notices that there would be a Christian service in the hotel dining room, then I scoured the country of the village and the valley beyond for about 6-8 miles — on foot, of course — advising them of the service. I was back in plenty of time to visit the Bar Room and invite the occupants into the dining room at 8 p.m. for the service. Several volunteered to sing solos for me and another said he'd take up the collection. I accepted and put them to work; sure, I let them sing and the fellow took my hat and passed it round — they insisted that he do that. I stayed at the hotel that night and the next morning I moved off to Owl Creek to hunt the next congregation. The Super of the Hatchery (the Fisheries maintained a salmon hatchery at Owl Creek during the late 'twenties and early 'thirties) was a wonderful help, offering me the use of the Hatchery dining room for that evening service. I went around Owl Creek to meet whom I could. I met the ever faithful Spetches, Samuel and Elizabeth, who offered me a bed for the night after the service was over. I next visited Harry and Frances McCulloch at their little ranch about half a mile by the trail in the bush from Spetch's store. These two loyal souls became my very loyal supporters every time I visited — approximately every month. During that first visit, I met Mr. and Mrs. Eddie [probably Doug Adie] who had their little home on the main trail between Owl Creek railroad station and Spetch's store. Mr. Eddie was, I believe, fire warden and patrol rider for that district; they were very hospitable people in deed and word . . . . In a day or so, the northbound P.G.E. train came in and I boarded it for Bridge River."

Frances McCulloch of Owl Creek writes too of those times:

"I remember Rev. Allen Pound and Rev. Rickaby. When they arrived at Owl Creek, they visited each family personally and helped with whatever work we were doing — haying — planting — milling — and stayed for a meal and told us about the time of the service and departed on foot. We all used to enjoy their visits and no matter what denomination we were, we all joined in the services held in the Hatchery dining room. Once when Rev. Rickaby was showing slides of African natives, Bill Spetch was putting the slides through while Rev. Rickaby read the story of them from a paper. Needless to say, Bill switched the slides and not until we could not suppress our giggles did Rev. Rickaby look up and find that the story did not match the picture. Sam and Elizabeth Spetch always gave these ministers a good welcome and accommodation; they mostly led us in singing the hymns, as we had no musical instrument to accompany us. These were happy days and life was so simple and without any modern conveniences, or modern mode of conveyance. Pleasures were simple and spontaneous."

For many years only very occasional visits of Methodist or Presbyterian ministers are recorded, until in 1954 Terry White was appointed student minister to the Lillooet charge of the United Church. He held services that summer in St. George's Anglican church in the Upper Valley, and returned the following summer, his services being attended by members of a variety of church affiliations. In July of 1956 Rev. George Searcy was appointed full-time minister to the Lillooet charge which included Pemberton. Services continued to be held at St. George's until the winter weather forced a move to the high school auditorium. That fall the congregation of Pemberton United Church was formed and from the following summer onwards services were held in the community hall.

On July 1st, 1959 the Board of Managers of the Pemberton United Church held their first meeting at the home of Kel and Peggy Harris. Elected to the chair was Rev. George Searcy, with Margaret Fougberg as secretary and Peggy Harris as treasurer; other members present were Gay Guthrie, Bertha Miller, Bill Spetch, Jack Nelson, Slim Fougberg, and Arthur Ruegg. The Board put plans into operation for the building of the first church in the village of Pemberton. The building was a true community effort, with contributions of both money and work coming from people of all denominations and, indeed, from those with no church affiliation. Construction of St. David's United Church was started in 1960 by local contractor Jack Nelson. The site on the hill above the village was well-chosen scenically but presented some winter parking problems. The building was sufficiently complete for the dedication service to be held on May 28th, 1961, by which time Rev. C. Torok

The Women's Auxiliary Provincial Archives, Victoria, B.C.

had replaced Rev. George Searcy; the latter, however, attended the dedication services. For many years the committee of stewards were concerned with the finishing of the inside of both the church and the basement below, not to mention the repayment of loans. Rev. C. Torok was followed by Rev. Douglas Archibald and later lay minister William Bell, and services were held on alternate Sundays for many years until an increased congregation felt able to support

The Girls' Choir Provincial Archives, Victoria, B.C.

weekly services. Many years were to pass before Rev. R. C. Matthews became the first resident minister.

On May 14th, 1933, at the home of Dorothy Girling, a group of women formed Pemberton's first women's organization: a branch of the Women's Auxiliary to the Missionary Society of the Church of England in Canada. The officers elected at that first meeting were President, Dorothy Girling; Vice-Presidents, Ada Taylor Smith and Maria Fraser; Secretary, Frances Decker; Treasurer, Lilian Shore; Dorcas Secretary, Margaret Green. Ruth Cooper, Gladys Ronayne, Mrs. Prendergast, Beatrice Girling, Joy Girling, Mary Taylor, Vivien Lokken were also present and some names mentioned at later meetings were Annie Ronayne, Adela Fowler, Dora Barbour, Mrs. Wilkinson, Rene Ronayne, Dorothy Waddell, Gladys Dermody, Violet Smith, Bertha Collins (Miller), Florence Cowell, Irene Blakeway, Sidsel Ross, Rose Collin, May Taillefer and Stella Shantz.

The fees were set at 35 cents a year and meetings were held in the homes of members or in the old Boys' Club Hall. Apparently the women paid no rent for this hall, yet frequently motions complained about the state of the roof, the windows and general cleanliness. The good ladies evidently intended to keep the "boys" up to the mark! The auxiliary was formed to assist the Anglican church council in furnishing the recently acquired St. George's Church, and it did purchase hymnals and doors for the little church and did keep up the appeals for more services. Church work included organizing "Sunday School by Post" for the Upper Valley children, assistance coming from Pat Wilson and Alice Fowler. Ada Taylor held regular Sunday School classes for the children in the village for many years.

But actual church work was by no means the end of the function of the W.A. The Dorcas Secretary was responsible for supplying clothes both old and new to needy families in other parts of the province, and the minutes refer to sending dresses and layettes to the Indian Community at Alert Bay. However, it was the Cariboo in the depths of the depression with many of its settlers destitute that claimed the greatest attention from the ladies of Pemberton. Bales of old clothing, layettes and "a few toys for Christmas" appear again and again in the minutes of the 'thirties and two of the members, Ruth Cooper and Frances Decker, had lived in the Cariboo and could speak of the conditions there from personal experience.

Local families in need were not forgotten: when the Rain family was burnt out, the W.A. co-operated with the Boys' Club in organizing a benefit dance, and collected suitable used clothing; when Alf Ridley had to go to hospital the W.A. found a housekeeper at $10 a month to care for his motherless children. Sometimes good intentions backfired: an offer to mend socks for bachelors brought from one man alone a grain-sack full of dirty holey socks. Social activities to help brighten the lives of settlers in those depression days also came within their sphere: card parties at both ends of the valley; evenings of games and dances; picnics for the children. The charges were modest at most functions: 25c for adults included refreshments, 5c for school children, and nothing for pre-schoolers. Together with the men of the Farmers' Institute the women made strenuous efforts to obtain the services of a nurse either through the Public Health Service or Victorian Order of Nurses, but evidently without success because not until 1948 did Lorraine Carruthers of the Squamish Public Health Service start regular monthly visits. In the early 1940's the little group was abandoned in favour of newly organized Women's Institute because the new organization was able to include women of all religious affiliations and therefore had a broader base.

On the occasion of Bishop Gower's first visit to Pemberton in the early 'fifties, a meeting was held at the home of Frances Decker to start St. George's Church Guild. Mainly concerned with raising money for the improvement of the little church, the Guild had members with both Anglican and United Church affiliations. Thanks to their efforts the inside of the church was redecorated, the roof repaired, and new altar linen supplied. Gay Guthrie and Mary Nakatani started a Sunday School at Pemberton Meadows School and the Guild supplied the hymn books and working materials; later this Sunday school moved to the village area so that more children could attend.

Hospitality for visiting ministers was quite a concern to the ladies because train schedules rarely fitted in with suitable service times. A rota was worked out and in theory members with spare accommodation took their turn; in practise families with hospitable hearts who lived near the station contributed much more than their share. Ministers are accommodating guests and particularly those who had served in the mission field often had a fund of interesting stories. Efforts were made from time to time to assist local families in distress and to contribute to the community at large. The guild, for example, sponsored Girl Guides and Brownies in the late 'fifties and donated money to enable these two groups to get started.

When the question of a new church building in the village was raised in the mid-'fifties, the guild members at first hoped for a community church. Unfortunately financial assistance from neither the Anglican diocese of New Westminster nor the United Church Board of Home Missions could be obtained for a church of this type. The group then changed its name to St. George's and St. David's Guild and continued to serve both churches until early in the 'sixties, when it was regretfully abandoned and in its place the Anglican Women's Auxiliary was revived, and to meet the needs of St. David's Church a new organization was formed. The United Church Women held their first meeting on January 28th, 1963 and the first officers were President, Gladys Phare; Vice-Presidents, Vera McCulloch and Marcella Halliday; Secretary, Sidsel Ross; Treasurer, Phemie Menzel; Programme committee, Saidee McCulloch; Social Committee, Grace Sinnes; Finance committee, Phemie Menzel; and Manse committee, Betty Talbot.

The Anglican women set to work to raise money for their new church with bake-sales, suppers and card parties. The United Church Women performed a similar function for their church, helping with the completion of the building and the paying off of loans. They co-operated with the church board in the organizing of talent shows and catered to the first Pemberton Loggers Sports Day organised by St. David's church in 1964, at which the grand aggregate prize was won by farmer Eddie Ronayne. The two church women's organisations supported each other's efforts and took care that dates of sales did not clash. Each year they co-operated with the Catholic Church of Mount Currie to hold a joint service for the World Day of Prayer.

During the early 'sixties the United Church's young people's group "Hi-C" was started under the able leadership of Rose Hamula, and the St. David's church board sponsored both Scouts and Cubs, with Slim Fougberg, Henry Menzel and Phillip Perkins as the first group committee.

The Roman Catholic families of Pemberton were served by the church in Mount Currie Indian village. In the mid-'sixties the Catholic Christian centre was built in Pemberton and services held there in the summer months. Many other denominations held services in homes from time to time, and Bible classes and summer Sunday Schools for children.

Norman and Muriel Woods, both staunch members of the Jehovah's Witness, arrived in the valley with their family in 1969 and very soon after their arrival had started holding meetings in their home. By 1971 they had enough members to form a congregation and to move to Signal Hill School for their meetings.

The Sunday School Provincial Archives

The Fall Fair Provincial Archives

1st July Celebrations

THE SOCIAL COMMUNITY

Entertainment available to the valley residents of the 'forties had changed little from the 'thirties, being very largely home-made. Visiting among neighbours, before the days of the telephone, was much more frequent and welcome than today. Information or help needed always necessitated a call and all callers had tea or coffee and discussed the latest gossip before finally coming to the purpose of the visit. By then most families had some sort of vehicle, but many older women could not drive. Upper Valley women making a trip to the store would often pick up a neighbour on the way and, in addition, take the opportunity to pay a call on a friend in the village who would be sure to offer refreshements. Pemberton was a very close and friendly community and during holiday seasons, particularly Christmas, many of the open-house type of evening party were held. In great demand were the musically talented: at the Shores, Lilian at the piano played a swinging beat for the dancers; Betty Wilson was another talented pianist; her husband Ed Wilson played the banjo; and both Bert Lundgren and Bert Summerskill were versatile on the accordion.

For the entertainment of larger groups, the Pemberton clubs could be relied upon. The community hall committee held dances on public holidays or other special occasions: Sadie Hawkins dances, Valentines dances, costume dances, or just plain dances, at all of which during the late 'forties and early 'fifties there was a chronic shortage of women. The music was supplied by the same local talent that entertained in private homes. In the mid-'fifties the "band" usually included Lilian Shore at the piano, Elmer Hellevang at the saxophone, Derry McEwan on the banjo, and Jack Fisher at the drums. The costume dances offered scope for the artistic, ingenious, or uninhibited to display their talents. Lil Sowerby in the remnants of a fake-fur coat strategically placed and clutching a large ham bone made a very effective "wolf girl" of the Dogpatch comics; Mary Crowston in a two-piece bathing suit augmented with sleeves and wide pants made from an old nylon nightdress made a fetching harem girl; Jimmy Decker in long dress and apron with blackened face as "Aunt Jemina" danced through half the evening before his friends recognized him; a salesman from the hotel as a "bedsheet" arab; ancient warriors with aluminum foil shields; a good-looking young woman in two diapers as a baby. The community hall, built in the 'thirties was reroofed in 1948 and ten years later acquired a kitchen and washrooms. Before that time, the tiny kitchen, which is the stage of the present hall, had a wood stove but no sink or water. The wood heater in the centre of the hall could not begin to heat it in cold weather, but vigorous dancing kept the blood circulating.

The coming of electrical power brought films on a regular basis instead of the very occasional showing using a private power plant. George Walker brought in some of the first films, but soon the community hall committee and the Farmers' Institute were showing weekly films in both the hall at the station and the Boys' Club hall in the Upper Valley. Immensely popular with the

The Celebration

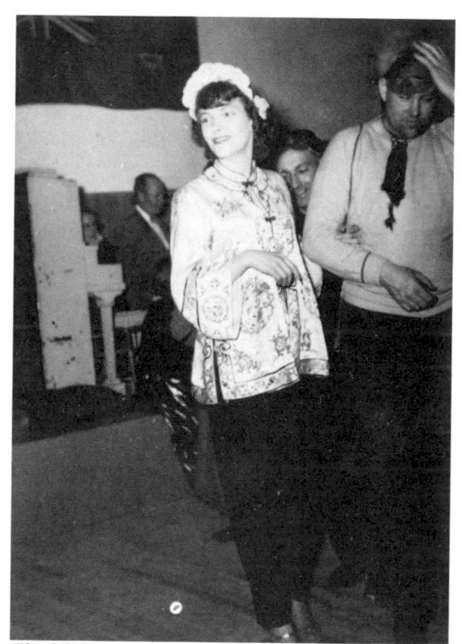

The Masquerade Provincial Archives, Victoria, B.C.

children the film show became the Saturday night meeting place for many. The community divided naturally into sections: the young in front; teenagers on the right, behind them; the adults on the left, with the very back row and the corners occupied by lovers. The Upper Valley hall catered to a smaller crowd and during the cold winter months the playroom of Pemberton Meadows School came into use. One night during a very scary film the children crept one by one from the front to the security of their parents, leaving their usual seats vacant. Projectionist George Mitchell finished the film with his own four children clustered close about him! But they all wanted to go back again the next week. Sometimes private individuals would bring in wildlife films to be shown in the hall, usually to an enthusiastic audience.

The hall committee also maintained a stock of crockery and cutlery which had been purchased by the joint efforts of four local organizations for use at suppers and banquets. The crockery was apparently broken by unseen elves and the same elves made the cutlery disappear in the same way. Minutes of the Women's Institute of this time are full of references to counting plates, or knives and forks, and variations in the count were sometimes the subject of acrimonious discussion between the different groups.

Early plays sponsored by the Women's Institute developed into a full-fledged Drama Club in the early 'fifties. Kindled by the enthusiasm of Lilian Shore and Eileen Brotherston, plays were presented at irregular intervals. Some of their most successful included *A Boy Named Beulah,* their 1958 centennial *Sadie Comes to Town, Second Honeymoon,* and *Clouds of Fear,* the last being the first effort at serious drama.

During the late 'fifties and early 'sixties entertainment groups like Evan Kemp and his band, and Taller O'Shay and his singers, included Pemberton on their regular circuit. They offered singing monologues and other variety numbers, and in addition played for the dance which always followed the entertainment.

Card parties held both in the halls and private homes were usually sponsored by the hall committee or one of the women's groups. The game most commonly played in earlier days was five hundred, but the Anglican Women later held bridge and canasta games.

In the spring of 1957 a C.B.C. film unit headed by producer Allan King and photographer Jack Long came to Pemberton to make a three-part film showing the life of a farm family, the activities in the village of Pemberton, and the Mount Currie rodeo. Doris and Lukie Van Beem, their two daughters Lucille and Julia, and foster children Vern and Elaine, were all featured in the film, as were Adolph and Marie Leo of Mount Currie whose young daughter was May Queen that year. Later shown at Pemberton High School the film provoked much comment, and not all of it favourable. One enthusiastic Pemberton booster was disturbed that the only private car shown was Lukie's Model A Ford. In 1957!

Mention should also be made of the J. Arthur Rank film "The Trap" starring Rita Tushingham and Oliver Reed which was filmed at Birkenhead Lake and Mount Currie in the early 'sixties and employed as extras many Mount Currie Indians. The company had chosen the Pemberton area for on-location shots in the expectation of plenty of snow, but unfortunately the snow was late coming that year and the company had to use artificial snow. In one scene, a discerning viewer could see snow on the ground by the cabin, snow on the higher mountainside, but between low and high land could see a band of dark green trees bare of snow.

In addition to talent nights organized by the United Church and plays put on by the pupils and staff of the schools on a more or less regular basis, other entertainments were often of the one-shot variety. The 1958 centennial dance brought all of Pemberton out in a wonderful selection of old-fashioned suits and gowns and the Hall Committee's first cabaret was the social event of the year, with the Valley people sitting around tables with liquor bottles actually in full view, dancing, and watching the can-can dancers perform in the supper interval.

Pemberton's most successful Pageant and Ball was held in the High School Auditorium on February 16, 1967 to celebrate the centennial of confederation. Reported on the front page of *The Vancouver Sun* and attended by Lieutenant-Governor Pearkes and his wife, the pageant presented some of the best-known events of Canadian history complete with songs and dances. As played by the boys and girls of Mount Currie, the Indians were truly real and their "scalping yell" shook the town visitors. Genuine deer-hoof rattles, skin drums, beaded buckskin and real beaver skins were some of Mount Currie's contribution to realism. Costumes from the previous Centennial, B.C.'s in 1958, were dug out of attics, added to, and improved. Bishop Harrington lent garments for the clergy, as did Father Scott of Mount Currie. In short, the whole community was involved in this inspiration of teacher David Codville who appeared in the pageant as John A. Macdonald with principal George Hayes as Georges Etienne Cartier. *The Vancouver Sun's* editorial of February 21st commented on us:

"THREE CHEERS FOR PEMBERTON"

"Let's admit it — little Pemberton has put us to shame. The folks up the valley rooted more centennial spirit out of their attics than has been mustered by the rest of us all put together.

"What a welcome breath of fresh air for our national birthday — that pageant with the kids of all colors whooping up history, and Lieutenant-Governor Pearkes and his missus at the hoedown, and the venison and smoked salmon and roast beaver tail and all the other great grub.

"Here we've had boards and committees and plans and projects and feasibility studies and heaven knows what all and we're about as festive as a funeral.

"It's taken Pemberton to show that the only indispensable ingredient is enthusiasm.

"Ready now? Three cheers for Pemberton, for showing us what a birthday party should be."

CAST

1. INTRODUCTORY REMARKS .... *Mr. G. Henry*

★

2. QUEBEC CONFERENCE ROOM—John A. MacDonald: .... *Mr. D. Codville*
George E. Cartier: .... *Mr. G. Hayes*

★

3. VIKING .... *L. Miller*

★

4. INDIAN LULLABY .... *M. Leo, L. Abraham*

★

5. INDIAN HARVEST DANCE .... *A. Ritchie, G. Dick, R. Sam, P. Sam, J. Wallace*

★

6. CARTIER MEETS DONNACONNA .... *C. Erickson, P. Sam*

★

7. DONNACONNA IN FRANCE .... *P. Sam*

★

8. CHAMPLAIN ESTABLISHES FUR TRADE .... J. Watson, A. Ritchie

★

9. JEANNE MANCE FOUNDS MONTREAL .... *M. Joseph*

★

10. BREBEUF PARADED BY CAPTORS .... *D. Harris, G. Dick, R. Sam*

★

11. DOLLARD ON THE OTTAWA .... *K. Fotsch, R. Shier*

★

12. MADELAINE DE VERCHERES .... *J. Miller, G. Hayes, G. Giguere*

★

13. FRONTENAC SIGNS PEACE TREATY .... *E. Talbot, P. Sam*

★

14. LONELY HABITANTS .... *L. Taillefer, B. Hardacre, D. Oberson, L. Cosulich*

★

15. BRIDESHIP DANCE .... *S. Priest, L. Alexander, I. Decker, S. Cosulich*

★

16. LaVERENDRYE BROTHERS ON PRAIRIES .... *P. Proudlock, P. Proudlock*

★

17. WOLFE MEETS MONTCALM .... *T. Lewis, C. Hellevang*

18. UNITED EMPIRE LOYALISTS .... *T. Lewis, N. Gott, L. Kuurne, W. Talbot, B. Fotsch, M. Abraham*

★

19. CAPTAIN VANCOUVER SURVEYS COAST .... *D. Spetifore, R. Fotsch*

★

20. MACKENZIE AND VOYAGEURS .... *F. Andrews, S. Kendall, B. Ayers, S. Matthews, G. Sankey*

★

21. FISHERMEN'S SCENE .... *M. Ayers, B. Walker, G. Mohs*

★

22. BROCK MEETS TECUMSEH .... *B. Potvin, J. Wallace*

★

23. LAURA SECORD .... *C. Ronayne*

★

24. ESCAPED SLAVE .... *L. Leo*

★

25. CHINESE IMMIGRANT ARRIVES .... *P. Wong*

★

26. BILLY BARKER .... *L. Brotherston*

★

27. CAN-CAN DANCERS .... *V. Shier, Judy McCulloch, L. Sankey, J. Menzel*

★

28. "O CANADA" .... *Assembled Company*

BRITISH SOLDIERS

E. McCulloch
A. Giguere
F. Menzel
D. Walker
C. Hellevang
G. Halliday
C. Jensen
D. Lewis
J. Ronayne
D. Menzel
B. Potvin

FRENCH SOLDIERS

R. Collins
C. Jensen
B. McCulloch
S. Andrew
F. Peters
S. Lester

Centennial Pageant cast

Waiting to perform Vancouver Sun

At the Pageant

Vancouver Sun

MENU

PICKLES AND CHEESES

LETTUCE AND TOMATO SALAD *JELLIED SALADS*

COLD SLAW SALAD *POTATO SALAD*

SCALLOPED POTATOES *SAUERKRAUT*

★ ★ ★

ROAST GOAT *ROAST TURKEY*

ROAST BEEF *ROAST VENISON*

ROAST BEAVER *ROAST ELK*

ROAST WILD DUCKS

PORK SPARE RIBS *BAKED STUFFED SALMON*

SMOKED SALMON

BEAVER TAIL WITH BOSTON BAKED BEANS

CHICKEN CHOW MEIN

★ ★ ★

HOMEMADE BREAD AND BUTTER

CENTENNIAL CAKES *CENTENNIAL PIES*

★ ★ ★

CENTENNIAL

TEA — PUNCH — COFFEE

Supper Menu

A Pemberton club contributing greatly to the social life of the community at this period was the Canadian Legion. In earlier years the World War I veterans of Pemberton belonged to the Squamish branch, but every Remembrance Day they organized a supper and dance at the community hall. Early Legionnaires included Arthur Mawbey, Chris and Barry Girling, Ernest Cooper, Eric Gethen, Gerry Cowell and Ernest Blakeway. Veterans returning after World War II formed Legion Branch 201 in 1946 under President Mawbey and Secretary Gethen. Charter members included Toni Bikadi, Len Fowler, Dick Green, Robert Kay, Fred Ridley, Peter Williams, Bill Spetch, Red Mahan and Ernest Blakeway. The Legion started with a small hut and

Legion Sports at Wellington Park 1951

PEMBERTON BRANCH NO. 201 CANADIAN LEGION B.E.S.L.

SPORTS DAY - 1st JULY 1947

AT WELLINGTON PARK - COMMENCING 2:00 p.m.

Sports

1. Race, Children, 6 years and under
2. Race, children, over 6 and under 12 years
3. Race, children, over 12 and under 18 years
4. Best decorated bicycle, children
5. Long jump, children
6. Race, 50 yards, women
7. Sack Race, children
8. Baseball Throw, children
9. Tug-of-War, women
10. High Jump, children
11. Three-legged Race, children
12. Race, 100 yards, men
13. Sack Race, adults
14. Cracker Contest (6 crackers), children
15. Egg and Spoon Race, children
16. Cracker Contest, adults
17. Thread and Needle Race, adults No 18 Relay Race.

All competitors in Children's Races to be under 18 years of age

Bean Guessing Contest **3 tries for 25c**

Boxing Tournament

(No decision bouts)

Under the direction of W. R. Green and H. E. McCulloch

Admission 25c

Dance

Commencing at 10:00 p.m.

Admission:- Gents 50c, Ladies 35c

Refreshments, cafeteria style

A conveyance will leave WILSON'S gate at 12:45 p.m. sharp and return after the Sports

---

Sports Programme

lean-to donated by Warren Taillefer. Later the enlarged premises included a shuffle board in the bar-room, a banquet room and kitchen facilities. From the start the Legion was a popular evening meeting place with its pleasant, friendly club atmosphere.

Apart from their special concern for veterans generally the Legion enthusiastically promoted every type of sport in the community. Every Dominion Day for many years they held a children's sports day, plain running and jumping; novelty races and races for adults too. Every entrant in the toddlers' class won a prize, a chocolate bar or ice cream cone — there were lots of ribbons and small money prizes for older children, prizes promptly spent at the concession stand. These early sports days took place in Wellington Park south of the track between Pemberton Plaza and Franks' Mill. Later the Ball Park in Signal Hill School grounds became the centre of activities with more concession stands and a refreshment stall. When the choosing of the Potato Queen became a community effort in 1957 the floats paraded and the queen was crowned on this same sports day. Rosemary Ronayne, the fourth Pemberton Potato Queen, was the first to ride a float down the main street.

In the first years of the Legion the Women's Institute often helped with catering for dances and made the curtains for the first hall, but such work was soon taken over by the wives of Legionnaires and in 1960, the sister organization, the Women's Auxiliary to the Legion was organized with charter members Fran Antonelli, Eileen Campbell, Eleanor Collister, Peggy Currie, Frances Decker, Edna Fegan, Margaret Green, Ada Graham, Peggy Harris, Edna Leach, Vera McCulloch, Elsie Miller, Doris Morozoff, Alice Penrose, Grace Sinnes, Agnes Taillefer, May Taillefer, Clara Walker, and Grethyll Watson. The Legion ladies were soon to be seen at concession stands not only at Legion functions, but at the Mount Currie Rodeo and other community gatherings, helping to pay for the enlarged premises completed in the early 'sixties. As with the Legion, youth was a special concern and the Auxiliary supplied trophies for clubs and gave scholarships for students as did the Legionnaires. Old people were also remembered and the Women's Auxiliary not only raised money for shut-ins in Vancouver, but also catered to pensioner groups who came on day trips to Pemberton.

Local interest in hunting and fishing prompted the Legion to sponsor the Rod and Gun Club which from its beginning had a strong appeal for the young men of the valley. The first Rod and Gun dinner, featuring wild game as the main dish, was held in the community hall in November 1961 and trophies awarded for the finest rack of deer horns shot that year and for the largest fish caught at the fish derby. Though other trophies were to be added, the kudos attached to the trophy for horns never diminished and the rivalry among the local sportsmen continued to be so keen that on at least one occasion the rack was hidden until just before the judging and produced only when others would be too late to better the effort. The Rod and Gun dinner-dance developed into a very popular yearly event as the members and their wives formed a lively fun-loving group.

The Hunter

The club's trap shooting range on the hillside above Pemberton proved very popular and turkey shoots became a regular feature of the year's activities. Safety training programs were offered to young hunters and the graduated became junior members of the club.

The principal target of the hunter's guns were the white-tailed deer which were to become scarcer as the logging destroyed much of their natural habitat and forced them into the less accessible areas. In the 'thirties moose moved into the Valley, particularly in the swampy bush of the upper reaches of the Lillooet River. For several years moose hunting was permitted, but when the numbers declined rapidly all moose hunting was stopped. Goat Mountain, as its name implies, is a haunt of the mountain goat on which there is a limited season in Pemberton. The use of telephoto sights has taken much of the skill and daring out of goat hunting.

Black bears abound in the area and over the years have developed a taste for oats, carrots, and even crabapples. Frequently seen by berry-pickers on the mountainsides, the bears are usually content to live and let live. The occasional grizzly seen in the back woods is more to be feared, and the trappers tell of being treed by them; in more recent times loggers have been menaced when a mother grizzly has been surprised. But grizzlies have been seen quietly pasturing on the back fields content to leave unharmed the cows and calves only a couple of hundred yards away.

On one of Bert Perkins' early journeys to Pemberton he saw a band of some seventeen wolves across Green River from his camp, but of recent years they have become a rarity, keeping mostly to the back country. Coyotes, though, are common enough to be a pest, cheekily approaching the barnyards in the early morning ready to pick off unwary poultry. Their choruses enliven the winter's nights and usually signify a change in the weather.

Other wildlife seen but not hunted include the occasional cougar, lynx, wolverine, and racoon. Skunks are common and frequently nest under houses — lifting a floor board to investigate a stopped sink, Irene Blakeway was startled to see the shiny black head of a mother skunk. Trapped for their fur are such animals as mink, beaver, muskrats, otters and the occasional fisher.

Before the drainage scheme mallard and pintails abounded in the swamp lands of the Indian reserve near Lillooet Lake, but in more modern days only a few are to be seen. Wild geese nest in the upper reaches of the Lillooet River and flocks often come onto Pemberton fields in the fall, but not in such numbers as formerly. Other non-game ducks like the mergansers often ride the turbulent waters of the Lillooet or Ryan with a band of ducklings bobbing along behind their mother. The rare bald eagles make this area their regular habitat, often nesting on the tops of dead cedar trees. More than eighty varieties of birds have been sighted, most on their spring and fall travels to and from their nesting areas.

In the 'forties and early 'fifties, with the game department and the police safely in Squamish, the game laws were kept in only a cursory fashion, hunters often shooting their deer before bothering to buy either license or tag, and fishing with no licenses whatsoever. As the population increased so did the visits of the game department and, after the completion of the road brought outside hunters in great numbers to the area, an office was set up in Pemberton and regular road checks became routine in the hunting season.

During the two summer months Federal Fisheries employed local fish guardians who were responsible for issuing permits to Indians to gaff or net fish in the area from D'Arcy to Port Douglas and for checking to see that nets were in the water only on certain days of the week. The fish guardians also reported to warden Art Reynolds of Squamish the runs of the different varieties of salmon, giving a rough estimate of the size of the run and the dates spawning salmon were seen. Slim Fougberg, Joe Taillefer, and Max Menzel were all employed as fish guardians for several years.

Sandy and Adela Fowler and their son Leonard

Indoor sports during the winter months of the 'forties were confined to badminton and table tennis at both the community hall and the Upper Valley hall. Informal clubs formed for the purchase of nets, shuttles and other equipment, competed at irregular intervals and the friendly rivalry between the Upper and Lower Valley continued. The Recreation Club started by a group of young people in 1956 brought in a new generation and replaced the old Boys' Club. This group also sponsored dances and organized summer camping trips to Tenquille Lake.

The rapid expansion in population of the early 'fifties brought many more groups into being. The Recreation Commission set up under the Provincial Government offered financial help and encouragement to many sporting activities: keep-fit classes, basketball coaching for adults, and swimming for children. Government funds proved to be insufficient for all these activities and much of the money needed to pay for swimming instructors was raised by local efforts like the variety show held at the Community Hall in May 1963.

PROGRAM

1. Shadow play by the pupils of Pemberton Meadows Elementary School

   Director: Wendy Baragar (teacher)

   Actors: Chris Hellevang, Janet Miller, Leena Kuurne, Lisa McNolty,

David Hellevang, Debbie Antonelli, Joe Ronayne and Doug Mitchell.
Stage Effects: Mark Kuurne and Bob Mitchell

2. A Women's Hunting Party — comedy presented by the Women's Institute
   Actresses: Wendy Baragar, Ruth Hellevang, Nell Van Loon, Leone Cosulich and Thelma Hamilton
3. 'Settling Down'' and ''Puff'' sung by the 4-squares
   Singers: Eddie McCulloch, Brent Pipe, Ray Shier, Jimmy Watson
   Accompanist and coach: Beth Pipe
4. ''Skip to My Lou'' and ''I Like to Be a Brownie'' sung by the Pemberton Brownies accompanied by Beth Pipe
5. Variety presentation by the Pemberton Girl Guides
   Highland Fling: Brenda Tindle
   Comedy Pair: Brenda Ayers and Barbara Fotsch
   Songs: Barbara Fotsch and June Halliday
   Piano Recital: June Halliday
6. Mount Currie Indian Brass Band: Selections.
7. ''If I Give My Heart to You'' and ''Among My Souvenirs''
   Singer: May Pascal of Mount Currie
8. ''Out in the Barnyard''
   Singer: Albert Nelson of Mount Currie

With the building of the gymnasium at the High School, the Pemberton ''Aces'' basketball team came into being; on the team in 1958 were Frank Shore, Ed Gilmore, Jim McKellar, Brian Ross, Fred Thompson, Ray Hass, and Mauri Hjelt. This young men's team became the ''Cascades'' of the 'sixties, playing the Mount Currie ''Braves'' and the Pemberton High School's ''Red Devils'', and travelling to Lillooet to compete with teams there. Baseball games between Pemberton and Mount Currie had always been a feature of the Legion sports days. In 1952 Frank Carrachelo of the Pemberton Hotel was sponsor of Pemberton's baseball team, purchasing their first uniforms; on the team that year were Paul Herendale, Henry Menzel, Roy Cowell, Max Menzel, Ernie Davis, Martin Taylor, David Taylor, Derry McEwan and Sonny Taylor. Four years later the first baseball banquet was held and awards given to Henry Menzel for the best batting average; Fred Thompson, the pitcher, as the ''most valuable player''; and Bobby Gilmore as ''rookie of the year''. Women's softball teams followed and by 1965 the Pemberton Hotel was sponsoring the ''Cabarettes'' who with the coming of the road began competing with teams from Squamish, Britannia and lower mainland. Pemberton's second softball team, sponsored by the C & S Logging Company, became keen rivals of the ''Cabarettes''.

The great Canadian sport of skating is only sporadically available during Pemberton's long winter, the heavy snow preventing the formation of firm ice, or if early strong ice does form before Christmas a three-foot dump of snow will effectively put an end to the skating. Birken residents are luckier, usually getting a long period of good ice every year. With the first irrigation pumps, people tried flooding level fields and, some years at least, the weather co-operated to allow several weeks of skating. The Pemberton Meadows pupils often skated while waiting for the home-bound school bus and men arrived for impromptu hockey matches at the week-ends.

In the early 'sixties Corporal Spray of the R.C.M.P. started classes in square dancing and filled the community hall with eager learners. A shortage of women in that first year meant that one of the ten squares would often be entirely composed of men who were always anxious to trade places, because "whirling" with a two-hundred-pound logger with a chest like a board was strenuous exercise rather than dancing. The keenest of the dancers formed the Mountain Dewers Square Dance Club, with Burnie Salter, Kel Harris, Jack Guthrie and later Len Pickell calling the rounds.

The Riding Club, developing from gymkhanas begun by the United Church, grew in popularity through the years. Soon it was an independent club with members of all ages taking part in trail rides, learning sessions, and annual gymkhanas. The horse population had declined rapidly with the advent of the tractors, but soon increased when pleasure horses appeared both on the working farms and on the smaller acreages near the village and shiny new tack replaced the old bridles and saddles.

Swimming, like skating, was limited in the Pemberton area. The glacier-fed rivers seldom warmed above 40 F and were usually too swift-flowing for safe bathing. The lakes too remained cold until late summer, leaving only small pools and backwaters shallow enough for the sun to warm: Salmon Slough, on Hellevang's farm in the Upper Valley and the pool near Zurcher's farm were popular spots in the 'fifties, and early 'sixties.

The Hockey Match

Swimming at Leach's Pool

On summer days in the 'forties a crowd of Pemberton children would gather at the pool under the old railroad trestle by Pemberton Station and in the centre of the crowd would be Lilian Shore helping the non-swimmers to get started. She would take the young ones for rides on her back and instruct the teenagers in diving. Former champion swimmer and winner of many awards she never mentioned, Lilian Shore was always ready to help and when swimming lessons of a more formal sort were started under the sponsorship of the Recreation Commission in the mid-'fifties Lilian was the one who took charge of the first classes held at Leach's Pool. After the first two years the classes for the senior children were moved to One-Mile Lake to a pool enclosed by a log raft. "We used Red Cross lessons and certification," Lilian writes, "and there was a very close relationship with Jack Scott of the Red Cross during those years . . . . The building of the raft was a community effort. I just 'bulldozed' everyone I knew to get that built, even to my son Gary's boss, Steve Blasco of Van West Logging, who gave us the necessary timbers, delivered to the lake shore. No money was involved. We had around 80 children in the first summer's effort, a third of whom couldn't swim, but all could when Sharon Esche, Vivian Carter and I were finished that year. Vivian's and Sharon's wages were paid by the Recreation Commission".

One-Mile, with its frigid water, presented quite a challenge to the participants because the weather that first July was unusually cold and cloudy. Two years later the water from the glacier-fed One-Mile Creek was diverted, and though certainly warming the lake the diversion encouraged the growth of weeds and produced unhealthy levels of bug count. In spite of all difficulties most of the children passed their tests and some went on to the Bronze Medal for lifesaving, returning in later years to teach in their turn. The beginners continued to be taught at Leach's pool by Lilian Shore with the assistance of her former pupils.

With beautiful mountain scenery on all sides Pemberton never lacked picnic sites, even when the one road stretched only from Perkins' ranch at the head of the Valley to D'Arcy on the southern end of Anderson Lake. On summer Sundays the Pemberton families would head for the favorite picnic spots on the Birkenhead River or, more ambitiously, to Birken or Anderson Lake, sure of finding some other Valley families with the same idea. Extended family picnics were the best fun for the children for they had plenty of playmates and a chance to sample another mother's cooking. With no road to the outside the few strangers were always someone's friends.

Holiday party at Tenquille Cabin

Tenquille Lake continued to be the preferred family holiday place for a longer stay. In 1942 a group of men headed by Sandy Ross and Morgan Miller decided to build a cabin because few families owned tents and camping under trees could be marred by rain. The balsam trees growing by the lake were used to construct a small sturdy cabin with a primitive table by the window and bunks along one end. Shingles packed up the mountain on horseback supplied the roofing, and windows were "liberated" from abandoned mines which also supplied the first stove and many of the kitchen utensils, cutlery, tin plates and mugs. Later miners using the cabin for prospecting trips left behind large tins of dried food which supplemented the supplies the holidaymakers brought up

Tenquille Lake

The Hikers

holidaymakers brought up on horseback. Set on the porch, a small cupboard with a screen was used for a larder. It was very handy for storing bacon, butter or jars of broken eggs, but for highly perishable goods such as meat or fish caught in the lake, the creek supplied a natural cooler. Each family left behind a supply of wood, including kindling, for the next comers and each family was supposed to leave the cabin tidy; standards of tidiness varied from family to family; it was usual, therefore, to hear that "the cabin was in a terrible mess when I got there, and I had to spend my first day cleaning up". To make an early start, pack the horse, round up the children, heat water to wash the breakfast dishes, and yet to leave the fire safely out, all took organizing and so dishes were sometimes dirty and clothes were left behind for subsequent parties to pick up. Mice and the occasional pack-rat did not help.

But this Tenquille Lake cabin offered a wonderful opportunity for families to take even quite young children for a holiday by a mountain lake for only the price of groceries and more than a bit of energy. Families shared the cabin, shared the chores, shared their food, and shared the bunk at night. As many as eighteen slept across the bunk, and usually the day's activities of hiking, fishing and climbing ensured a good sleep. When the old boat on the lake finally collapsed John Ronayne built a new one which was air-lifted under the belly of a helicopter. Most school-age children managed the eight miles up the mountainside under their own steam, the younger ones rode at least part of the way, the smallest in a packboard on Dad's back. Mother brought up the rear, sometimes hanging onto the horse's tail for extra lift, for the bedding and groceries came on horseback as did the clothes for the younger children.

Horses often proved a trial at Tenquille, particularly borrowed horses which were frequently unused to packing and resented the strange hands. Like people, horses get homesick and usually in the middle of the night they would set off down the mountainside. The common practice was to tether them to a large dead-wood log, but the horse would often manage to break the tethers and more than one man had a wild midnight run after a horse, for much worse was the prospect of packing bedding, clothes and saddle down the mountain. Some horses, those trained originally for logging, set off dragging the log tethers, but the noise usually roused the sleeping family.

In August 1962 the Pemberton Girl Guides under the leadership of Captain June Perkins and Lieutenant Jean McEwan joined with the Squamish Guides led by Captain Margaret Flack for a week's camping at Tenquille Lake. The plan was to pack in the food, tents and sleeping bags; the girls were to carry their own clothes. Pack horses or, rather, horses to pack were rounded up and several men to take charge of the "pack train". Derry McEwan, one of the packers, described the trip some years later:

"The packers were Don Miller, Phillip Perkins, Derry McEwan, Bert Lundgren and possibly others. By 6 a.m., they had led the horses across Fowler's Bridge, and carried the girls' supplies over. They started to pack. But none of them could remember the diamond hitch. Not Phillip, son of a well-known packer; nor Bert, who had worked with Bert Perkins. Somehow the packs were tied on with any kind of knots and finally the pack train started off. But the horses lost packs all the way; first when they stopped to drink, later when they grew thinner with the exertion of climbing. So the men would hang onto trees the packs that fell off, expecting to come back later. The Girl Guides had done the same earlier, leaving personal items they found too heavy, confident that the men with the pack train would pick them up. The weary horses and packers finally reached the lake at 7 p.m. The next day the men went back for the goods left behind. The tents and the bleach intended to purify Tenquille's pristine streams never left the banks of the Lillooet, the men judging correctly that the clear weather would continue.

"Then for three evenings Derry McEwan and Burnie Salter went to Bill Spetch for instruction in packing, Clara Salter's horse acting as model. When the time came for the return trip, all was simple. In about four hours the packers had the horses down the mountain and over Fowler's Bridge, packs still on."

Fowler's Bridge had been built that same summer by local volunteer labour because the old cable ferries had gradually become unsafe and fallen into disuse. Before the bridge was built the horses were swum over the river, the families travelling in dug-out canoes, at least one mother insisting that her children were to travel in separate trips, not all together. Most of the Valley-raised men were very competent in these canoes, but the Lillooet swollen by the melting snows of summer could look very alarming.

Crossing the Lillooet

The Girl Guides had formed under the sponsorship of the Church Guild in the early 'sixties and were first led by Rene Carradice whose enthusiasm gave this group a good start. Other leaders of the Guides included June Perkins, Jean McEwan, Dianne Tetrault, Leone Cosulich, Dawn Ross, Joan Brown, and Dorothy Morgan. Every summer in the early years the girls attended camp with other companies, and Dawn Ross recalls pleasant summer picnics accompanied by Mount Currie guides with leader Sister Mary Immaculata. The Brownies organized at the same time had Frances Antonelli briefly as their first leader; she was followed by Beth Pipe who was Brown Owl for a number of years.

The Boy Scouts, organized at the same time under the sponsorship of the United Church Board, drew on both the R.C.M.P. and the forestry for their leaders, as well as on local men. Names associated with the Scouts include Sonny Taylor, Burnie Slater, Perry McCulloch, and Don Hardacre. A local campsite obtained for Guides and Scouts near the Owl Creek Hatchery proved a limited success — Mosquito Portage lived up to its name and not even daily spraying could keep the campsite enjoyable. The Scouts also camped at Gun Lake twice and at Shalalth during the 'sixties, but a campsite at Blackwater Lake was later obtained from the government. The Cubs were also started about the same time and early leaders included Dale DesRosiers, Dianne Tetrault, and Grace LeBlanc. The Scouts and Cubs obtained the right to cut trees on the powerline and for several years used this as a source of income.

Pemberton and District Board of Trade had been the driving force behind the drainage program and during the war years, assisted at times by the Women's Institute, sponsored salvage drives, showed films at the Community Hall and continued to boost Pemberton and to harass the Government about the local roads and the lack of a through train to Vancouver. In 1944 Vivien Lokken and Kathleen Lundgren were accepted as the first women members. By 1949 Board members were concerning themselves with the water supply for the village, and endorsing a request of the Lillooet Lake Trading Company for the establishment of a post office at Creekside. In their concern over the lack of a road they let no opportunity for publicity pass — in 1958 they distributed 5,000 pamphlets in Vancouver on this subject. The report in Vancouver that 4,900 of these were given out in beer parlours was hotly denied! The Board of Trade strongly supported Pemberton's drive for incorporation, and through the years made many attempts to interest large mill firms in the area and even to persuade the federal government to establish a heavy-water plant. Though in earlier days the Board of Trade was mainly concerned with the needs of the farming community, as the population expanded their concerns turned towards the business community and the need for a locally based industry offering year-round employment. This very real need has yet to be fulfilled and the Board of Trade, now the Chamber of Commerce, is still working on the problem.

On the social side the Board of Trade held an annual banquet which was a very popular local event in the 'fifties and 'sixties. In 1957 they entered the P.N.E. parade with Princess Mary Miller riding a float decorated with paper potato flowers. Earlier they entered the District Display at the PNE and filled a stall with local produce from sheaves of oats to jars of locally preserved fruits. The Taylor family and Eric Gethen were closely associated with this effort, and Granny Taylor spent many hours at the stand answering questions about this area which was then largely unknown to the lower mainland.

By 1966 Pemberton men came to feel the need for a service club which would offer to men a broad range of interests, an opportunity to meet socially and plan for much-needed services for the rapidly growing community. Pemberton Lion's Club, sponsored by the Squamish Club, was inaugurated in the High School Auditorium on February 19, 1966. More than three hundred guests from Vancouver, Vancouver Island, Cheakamus, Squamish, Kitimat, Bellingham, Olympia, Aberdeen and even Lion's Club International President from Chicago, George Campbell, crowded into the hall to be served a dinner prepared by the united efforts of the women of the Valley, to join in the opening ceremonies, and to be entertained by a choir of local ladies singing a welcome, by Swiss-born Gus Zurcher playing the Alpenhorn, and by Indian dancers from Mount Currie. Marie Joseph, Mrs. Stanley Dan, Barbara Dan, Lyle Leo, Pauline John, Ronald Dan, Mary James, Henry Dan and David Dan performed a variety of Native dances.

In the hall the entertainment went with a swing and without a hitch, but behind the scenes was another story. The much added-to Pemberton High School has a corridor more than a hundred yards long: at one end is the Home Economics Room where the food was cooked, and at the other was the top door of the auditorium. Food in ample quantity was ready in the kitchen and down that hundred yard hall by a long service table a gang of waitresses was ready to go. To carry the food down from the kitchen was only one small food trolley and woman-power. Back and forth the servers went carrying trays of cut meat, big pots of vegetables, piles of plates, until finally the food was all out. Bedlam ensued: waitresses in a milling crowd on both sides of the table, a more than serious shortage of serving spoons, the servers filling plates in a hectic rush, reinforcements with more food running up and down that long hall. Everyone in everyone's way. Dessert followed the earlier bedlam. And then the carrying of the dirty plates back to the kitchen. Fortunately, the hot water soon ran out and helpers could go home. To the Lion's Club — triumph; to servers and waitresses — sore feet.

The Lions elected Bob Priest as their first President, and Vice-Presidents Tom Allen, Slim Fougberg, Bob Herron; Secretary, Brian Edwards; Tail Twister, Perry McCulloch; Lion Tamer, Bill Olsen; Directors, George Henry and Wendell Watson. Sixteen other charter members joined at the same time. In their first two years the Lions purchased and operated Pemberton's first ambulance, sponsored a village spring clean-up drive which became an annual event, held a Loggers Sports Day, entered a float in the Squamish Loggers Parade, helped to organize a blood donor's clinic, cut Christmas trees from B.C. Hydro land and made serious plans for the building of a fire hall. The ideal of service was certainly put into action, but the social side was not forgotten, with ladies' nights, picnics, and other jollifications, including a special picnic for the graduating class of '66.

On January 31st, 1940 twelve women met at the Upper Valley club house to discuss war work and the possibility of setting up an organization with as broad a base as possible, open to all women of the Valley. The Women's Auxiliary with its close Anglican connection had a limited appeal to women of other religious affiliations. After considering information of both the Women's Institute and the Red Cross Society, the women decided on the former with Frances Decker as the first President; Gladys Ronayne, Vice-President; Margaret Fougberg, secretary; and Joy Girling and Margaret Green as directors. To express their support of Ada Taylor and the Red Cross group of the Lower Valley, Maria Fraser was appointed convenor for Red Cross work. Directors' meetings were held to discuss the organization and the following month the first regular meeting was held. Among those who attended the first year's meetings were Sidsel Ross, Irene Blakeway, Annie Ronayne, Mrs. Prendergast, Edith Lansdowne, Mrs. Blattler, May Taillefer, Dorothy Girling, Adela Fowler, Clarice Urdal and Maud Ronayne.

The early efforts of the Women's Institute, or W.I. as it was usually called, concentrated on contributing to the war effort by making garments and

Women's Institute Picnic 1949

Fishing at Lillooet Lake

canvassing for funds for the Red Cross, preserving food for relief purposes, collecting salvage, wool for blankets and comforter batts, donating clothing, comforters, and money for Russian relief, sending comfort parcels to local boys serving overseas and to other Canadian soldiers in overseas hospitals, appealing for free transportation for soldiers so that leave could be spent at home and, at the end of the war, joining with the Rangers in holding a VE Day celebration which included ceremonies, speeches, songs, field sports and a ball game. With all their war work the women found time to hold quilting bees, cater to Field Days at the Illustration Farm, organize dances, picnics and sports days. As early as 1943 Frances Decker appealed at a W.I. meeting for a permanent record of the Pemberton pioneers.

In November 1946 the first W.I. banquet held in the Upper Valley Hall offered, in addition to the food, raffles, a quiz program, a bazaar and dancing with music supplied by Bert Lundgren, Bert Summerskill and Ed and Betty Wilson. This banquet, moved to the Community Hall the following year, became a popular yearly event offering a fine menu of varied dishes followed by entertainment and dancing, for it was a family affair with everyone from grandmothers to babies in arms attending. To recall those banquets of the late 'forties and early 'fifties, it must be remembered that the lack of phones made careful planning ahead of time essential.

On the morning of the banquet one or two women from the Upper Valley would be responsible for collecting all the pies and buns, but would leave most of the hot food to be brought down later. Pies rode precariously on the back seat of the car or in the back of a pick-up carefully covered against either road dust or snow — slipping back and forth on a foot of fresh snow often meant that meringue pies lost their topping on the way. The community hall was already the scene of great activity when the upper valley group arrived. The heater and cookstove, both wood-fired, were lit as early as possible by the Lower Valley women in order to cook the roasts and also to warm the frigid hall. The wood available was usually still in blocks, and the axe missing. One woman would hopefully go out to round up an axe and to bribe a husky young man to split wood for a free supper later in the day. Next they set up the tables and always met with delays when finding broken tables which had to be mended. White cotton sheets or building paper covered the tables. Chairs and benches were put in place. Food, served buffet style, was usually plentiful with a strong emphasis on local produce such as potatoes and turnips. One year, however, the convenor had her quantities badly out, and when Sandy Ross arrived late with a previously purchased ticket, he was offered a plate of turnips or his money back!

The rapidly increasing membership of this period enabled the W.I. to launch a variety of projects for entertainment and social improvement. A Coronation Pageant showing the variety of ethnic groups among Canadians held in 1953 was the start of annual citizenship programs involving Gay Guthrie and the pupils of the elementary schools.

Late August Flower Shows held in the community hall from 1953-56 and convened by W.I. members Margaret Fougberg and Kathleen Lundgren revived interest in Fall Fairs. The Pemberton Fall Fair Committee was brought back to life under the chairmanship of Slim Fougberg with Margaret Nielsen as secretary. The W.I. members, particularly the farmers' wives, contributed greatly to the success of these fairs which later were transferred from the community hall to the more spacious High School Auditorium. The centennial fair of the 'sixties included a competition for old-time dresses and a display of museum articles owned by W.I. members.

Though the old Boys' Club had included teenage boys among its members, the 4H club sponsored by the W.I. in 1951 was the first club for children in Pemberton. Under the leadership of Doris Van Beem, this club was involved in a variety of projects, including potatoes, calves, chickens and gardens. The annual achievement day held at the Upper Valley Hall gave the children an opportunity to show off their prize ribbons and the square dancing they had learned. The 4H club also started the first competition for the Pemberton Potato Queen, the senior girls of the club canvassing the valley for votes. First Potato Queen, Noreen Shier, was crowned in August 1953, attended by Princesses Jean Miller and Maureen Ross, flower girls Rosemary Ronayne and Ida Miller, and by Ralph Fowler as pageboy. Pat Harwood followed Noreen and then Pat Young in the three years before this ceremony became a community event. Doris continued as leader until 1963 when the club was disbanded and reorganized by Gordon Ferguson in 1966. The W.I. also sponsored the Pemberton Perky Pins 4H sewing club started by Edythe Bokstrom in 1967 and later under the leadership of June Perkins assisted by Grace and Lesells LeBlanc.

First Potato Queen and 4H Club

Money was raised for the various W.I. activities by bazaars, serving refreshments at community hall dances, catering for banquets, raffles, plant sales, bake sales, plays and talent shows, and sales of work. Under the energetic leadership of Lilian Shore the W.I. was involved in health programs such as dental clinics for children and the well-women cancer clinics, and in the Health Centre itself which was the W.I.'s proposal for a centennial project and which had received enthusiastic support from the other community organizations. The 1958 Centennial Committee on which Lilian Shore served obtained a federal centennial grant as well as assistance from the Public Health Service and the Red Cross and the center opened that centennial year; considerable sums were also raised locally, every club sponsoring a money-raising project. Other members of this committee were Toni Bikadi as chairman, Gunnar Nielsen, Don Dufault, Bill Spetch, Bill Davis and Jack Guthrie. At this time the Red Cross separated from the W.I. and formed the first Pemberton chapter under the Presidency of Ada Graham, with Vice-Presidents Sidsel Ross, Bill Pascal and Peggy Currie; secretary was Mrs. Larry Adolph, Treasurer Eileen Brotherston, and other officers Mrs. Don Neil, Fran and Harry Erickson, Father Coffin and Margaret Mitchell for the juniors.

The W.I. also took care of the social amenities with Christmas gifts for the younger children, flowers for the sick, greetings to new residents, friendship teas, showers for burnt-out families, and even centennial spoons for babies born in 1958. For the community welfare they badgered the B.C. Electric and B.C. Telephone for service, helped to provide a wheelchair for Squamish station, furnished a ward in Squamish hospital, pushed the P.G.E. into offering reduced fares for High School students for week-end trips home, supported the men's organizations in their appeals for dyking and drainage, better roads, rural mail service, and all and any improvements that the government might be persuaded to make.

The Women's Institute provided an outlet for the energies of Pemberton women when they were isolated from the lower mainland by the lack of a road, and offered a much needed information centre in an era of poor radio reception and no television at all. The meetings were far from formal, the discussions lively, as on local issues feelings ran strong. The social over tea provided a chance to visit with neighbours and catch up on local gossip.

In 1949 Frances Decker won the Tweedsmuir Cup presented every three years by the Federated Women's Institutes of Canada on a Canada-wide basis for the best essay on a selected topic.

"We will endeavour, in all ways, [she said, at the end of her essay] to keep harmony in our Institute and our community; to work for tolerance and co-operation amongst those of diverse creeds and nationalities.

"Thus we will take a forward look in these anxious days, remembering the one who said 'fear not', and remembering when we think of our motto FOR HOME AND COUNTRY that 'HOME' in the present day world means sanctuary for all in need of comfort, security and the outstretched hand of friendship; and that 'COUNTRY' extends far beyond the boundaries of our beloved Canada."

First Bank in Pemberton Provincial Archives

THE BUSINESS AND LOGGING COMMUNITY

Pemberton village of the 'forties was still quite small, with all its businesses on the main street: community hall, Taylor's garage, Taillefer's store, the hotel and Prendergast's log cabin facing the station and agent's house; the section house, as now, at the end of the road; at the opposite end, across from the hall, Jack Taillefer's garage and later Joe and May Taillefer's new home, and behind it the first, very modest Legion building. By the railroad was a small cabin used by the Forestry during summer months, a couple of old log cabins, and the bunkhouse where the unmarried members of the section crew lived.

The Pemberton Express garage was both home and business premises to Bob Taylor and his family. The PX, as the business was known throughout the Valley, not only delivered the express parcels and general freight from the station, but also the private mail sacks and groceries on a twice weekly basis. The mail run went as far as the Van Beem farm, waited two hours, and collected outgoing mail and grocery orders on the return trip. The PX sold gas from the pump, and bulk gas and oil from a warehouse by the railroad track. In addition, the PX hauled potatoes, turnips and cattle to the station for shipment to Vancouver and beyond, ran a taxi service, rented the car or pick-up to visiting salesmen and officials, was the agent for farm machinery, and sold real estate. As they grew up the older Taylor boys, Sonny and Martin, became involved in the business, driving the trucks and running the gas pump.

Unofficially, and quite unpaid, the Taylors ran a news service. On their regular trips up the Valley they collected and dispensed all the local news. News then travelled up and down the Valley faster than it does now with all the convenience of the telephone. Mr. Farmer learned that his reefer car had arrived and was ready for loading at the station, and back down the Valley would go the news that Farmer children had brought measles back on their last trip to town.

Pemberton Hotel had changed little from earlier days. The only structural alteration was a lean-to addition which served as the men's section of the beer parlour, and a large storage shed built in 1948. The owner's family lived in the upper rooms of the hotel, dined in the kitchen and used the lobby as a living room. During Frank Carrachelo's ownership in the late 'forties his daughter Frances served in the dining room while son Billy kept the cook's woodbox filled; Bob Sowerby worked in the bar and his wife Lil was chambermaid. Some of the bedrooms had running water, but the only bathroom and toilets were on the main floor, and used by the bar customers during open hours. The bar parlour, partially divided into "men only" and "ladies and escorts" occupied the space later used for the cabaret. On busy nights the tables from the mixed side overflowed into the men's section; on Friday pay nights often the reverse. On weekday afternoons the place was so quiet that the owner would call a round on the house!

A large wood range dominated the hotel kitchen. The small sink, where family, restaurant and kitchen dishes were washed, had one tiny draining board and a far-from-adequate supply of hot water. Storage shelves and a large cook's table ran down the centre of the room and at the end under a long window was the family's eating table and benches. Wood was stored on the back porch where meat was hung in the winter months. The large beer cooler in the bar was also used to store kitchen supplies. "Out back" was a small hen house, rabbit hutches and an open garbage dump which was the winter haunt of bluejays. A gasoline-fueled power plant supplied lighting, and water came from the village supply. Because the hotel bath was one of the few in the community, it was often booked on dance nights for 50 cents. One young man came to claim his bath only to find one of the bar customers asleep fully dressed in the water! Meals were served at one long table in the lobby-cum-dining room; if more than eight customers were expected small side tables were pressed into service. No choice of menu was offered, there being a straight charge for the meal, the family and staff having essentially the same meal in the kitchen. On Sundays, the cook's day off, the hotel family took care of the cooking, Frank Carrachelo often making his "speciality" — spaghetti with meat balls or fried pork. The hotel owners of this period always gave a Christmas dinner for the bachelors of the village: one cold Christmas the guests slept on the lobby chairs rather than return to their cabins and the cook had to rout them out the next morning by the simple expedient of opening the windows and letting in the below zero air from outside.

When Bill Davis took over the hotel he changed the dining room into a modern-type cafeteria, modernizing the kitchen at the same time. From then on the cafe became a concession operation by a succession of couples, including Jim and Peg Currie, the Flints, and the Wings, who later purchased the store from Hardacres.

Taillefers, like the early hotel owners, had added a lean-to shed at one side, but the family still lived above the store. A roothouse at the back served as vegetable storage and cooler. The pot-bellied wood heater was replaced by oil in the late 'forties, but the customers still stood and warmed their backs around it, gossiping while waiting for the mail to be sorted. Joe and May

Taillefer were joined in the operation of the store by their son Warren on his return from the Air Force. May ran the Post Office, sorting the mail which arrived by train three times a week, and filling the individual mail sacks which the PX delivered to the Valley farms twice a week. By 1949 the elder Taillefers had moved into their fine new house across the road from the community hall and Warren was managing the store.

Like most general stores, Taillefer's stocked a wide variety of goods: groceries, basic work clothes, hardware, tools and feed. Supplies arrived on the Wednesday afternoon wayfreight; fresh meat and vegetables came by express, packed in dry ice, usually every couple of weeks. These luxuries were available for only a few days. Orders for groceries were sent down with the mail and often included post office transactions:

"Please send me 100 lbs. White Flour, 20 lbs. Brown Sugar, 5 lbs. one inch nails, 2 spools White Cotton. Also I want a money order for $5.95 put in the letter to Eaton's and my letters stamped. Put $10.00 on the store bill and send me the change in 4c stamps. Cheque for $20 enclosed."

As cheques could not be included in the post office accounts, transactions such as this required some juggling with the tills. Substitutions were common and no one was surprised to receive Corn Flakes instead of Rice Krispies or yellow instead of brown sugar. Additional complications came up when farmers claimed credit for eggs or vegetables sold to the store. Some families purchased their supplies in bulk from Woodward's to be shipped up by wayfreight. That transaction was strictly cash, of course, and the storekeeper, who inevitably saw these parcels in the station freight shed, was often considerably provoked to notice groceries arriving for customers who had long outstanding accounts.

At the south end of the main street Mrs. Prendergast ran a small store in a log cabin, for a short time in conjunction with the Co-op. By 1948 the little log cabin was the home of Warren and Mary Taillefer with the front portion being used as a storage place for feed and bulk supplies for Taillefers.

Warren's brother Jack ran a garage and Ford agency across from the community hall, but sold out to Brotherston and McNally in the spring of 1952 because by that time electricity had arrived and Jack was fully occupied with a flourishing electrical and plumbing business.

The general expansion of the area of the early 'fifties brought new business enterprises to the village of Pemberton, including Rolf Fougberg of Pemberton Valley Distributors who sold machinery and ran a small construction outfit; Dan Antonelli of Top Spot Appliances; and Prendergast's log cabin underwent another transformation and became a cafe run by Wendell and Grethyll Watson.

Apart from the trucking run by Taylors, several other men "took a whirl" at hauling gravel for the P.F.R.A. or the Public Works and at hauling farm produce such as potatoes, turnips or cattle down the Valley road to the station. Early truckers included Bob Sowerby, Jack Matthews, Jack Taillefer,

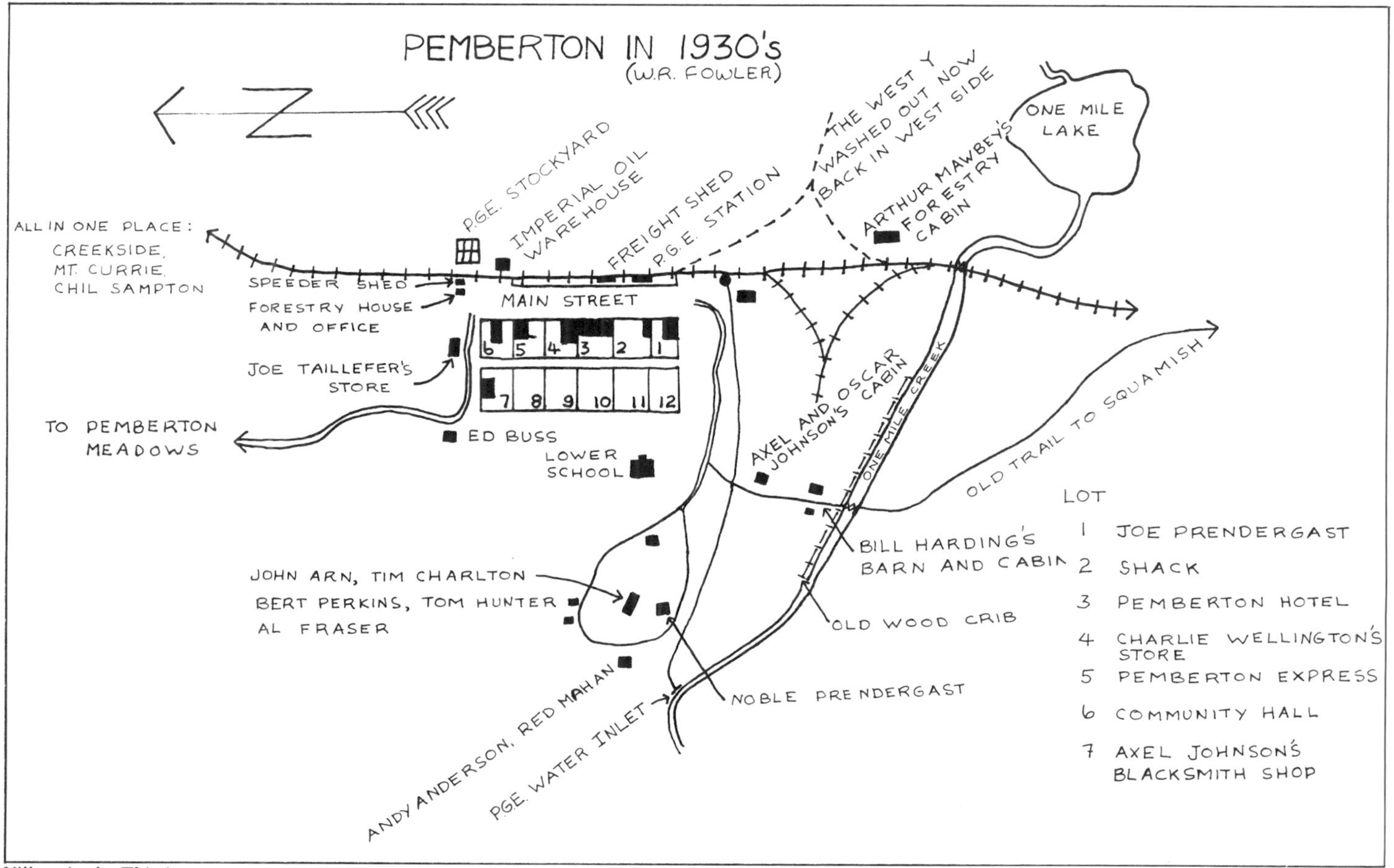

Village in the Thirties

W. Fowler, J. M. de Suarez

Bud Fraser, Bob Spetifore, Martin Beks, Gunnar Gimse, Brian Ross, Fred Collister, Earl Rivett, Joe Antonelli and Wendell Watson. Hauling from the farms was very much a seasonal business, particularly the livestock side which only involved a few loads of cattle each year. The racks were make-shift affairs hastily added to a flatdeck truck, often sheets of plywood held in place by very flimsy stays. More than once cattle escaped on their way to the station, the bewildered animals taking off into the bush. One steer evaded all efforts at recapture, but after the first snowfall two months later appeared in a local barnyard looking for a feed of hay. As no farmers of the early 'fifties owned loading equipment, the trucker usually had to help load the sacks from the low-built log roothouses of that period, and then at the station the sacks had to be reloaded and stacked high in the reefer.

In 1956, Robbie Miller, whose slaughter house was located at his farm, started the first retail meat business in a small building between the B & M garage and another small building which, like Prendergast's cabin, was to have a series of uses, including use as a telephone switching system, a private house, a bank and a real estate office. That same year Harold Pipe started construction of the Pemberton General Store, a single-storey building with a small apartment behind for the family. Pemberton's second grocery store opened for business in 1957, offering a similar type of service to Taillefer's. Pemberton General Store was a family business with the older children helping out after school. As business increased, Harold built an apartment above the store, taking the original apartment for storage, and later ran a bulk propane service.

The first locally based savings and lending institution, the Pemberton and District Credit Union was founded in March 1956, officers being Slim Fougberg, Bill Spetch, Warren Taillefer, R. W. Thomas, Kel Harris, Jack Nelson, Jim Currie, Roy Penrose, Fred Meen, Frank Carrachelo, Wendell Watson, and treasurer Ken Kenward. In its early days, opening only one afternoon in a tiny office of the building also used by Rolf Fougberg, the Credit Union was to grow to a full-time operation with chequing facilities and a modern office. Both Audrey Oberson and Marg Deering worked for the Credit Union during its growing years. Centennial year 1958 saw the opening of the Bank of Nova Scotia as a twice-weekly operation.

Meanwhile the old established businesses had not stood still. Pemberton Express completed its new garage and gas station in 1957, and the bulk sales were taken over by the new $15,000 bulk plant built by Imperial Oil, and managed by Lorne Monford. Warren's Department store, formerly Taillefer's, expanded into two parts — a modern style grocery store on one side and the hardware department on the other, in the original building. Robbie Miller and his wife Millie took over the grocery business from Warren who then concentrated on hardware and appliances. At this time the post office was separated from the store and Ben Cherry became Pemberton's first full-time postmaster. In fact the little village was expanding in all directions and in all ways, the old shacks up back being replaced by the neat row of B.C. Electric houses, and new homes being started on the mountainside above the village. Pemberton had the beginnings of a Nob Hill!

The next large business expansion came in the mid-'sixties, when the road became more than a rumour and daring souls were dodging the highway crews to drive in from the city. At the Pemberton Hotel new owners Tom and Helen Allen, in partnership with their two sons Larry and Dale, embarked on an expansion program which transformed the small frame hotel with its very basic services into a modern building with coffee shop, dining room, cabaret, a greatly enlarged beer parlour, and many more bedrooms. The hotel now extended to the end of Frontier Street, for the old Prendergast cabin had met its end by fire, and the residence built by former hotel owner Frank Carrachelo had been moved to a new site in the village.

The old Brotherston and McNally garage underwent remodelling and renovation to become Pemberton's first drugstore, opening for business in May 1964 with Bob and Pat Priest moving into the apartment above the store with their four children. For the first few years Bob worked part-time teaching science at the High School and opened the store for business in the afternoons, in early evenings, on show nights, and on Sundays for the tourist traffic. The older Priest children were put to work in the store at weekends and evenings after school. As business expanded Bob was able to become a full-time druggist and later to eliminate the Sunday and evening openings. In later years Bob replaced the old building with a fully modern store, and moved his family to a home on the hill above Pemberton.

Warren Taillefer, who had built a new hardware store early in the 'sixties, expanded his premises in 1964 to include a coin-operated laundromat with four washers and two dryers. The first business of its kind in the community, it proved very popular with both Pemberton and Mount Currie residents, doubling its size in only a few years. Like most laundromats it became a centre for local gossip and a notice posted there was sure of the attention of the community.

The taxi service in Pemberton started by the Pemberton Express underwent many changes. Earl Rivett and wife Norma ran a taxi service out of Pemberton, and Gerry Belanger operated out of Mount Currie. Bob Matthews consolidated and expanded the service with two cars and radio communication, the bulk of his business being the run between Pemberton and Mount Currie.

By 1962 the grocery store had changed hands again and was under the management of Don and Dorothy Hardacre who, as other storekeepers before them, lived in the apartment above the store with their two sons. With considerable experience in marketing, the Hardacres brought a more modern concept of marketing to Pemberton with a better selection of fresh produce and quick efficient service.

Difficulties in obtaining a reliable water supply in Pemberton village first started the residents to organize as a group, and eventually to think of incorporation as a village. In 1949 they petitioned the trustees of the Pemberton Valley Dyking District to install and maintain a water main and to supply the townsite with water. The P.G.E. railway had a pipe line from One Mile Creek which formerly supplied the water tank and later the section house and agent's house. For years this pipeline had been tapped both legally and illegally, but because the supply was inadequate a new line was needed. Wooden pipe and the necessary valves and plugs were purchased by the Dyking District for $629.37. The fee for each outlet was $59.00 and users supplied their own lines, paying in addition a consumption fee. By 1953 the residents were petitioning for incorporation as a water improvement district under the Water Act. Frank Carrachelo, Warren Taillefer, Bill Brotherston, Harvey McNally, Len Fowler, Joe Taillefer, Frances Taillefer, Bob Taylor, Hector Harwood, Jack Taillefer, Eileen Taillefer and Henrietta Boeur were the residents signing, with general support from the Canadian Legion, Community Hall, Public Works, Pemberton Valley Dyking District and B.C. Electric. At first the plan was to organize street lighting, drainage, sewerage and fire protection as well as water service and the residents wanted to be able to tackle these problems as they arose, but unfortunately the B.C. Electric felt that because its property was valued at $33,168 as compared to $17,800 for the remainder of the village, the B.C. Electric would in reality be footing much of the bill. The Company did agree to the water and street lighting, but baulked at the rest. When the local group investigated further, however, they found that the B.C. Electric would only supply lighting if the residents would be personally responsible for the maintenance charge.

Village Council 1959

Then strongly backed by the Board of Trade, the villagers pressed for incorporation which became a fact on July 20, 1956. The first meeting of the Pemberton Village Council was held on August 2, 1956 with Frank Carrachelo in the chair, and Ken Kenward acting as secretary. A nine o'clock curfew for children under sixteen was one of the first by-laws passed by the village council and water and lighting its first priorities.

The Ball Team

Vice-chairman Warren Taillefer took charge of lighting, Bob Taylor water, Fred Menzel roads and Wendell Watson fire protection. By the second meeting Frank Carachelo had resigned and was replaced by Walter Green, and Frances Antonelli replaced Ken Kenward at the princely fee of $75.00 a month. Jack Nelson was appointed building inspector and by November of that year the water system, with all its accompanying headaches, was turned over to the village.

In the early 'sixties a group of residents living in the area round the High School formed the Pemberton North Water District. The water for Pemberton

First Sports Day at Signal Hill

North District also came from One-Mile Creek and this new group had to co-operate with the village water commissioner. The seasonal variations in water level and accumulated snow and freezing pipes in the winter provided plenty of problems, as did the greatly increased water use of an increasing population. The water commissioner, who did not have the most popular job on the village council anyway, found himself spending his Sundays on volunteer labour on the line. For Pemberton North, Bert Lundgren had "free" water for his efforts in keeping the line running.

Horse Logging

The unprecedented expansion of Pemberton, both the village and surrounding area, during the 'fifties and 'sixties was the result of a number of factors: the opening up of new farm land and improvement of existing farms because of the drainage project; the improved services brought by the B.C. Electric and the B.C. Telephone; the completion of the railroad and later the road to Vancouver; and, most of all, the start of the logging industry which later took the place of farming as the main income base of the valley.

Apart from the Blackwater Timber mill at Devine, operated by Andy Devine, logging operations in the 'forties were restricted to small sawmills, one horse logging outfits and pole cutting. George Walker and Bill Spetch went into partnership in a sawmill in 1945 and were typical of the operators of that era. George ran the mill, assisted during the summer months by his brothers and father who later ran the planer. Bill, a great horseman and an expert in training a team, ran the logging end. The trees, mostly fir, were hand felled

Modern Logging

with six-and-a-half foot cross-cut saws which required the energy of two husky men. John Punch, the axe expert, hewed out the trails for the teams and sniped the logs, sharpening the ends to a point so that they would travel more easily down the hillside and along the skid road. Skinners like Victor Frank and Seymour Wallace handled the teams expertly, teams so trained that when they felt the tension on the chains slacken they would leap to one side as the loosened logs shot down the mountainside and the torn out dogs rattled on the end of the chains. Once on the flat, the logs were too heavy for the teams, unless on a skidroad built of small logs lying crosswise. Barkers were not so essential then because the bark was cleaner without the embedded stones typical of bulldozed logs. George Walker purchased his last team of horses as late as 1952 for $500. A champion lead pair from a team of Clydesdales that had competed in exhibition across Canada, they weighed between 1700 and 1800 pounds each, and proved their worth in the woods. It was possible in the days of horse logging, to buy a team, train and use them for a year, then sell them for as much as or more than they had cost — and that, commented one old horse-logger, is "more than you can do with a skidder". And the woods were quieter then, and though nobody made a fortune, most made a reasonable living.

Cedar pole cutting went on side by side with the fir logging, similar methods being used to haul the poles out of the woods. Among the pole men were Bud and Dan Fraser and the Fowler boys, Leonard and Laurie, the latter a very husky young man who would often drag out a pole when he came down the hillside for his lunch. Pole cutters came and went. Two or three men would take a contract having first successfully bid for a pole-limit, fell, limb and peel cedar trees young and straight enough to pass inspection and then ship them out to make a large or small profit. If the latter, they would complain bitterly of the market or the unfairness of the government scaler, and move on to some other job. Many farmers, like Lukie Van Beem, Ron Ronayne and Ben Kay, were able to supplement their farm income with poles cut on their own land or obtained a short distance away. By 1949, when Bud Fraser, Charlie Wallace and Vern Lundstrom were pole cutting on the hillsides above Lillooet Lake, the two-man chain saw was coming into general use. These saws were as long as the old cross-cut saws and weighed over 100 pounds. Around the same time Wally Wagner, Jack Matthews and Gerry Wolf were logging fir, using a spar tree, the lines powered by a donkey motor to bring the logs together in piles on the hillside. An A-frame mounted on a log raft was used to pull the logs into the water and they were floated to the end of the lake to be shipped by road to the Creekside railway spur, and thence to Vancouver. The pole cutters on the lake used a similar method.

The coming of the B.C. Electric brought slashing contracts to Bud Fraser and partners from Seton Portage to McGillivray; Thevarges, from McGillvray to Birken; Menzel brothers, from Birken to the Cariboo road; and Fleetwood Logging from the Cariboo Road to the lower end of Lillooet Lake. Unemployment Insurance was not so easy to get then and "where there was a buck to be had the local boys were out looking for it".

During this same period a number of small saw mills operated: in the Upper Valley, Hines and Sorge who later sold out to Wilf Doyon, Roger Dickey on the Cariboo Road south of the Birkenhead River, Arthur Thevarge in the D'Arcy area, Gunnar Gimse in the Birken district and Miller Creek watershed, Toni Bikadi, near Creekside, and John Ronayne in Pemberton Meadows. By the early 'fifties Toni Bikadi, in partnership with Bill Brotherston and Harvey McNally, was working near Miller Creek, Joe Antonelli near Tisdale, and Ed Morgan in the Birkenhead district near the old fish hatchery.

Some worked from their homes and others operated from small camps set up in the bush. Up the narrow twisting Soo Valley road travellers today can see the remnants of a small camp. The rusting skeletons of two trucks almost hidden in the underbrush, the cleared space where the sawmill stood and the old, high greying stumps are all that is left to show that men once lived and worked here, falling trees with cross-cut saws, yarding with a donkey engine or spar tree and trucking their logs to the railroad ten miles away. From the railroad they would collect their groceries and machine parts and drive back to their lonely camp.

Starting in the late 'fifties, Danny and Mabel Franks ran a sawmill, two shake mills and three shingle mills, the last two operations being destroyed by fire in the mid-'sixties. Financed at different times by Vancouver Warehousing, Tyee Forest Products and Robson Plywood, Franks' Mill continued off and on into the late 'sixties. John Cosulich worked as bookkeeper, Rhea Sankey in the office, Magnus Urdal at both construction work and in the mill, and A. Danyliuk as sawyer. The first shingle mill in Pemberton was built by Dick Green in partnership with Harry Weber and Emery Doyon. Emery's sister Terry worked side by side with the men and put in a "man's" day at the mill.

The arrival of the Fleetwood Logging Company around 1950 signalled the start of bigtime logging in Pemberton. Fleetwoods set up a camp on the upper end of Lillooet Lake, built a bridge and some roadway, and used crawler tractors to supplement the spar trees and A-frame. By 1956, George Walker had left his sawmill and with Howard Anderson of Fleetwood formed the new company of Cascade Fir Logging, working first at Tisdale along the Green River and later at various locations including One-Mile Creek, Mosquito Lake, Ure Creek, Ryan Creek, Keirstead Creek and Rutherford Creek.

The first steel spar in Pemberton was brought in by Cascade Fir and that steel spar, with the other heavy machinery, transformed logging in Pemberton.

Miller Creek Lumber Co.

The higher slopes of the hillsides could be reached by bulldozed roads, the new lighter chain saws could be operated by one man, and the steel spar could be set up in a matter of hours, as opposed to the two days needed to prepare a spar tree. Soon Anglo-Canadian Forest Products, earlier known as Gillespie Logging and later as Van-West, had started operations on the south side of Green River at the foot of Mount Currie, and Empire Mills was working near Tisdale. The loggers were everywhere. The woods screeched with the high-pitched whine of the power saws, bare patches appeared on the mountainsides, and logging trucks raised clouds of dust on the gravel highways.

The Loggers

Side by side with the giants worked the smaller, usually locally based outfits: LeBlanc Brothers, who started near D'Arcy and later moved to the slopes above Ryan Creek; Perkins Brothers, mainly in the Upper Valley; Talbot's Logging on the slopes near Miller Creek; Larry Hamula in the Soo Valley. Others like Lizard Logging, and Crivea and Shenko, flourished only briefly. Mount Currie Contractors were operated by two Valley-raised men, Len Fowler and Pete Shore. Jim Collins, who turned from farming to pole-cutting in the early 'fifties, was later to join Pete in order to form the C & S Logging Company.

As well as at the Creekside spur, logs were loaded at three loading yards near to Pemberton Station. The coming of the road in 1965 saw the first logs being shipped direct by LeBlanc Brothers, and from that time on more and more logs were trucked from Pemberton to Squamish. Though most of the wood shipped was fir, in the early 'sixties Scott Paper Company began buying cottonwood which was shipped directly by road to New Westminster.

Large scale logging brought full employment to the young men of the district, at least in the summer months, a profitable alternative to farming and much more money in the village. Derry McEwan opened a small repair shop specializing in chain saw sales and service. New families moved into the district to work for the logging companies or in the subsidiary occupations like truck driving and machinery repair. Between 1951 and 1966 the population of the area, excluding the Reserve, increased from 250 to 768.

Expansion of the logging industry brought more Forestry personnel. Prior to 1958 it was customary for an Assistant Forest Ranger from the Squamish Ranger Station to spend the summer months in Pemberton. A small cabin constructed on the P.G.E. right-of-way served as both home and office until the building of the warehouse and residence in 1957. The next year Jack Carradice took over his duties as the first Forest Ranger in charge of the Pemberton area. As the forest industry expanded further, assistant rangers were appointed and another residence was built. Fire suppression crews of university students occupied a camp run by Al Staehli with his wife, Marti, who was cook, and often with a local girl hired to help her. Later many of the hillsides denuded by logging operations were replanted by crews working either on contract or directly under the Forest Service.

And what of the future? The seed potato business had brought prosperity to the farms; the logging industry had offered jobs and a solid income, particularly to the young men; employment opportunities had increased in the village in cafes, stores, bank, offices and forestry. The road to Vancouver was now all blacktop and being improved year by year, bringing both goods and tourists to the valley. A radio transmitter in the village had improved local reception; and even one shaky TV channel brought in news, police shows and commercials to amuse and aggravate the population. Pemberton was now part of the lower mainland. Its citizens bought their groceries in Squamish or Vancouver and had every modern advantage. And yet, with all the advantages of more industry, many of the older residents look back on the old days with affection. The inconveniences forgotten, they remember the closeness of an isolated community: Tenquille Lake in its splendid pre-tourist virgin beauty; the family picnics by the Birkenhead; the summer trips to D'Arcy when half a dozen families would gather by the lake; the impromptu swimming parties in the summer at Salmon Slough or One-Mile Lake; and skating parties in winter whenever there was a patch of ice on a field. They remember too, the instant help in time of trouble: the chores done, the children cared for, any neighbour's car available as an ambulance to go to the station; and the train would always wait. They forget the hard work of churning and remember the good taste of summer butter; they forget the milking, and remember the home-made ice cream. Land clearing had brought wonderful bonfires, but baled hay saw the end of the children's hayrides.

Some of that closeness still remains and, one hopes, will always remain, because Squamish is still fifty miles away and a winter snowstorm can make those fifty miles seem very long indeed. The high mountains prevent the building of many roads, though a through road north, by one route or another, seems inevitable. The new roads have already made new areas more accessible, but the backwoods are little changed, and the hillsides denuded by the loggers now provide space and air for wild fruit — there are still huckleberries on the hill.

Pemberton Village in the 'fifties

Will Miller's farm in the 'thirties

SELECT BIBLIOGRAPHY

Anderson, J. R. "Memoirs". 1878.

Begg, Alexander. *History of British Columbia from its Earliest Discovery to the Present Time.* Toronto, Briggs, 1894.

British Columbia. Department of Highways. *Notes on the Road History of British Columbia.* Victoria, 1953.

British Columbia, Legislative Assembly. *Journals.* Reports of Department of Lands and Works, 1873-1917.

Brown, R. C. Lundin. *British Columbia. An Essay.* New Westminster, printed at the Royal Engineer Press, 1863.

Cairnes, C. E. "Pemberton Area, Lillooet District, British Columbia". From *Summary Report, 1924. Part A. Geological Survey of Canada.* Ottawa, Government of Canada, 1935.

Canada, Department of Indian Affairs. *Annual Report,* Part 1, 1882. pp. 778-781.

Cheadle, Walter B. *Cheadle's Journal of a Trip across Canada, 1862-63.* Edmonton, Hurtig, 1971.

Chipman, Renee Haweis. "Lundin Brown of Lillooet", in Millicent A. Lindo, ed., *Making History. An Anthology of British Columbia.* Victoria, Lindo, 1974. pp. 63-69.

Corporation of the Village of Pemberton. Council Minutes.

Downton, G. M. "Extract from the Report of 1913"; "Report, 1919"; "Extracts from the Report of 1921". *Reports of Surveyors of Lillooet District.* Victoria, Department of Lands, 1913, 1919, 1921. pp. 30-34, 74-76, 88-90.

Elliott, Gordon Raymond. *Quesnel, commercial centre of the Cariboo Gold Rush.* Quesnel, Cariboo Historical Society, 1958.

Elliott, Margaret. "Revisiting Pemberton". *B.C. Motorist* 9(3): 14-15 April 1970.

Faulknor, C. V. *Pemberton Valley Land Utilization Survey.* Victoria, Department of Lands and Forests, 1951.

Girling, Dorothy. "Flood — 1940". C.B.C. Script.

Girling, Dorothy. "Those not-so-bygone days". C.B.C. Script.

Great Britain, Parliament, House of Commons, J. W. McKay's "Journal of a journey through part of Fraser's river; also register of bridges on Harrison's river road". *Papers relating to the Affairs of British Columbia.* Part 2. London, 1859. pp. 30-32.

Green, Robert Blakely. "Camels in the Cariboo". *Museum Notes.* Second Series. 1:26-30. March 1950.

Hartzell, C. A. Fragment from weather record, November 1895 to November 1909. "From Diary kept on Lot 181 Pemberton Meadows about 10 chains in from the river bank".

Howay, Frederic. *British Columbia, the Making of a Province.* Toronto, Ryerson, 1928.

Howe Sound School District. School Registers.

Keith, J. C. Copy of a letter to the Honourable Mr. McBride, including data laid before the Executive Council, 1909-10. Vancouver, 1911.

Lindsay, F. W. The Cariboo Story. Quesnel, *The Quesnel Advertiser,* 1958.

McEvoy, A. An open letter on the incorporation of Squamish and the P.G.E. Vancouver, 1919.

Mayne, R.C. *Four Years in British Columbia and Vancouver Island.* London, John Murray, 1862.

Morse, Eric W. *Fur Trade Canoe Routes of Canada Then and Now.* Ottawa, National and Historic Parks, 1969.

Ormsby, Margaret A. *British Columbia: a History.* Toronto, Macmillan, 1958.

Parsons, Otis. Diary, June 29 to September 19, 1858.

Palmer, H. Spencer. "Report on the Harrison and Lillooet Route", in *Papers Relating to British Columbia.* Queensborough (Royal Engineer Press), 1859.

Pemberton and District Board of Trade. First Minute Book, 1931-1952.

Pemberton and District Co-operative Association. Minutes, July 1941-June 1960.

Pemberton Dyking District. Correspondence.

Pemberton Meadows Athletic Club. Minute Book, 1925-1953.

Pemberton Valley Farmers' Institute. Minute Book, 1942-1962. Document of incorporation, 1925.

Pemberton Women's Institute. Minute Books, 1940-1966.

Perkins, Herbert. Trapping Diary, 1922.

Perkins, Herbert. Time Book, a record of trail building and trail repairs, 1926-1927.

Ramsay, Bruce. *P.G.E. Railway to the North.* Vancouver, Mitchell Press, 1962.

Reid, H. Stewart. *Mountains, Men and Rivers.* Toronto, Ryerson, 1954.

Ronayne, Annie. "Journey to Pemberton". C.B.C. Script.

Ronayne, Annie. "Bringing Kathleen Home". C.B.C. Script.

Ronayne, Jack. Diary, 1909-1916.

Slaymaker, O. and R. E. Gilbert. "Geomorphic process and land use changes in British Columbia". *Processus Périglaciaires Étudiés Sur Le Terrain.* Liége, Université de Liége, 1972. pp. 269-279.

Smith, Dorothy Blakey, ed. "Harry Guillod's Journal of a Trip to Cariboo, 1862". *British Columbia Historical Quarterly* 19:187-231 July-October 1955.

Smith, Marcus. "Detail Report on the Surveys in British Columbia for the year 1873". *Report of Progress on the Explorations and Surveys up to January 1874.* Ottawa (MacLean, Roger & Co.), 1874. pp. 174-193.

Squamish Centennial Committee. *A Centennial Commentary Upon the Early Days of Squamish, British Columbia.* 1958.

St. David's Church Board. Minute Books.

St. George's Church Board. Minute Books.

St. George's and St. David's Guild. Minutes.

Tatlow, Rose. "B.C.'s Cattle Trail". C.B.C. Script.

Teit, James. "The Lillooet Indians". *Publications of the Jessup North Pacific Expedition.* New York, Steckert, 1906. vol. 11, pt. Y, pp. 193-300.

United Church Women. Minute Book.

Walkem, W. Wymond. *Stories of Early British Columbia.* Vancouver, News-Advertiser, 1914.

Walker, E., Chairman. Report: Pemberton Valley Production, 1974.

Wedley, William C. Community and Corporate Development in the Pemberton Valley. A report prepared for the Pemberton Valley Labour Force Development Committee, 1975.

Women's Auxiliary to the Anglican Church. Minute Books.

NEWSPAPERS

Bridge River-Lillooet News, Lillooet

British Columbian, New Westminster

British Colonist, Victoria

Daily Colonist, Victoria

The Province, Vancouver

Squamish Times, Squamish

The Vancouver Sun, Vancouver

Victoria Gazette, Victoria

Lower Hatchery — spawning salmon

Float in parade

INDEX

PHOTO GALLERY

Ronie Miller on last leave, 1942, with nieces Laura and Jean Miller

Pat Wilson on leave, 1940, with friends Bussie Pomeroy and her children, Anne and Dick

Left to right, Dick Green and Johnny Decker on their last leave, 1941

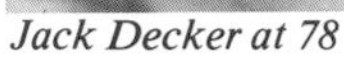

Jack Decker at 78

May and Joe Taillefer in the mid-'fifties

The Taylor family in the late 'thirties: from left, Bob, Molly, May, David, Martin, Sonny, Mary

Bert and Kathleen Lundgren heading for the trap line

Henry and Phyllis Erickson ready for their trap line; Elsie Miller on horseback

Edmond and Gladys Ronayne

Provincial Archives, Victoria, B.C.

Watching the game — back row, from left: Tessie Ronayne, Kathleen Ronayne, Lilian Shore; middle row, from left: Mrs. "Red" Mahan, Gladys Dermody, Teresa Miller, Vivien Lokken, Sidsel Ross, Bertha Collins, Mrs. Broadfoot, unidentified child; front row, from left: Rene Oman, Gladys Ronayne

Provincial Archives, Victoria, B.C.

Mount Currie soccer team, from left, Martin Williams, Steve Pascal, unidentified, Bill Pascal, Harry Dick's father, ______ Wallace

Provincial Archives, Victoria, B.C.

Pemberton soccer team — back row, from left: Sandy Ross, Slim Fougberg, Gerald Ross; middle row, from left: Bob Taylor, Ronie Miller, Johnny Ronayne; front row, from left: Leon Keyes, Scotty Bennett, Ernie Cooper, Morgan Miller, Allison Johnston

The Spetch School with teacher Molly Garvin and, left to right, Muriel, Bill, and Elizabeth

Teresa Miller and her family in 1917: back row, Gerald, Sandy, and Vivien Ross; front row, Robbie, Ronie, and Morgan Miller

Teacher Greta McDonald, about 1920

May, Tats, and Norman Dermody in 1917

Harold Wyatt-Purden, about 1930

Thomas R. Greer in 1910

Herbert Perkins Provincial Archives, Victoria, B.C.

Leonard Neill in 1910 Provincial Archives, Victoria, B.C.

Indian Dancers, July 1959

Squamish Times

Vancouver Sun

French soldiers at 1967 pageant, from left: Florence Peters, Christine Jensen, Sylvia Lester, Barbara McCulloch, Sharyle Andrew, Becky Collins, Chris Hellevang

Ray Elliott

Margaret Mellish (Mrs. Ray Elliott) in 1917

Nelson and Maria Fraser

Dora Barbour in 1917 Provincial Archives, Victoria, B.C.

Skaters, 1920, including the Joe Ronayne and van der Hoop families Provincial Archives, Victoria, B.C.

The big snow

At the Halfway House on Pemberton Portage

1927 First of July picnic at Agerton

In foreground, from left: Bill Pascal, Sandy Fowler, Count van Rechteren

Mr. and Mrs. Sid Spetch

Tommy Hurley, V. Lloyd-Owen, Ray Elliott

A. McLeod and C. Barbour at entrance to Crown Mine, August 1924

Margaret Green in 1935 with daughters and granddaughters; on left, B. Pomeroy with Anne; on right, L. Gowan with Marilyn. Men at rear, Harvey Derrick, left, and Charles Wellington

Provincial Archives, Victoria, B.C.

Teresa and Will Miller with Robbie, on left, and Don

1949 picnic at the Birkenhead; left to right, Ernie Cooper; Maureen, Brian, and Lex Ross; Sidsel and Sandy Ross (in smoke); Slim Fougberg, Ruth Cooper, and little Anne Jamieson

1948 Women's Institute picnic — back row, from left: Vivien Lokken, Maud Ronayne, Henrietta Boeur, Phemie Menzel, Teresa Summerskill, Maria Fraser, Lilian Shore, Margaret Fougberg, unidentified, Mollie Ronayne; front row, from left: Frances Decker, Margaret Green, Stella Gummow, Vera Miller

Evening

Edith and Tommy Fowler with Francis Joe children

Provincial Archives, Victoria, B.C.

Upper Valley School, about 1924; from left: Kathleen Ronayne, Eddie Ronayne, Bart Ryan, unidentified, Dorothee van der Hoop with apple, Dick Green, Tessie Ronayne

Far left, Mary Miller; group of Lower Valley pupils in the mid 'forties — back row, from left: Mollie Taylor, Jean Miller, Laura Miller, Norma Shore; front row, from left: David Taylor, Nancy Shore, David Shore

Teacher Ab Wilson, 1920's

Teacher Molly Garvin

Lower Valley School, built in 1929

Provincial Archives, Victoria, B.C.

From left, Leonard Fowler, Clifford Ronayne, Billy Fowler

At John Jack's cabin, 1937; from left, Teresa Lokken, Winnie Cooper, Kathleen Ruddock, Gunna Gimse, Bert Lundgren

Betty Ronayne

Eddie Ronayne, Bert Summerskill, Kathleen Lundgren

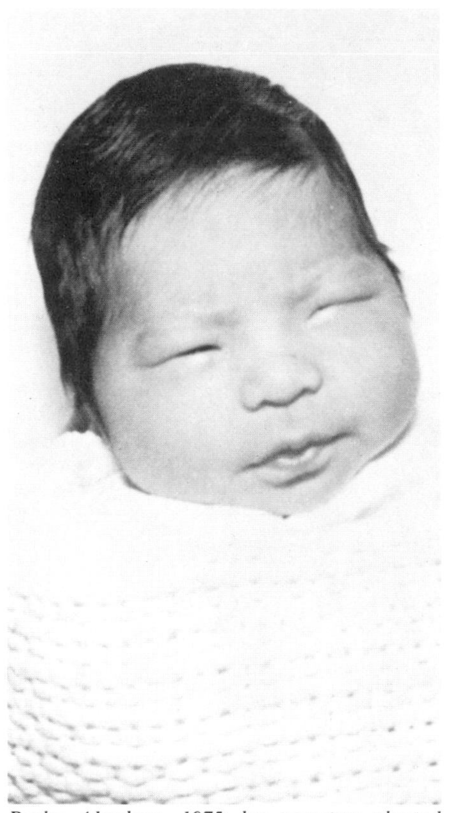

Becky Abraham, 1975; her ancestors planted the Valley's first potatoes

Jim Ryan with a grandchild

Mrs. Martin Williams, left, and Mrs. Baptiste Ritchie at a Fall Fair

"Red" Mahan in 1959 Provincial Archives, Victoria, B.C.

Jim Landsborough at V.E. Day observances, 1945

William Currie Provincial Archives, Victoria, B.C.

Charlie Barbour Provincial Archives, Victoria, B.C.

Annie Ronayne cutting ice

Billy Fowler with wolf pelt, 1930's

Provincial Archives, Victoria, B.C.

Neill ranch, 1910

Provincial Archives, Victoria, B.C.

Packed up and ready to leave

At the van Loons'

The Halfway House on Pemberton Portage

Ray Elliott's pack train

Provincial Archives, Victoria, B.C.

At "Coffee" or "Mahogany" John Miller's stopping house on the Pemberton Trail, 1911; from left, Charlie Barbour, land seeker, John Miller, Myrtle Philip

On top of the mountain

Tenquille cabin, late 1940's

Ready for the trail

Clara Jones, left, and Adela Fowler Provincial Archives, Victoria, B.C.

At Pemberton Meadows, about 1920

Mr. and Mrs. Francis Wallace, early 1970's

Bridge at the Hatchery

River bank protection, about 1920
Provincial Archives, Victoria, B.C.

The Fowler brothers' snowplane, 1938

Herb Steinbrunner freighting lumber

Raising a barn

Hellevangs' first house

Provincial Archives, Victoria, B.C.

One of the oldest houses in Mount Currie

Helping Dad with the turnips

The Maypole dance

Pacific Coast Militia Rangers, 1940's

November 1921

Tues 1 Anderson started for Pemberton this morning. I cleaned out house, filled some wood in shed and took bath. doctored my boil weather rain last night, cloudy all day caught 2 bush rats last night and 2 mice this evening while I was sewing my shoes.

Wed 2 Finished putting wood in shed washed clothes
2 1/2 suits underwear
3 top shirts 1 handkerchief
2 face towels 19 socks
3 dish towels
2 flour sacks
9 little sacks

November 1921

cont. Wed 2 Wind still in S.W. but did not storm sun came out several times Clear to-night Baking Bread.

Thur 3 made pieces for window for H.S. Cabin took deer hide out of tanning liquor and put goat skin in put beef hide in and soaked it and stretched it out to freeze so as to cut snow shoe string Went down to Graveyard Point a little cloudy this A.M. but clear to-night. Wind in S.W.

From Bert Perkins' diary, 1921